BOXED IN

BOXED IN

THE CULTURE OF TV

MARK CRISPIN MILLER

NORTHWESTERN UNIVERSITY PRESS
Evanston, IL

Northwestern University Press
Evanston, Illinois 60201

© 1988 Mark Crispin Miller
First published 1988 by Northwestern University Press
All rights reserved
Printed in the United States of America

96 95 94 93 92 91   9 8 7 6 5 4

LIBRARY OF CONGRESS
Library of Congress Cataloging-in-Publication Data

Miller, Mark Crispin
    Boxed in : the culture of TV / Mark Crispin Miller.
        p. cm.
    Includes bibliographies and index.
    ISBN 0-8101-0791-0: ISBN 0-8101-0792-9 (pbk.):
    1. Mass media—United States. I. Title.
P92.U5M55 1988
302.2 ′34′ 0973—dc 19   88-16959
                                                            CIP

The paper used in this publication meets the minimum requirements of
American National Standard for Information Sciences—Permanence of
Paper for Printed Library Materials, ANSI Z39.48-1984

For Jean McGarry

CONTENTS

. . . .

ILLUSTRATIONS

■ ■

ACKNOWLEDGMENTS

■ ■

I would like first of all to thank those old friends who have long sustained me with their critical sympathies, their conversation: Ross Posnock, Bill Warner, Bruce Miller, Geoff Baere. I also want to thank Jack Beatty, who first urged me to write about TV, and who then—along with Ann Hulbert—encouraged me with the best kind of editorial attention. David Diamond has been immeasurably helpful in a number of capacities. Also, Karen Runyon subjected many of these writings to an exacting eye.

At Johns Hopkins, three colleagues in particular have shown abundant generosity, intellectual and otherwise: John Irwin, most tolerant of chairmen; Richard Macksey, perhaps the last of the great patrons; and George Wilson, whose critical grasp of cinema has been both an inspiration and a steadying influence.

Securing the illustrations for this book was a big and vexing job, but one made easier by the careful efforts of several people: Moses Hunter; the staff at Regester Photo Services in Baltimore; Marc Platt of RKO, Inc.; Stewart Linder of Films, Inc.; Jill E. McGovern, Senior Assistant to the President at Johns Hopkins; and Janet Chase at the Library of Congress.

I want also to thank Jerry Graff, for his persistence in soliciting this collection, and for his patience as I labored over its completion. Susan Harris of the Northwestern University Press was prompt, meticulous, and tactful in editing a complicated manuscript. And, finally, I thank Roberta Pryor, my agent, for all her friendly counsel.

The essays collected in *Boxed In* were revised and often expanded from the following original publications and are used here with permission.

"Massa, Come Home" from *The New Republic*, 16 September 1981.

"Getting Dirty" from *The New Republic*, 2 June 1982.

"Family Feud" from *The New Republic*, 18–25 July 1983.

"Off the Prigs" from *The New Republic*, 18 July 1981.

"Cosby Knows Best." Excerpt from "Deride and Conquer" in *Watching Television*, Todd Gitlin, ed. (New York: Pantheon, 1986).

"Virtù, Inc." from *The New Republic*, 7 April 1982.

"A Viewer's Campaign Diary, 1984" from *The Missouri Review*, Vol. 9, No. 1, 1985–86.

"Sickness on TV" from *The New Republic*, 7 October 1981.

"Patriotism Without Tears" from *The New Republic*, 14 April 1982.

"The Air of Expectancy Was Bursting at the Seams" from *The New Republic*, 22–29 August 1981.

"Black and White" from *The New Republic*, 28 October 1981.

"How TV Covers War" from *The New Republic*, 29 November 1982.

Introduction

The Hipness Unto Death

"I think probably the biggest sin of the medium as it exists is that so little sticks to your ribs, that so much effort and technology goes into—what? It's like human elimination. It's just waste."

—Grant Tinker[1]

"How many times can I make this face, this smirk, before somebody says, 'Let's see what's on the other channel'?"

—Bruce Willis[2]

SOMETHING ON THE SIDE

I wrote the first few of these essays on mass culture while also toiling within the profession of English, first as a graduate student, then as an assistant professor. Renaissance poetry was my primary specialty; and so, while crafting a number of "close readings," and working daily, nightly, on the dissertation, I was also trying to amuse and discomfit a public audience, with critical essays on cinema, rock and roll, TV, advertising. Thus my early bibliography had a certain jaunty schizophrenic air, associating "Welcome Back, Kotter" with *The Faerie Queene*, or Castiglione's notion of *sprezzatura* with Elvis Presley's weight problem.

It was not easy to sustain this dual project. In fact, it soon turned out to be impossible, because of numerous subtle pressures. For one thing, most of my superiors could see little excuse for the public writing, which struck them as unseemly, trivial, too "journalistic" an enterprise for one trained to be a scholar/critic. Around the department, the magazine pieces would often inspire unpromising responses from the father figures: outright disdain, or—more often—a kind of smirking disbelief.

I found that mild derisiveness a bit insulting, but I could understand it. Toward those nonliterary subjects I did not feel much of that defensive piousness evinced by many a "pop culture" maven—the solemn archivist of "I Love Lucy" episodes, or the connoisseur of prewar billboards. Nor did I ever see myself as a bold young rebel, hurling his rude works against the staid Academy as if they were so many Molotov cocktails, or custard pies. Without any such heroic illusions, I was free to grasp the comic principle that then informed my bibliography, which (for example) placed John Milton just below Sam Peckinpah.

While I could see the comedy, however, it did not exactly slay me, since I could also see, or sense, that there was a subterranean relationship between the two kinds of analysis. Those quick to chuckle at the seeming incongruity might not have noticed that connection, since they preferred to honor only the differences between high literary art and low commercial spectacle. This preference had (has) much to do with ancient notions of the written word, the requirements of professionalism, the class bias of higher academia, and other forces too complex to be treated here. My purpose at this point is simply to counter that presumption of total difference, that firm belief in the cultural antithesis of High and Low, by tracing the history of these collected essays; for these writings did not and do not represent a movement clean away from or against the practices of academic literary criticism.

I WENT TO GRADUATE SCHOOL AT JOHNS HOPKINS, IN ITS twilight as a bastion of the old *explication de texte*. There I learned to know the poem, to (try to) divine its every implication, to trace its terms and images back through their respective secret histories, and then finally to compose a reading, so that the old text might dance clear of the impediments of age. Such, at any rate, was the ideal, and in graduate school I started to pursue it, even though the Hopkins mode of textual analysis was, by and large, a grim procedure, more like an autopsy, with the able exegete systematically detaching every *topos*, trope, and symbol from the corpus lying there before him, and expertly naming the remote origin of every bit. As oppressive as it often was, however, that hermeneutic mode could also illuminate what had been dark, for there was, in the erotic sense, a certain madness in that method, which demanded the near-maniacal attentiveness of a yearning lover.

And so, in that challenging atmosphere, I learned the necessary critical absorption, and took a monastic sort of pleasure in so doing: in the long, orderly researches down in the quiet of the library, and in the opportunities to craft an intricate argument, returning, over and over, to delve among the subtleties of Hamlet's sly assault on King Claudius, of Beelzebub's inept flatteries of his master Satan, of Lodovico's self-effacing brilliance that first night, in the attentive circle of his peers.

MEANWHILE, THROUGHOUT THE PROFESSION, THE BUSINESS of criticism was undergoing renewal and expansion, shaken up by the new interpretive theories from abroad: structuralism, semiotics, analysis neo-Freudian or neo-Marxist—approaches that legitimized a textual analysis beyond the usual texts. Thus encouraged, I began to notice how—despite the original tenets of New Criticism—the New Critical impulse points beyond its seeming province: away from the purely literary object, toward other kinds of texts—first of all, toward cinema.

Out of this application came a new kind of pleasure: to discover

masterpieces in the most unlikely places—among one's own lifelong
favorites, or on TV late at night, or simply in some movie theater. Thus,
by sustaining off-campus that critical attention taught me by the guardians of the canon, I came to notice that the canon was far too limited,
for it ought to have included, along with Conrad and Faulkner, Fritz
Lang, Josef von Sternberg, Orson Welles and (above all, as some of
these essays argue) Alfred Hitchcock; John Ford along with Yeats and
Dos Passos; Max Ophuls along with Virginia Woolf; Nicholas Ray and
Sam Peckinpah along with Flannery O'Connor; along with James
Joyce, Stanley Kubrick. It seemed to me that, if the liberal arts curricu-
lum is meant to introduce students to the outstanding narrative works
of their own culture, it must be grossly deficient if it neglects *China-
town, Nashville*, and the *Godfather* films, and omits, or barely toler-
ates, any guidance in the art of watching them.

My elders, however, laughed this one off, just as they had derived
(too) much amusement from my bifurcated c.v. Of course, they were
willing to put up with some such foolery if it would help get me a job
somewhere (as it finally did). "This is good, this is good," muttered the
Director of Graduate Studies, as he cast his practiced eye over my letter of inquiry, during our strategy session early in my job-seeking year.
"You're solid in the Renaissance, and you do this film stuff. It's always
good"—he looked up at me with a steely twinkle—"to have a traditional
field, and also do some bullshit on the side." ". . .'bullshit?' " I croaked
back, with a tight half-smile. "Yeah. You know: 'film studies.' Feminism. 'Children's lit.' It looks good. On the side."

I found such dismissiveness especially galling because I knew that it
was more than justified. At many schools, "film study" entered the cur-
riculum not out of any new awareness of the subject's value, but—like
"peace studies" or "pop culture" courses—only as a way to calm down
the aroused student body. By the late Seventies, the "film course" had
become, on many campuses, a standing joke: an easy entertainment,
very crowded, and often supervised by some boyish charlatan with a
rich fund of countercultural quips. Although none of his colleagues
would go near him, his department would never dump him, because of
his magic influence on enrollment levels.

As far as my professors were concerned, however, it was not the
occasional fraudulence of "film study" that was the problem, but film
itself, which they would see as illegitimate in any case—useful as a
personal selling point, maybe, or as a way to goose up the enroll-
ments, but still just a bit of "bullshit on the side." This attitude was
and still is determined by a deep bias common among literary humanists: essentially a religious bias, for it exalts the humanist's own
province—his/her concerns and practices—to the level of the sacred,

while disvaluing all else as irredeemably profane. The profession is therefore conceived as a priesthood, both by its canniest prelates—as at Hopkins—and by its most earnest clerks and pastors. As an assistant professor at the University of Pennsylvania, I would often find myself assailed by the latter sort of piety. Once, speaking at a departmental "collation" meant to introduce the faculty to the new graduate students, I described my work on film. The chairman-to-be then rose and, delivering an impassioned sermon on the moral value of literary research, actually began to weep: "I am a *textual* person!" he exulted ambiguously, then wondered aloud, with trembling lips: "Is Mark Miller a *textual* person?"

And yet, while my elders thus lamented cinema, or smirked at the thought of it, as if it were some foul betrayal of their activity, my students were discovering the value of that same kind of activity—in the study of cinema. Faced with those intricate and moving images, and oriented now to take them seriously, the students undertook to read them with a rigorous enthusiasm that, by and large, they simply (and unfortunately) could not muster over *Samson Agonistes* or *Middlemarch*. Here it was no arduous duty to try reading carefully, but a new kind of exhilaration: for in the movies—certain movies—they discerned the radical suggestiveness of art in what had only seemed, to them, a mere diversion; and thus they now began to grasp the anarchic spectacle that is our culture, or at least to comprehend some of its finer elements.

To read is not just to undo. Critical analysis can just as easily reclaim a marvel, reveal—in all humility—some excellence obscured by time or preconception, as it can devastate a lie. And it is not only the artwork that the analyst might thus restore; for the critical impulse can help also to replenish the minds within its sphere. Contrary to an old McLuhanite canard, those who have grown up watching television are not, because of all that gaping, now automatically adept at visual interpretation. That spectatorial "experience" is passive, mesmeric, undiscriminating, and therefore not conducive to the refinement of the critical faculties: logic and imagination, linguistic precision, historical awareness, and a capacity for long, intense absorption. These—and not the abilities to compute, apply or memorize—are the true desiderata of any higher education, and it is critical thinking that can best realize them.

SOMETHING OUT THERE

And yet the New Critical tendency—the impulse toward close reading—seemed to be pointing further still beyond its usual sanctum, way out toward alien ground. This was the mid-Seventies. While we young exegetes were contemplating our chosen books (or movies) within the

6

quiet of the campus, outside there was a different sort of text piling up all over the place, covering the world like snow, or uncollected trash. Now wherever you looked or listened, there it was—flashing by on the side of a bus, or winking from the storefronts, or gazing back from page after page of the magazines and newspapers, or playful on a passing t-shirt, or grandiose across a billboard, or crooning in an elevator: and all of it echoing and/or reflecting the faces and the voices, cars, interiors, luminous bodies jerking, presidential strolls, dark terrains of pastry, smart packages, labels turning your way—the interminable text of television, usually somewhere in view, and never out of earshot.

Of course, this was not the first time that the Western cultural atmosphere had begun throbbing with the din of mass entertainment, journalism, advertising—that prolific mechanism which we call "the media." Much the same din resounded through the culture of the Fifties, as Humbert Humbert finds in his aimless travels with Lolita, and as (for example) George Kennan pointed out in 1953, deploring "the immense impact of commercial advertising and the mass media on our lives"; certainly through the bombarded culture of the Forties, as Auden suggests through the sinister radio, "with its banal noises," in *The Age of Anxiety*, and as Orwell dramatizes it through the omnipresent telescreens in *Nineteen Eighty-Four*; through the culture of the Twenties and the Thirties, as Dos Passos recalls in the anarchic "newsreels" running throughout *U.S.A.*, and as the Lynds explain in *Middletown* and its sequel, and as Aldous Huxley satirizes it in *Brave New World*, and so on. Indeed, the uneasy sense of an oppressive mediation was often manifest long before the inventions of radio and television: "We live surrounded by the advertisement," wrote Samuel Hopkins Adams in 1909. "Our notions of art, and even of literature, must be insensibly modified by this enormous mass of inescapable display." And in 1876, after visiting this country, Jacques Offenbach noted that "the American advertisement plays upon the brain of a man, like a musician does upon a piano."[3]

Ordinarily, the fact of all that earlier satire and polemic would serve as a basis for denying that the media has ever changed: "People have been saying this kind of thing for years," etc. Those writings, however, indirectly reinforce the claim that something new had happened in the Seventies—for they largely ceased at just that time. All that prior alarm referred to a flood of propaganda that had not yet covered everything, but was only rising, each unprecedented wave or current eliciting fresh outcries from the generation almost drowned by it. By the late Seventies, however, there were virtually no more public outcries from a critical intelligentsia, but only TV's triumphal flow.

Here was the completion of an enormous transformation, all the more striking for the fact that no one was struck by it. Whereas the earlier critics could track the flagrant spread of advertising and its media through the cities and the countryside, and even into common consciousness, one could not now discern TV so clearly (if at all), because it was no longer a mere stain or imposition on some preexistent cultural environment, but had itself become the environment. Its aim was to *be everywhere*: not just to clutter our surroundings, but to become them; and this aim had suddenly been realized by TV, which was not only "on the air," but had become the very air we breathe.

How, in retrospect, do we perceive that imperceptible diffusion? It was not merely that everyone out there seemed always to be watching. This was, in general, nothing new, since television had long since become the national pastime. By the mid-Seventies, however, there was one demographic group now "totally into it" for the first time: America's undergraduates, who watched much more and knew much less than any of the student cohorts that had preceded them. So it seemed, at least, to those of us now teaching. No longer, certainly, could you assume that your lit classes would recognize, say, Donne's Holy Sonnet XIII, or the Houyhnhnms, or the first sentence of *Pride and Prejudice*, or any of the other fragments that had once been common knowledge among English majors. Many majors had been thus ill-educated since the mid-Sixties. By the mid-Seventies, however, I could not even expect my undergraduates (except for a pale few) to catch broad allusions to *Citizen Kane* or *Dr. Strangelove*, or to recall the last scene of *Sunset Boulevard*, or to know who Frank Capra was. And yet, while a roomful of students might just sit there, mute and wondering, at the quotation of any film or novel, they could also, without pausing, and in one firm voice, recite any advertising slogan, or hymn the last half of any jingle: "You dee—?" "—ZERVE A *BREAK* TOO-DAY!!"

This receptivity was very different from the undergraduate stance of just ten years before. Back then, TV had seemed to us as something alien and unbelievable, like enemy propaganda—the smiles too broad, the music all wrong. Indeed, the prime-time spectacle of the Sixties already looked to us as silly as it looks to everyone today, now that the parody of past TV has become the very content of TV in the present. Thus we were ahead of our time, while TV kept trying earnestly to "reach" us, offering us laughable depictions of the way we weren't: the stiff bell-bottoms, the calculated bangs, the nice faces solemn with "commitment," and everybody saying "man" and "groovy."

We could see through all of that. And yet, despite such immunity, the Sixties were no absolute heroic deviation from our culture's movement toward TV, but were in fact a moment in that process—for television had itself, in part, created the subculture that upset the decade.

8

That "youth culture," first of all, was an indirect derivative of the "youth market" encouraged in the Fifties, when the young acquired a nascent group identity from TV and its eager advertisers. Furthermore, the "counterculture" was dependent on the mass media—contrary to the Luddite and/or pastoral mythology of the era. The familiar symbols and catchphrases of the young gained currency through films, through radio and television, through albums and rock concerts deftly engineered. And television left its traces even on the high ground of countercultural ideology. The psychedelic fantasy of universal, instantaneous communication, of every head attuned to every other head, was, among other things, a metaphysical projection of the national TV audience—everyone watching Ed Sullivan at once.

Thus television had imbued even its most disaffected audience. Nevertheless, that disaffection was important, for it expressed a new distrust of TV's relentless sales pitch. And that now-forgotten feeling of estrangement points us toward another telling difference between then and now. Not only did TV seem strange throughout the Sixties, but it was also easily disruptible, despite all the precautions of its ever-vigilant bureaucracy. By and large the spectacle seemed just as inane as it does today, but at times it could be shattered memorably, the televisual surface broken open, by some edifying loss of control: Captain Loan abruptly murdering a handcuffed suspect; Chicago's police running riot at the corner of Michigan and Balbo, and Mayor Daley's catcalls in response to Senator Ribicoff's exalted reprimand; William Buckley in a foulmouthed rage, trying to get tough with Gore Vidal; Norman Mailer trying to get tough with Gore Vidal; Little Richard yelling a satiric gibberish at John Simon.

Those who defend TV will often single out scenes such as these, praising television for its on-the-spot historical veracity, "and you are there!" What a loss (they insist) if we had not witnessed the Army-McCarthy drama, JFK's funeral cortege, the march on Selma. This is, however, an ex post facto argument, so out-of-date as to be irrelevant: for TV today almost never comes across with such unplanned events or unexpected moments. It is now too well-controlled—and so are its performers (the public included)—to permit the sort of outburst that once enlivened it. This change is manifest in the difference, say, between the frequent wildness of the old "Dick Cavett Show," and the highly regulated tit-for-tat on "Nightline"; between the ungainly mob that booed down Nelson Rockefeller at the Cow Palace in 1964, and today's far smoother ultrarightists, smiling through their expert conventions; between the revelations of the Watergate inquiry, and the Iran/contra panel, out-faced by the telegenic Colonel North; between Richard Nixon and Ronald Reagan.

9

The culture of the Sixties, then, gave way to our culture of TV: a great change that—literally—*made no difference*, for it meant that prior differences were now dissolved within TV's new and improved universe. Now students no longer felt themselves estranged from TV, but only felt at home with it, as TV itself became a perfect shelter, a dream container, unbreakable, antiseptic and without surprises. By the mid-Seventies, in short, TV had started to resemble what it is today: a good "environment" (as the admakers say) for advertising.

This development was a long time coming, as network television gradually purified itself of all antithetical tones and genres, i.e., any kind of spectacle that might not offset and complement the advertising: the independent documentary, officially proscribed in 1960, and then the network documentary as well, lately phased out for "budgetary reasons"; the Western, with its preconsumeristic milieu; the live drama, too unpredictable for TV's tight schedule, and (sometimes) so intense as to disgrace the sudden jabbering pitchman; the old movie, reminiscent of an earlier, grander form of spectacle, and therefore supplanted by the adlike telefilms; the talk show actually comprised of talk, and not of plugs and gags; the patriarchalist sitcom, with its absurd solemn Dad standing tall for honesty, sobriety, self-discipline, and other virtues long since superannuated by the market.[4]

And as it thus modernized itself within, transforming the old partitioned spectacle into one wide bright aisle, where ads and news and sports and shows and politics all run together, so did TV simultaneously suffuse the world with the same commercial glow and hubbub—the weird deluge that I first half-heard as a graduate student, down in the library. Repeatedly you found that you had picked up more than you might ever want to know about the newest look in burger ads, Michael Jackson's clothes, the candidates' faces, Dolly Parton's build, Arnold Schwarzenegger's screen career, etc. Certainly you could choose not to own a television set, but such a refusal would condemn you to a life of touristic ignorance, for TV had now become the native language. While variously emulating TV's look and tempo, the other media—films, books, magazines, newspapers—were also referring endlessly to TV's ephemeral content: the only referent of our "public discourse" in the Eighties, when TV finally became the one subject of stand-up comedy, the context of rock music, a frequent news item, a common talk show topic, the scene and arbiter of politics and the major source of political rhetoric ("Where's the beef?" "How do you spell relief?" "We make money the old-fashioned way," etc.). And this containment has been subtly reconfirmed by the closed habitat wherein everyone goes shopping, and where many also work and live—the network of malls and high rises, a cool conduit for the flow of TV's goods, and (therefore) the architectural matrix for more of the same.

RECOVERING FROM THE DEPRESSION

The arrival of the culture of TV, then, was the imperceptible result of many factors—material, commercial, demographic, technological. This culture, however, represents not only the convergence of those disparate developments, but also—or primarily—the fulfillment of an old managerial ideal: to exact universal assent, not through outright force, but by creating an environment that would make dissent impossible. Since World War I, such had been the enlightened aim of management for the workers in America's factories and office buldings; and such too has been the enlightened aim of advertising for as many years—and for the whole public, on the job and off: "The Advertising man," wrote J. George Frederick, one of the industry's most prolific boosters, in 1925, "can mass the thousand and one methods of advertising into a concentrated volume of appeal that will make the people absorb his thought as though through the air they breathe, and as naturally."[5]

Like propaganda generally, advertising must thus pervade the atmosphere; for it wants, paradoxically, to startle its beholders without really being noticed by them. Its aim is to jolt us, not "into thinking," as in a Brechtian formulation, but specifically *away* from thought, into quasiautomatic action: "To us," as an executive at Coca-Cola puts it, "communication is message *assimilation*—the respondent must be shown to behave in some way that proves they [sic] have come to accept the message, not merely to have received it."[6] This Pavlovian (or Oceanic) project requires that "the respondent" not be confronted by the messages head-on and in an alien context, because so direct and vivid an approach might snap him out of his receptive trance and into an unprofitable meditation. Rather, advertising must come down on everybody like the scents of spring, "as though through the air they breathe, and as naturally"; for, once isolated and deliberately interpreted, an ad will betray not only the devices that may enable it to work, but certain larger truths about the system that requires it, and that (therefore) requires that you not think about it.

In short, it has long been the aim of advertising to be everywhere, and yet to seem fundamentally illegible—and TV has realized that complex aim. On (and as) TV, mass advertising is ubiquitous, and yet it also hides behind that very flagrancy, half-camouflaged within surroundings that offset it and yet also complement it. We can now discern this televisual illegibility only by revisiting an earlier period,

11

when advertising was briefly vulnerable to certain critical devices that could make it legible: subversive contrast; mockery; a willful and politicized "misreading." Such perverseness was very common during (and only during) the Thirties, when the advertising images suddenly looked grotesque against the backdrop of a depressed reality.

Of course, even before the Crash, there were certain writers who attempted to deflate the affirmations of the day by throwing the omnipresent puffery into violent relief. In *The Great Gatsby* (1925), for instance, there are "the eyes of Dr. T.J. Eckleburg," "blue and gigantic," gazing from a ruined billboard in "the valley of ashes," offering a prospect wholly unlike "the white palaces of fashionable East Egg." And toward the end of *Sister Carrie* (1900), "a large gilt-framed posterboard," displaying "a fine lithograph of Carrie, life-size," confronts the broken Hurstwood as he wanders down Broadway, freezing in a "cracked derby hat" and "an old, thin coat."

It was not until the Depression, however, that the essential discordancy of advertising struck the attention of great numbers of Americans. Now many noticed the nightmarish divide between the ads' easy vision and the misery of numerous real lives—a mass perception that sparked the consumers' movements of the period, and that inspired the coincident emergence of antiadvertising satire as a journalistic subgenre. And now the ads' jarring incongruity was emphasized repeatedly by artists of all kinds.[7] It was mainly those working through the visual media, however, who discredited the over-cheery advertising vision. Working for the WPA, many of the best-known photographers of the period subverted the posters and the billboards by shooting them against neglected fields or peeling tenements, or surrounded by the ragged children of the Dust Bowl, or towering above a long bread line. Recorded by, among others, Dorothea Lange, Walker Evans, Arthur Rothstein, and Margaret Bourke-White, this sort of image soon became something of a cliché, often cropping up among the illustrations of leftist tracts, and appearing even in certain Hollywood movies.

Trite though it may have become, however, such contrast was a powerful iconoclastic method; and it has been neutralized completely by the rise of television. The commercials, first of all, are simply not at risk the way the outdoor icons used to be. On TV, advertising streams along unmenaced by the sight of public suffering or material dilapidation, exhibiting itself in its own home—the viewer's home—buffered, like the viewer, against all the contrary evidence out in the streets and beyond. Whereas the ads must each stand out in order to succeed, advertising must not itself stand out, must not itself get caught in the glare of unexpected contrast—as so often happened in the Thirties, by propagandistic design, and often also in the Sixties, by the accidental revelation of atrocity or tantrum. What advertising needs is precisely what TV provides: a site secured against all threatening juxtaposition, so that, within it, the ads may proceed to juxtapose one high-contrast image with another, in order to offset the goods—the can of Pepsi in extreme close-up; the Buick (or Volvo, or Mercedes) speeding low and dark among the dunes, or along an empty lunar highway; the tight Levi's, shapely denim on the tall girl leaning, braless and red-lipped, against a concrete wall in Nowhere City.

TV's spectacle of superficial contrast did not develop automatically, but has been the achievement of the sponsor, who has worked for over three decades to cleanse the spectacle of cowboys, independent documentaries, too-sober Dads, and other incommensurable elements. In 1959, for example, one adman wrote a letter to Elmer Rice, explaining why the agency would not support a series based on the playwright's early realist drama *Street Scene*:

> We know of no advertiser or advertising agency of any importance in this country who would knowingly allow the products which he is trying to advertise to the public to become associated with the squalor . . . and general 'down' character . . . of *Street Scene*. . . . On the contrary, it is the general policy of advertisers to glamorize their products, the people who buy them, and the whole American social and economic scene.[8]

And to this day the spectacle is carefully policed by the admakers, who make sure, on the clients' behalf, that the commercials are not broadcast after any pertinent bad news—the only sour note left on TV, now that the programs reexpress the oceanic ad. As a precaution against even this rare infelicity, the agency will often send out to the stations, along with the latest reel of ads, a "TV Spot Instruction Letter" stipulating which kinds of news bulletins would require that this or that commercial be postponed or canceled. (And the shopping malls—TV's outposts—are often similarly bolstered, as management denies all dissident groups the right to leaflet in those antiseptic corridors—an activity that might unduly bum the shoppers out.[9])

By now, however, such cautiousness may not be necessary, for it is possible that no contrast, however violent, could jolt TV's overseasoned audience, for whom discontinuity, disjointedness are themselves the norm; a spectacle that no stark images could shatter, because it comes already shattered. TV ceaselessly disrupts itself, not only through the sheer multiplicity of its offerings in the age of satellite and cable, but as a strategy to keep the viewer semihypnotized. Through its monotonous aesthetic of incessant change, TV may make actual change unrecognizable, offering, in every quiet living room, a cool parody of the Heraclitean fire.

Contrast per se, however, was not the only problem that once beset America's business leadership. The spirit of mockery also offended them. Indeed, it was the possibility of enlightened ridicule that made them see such contrast as subversive. The heads of Johns-Manville, General Motors, and other major companies, for instance, sought to reverse the mass animus against big business by starting with the more irreverent members of their own work force, who would (it was hoped) adopt the proper attitude if immersed in the proper social element. As two business journalists put it with approval:

> It is felt that whereas a man may read an advertisement about the "American Way" and laugh at it, or draw from it a conclusion opposite to the one its author intended, he will find great difficulty in acting contrary to the beliefs of the organizations to which he belongs or of the social-pressure groups within whose range he lives. To generalize, it is felt that if a man belongs to the "right" groups his thinking will be "right," and that otherwise the "right" ideas cannot be sold to him.[10]

Here, explicitly reported, was the desire of management to submerge the employee's sense of irony, to rinse his mind out in a tide of boosterism, so that he might not "misread" the company's p.r.: i.e., make fun of it, or—like the quasi-radical photographers—"draw from it a conclusion opposite to the one its author intended."

Finally, however, it was not calculated peer pressure that protected advertising against the ironic viewer, but TV: for TV preempts derision by itself evincing endless irony (a reflex that I analyze below, in the final essay, as a manifestation of Enlightenment). Thus TV co-opts that smirking disbelief which so annoyed the business titans of the Thirties. "Whereas," they feared, "a man may read an advertisement for the 'American Way' and laugh at it," TV protects its ads from mockery by doing all the mocking, thereby posing as an ally to the incredulous spectator. "It seems to me," says one creative director, whose agency devised some comic ads for Kronenbourg beer, "that when an advertiser makes fun of advertising it endears him to the consumer, who says, yeah, they're right. It's a way of getting the consumer on your side."[11]

The admen first deployed such preemptive irony during the Depression, in response to the rising distrust of big business; and yet the televisual irony is more than a mere commercial tactic, for it suffuses the whole spectacle, whose viewers and performers are alike protected by the sense of their own knowingness. "I call it talk-back TV," says actor

John James, a regular on "Dynasty." "You turn on the set, sit back and, between scoops of Häagen-Dazs, you say, 'Do you believe he said that?' "[12] Thus, within the televisual environment, you prove your superiority to TV's garbage not by criticizing or refusing it, but by feeding on it, taken in by its oblique assurances that you're too smart to swallow any of it.* And as it permeates TV, so does this prophylactic irony now suffuse TV's culture, whose main attractions, however gross, seem admirable, as long as—like Hulk Hogan, "Sledge Hammer," Joe Isuzu— they play their grossness "tongue-in-cheek." Thus *Vanity Fair* somehow seems a classier item than the *National Enquirer*, Madonna seems savvier, somehow more advanced, than Betty Grable, Sam Kinison seems like an improvement on Don Rickles or Benny Hill, and so on.

Through such easy irony the generation that upset the Sixties now distracts itself with an illusion of exceptionalism; for it is that generation, or its wealthiest subgroup, that maintains the spectacle today, both as its authors and as its most esteemed consumers. The generation that once laughed off TV, in short, is trying still to laugh it off while disappearing into it. In Bruce Willis, and/or in David Letterman, and/or in Mariette Hartley, or in any of a hundred other aging wise guys, the old children of the Sixties half-recognize an emanation of their own self-irony—the corrosive cynicism of those who have had to trash the ideals of youth so as to keep on shopping. For this generation, now inside the mall along with everybody else, the televisual irony is at once a reassurance that they are still as hip as ever, and yet a way of laughing off the earnest, groggy hipness of the past.

TV's irony has been universalized, however, not just because of the day-to-day ambivalence of an axial group of viewers, but because of a self-disgust subtler and more widespread, induced by an ideal now implicit in almost every moment of the spectacle. Consider the human figure celebrated on TV: the "smart shopper," perfectly dressed, "calm" and "confident," always much the same cool presence, whether we call it Sonny Crockett, or Fallon Carrington, or the Equalizer, or whether it gazes back at us anonymous, and only once or twice, from some commercial; "Be like me," the brand-new gaze of each such figure tells us— which means not just "Buy the product," but actually: "Be like it." We are meant to look back at that impassive face with a longing that s/he has long since transcended, now that s/he has found a place in the refrigerated heaven of commodities. Beyond desire, and with a perfect

---

*In no way do these observations amount to an attack by *homo seriosus* on irony per se— nor could they, given my own practice. Irony can be an invaluable rhetorical means toward real enlightenment: the televisual irony is a sort of commercial antibody against just such a possibility, and therefore the object of this critique.

body, s/he must view us hungering viewers with irony, seeing how ludicrous it is to be mortal and a person, and therefore having something left to lose. Against the imagined hauteur of the commodity, humanity seems like a joke; and so, within the culture of TV, it makes a certain sense that we admire, "between scoops of Häagen-Dazs" (or Sealtest), TV's pure and total irony, the hipness unto death.

Fragmented and ironic, then, TV cannot be made legible through further contrast. Thus TV has defeated the Depression-era weapons against advertising; and there is one more way in which TV is now immune to the general critical approach of yesteryear. Formerly, the numerous opponents of mass culture cast their various critiques as indictments for conspiracy. Dwight Macdonald's excoriation of "the Lords of *kitsch*," for instance, or Adorno's and Horkheimer's animadversion on "the deceived masses" is exemplary, denouncing an enormous ruse contrived deliberately by those on top. "Advertisers," wrote F.R. Leavis and Denys Thompson in 1937, "know very well what they are trying to do and what they are actually doing." And even Marshall McLuhan—before his mock-ecstatic phase—observed that "many thousands of the best-trained individual minds have made it a full-time business to get inside the collective public mind. To get inside in order to manipulate, exploit, control is the object now."[13] Nor was this apprehension peculiar to the intelligentsia, moreover, for it was a common public attitude, expressed through, among other things, the immense popularity of Vance Packard's *The Hidden Persuaders*, published in 1957.

Certainly the admen, p.r. experts, and media moguls of the past often schemed, and often with success, to put one over on the public. In general, however, the "scheming" was overt. As far as their overall intentions were concerned, they were—at least into the Forties—not conspiratorially sly, but ebulliently forthcoming, given to proclaiming outright, and in good conscience, their project of eventual hegemony; J. George Frederick's blithe boast is only one example among thousands from those early days. The conspiracy theory was therefore half-correct: it could indeed be said that those at the top "know very well what they are trying to do," and yet they made no secret of that enterprise.[14]

Within the culture of TV, however, there is no such easily legible intention, for the marketing imperative does not now originate within the midst of some purposeful elite, but resides in the very consciousness and day-to-day behavior of the media's general work force. Contrary to the dark guesswork of the vulgar Marxist, the TV newsman, for example, usually needs no guiding phone call from his higher-ups in order to decide the bias of his story, but will guide himself, as if on automatic, toward whatever formula might "play," i.e., fit TV's format, goose up the ratings, maintain (or boost) his salary. Similarly, the admaker need not

16

consult, wizardlike, the secret findings of some motivational researcher (although there are plenty of such findings), but need only look into his/her own racing heart in order to discover a scenario that might startle and attract fifty million other hurrying consumers—all ironists, as s/he is. Thus the imperfect self-delusion of J. George Frederick and his ilk has reached perfection in the busy cadres of the media, who have no time for much ambivalence, and who could not rhapsodize the media's larger purpose, because there isn't one. The culture of TV goes on and on because it must go on and on. More disquieting even than the old nightmare of conspiracy is the likelihood that no conspiracy is needed.

HECTIC, IRONIC, AND SEEMINGLY UNINTENDED, THE ADS DO not stand out—and so TV has all but boxed us in. Whereas, out on the walls and billboards, the ads were once overt and recognizable, TV has resubmerged them, by overwhelming the mind that would perceive them, making it only half-aware—as every adman knows: "People don't watch television like they're taking notes for an exam," says Lou Cent-livre, Executive Creative Director at Foote Cone Belding. "They're half-conscious most of the time when they're watching television." "People don't really attend to TV commercials. It's more of a subconscious or subliminal effect," observes Fred Baker, a Senior Vice-President at McCann-Ericksen.[15]

Management has lately recognized the usefulness of TV's indoor sway. Whereas the nation's top executives once looked for ways to keep their employees from snickering at the companies' own ads, today's CEO often uses TV as a morale-booster, establishing an in-house network whose programs adopt the formats of prime time to spread the corporate word internally. Over 8,000 U.S. businesses now operate their own TV networks. "Most of our employees are used to getting information off the job from television," says a manager at Pacific Bell. "So, we're seeing it as a natural way of communicating inside the company." "They'll watch anything," says the training director at Tab Products, Inc. "They are conditioned to TV." On the company's own monitors, management can now seem just as laid-back as their ironic audience of employees. Tandem Computers produces a monthly show called "First Friday," "which borrows some of the zaniness of 'Saturday Night Live' and mixes it with the format of a light daytime talk show." When the company's executives appear on this program, "our people," says Tandem's human resources director, "get to see them as approachable, fun human beings."[16]

Thus TV has turned the cultural atmosphere into one big ad, whose appeals, therefore, now seem illegible, whether we absorb them, only half-aware, in our own homes, or laugh and nod along with them at

work. In our containment TV is so successful that it has not only surpassed the grandest expectations of the early admen, but in fact it
would now also horrify them, if they had lived to see it. "Modern electric machinery could make a hermit's life a paradise of comfort and
isolation," writes Edgar H. Felix at the end of *Using Radio in Sales Promotion* (1927). "But the normal individual looks forward to no such
paradise. He wants to shine among his fellow men, work with them and
play with them. Man is definitely gregarious." Therefore, "broadcasting
and television," while they will surely "brighten home life and make a
happier and better world, . . . will never supplant the university, the
motion picture theater, the stage, the opera, or the newspaper."[17]

Sixty years later, a full-page ad in the *New York Times Magazine*
demonstrated both the naivete of the uneasy Felix, and the fulfillment
of the great enterprise which he had helped to promote.[18] A handsome
man and woman, in their thirties, lounge impassive, watching TV in
their living room. He lies full-length on the couch, she half-reclines
against it on the floor before him. Swathed in dark silk pajamas, each is
also all but enveloped in a billowing white article, a sort of comfy
shroud, out of which each seems just to have worked his/her head and
shoulders before falling still, sedated in TV's glow.

This is an ad for "the Couchpotato," "an ingenious combination of a
plump featherbed and a cozy down comforter." The copy devastates
Edgar Felix's hopeful notions about public culture and gregarious
"man":

> If you're anything like us, you push yourself to the limits. Aerobic
> channel changing. Video cassette juggling. Maybe you're in train-
> ing for the triathlon—you know—watching LA Law, reading a
> book, and eating popcorn without getting butter on the pages.
>
> Well, we think you deserve the proper equipment for these sed-
> entary sports. That's why we've dedicated our newest invention
> for the indoor athlete to you [sic]: The Couchpotato. . . .
>
> This warm cocoon is perfect for all your favorite indoor sports,
> or as a gift for the significant spud in your life.

Here, encapsulated, is the culture of TV: a vision of upscale entomb-
ment, offered in dead earnest and yet played for laughs.

BOXED IN

Now, at the dead end of the consumer culture, it is both necessary
and, finally, possible to read against TV, "drawing from it a conclusion
opposite to the one its author[s] intended." For, despite its various

self-protective moves, TV is in fact more legible than ever; or rather, those very moves have made it legible: TV's success has, paradoxically, made it revealing in its every particle.

Now that TV's content has itself been determined and homogenized by the commercial impetus that once merely underlay the spectacle, and now that TV's basic purpose is to keep you watching, the images all point back toward that now-imperceptible managerial intention. And because TV is, on the whole, devised by and for the same class and generation, it constitutes a vehicle of collective self-allurement and self-solace, so that the spectacle has all the eerie resonance of a great bad dream. TV's images, furthermore, are all the richer in unconscious meanings for the increased sophistication of the visual technology that represents them. Calculated always to jolt the nerves of the half-attentive, the spectacle is less and less elaborately scripted and plotted, while more and more reliant on stark pictures and a lightning pace (along with infectious music), and on words as blunt as pictures. Such is the imperative behind all the ads and newscasts, game shows and cartoons, and nearly all the talk shows, dramas, and sitcoms, so that TV's "concentrated volume of appeal" actually gives more and more away the more it tries to rush and dazzle us beyond understanding what it's all about.

What the spectacle reveals, then, are not only the commercial forces that demand our continual consumption, but these largely unacknowledged facts of American life: the degradation of experience by technology; the demise of public culture in all its forms; and the warlike relations between men and women, between blacks and whites, and the complicated, hidden animosity between the upper stratum and the spreading underclass—tensions that TV reveals even as it both sentimentalizes and exacerbates them. Thus TV edifies precisely where it seeks most to conceal, and through its very means of concealment.

To read is, in this case, to undo. Such a project, however, demands that we not simply snicker at TV, presuming its stupidity and our own superiority. Rather, we need a critical approach that would take TV seriously (without extolling it), a method of deciphering TV's component images, requiring both a meticulous attention to concrete detail, and a sense of TV's historical situation. Genuinely seen through, those details illuminate that larger context, and vice versa, so that the reading of TV contains and necessitates a reading of our moment and its past.

The essays in this book represent my efforts to set such a critical example. They constitute the record of my discovery, begun down in the library, that there was also a lot of reading to be done outside. To look and look again into the glowering features of a Winston smoker ("I

like the box"), or into a thirty-second ad for Shield ("I *do* feel cleaner!"), or into a certain three minutes of convention coverage ("Mr. May-
or, I work with my colleagues"), or at Bill Cosby's pseudo-impish grin,
or at Darth Vader's mutilated head, or at Ronald Reagan, has been to
train the New Critical attentiveness on some of the ephemeral details of
a spectacle approaching total closure, yet at the same time pointing
some way out.

CRITICISM AS THE CULTURE OF TV

The impending closure of the world by TV entails not just the homogenization of the spectacle, and the capitulation of the whole public,
young and old, and the incorporation of all once-wayward elements,
and the renovation of our country into one transcontinental shopping
mall. More damaging than these developments, perhaps, has been the
subtle and coincident trivialization of criticism—the one action that
could still counteract TV. Mass culture itself disvalues criticism by reducing it to a mere binary mechanism—the thumbs up/thumbs down of
Siskel/Ebert, the "Picks & Pans" in *People*, the "Cheers 'n' Jeers" in *TV
Guide*. Reporting on a new "audience measurement technique," *The
Wall Street Journal* tells us that "the Voxbox test allows viewers to play
critic. They can hit buttons that read 'funny' or 'boring' or 'dumb.' "[19]
These versions of "criticism" are, of course, entirely televisual, for they
are not only crude enough to apprehend in a flash, but are essentially
consumeristic, representing the "criticized" material only as a commodity that you should either buy or leave up on the shelf.

Such is the notion of criticism that we should expect from TV and its
satellites; but even among our intelligentsia—i.e., journalists and aca-
demics—the critical analysis of mass culture is scarcely more advanced. As on "At the Movies," so at the symposia and in the magazines
and journals (as well as over lunch), the discussion of TV fails to illuminate its subject because that discussion replicates TV itself. To take TV
seriously is often to invite responses no less automatic than the car
chase, the laugh track, the news team's zoom-in on the tearstreaked
face of the bereaved.

Like the "Picks & Pans" mode of criticism, the general discussion of
mass culture is a binary affair: pro or con. Thus the discussants fall into
one or the other of two broad categories. (Here I resort, albeit with
accuracy, to a little satire.) On the one hand, there are those academ-
ics—now in the minority—who despise mass culture in all its forms
and phases. Some of these critics hold to an apocalyptic ideology—a
blend of Marxism and feminism, say, or the relentless Situationism of
Guy Debord. Others are traditional highbrows, like my lachrymose

colleague at Penn, and others who regard any sustained attention to mass culture as a form of heresy or sinful trifling. Often the highbrow will exempt from his disapproval certain mass-cultural products—movies with subtitles, for example, or some careful adaptation of a literary classic, broadcast on PBS. Although gradually disappearing from the academic scene, this scornful stance has lately been reexalted by the influence of neoconservatism, as we now see in the celebrity of Allan Bloom, decrying all mass culture as one long burst of barbarism, the fault of Science and the brainless young.

This position is—to say the least—questionable. First of all, such a critic tends to ignore the historical context of mass culture, preferring to groan long and loud for the reinstatement of some vague code of yore. Furthermore, the highbrow militant—like his unacknowledged cohort, the apocalyptic radical—usually cannot or will not tell the important differences between one movie and another, or between movies and comic books—a problem besetting not only Bloom's screed, but many earlier and more astute critiques, such as Adorno's and Horkheimer's seminal attack on Hollywood. For the most part, these grandiose denunciations of mass culture—whether they derive from Marx or Plato—promote a pleasureless view of modern life, whose entertainments have provided much that is provocative and even beautiful, and which therefore require the critic to discriminate among them.

The most serious fault in this position, however, is not that it is anhedonic, or elitist, or nostalgic, but that it actually preempts any critical analysis of mass culture by positing a gross negativity with which all critiques can then be identified, and so dismissed—as anhedonic, or elitist, or nostalgic. Whereas the apocalyptic critic simply never leaves the marginal preserves of the lesser learned journals and the conference circuit, the highbrow Jeremiah is—if he makes the Big Time—erased through his success. Mass culture needs such glowering figures, the Mrs. Grundy and the Gloomy Gus, certainly not as a way to usher in a new repressiveness, but as a way to forestall any serious criticism of itself, turning the would-be Ruskin into a media sideshow: John Simon (an ex-comparatist) played this role in the Sixties and the Seventies, and did it well enough to end up parodied in the movie *What's Up, Doc?* and on an episode of "The Mary Tyler Moore Show"; and now Allan Bloom, having taken on the same persona, is both played up and belittled in the same way: a profile in the *New York Times Magazine* bears the subversive title, "Chicago's Grumpy Guru."

As opposed to those who sweepingly condemn the spectacle, there are various intellectual factions who now write in its defense—as if mass culture, now triumphant, needs somehow to be shielded from criticism (and yet these very defenses are mere further proof of TV's

21

triumph). Like mass culture itself, its proponents will invariably choose (or concoct) some critical straw man in order to jeer him down, thereby offering a fine display of enlightened populism. Here is an example from the world of journalism, written, in 1979, by Robert Asahina, in an article subtitled "Why intellectuals hate television":

> The medium—never a favorite of social critics—has in the past three or four years come under yet another wave of attacks—by some earnest guardians of America's children (like Marie Winn, in *Plug-In Drug*), staunch upholders of civic virtue (like Frank Mankiewicz and Joel Swerdlow, in *Remote Control: Television and the Manipulation of American Life*), and fire-breathing advocates of revolutionary action (like Jerry Mander, in *Four Arguments for the Elimination of Television*).
> Their complaints are familiar, and overwrought . . .[20]

This is not so much a defense of TV as an *imitatio televisionis*, the cool critic making light of the "staunch upholder," the "earnest guardian" and the "fire-breathing advocate," exactly as TV's authors will present, in an ad or sitcom, some tense do-gooder, stuffy bureaucrat, or humorless Soviet, and then deflate him, as "a way of getting the consumer on their side."

Since that piece was written, the academy has changed, the faint contempt that I once sensed in my superiors slowly giving way to a more tolerant attitude toward the spectacle—a tolerance no less hostile to critique than their original high-handedness. The sort of televisual scapegoating exemplified above is a device now used as frequently by academic humanists as by TV's natural allies—the journalists, admen, futurologists, and other boosters of the consumer culture. Thus Stanley Cavell writes in TV's defense (seemingly), using Jerry Mander's broadside as an easy mark.[21] And thus T.W. Adorno is invoked routinely as a committed enemy of pleasure, condemned over and over for his infamous antipathy to jazz, as if that quirk of taste defines that complex thinker—a handy representation for the critic feigning populism, but one that seriously distorts Adorno's views.

There are, roughly speaking, two academic factions that now support TV. One may be termed the liberal faction, whose members automatically come back at any critical utterance with one or another of a certain range of dismissive commonplaces, none of them defensible in light of TV's actual *modus operandi*. "So you don't like television," they might reply. "Then you must think very little of the millions who watch it!"—as if TV and its viewers were the same, and as if "the people" all enjoy TV immensely, just because they're stuck with it.[22]

Or: "Nobody really falls for TV!"—a claim that is partly true, but which fails to perceive the fact of TV's reliance on, and exploitation of, that very posture of distrust. "So TV is mediocre. But surely there was never any Golden Age of mass entertainment." This enlightened observation implies that TV is perfectly continuous with all prior forms of amusement, and that, therefore, one ought not to knock it—an assumption that is not only false, given TV's wholly corporate character, but cynical, since it suggests that one should never get upset over an abuse of long duration. And finally: "If you don't like it, why not turn it off?"—a suggestion that is not only vaguely impolite, but impossible to honor, now that TV is everywhere.

Each of these nonarguments is an attempt to shut off all discussion of TV, so that TV might be exonerated. The other, younger faction of televisual humanists—a group better informed and more self-conscious than the diffuse network of apologists—seek not simply to exempt TV from criticism, but to promote it as a means of liberation. According to this postmodernist view, TV and the market generally provide "the people" with a fresh opportunity to refashion their own identities, thereby throwing off the dead hand of the past. Because it apparently ironizes all older social codes, the outdated demands of church, state and family, the sway of militarism and the rigidities of patriarchy, TV and the market free the shopper to choose, from among the images and products now abundantly available, his/her own personal style. Like the liberals, the postmodernists reject the notion that TV is in any way a suasive force, insisting that everyone is in the know already, so that there is no need for any pushy critical directives from on high.

Like TV itself, this post-Frankfurt argument has lately permeated academia. It recurs in Fredric Jameson's reverent observations on the Hotel Bonaventure in Los Angeles, a structure that, he argues, frees its visitors from the oppressive monumentality of nineteenth-century architecture. It recurs in feminist defenses of the department store or the Harlequin Romance, each supposedly a refuge from the batterings of daily life under male authority. It recurs in the writings of David Marc and other students of communications, who claim that today's spectator can, just by changing channels, turn TV-viewing into a creative action, the continual redesigning of a do-it-yourself postmodernist collage. And it recurs throughout the current symposia now devoted to TV, such as one I recently attended at Johns Hopkins, in the course of which a man from Princeton read a paper, without a trace of irony, and to much applause, asserting a profound subversiveness in "Pee-Wee's Playhouse."[23]

Certainly the postmodernist argument offers a valuable corrective to the Stalinist tendency in certain leftist critiques of mass culture. Nevertheless, there is a disquieting similarity between this new position and

23

the typical effusions of those who manage the spectacle, and of those who extol it from the right. The admakers too are quick to insist on the advanced shrewdness of Americans today: "People today are adwise," says adman Hal Riney. "They know what we are trying to do." "We're an advertising-oriented country," says adwoman Mary Wells Lawrence. "People have seen so much advertising that they're quite professional about it." And, much like the postmodernists, Daniel Boorstin sees TV and the shopping mall as the great guarantors of individual freedom. In a recent speech delivered to an advertising group, he described his return from a visit, with his wife, to the Soviet Union: "And when we came back and turned on our American television set, instead of feeling the familiar irritation at the interruption of commercials, . . . we bought a little box of tapers and we lit a taper any time a commercial appeared, since the commercial was an icon of freedom . . . a sign that we had the opportunity to choose."[24]

In this convergence of managerial wisdom, Cold War piety and avant-gardist criticism, the culture of TV would seem to be complete, and therefore unassailable. Against this possibility, it is necessary to reemphasize certain truths. Contrary to the assumption both of its highbrow detractors and its self-conscious devotees, TV is not an expression "of the people," not "vulgar" in any traditional sense, but an effective corporate instrument, whose sole purpose—as its executives will tell you—is to sell you to the advertisers; and it does so, in part, precisely through the very irony which some now celebrate as the proof of mass immunity. TV would "liberate" us only from the notions that impede its own advance, and the advance of the market, which, while promising a world of pleasure, finally offers nothing but its own relentlessness.

At their best, both the critics and the celebrants of TV argue on behalf of pleasure: Adorno, even in his most acid observations on the spectacle, and the postmodernists, looking for those moments that can startle us with something that resembles joy. And indeed, there is such a thing as art even on TV, and for those rare exceptions we should be grateful. But it is not the purpose of the cultural critic merely to accentuate the positive, neglecting the inquiry into TV's vast badness, and the reasons for it, which TV itself betrays. This inquiry, which once could be regarded by my teachers as "some bullshit on the side," must now move to the center of our marginal profession, as a last defense against the flood of offensive matter rising all around us. Reading the culture of TV for its inadvertent revelations, we can glean the only possible advantage from a system whose intention is to disadvantage everyone, including those who profit from it.

NOTES

■ ■

1. Quoted in Todd Gitlin, *Inside Prime Time* (New York: Pantheon, 1983), p. 16.

2. Quoted in "People, Etc.," *The Baltimore Sun*, 24 January 1988.

3. Samuel Hopkins Adams, "The New World of Trade," *Collier's*, 22 May 1909, p. 15; Jacques Offenbach, *America and the Americans* (London: William Reeves, 1876), p. 52.

George Kennan included his remarks in a speech delivered at Notre Dame University on 15 May 1953. The pertinent passage is worth quoting in full: "The immense impact of commercial advertising and the mass media on our lives is—let us make no mistake about it—an impact that tends to encourage passivity, to encourage acquiescence and uniformity, to place handicaps on individual contemplativeness and creativity."

For an ample collection of other postwar writings against the media, see *Mass Culture: The Popular Arts in America*, ed. Bernard Rosenberg and David Manning White (New York: The Free Press, 1957).

4. For a fuller discussion of TV's gradual self-purification, with emphasis on the revealing history of the sitcom, see Mark Crispin Miller, "Deride and Conquer," in *Watching Television*, ed. Todd Gitlin (New York: Pantheon, 1986), pp. 183–228.

5. J. George Frederick, "Introduction" to *Masters of Advertising Copy* (New York, 1925), p. 21.

6. From "Redefining Communication," a talk delivered to the Association of National Advertisers on 13 December 1983 by Joel S. Dubow, Communications Research Manager of Coca-Cola USA.

7. Thus Hart Crane, in "The Bridge," evokes the cruel difference between the ad slogans flashing, upbeat, past the windows of a train, and the bleak after-image of "three men, still hungry on the tracks, ploddingly / watching the tail lights wizen and converge, slip- / ping gimleted and neatly out of sight." And thus in Orwell's *Keep the Aspidistra Flying*, the hero, as he contemplates the "grinning yard-wide faces" of "the ad-posters," senses "the great death-wish of the modern world. Suicide pacts. Heads stuck in gas-ovens in lonely maisonettes. . . . And the reverberations of future wars."

8. This letter, part of which appeared in *Theatre Arts*, November 1959, is quoted in Erik Barnouw, *The Sponsor: Notes on a Modern Potentate* (New York: Oxford Univ. Press, 1978), p. 196 n.6.

9. For a brief overview of this situation, see Keenen Peck, "Just Shut Up and Shop," *The Progressive*, October 1987, 23-25.

10. S. H. Walker and Paul Sklar, "Business Finds Its Voice," *Harper's Monthly Magazine*, vol. 126 (December 1937-May 1938), 430. The

entire three-part article was published in book form by Harper and Bros. in 1938.

11. "Kronenbourg puts the accent on humor," *Advertising Age*, 13 September 1984, 14.

12. Quoted in "Insider," *TV Guide*, 10 January 1987, p. 18.

13. Dwight Macdonald, "A Theory of Mass Culture," in Rosenberg and White, p. 60; Max Horkheimer and Theodor Adorno, *Dialectic of Enlightenment* [1944], tran. John Cumming (New York: Continuum, 1982), p. 133; F. R. Leavis and Denys Thompson, *Culture and Environment: The Training of Critical Awareness* (London: Chatto & Windus, 1937); Marshall McLuhan, *The Mechanical Bride* [1951] (rpt. London: Routledge & Kegan Paul, 1967), p. v.

14. Furthermore, those eager propagandists, the so-called "captains of consciousness," were often not entirely resolute, like Zinoviev or Goebbels, but acutely ambivalent about the very system which they were furthering so energetically. Here again, the old conspiracy theory must be qualified, inasmuch as those early manipulators did not work just to fool (or to "uplift") the public, but were also trying to put one over on themselves. For a subtle analysis of such ambivalence in the case of Bruce Barton, see T. J. Jackson Lears, "From Salvation to Self-Realization: Advertising and the Therapeutic Roots of the Consumer Culture, 1880-1930," in *The Culture of Consumption*, ed. Lears and Richard Wightman Fox (New York: Pantheon, 1983), pp. 1-38.

15. Centlivre quoted on "The Nightly Business Report," WPBT, Miami, Fl., 29 August 1985; Baker quoted in *The Wall Street Journal*, 25 July 1985, p. 23.

16. "Calif. companies find in-house TV holds key to attitude adjustment," a Knight-Ridder wire story, *The Baltimore Sun*, 23 November 1986.

17. Edgar H. Felix, *Using Radio in Sales Promotion: A Book for Advertisers, Station Managers and Broadcasting Artists* (New York: McGraw-Hill, 1927), p. 350.

18. *The New York Times Magazine*, 11 October 1987, p. 43.

19. "Marketing," *The Wall Street Journal*, 1 November 1984, p. 33.

20. Robert Asahina, "Blame It on the Tube," *Harper's*, November 1979, p. 106. Oddly enough, Asahina, as an editor at Simon & Schuster, went on to edit Allan Bloom's *The Closing of the American Mind*.

21. "The Fact of Television," in *Themes out of School: Effects and Causes* (San Francisco: North Point Press, 1984), pp. 235-68.

22. For a thorough and intelligent consideration of this issue, see Todd Gitlin, *Inside Prime Time* (New York: Pantheon, 1983), pp. 17-30.

23. Fredric Jameson, "Postmodernism, or the Cultural Logic of Late Capitalism," *New Left Review* 146 (July/August 1984), 54-55; Janice A. Radway, *Reading the Romance: Women, Patriarchy and Popular Culture* (Chapel Hill: University of North Carolina Press, 1984); David Marc, *Demographic Vistas: Television in American Culture* (Philadelphia: Univ. of Pennsylvania Press, 1984). The paper at Hopkins was entitled "Tracing the Signifier: A Micrological Reading of 'Pee-Wee's Playhouse.'"

24. Hal Riney, quoted in an interview comprising the copy of an ad for *The Wall Street Journal*, in *The New York Times*, 9 September 1986, D28; Mary Wells Lawrence, quoted in an interview in *Vogue*, January 1985, p. 276; Daniel Boorstin's speech, "The Good News of Advertising," is available from the archives of the Library of Congress.

What's On TV

Family auditioning for "Family Feud"

Massa, Come Home

· ·

THIS SUMMER [1981] HAS SEEN THE RELEASE OF A NEW commercial for Jamaica. It lasts one minute and contains 14 shots. If you watch much television, you have probably seen this little travelogue, which appears at all hours, on every channel, often enough to reach millions of would-be tourists. It presents a series of happy black Jamaicans, each in a different picturesque setting, each making some soothing offer: "Come back to gentility"; "Come back to romance," "to our beauty," "our bounty," "tranquility," etc. Finally, an old man with a walking stick, a crowd of well-dressed toddlers frisking at his feet, ambles past an ancient tree, and says, "Come back to the way things *used* to be. Make it Jamaica again, and make it your own." After a reprise of faces in smiling close-up, there is a high helicopter shot of a glittering beach, a horse and rider pausing in the surf. A legend then appears over this last image: "Make it Jamaica. Again."

Half-noticed, this commercial might seem just the usual empty allurement, merely one bright bubble from the great boiling cesspool of daily television. That inundation, however, is precisely what allows commercials to succeed: they come at us in stupefying numbers, each one overcharged and utterly forgettable, so that we find ourselves lulled into the receptive state of the well hypnotized. Although the process seems like an enormous imposition, it depends on our own complicity. "It's only a commercial," we say to ourselves, then settle back, watching without really watching, thereby letting each image make its deep impressions. Although we have learned to distrust commercials automatically, this sort of knee-jerk skepticism is a poor defense against the subtleties of advertising, which can affect you whether or not you believe their ostensible claims.

We are accustomed to think of these subtleties in quasi-Pavlovian terms, as hidden stimuli that "turn us on" without our knowing it: nipples airbrushed into sunsets, lewd words traced into some ice cubes, etc. But this conception of the way ads work, and of the way we apprehend them, is much too crude. They function, not mechanically, but poetically, through metaphor, association, repetition, and other devices that suggest a variety of possible meanings. The viewer, therefore,

31

does not just watch once and start salivating, but senses gradually, half-consciously, the commercial's welter of related messages.

And just as the viewer needn't recognize these subtleties in order to take them in, so, perhaps, the advertisers themselves may not know their every implication, any more than a poet or filmmaker is fully aware of all that his work implies. Of course, most of what we see in a good commercial was probably calculated by its makers, who are quite sophisticated, and who spend immense amounts of time and money on each thirty- or sixty-second bit. Nevertheless, some of these nuances might have been unconsciously intended, details that just "seemed right" as part of the commercial's general drift. Ultimately, however, these questions of intention are irrelevant. If criticism can demonstrate convincingly that a commercial uses certain strategies, then we can assume that those strategies are, in fact, at work, whether or not the advertisers might acknowledge them. This new commercial for Jamaica offers an example of advertising at its most artful. Its various strategies are worth analyzing in order to demonstrate how carefully these little works are put together.

The new ad differs from its predecessor, which ran from 1979. That commercial worked through physical appeal. It was arousing, mouth-watering, irresistibly rhythmic—watching it, you could barely keep from dancing over to the telephone to call your travel agent. The score was an infectious blend of reggae and Broadway, worked into a sort of overture that promised infinite renewal; every seeming cadence only opened out into a new and different phrase. As the song seemed never ending, so did those sun-kissed delights that flashed onto the screen in tempo with the music—girls, melons, golf courses, flowers, champagne, horses, lunches, girls. "We're not just a beach!" the voices finally sang, *"we're a countreeeee---!!!"*

That motto gave the game away. Taken by itself, it sounds bellicose and nationalistic, like a slogan for revolutionaries. Michael Manley might have used it to denounce the humiliations of tourism: a beach is just a stopping-place for rich transients; a country belongs to its people. It may be nice to go wading, but it is sweet and proper to die for one's country. In short, the motto expressed that very possibility of violence which may keep people *away* from Jamaica, land of "rude boys" and enchanted potheads. Of course, this off-putting implication was overwhelmed by the music and the images, which turned the threat into a temptation: "We have all that a beach can have, and a whole country full of other goodies, too." In other words, the commercial teased the tourist's fears away with an upbeat promise of inexhaustible bounty.

But some tourists have lately been attacked in Jamaica, and the Socialist regime has been replaced by the Conservatives under Edward

Seaga. These facts may help account for the peculiar tone and rhetoric of the new commercial, which uses no titillating come-ons. Its basic message, rather, is a deeply emotional entreaty: "come home." This is a familiar pitch in these days of right-wing symbolism. Ronald Reagan's speeches, *Time's* call for "American renewal," and numerous ads ("I'm comin' on home—to Wyler's!") currently use the myth of homecoming to enjoin our sentimental acquiescence in the general betterment of the rich. "Home" refers to an imagined past, a hazy paradisiacal interlude that fell sometime between Reconstruction and the Beatles' first appearance on Ed Sullivan. We were happy, back then. Watched over by God and a few other kindly tycoons, we understood the meaning of hard work, a dollar, life itself; colored people knew their place, and nobody pushed us around. We inhabited a paradise that we can have again, the myth implies, if we just wish very hard and make no noise.

The myth of homecoming informs this commercial in a complicated way. First of all, Jamaica herself appears to have "come home." The election of Edward Seaga, we infer, has brought the country back to its senses. Forget Havana, and those hoodlums with their odd patois. Jamaica is once again genteel, tranquil, and romantic, a colonial idyll in need of one thing only: white masters.

"MAKE IT JAMAICA. AGAIN." THIS MEANS BOTH "CHOOSE Jamaica" and "Only *you* can turn this place into *Jamaica* once again." Or, in other words: "We're not really a country, we're just a plantation." These Jamaicans grin deferentially (and with perfect teeth) at the camera, their clothes recall the slaves' wardrobe in *Gone With the Wind*— no stark rags or dreadlocks here. And as they have "come home," so are we invited to "return" to a fantastic past: "Come back to the way things used to be," referring not just to "the way things used to be" in the Caribbean, but to the way things supposedly used to be in our own midst, right here at "home." From beginning to end, the commercial plays brilliantly on the repressed fears and desires of white consumers, and even hints at darker, more general longings. It subtly excites those fears in order to allay them, thereby countering the viewer's misgivings before they surface into consciousness.

The opening shot presents an image of impending violence converted into recreation. A group of blacks, wearing helmets, waving sticks, gallop on horseback toward the camera. One of them pulls ahead of the others, swinging his instrument down like a sabre, and strikes—a polo ball. It is an archetypal vision of imminent destruction (there are, in fact, four horsemen here), but the martial implication is simultaneously denied, as if to say, "You expect to be killed by our natives? Sit back and relax! This is only an athletic display!"

33

BOXED IN

■ ■ ■ ■ ■ ■

THUS WE ARE COMFORTED WITH AN IMPLICIT PROMISE OF unassailable spectatorship, as if Jamaica were as safe as our own living rooms. Various techniques further mitigate the sense of threat, without entirely dispelling it. The riders lumber forward, hindered in slow motion; they are also shot with a long lens, in shallow focus, so that they have no spatial depth and appear to make no progress, like painted figures. And the music—mellow steel guitars and crooning voices—lends the scene a sweet narcotic aura. The tune, moreover, is the one used by John Lennon and Yoko Ono for their song "Happy Xmas (War is Over)," and therefore evokes, for millions of young spenders, a peaceful mood:

Come back to Jamaica:
What's old is what's new.
We want you to join us,
We made it for you.

So make it Jamaica,
Make it your own.
Make it Jamaica,
Your new island home.

The riders look like police or a "peacekeeping force," yet they are neither: "Jamaica is *not* a trouble spot!" the image insists. "We have beaten our machetes into polo mallets." Polo is a gentlemanly pastime with imperialistic overtones, having been revived in the nineteenth century by British officers stationed in India. This hint of a national "return" to colonial status becomes explicit in the next shot. Three of the horsemen appear in medium close-up, facing us while cantering along to the right, and one of them says, "Come back to gentility." Whoever would extol "gentility" should himself evince refinement, and this light-skinned black, bouncing along on his steed in knightly fashion, accompanied by silent (and much darker) companions, seems aloof enough to make his endorsement credible. At the same time, this black pride is still a threat. Therefore, the second shot, like the first, flattens out that threat with shallow focus (all the subsequent shots are in deep focus, with their backgrounds clearly in view), and then removes it entirely by having the horsemen ride on to the right, exiting the frame: "Come back to gentility. [And now we'll be running along.]"

From this point on, Jamaica seems like a country made docile by defeat, its young men killed off in some disastrous war. The commercial's subsequent speakers are either women or old men. Moreover, while the horsemen were mobile, numerous, and unflinching, each of the following speakers is fixed and (even when among others) solitary, and looks up at the viewer discreetly, responding only *after* the camera has approached, as if not speaking until spoken to. It is a fantasy for the armchair buccaneer. Her vigorous males having vanished, Jamaica is now free to please her plunderers again.

A pretty young girl appears in a blooming jungle, up to her chest in exotic flora. She wears a bright red sarong ("I am . . . *Tondelayo!*"), has flowers of the same color in her hair, and holds a bunch of more such flowers in her hands. "Come back to our beauty," she says with a shy smile, extending the bouquet as if offering tribute. In fact, she is offering herself, now that her brothers are out of the way: the flowers are a symbol of her available womanhood. It is an old association, confirmed here by the common color red, and by her wearing a flower just like the one she offers. "Come back to our beauty," then, really means: "This dark blossom is for *you*, white man."

AS IF TO ASSURE THE VIEWER THAT THIS OVERTURE IS NOT taboo, in the next shot a burly, white-haired old fisherman, sitting at dockside, looks up and says, "Come back to our people." He could be the father of the willing jungle girl, but he obviously won't mind her having fun with the right folks: he has an air of gentle resignation, and sits winding a rope around one hand, in a gesture of self-restraint. Nevertheless, he is still a potential menace, like the youths in the opening shot. He could use that rope in unpleasant ways, and his phrase "our people" is unsettling; it suggests that Jamaicans are both alien and homogenous, a colored horde.

That slight threat must be nullified, and so the next four shots counteract it with intricate denials of strife; all four characters are women, making unequivocal offers. After the allusion to "our people," there is a dissolve from the harbor to an elegant dinner table, the camera gliding across its lustrous surface to show us how Jamaica feeds her guests: silver, crystal, candles, and a huge lobster on a platter at the center. (Thus it turns out that the fisherman has grown old in our service.) As the camera comes to rest, a woman in native headdress and ample skirts, standing at the table to perform some preprandial task, turns in our direction and says, "Come back to hospitality," with a gesture that implies "All this is yours." This is, first of all, an assurance that "our people" will protect, not harm, their visitors. But the real assurance is more bizarre than this. By dissolving from "our people" to a waiting meal, the commercial implies that even the Jamaicans themselves, like their foodstuffs, are delicious and readily available. It is a metaphor for the island's total exploitability—this really is a great place for *consumers*.

35

The same implication pervades the next shot: "Come back to our bounty," smiles a plump old woman sitting at a fruitstand. She herself is "bounteous," as round and ripe as the heavy melons piled beside her. (Her girth is a sign of contentment as well as fecundity, implying that, although poor, this jolly soul has no complaints.) Her light blue dress bears a motif of yellow fruit, which identifies her further with her wares. And she sits beneath a parasol, shielded from the sun like a giant mango for sale under an awning.

At this point, the appeal becomes less sensual, more escapist. A woman stands at a railing above a sylvan waterfall, and murmurs, eyes half-closed: "Come back to tranquility," beckoning with languorous fingers. Her pose and manner suggest an invitation to the perfect orgy, but what she offers is not straightforward pleasure. "Tranquility" is hardly stimulating, and this woman, in fact, looks more ascetic than sensuous. In this context, "tranquility" is the calm that a strong ruler can impose on "our people."

SHE IS UNTHREATENING BECAUSE SHE LOOKS WESTERNIZED. Unlike the previous two women, she is bone-thin and bareheaded, and wears bulky jewelry. These marks of high fashion imply that she is rich, or kept by a rich man. (She is the only skinny person in this ad for a poor country, and her thinness is a sign of chic rather than starvation.) Since she would appear to depend on the island's staying "tranquil," we should find her especially trustworthy, while those women less detached from their own culture could revert to savagery at any time, and turn against their civilized overlords.

But we needn't worry about any of these dark, elemental beauties. All Jamaica's women live to serve and service *us*; their menfolk may be lithe and well endowed, but these bestial qualities just can't compete with our accomplishments and bank accounts. This suggestion becomes explicit in the next shot. In another polished room, four couples, standing in a circle, execute one step in a courtly dance. As the men stand still, the women neatly whirl in place, and then the one closest to the camera says to us, "Come back to romance."

If this proposition carries a hint of recklessness, the general image counteracts it with a vision of complete containment. These are no wild natives freaking out under the stars, but a sober indoor gathering of domestics; they wear chaste white, and move like the automata that decorate old European clocks. They seem entirely in our power, dancing for us, not for themselves, sacrificing ecstasy for the sake of orderly display.

WHEN SHE TURNS IN OUR DIRECTION, MOREOVER, IT IS AS IF we have successfully cut in. In facing us, the woman turns back on her partner, who waits willingly, yet with a tense, covetous air; he wants her, yet has to wait his turn. This subtle detail intensifies the moment's "romance" with some gratifying implications: his desire increases ours; she wants us more than she wants him; his defeat is our victory. Of course, this triangle is not the least bit risky—if a few young men have reappeared on the scene, they are housebound and discreet, and know enough to yield to their betters.

This Jamaica is, indeed, a land of "romance": a vicarious delight, as vivid and safe as a daydream. Although this offer looks like a sexual enticement, it actually tempts us *away* from all stimulation, into a cool and silent twilight. The dim elegance of the setting, the dancers' conspicuous propriety, the atmosphere of bygone days, all evoke Jamaica as a lush retreat for those who are tired or afraid of living.

We might have thought, midway through the commercial, that we were being summoned to a "pleasure spot," a place that gets the juices flowing—a land of easy girls and lots to eat. But this is no country for young men, black *or* white. After the fisherman appears, we move away from arousal, toward a more lulling and sinister allure. Ostensibly tantalizing, the ad appeals to a longing for escape—from the flesh, from conflict, from adulthood. Blacks, ordinarily so threatening to whites, are here transformed into protective parents.

Both Hospitality and Bounty evince an old-fashioned maternal warmth; they are large and sweet, and wear kerchiefs on their heads, like mammies. The "food" itself—lobster, melons, edible natives—matters less than our sense that these abundant servants will feed us, protect us, and otherwise cater to our rediscovered infancy. The repeated invitation to "come home" is therefore an appeal for regression, as well as a request that we "make it Jamaica again."

And what is the real end of this return to infancy? Just what does this Jamaica hold for the man who wants to come all the way back home, even as far as the sheltering womb? This desire for perfect equilibrium suggests a deeper longing for a quietude still more absolute: "Come back to tranquility." The ultimate calm, which no "unrest" can violate, is *this* Jamaica's real attraction. The woman at the railing stands *above* the jungle, as if to tempt us up and away from that worrisome lower region, toward an ease that is complete, unlike the fleeting joys of girls and flowers. The waterfall behind her plashes noiselessly, like one of the sights at Forest Lawn. This Jamaica is, in every sense, the last resort.

These grim innuendoes tell us something about the contradictory character of the whole commercial, and about the consumeristic world view which it represents. The repeated exhortation to "come back" is both a plea and a command; and this tonal ambiguity reflects another,

37

deeper ambiguity in the message itself, which offers old strength while confirming recent weakness. We are asked to rule once more, and yet this very vision of a homecoming is, necessarily, a temptation to surrender, since it assumes that the world away from home is too much for us. More to the point, the notion of "return," Freud suggests, always exerts this morbid fascination, because it gratifies the death instinct, that impulse to revert to "an initial state from which the living entity has at one time or other departed and to which it is striving to return by the circuitous paths along which its development leads."

THIS STATE OF INFANTILE OR MORBID HELPLESSNESS IS, paradoxically, the ultimate condition of the perfect consumer, who energetically spends. If he is entirely "free to choose," to buy anything, satisfy any longing, without any constraints of time, nature, income, or federal government—if he is, in other words, that wandering and insatiable maw which commercials constantly image forth as the ideal human being—then he must finally become a mere pulsating node, something to be hooked up to sustaining appliances, like the comatose or cryogenically preserved, those fetal entities that might as well be dead.

All the paeans to "home" and "renewal" currently saturating American culture may sound like calls to arms, but they are only asking us to lie down and die. This Jamaica would be just the place to follow that fatal order, a sort of Jonestown and Fantasy Island combined. Its pleasures involve no risks whatsoever: you can't get hurt, bored, or disappointed, because here time stands still and conflict is unknown. The commercial ends with one last promise that Jamaica will restore us to this static dominance—over her blacks, over her resources, over time itself.

The old man with the walking stick sums up for all the menials who have preceded him. He is *very* old, and so represents the culmination of the aging process for Jamaican males, which dispels the threat of potency: young polo player, young and proud/old fisherman, still vigorous but humbled/ancient sage, loyal and weak. He is debilitated not simply by his age, but by his posture of servility. He is himself a picture of "the way things used to be," tottering along with a smile of broad benevolence, and wearing the uniform of the devoted pappy: white shirt and trousers, modest necktie, dark suspenders, white hat, gold inlays. He is peaceable, and, like a privileged retainer, enforces the peace among his own. The tykes at his feet wear party clothes, and they frolic with a markedly unchildlike cautiousness, like a flock of drugged sheep.

These strange details offer more assurance that Jamaica's young are content and tractable, unlike the uppity polo players (and many real

Jamaicans). It is significant that the old man and his little charges move leftward, thus visually countering the polo players, who moved toward the right. "Come back to the way things used to be": it is a moment that appears to celebrate tradition. These young seem to revere their elders; while their guardian speaks, they climb respectfully onto the gnarled base of the old tree, as if playing homage to that symbol of duration and stability.

And, of course, the commercial encourages dependency as surely as it seems to offer power. It courts us as potential masters by tempting us with a vision of our own potential helplessness. In Jamaica, we will be so strong that the natives will take care of all our needs; we will be as mighty as any baby. This paralyzing contradiction lies at the heart of the tense relations between master and slave, each seeming weak and strong at once. Not by coincidence, the same contradiction underlies the strategies of advertising, which promise an impossible advantage: through enfeebling dependence on "services" and products, you can become autonomous and powerful.

In order to make this offer convincing, advertisers put together costly little narratives far more inventive and sophisticated than anything else on television. The works succeed like clever servants, flattering us with all sorts of attention, winning small victories through blandishments that we don't quite notice, approaching us with a deference that can barely hide their deep contempt. They make a fortune off our negligence, and so we really ought to keep an eye on them.

Afterword

. . . .

SOME MONTHS AFTER THIS ESSAY APPEARED IN 1981, Young & Rubicam aired a revised version of the Jamaica fantasy. The structure, pace, and music were the same, but now the sun was shining brightly on the island, the wind and waves were active, the natives beckoning in a snappier and more athletic way. The subsequent ads in that campaign (a huge success) have all been thus superficially enlivened—and yet all have retained the sinister atmosphere of the original, the same eerie tranquillity that enwraps the captive slave ship in Melville's "Benito Cereno." This is understandable, since the appeal of this mythical "Jamaica" depends on just such ambiguity. The first ad was too dark—not quite ambiguous enough.

According to a few insiders, the campaign was deliberately lightened up in part because this essay had publicized the excessive gloom of the first commercial—one more example of advertising's impulse not to be too noticeable (see pp. 12–13 above).■

Getting Dirty

E ARE OUTSIDE A HOUSE, LOOKING IN THE WINDOW, and this is what we see: a young man, apparently nude and half-crazed with anxiety, lunging toward the glass. "Gail!" he screams, as he throws the window open and leans outside, over a flowerbox full of geraniums: "The most important shower of my life, and you switch deodorant soap!" He is, we now see, only half-naked, wearing a towel around his waist; and he shakes a packaged bar of soap—"Shield"—in one accusing hand. Gail, wearing a blue man-tailored shirt, stands outside, below the window, clipping a hedge. She handles this reproach with an ease that suggests years of contempt. "Shield is better," she explains patiently, in a voice somewhat deeper than her husband's. "It's extra strength." (Close-up of the package in the husband's hand, Gail's efficient finger gliding along beneath the legend, THE EXTRA STRENGTH DEODORANT SOAP.) "Yeah," whimpers Mr. Gail, "but my first call on J. J. Siss [sic], the company's *toughest customer*, and now *this*!" Gail nods with broad mock-sympathy, and stands firm: "Shield fights odor better, so you'll feel *cleaner*," she assures her husband, who darts away with a jerk of panic, as Gail rolls her eyes heavenward and gently shakes her head, as if to say, "What a half-wit!"

Cut to our hero, as he takes his important shower. No longer frantic, he now grins down at himself, apparently delighted to be caked with Shield, which, in its detergent state, has the consistency of wet cement. He then goes out of focus, as if glimpsed through a shower door. "Clinical tests prove," proclaims an eager baritone, "Shield fights odor better than the *leading* deodorant soap!" A bar of Shield (green) and a bar of that other soap (yellow) zip up the screen with a festive toot, forming a sort of graph which demonstrates that Shield does, indeed, "fight odor better, so you'll feel *cleaner*!"

This particular contest having been settled, we return to the major one, which has yet to be resolved. Our hero reappears, almost transformed: calmed down, dressed up, his voice at least an octave lower. "I *do* feel cleaner!" he announces cheerily, leaning into the doorway of a room where Gail is arranging flowers. She pretends to be ecstatic at this news, and he comes toward her, setting himself up for a profound humiliation by putting on a playful air of suave command. Adjusting his tie like a real man of the world, he saunters over to his wife and her flower bowl, where he plucks a dainty purple flower and lifts it to his lapel: "And," he boasts throughout all this, trying to make his voice sound even deeper, "with old J. J.'s business and my brains—" "—you'll . . . *clean up again*?" Gail asks with suggestive irony, subverting his authoritative pose by leaning against him, draping one hand over his shoulder to dangle a big yellow daisy down his chest. Taken aback, he shoots her a distrustful look, and she titters at him.

Finally, the word SHIELD appears in extreme close-up and the camera pulls back, showing two bars of the soap, one packaged and one not, on display amidst an array of steely bubbles. "Shield fights odor better, so you'll feel *cleaner*!" the baritone reminds us, and then our hero's face appears once more, in a little square over the unpackaged bar of soap: "I feel *cleaner* than *ever before*!" he insists, sounding faintly unconvinced.

Is all this as stupid as it seems at first? Or is there, just beneath the surface of this moronic narrative, some noteworthy design, intended to appeal to (and to worsen) some of the anxieties of modern life? A serious look at this particular trifle might lead us to some strange discoveries.

We are struck, first of all, by the commercial's pseudofeminism, an advertising ploy with a long history, and one ubiquitous on television nowadays. Although the whole subject deserves more extended treatment, this commercial offers us an especially rich example of the strategy. Typically, it woos its female viewers—i.e., those who choose the soap in most households—with a fantasy of dominance; and it does so by inverting the actualities of woman's lot through a number of imperceptible details. For instance, in this marriage it is the wife, and not the husband, who gets to keep her name; and Gail's name, moreover, is a potent one, because of its brevity and its homonymic connotation. (If this housewife were more delicately named, called "Lillian" or "Cecilia," it would lessen her illusory strength.) She is also equipped in more noticeable ways: she's the one who wears the button-down shirt in this family, she's the one who's competent both outdoors and in the house, and it is she, and only she, who wields the tool.

These visual details imply that Gail is quite a powerful housewife, whereas her nameless mate is a figure of embarrassing impotence. This "man," in fact, is actually Gail's *wife*: he is utterly feminized, striking a posture and displaying attributes which men have long deplored in women. In other words, this commercial, which apparently takes the woman's side, is really the expression (and reflection) of misogyny. Gail's husband is dependent and hysterical, entirely without that self-possession which we expect from solid, manly types, like Gail. This is partly the result of his demeanor: in the opening scene, his voice sometimes cracks ludicrously, and he otherwise betrays the shrill desperation of a man who can't remember where he left his scrotum. The comic effect of this frenzy, moreover, is subtly enhanced by the mise-en-scène, which puts the man in a conventionally feminine position—in dishabille, looking down from a window. Thus we infer that he is sheltered and housebound, a modern Juliet calling for his/her Romeo; or—more appropriately—the image suggests a scene in some suburban red-light district, presenting this husband as an item on display, like the flowers just below his stomach, available for anyone's enjoyment, at a certain price. Although in one way contradictory, these implications are actually quite congruous, for they both serve to emasculate the husband, so that the wife might take his place, or play his part.

Such details, some might argue, need not have been the conscious work of this commercial's makers. The authors, that is, might have worked by instinct rather than design, and so would have been no more aware of their work's psychosocial import than we ourselves: they just wanted to make the guy look like a wimp, merely for the purposes of domestic comedy. While such an argument certainly does apply to many ads, in this case it is unlikely. Advertising agencies do plenty of research, by which we can assume that they don't select their tactics arbitrarily. They take pains to analyze the culture which they help to sicken, and then, with much wit and cynicism, use their insights in devising their small dramas. This commercial is a subtle and meticulous endorsement of castration, meant to play on certain widespread guilts and insecurities; and all we need to do to demonstrate this fact is to subject the two main scenes to the kind of visual analysis which commercials, so brief and broad, tend to resist (understandably). The ad's visual implications are too carefully achieved to have been merely accidental or unconscious.

The crucial object in the opening shot is that flower box with its bright geraniums, which is placed directly in front of the husband's groin. This clever stroke of composition has the immediate effect of equating our hero's manhood with a bunch of flowers. This is an exquisitely perverse suggestion, rather like using a cigar to represent the Eternal Feminine: flowers are frail, sweet, and largely ornamental, hardly an appropriate phallic symbol, but (of course) a venerable symbol of *maidenhood*. The geraniums stand, then, not for the husband's virility, but for its absence.

More than a clever instance of inversion, furthermore, these phallic blossoms tell us something odd about this marital relationship. As Gail, clippers in hand, turns from the hedge to calm her agitated man, she appears entirely capable of calming him quite drastically, if she hasn't done so already (which might explain his hairless chest and high-pitched voice). She has the power, that is, to take away whatever slender potency he may possess, and uses the power repeatedly, trimming her husband (we infer) as diligently as she prunes her foliage. And, as she can snip his manhood, so too can she restore it, which is what the second scene implies. Now the flower bowl has replaced the flower box as the visual crux, dominating the bottom center of the frame with a crowd of blooms. As the husband, cleaned and dressed, comes to stand beside his wife, straining to affect a new authority, the flower bowl too appears directly at his lower center; so that Gail, briskly adding flowers to the bouquet, appears to be replenishing his vacant groin with extra stalks. He has a lot to thank her for, it seems: she is his helpmate, confidante, adviser, she keeps his house and grounds in order, and she is clearly the custodian of the family jewels.

Of course, her restoration of his potency cannot be complete, or he might shatter her mastery by growing a bit too masterful himself. He could start choosing his own soap, or take her shears away, or—worst of all—walk out for good. Therefore, she punctures his momentary confidence by taunting him with that big limp daisy, countering his lordly gesture with the boutonniere by flaunting that symbol of his floral status. He can put on whatever airs he likes, but she still has his fragile vigor firmly in her hand.

NOW WHAT, PRECISELY, MOTIVATES THIS SEXLESS BATTLE of the sexes? That is, what really underlies this tense and hateful marriage, making the man so weak, the woman so contemptuously helpful? The script, seemingly nothing more than a series of inanities, contains the answer to these questions, conveying, as it does, a concern with cleanliness that amounts to an obsession: "Shield fights odor better, so you'll feel cleaner!" "I *do* feel cleaner!" "Shield fights odor better, so you'll feel *cleaner*!" "I feel *cleaner* then *ever before*!" Indeed, the commercial emphasizes the feeling of cleanliness even more pointedly than the name of the product, implying, by its very insistence, a feeling of dirtiness, an apprehension of deep filth.

And yet there is not a trace of dirt in the vivid world of this commercial. Unlike many ads for other soaps, this one shows no sloppy children, no sweatsoaked workingmen with blackened hands, not even a bleary housewife in need of her morning shower. We never even glimpse the ground in Gail's world, nor is her husband even faintly smudged. In fact, the filth which Shield supposedly "fights" is not physical but psychological besmirchment: Gail's husband feels soiled because of what he has to do for a living, in order to keep Gail in that nice big house, happily supplied with shirts and shears.

"My first call on J. J. Siss, the company's *toughest customer*, and now *this!*" The man's anxiety is yet another feminizing trait, for it is generally women, and not men, who are consumed by doubts about the sweetness of their bodies, which must never be offensive to the guys who run the world. (This real anxiety is itself aggravated by commercials.) Gail's husband must play the female to the mighty J. J. Siss, a name whose oxymoronic character implies perversion: "J. J." is a stereotypic nickname for the potent boss, while "Sis" is a term of endearment, short for "sister" (and perhaps implying "sissy," too, in this case). Gail's husband must do his boyish best to please the voracious J. J. Siss, just as a prostitute must satisfy a demanding trick, or "tough customer." It is therefore perfectly fitting that this employee refer to the encounter, not as a "meeting" or "appointment," but as a "call"; and his demeaning posture in the window—half dressed and bent over—conveys, we now see, a definitive implication.

Gail's job as the "understanding wife" is not to rescue her husband from these sordid obligations, but to help him meet them successfully. She may seem coolly self-sufficient, but she actually depends on her husband's attractiveness, just as a pimp relies on the charm of his whore. And, also like a pimp, she has to keep her girl in line with occasional reminders of who's boss. When her husband starts getting uppity *après la douche*, she jars him from the very self-assurance which she had helped him to discover, piercing that "shield" which was her gift.

"And, with old J. J.'s business and my brains—" "—you'll . . . *clean up again?*" He means, of course, that he'll work fiscal wonders with old J. J.'s account, but his fragmentary boast contains a deeper significance, upon which Gail plays with sadistic cleverness. "Old J. J.'s business and my brains" implies a feminine self-description, since it suggests a variation on the old commonplace of "brains vs. brawn": J. J.'s money, in the world of this commercial (as in ours), amounts to brute strength, which the flexible husband intends to complement with his mother wit. Gail's retort broadens this unconscious hint of homosexuality: "—you'll . . . *clean up again?*" Given the monetary nature of her husband's truncated remark, the retort must mean primarily, "You'll make a lot of money." If this were all it meant, however, it would not be a joke, nor would the husband find it so upsetting. Moreover, we have no evidence that Gail's husband ever "cleaned up"—i.e., made a sudden fortune—in the past. Rather, the ad's milieu and *dramatis personae* suggest upward mobility, gradual savings and a yearly raise, rather than one prior killing. What Gail is referring to, in fact, with that "again," is her husband's shower: she implies that what he'll have to do,

47

after his "call" on J. J. Siss, is, quite literally, wash himself off. Like any other tidy hooker, this man will have to clean up after taking on a tough customer, so that he might be ready to take on someone else.

THESE SUGGESTIONS OF PEDERASTY ARE INTENDED, NOT AS a literal characterization of the husband's job, but as a metaphor for what it takes to get ahead: Gail's husband, like most white-collar workers, must debase himself to make a good impression, toadying to his superiors, offering himself, body and soul, to the corporation. Maybe, therefore, it isn't really Gail who has neutered him; it may be his way of life that has wrought the ugly change. How, then, are women represented here? The commercial does deliberately appeal to women, offering them a sad fantasy of control; but it also, perhaps inadvertently, illuminates the unhappiness which makes that fantasy attractive.

The husband's status, it would seem, should make Gail happy, since it makes her physically comfortable, and yet Gail can't help loathing her husband for the degradations which she helps him undergo. For her part of the bargain is, ultimately, no less painful than his. She has to do more than put up with him; she has to prepare him for his world of affairs, and then must help him to conceal the shame. Of course, it's all quite hopeless. She clearly despises the man whom she would bolster; and the thing which she provides to help him "feel cleaner than ever before" is precisely what has helped him do the job that's always made him feel so dirty. "A little water clears us of this deed" is her promise, which is false, for she is just as soiled as her doomed husband, however fresh and well-ironed she may look.

Of couse, the ad not only illuminates this mess, but helps perpetuate it, by obliquely gratifying the guilts, terrors, and resentments that underlie it and arise from it. The strategy is not meant to be noticed, but works through the apparent comedy, which must therefore be studied carefully, not passively received. Thus, thirty seconds of ingenious advertising, which we can barely stand to watch, tell us something more than we might want to know about the souls of men and women under corporate capitalism.

Afterword

· ·

ADVERTISING AGE CAME BACK AT THIS ESSAY WITH AN edifying two-pronged put-down. In the issue for 7 June 1982, Fred Danzig (now the magazine's editor) devoted his weekly column to the Shield analysis: "The professor prunes a television trifle," ran the headline. After a genial paraphrase of my argument, Danzig reported a few of the things I'd told him in a telephone conversation, and then finally got down to the necessary business of dismissive chuckling: "[Miller's] confession that he had watched the Shield spot more than 15 times quickly enabled me to diagnose his problem: Self-inflicted acute soap storyboard sickness. This condition inevitably leads to a mind spasm, to hallucination." The column featured the ad's crucial frames, over a caption quoting an unnamed "Lever executive": "We can hardly wait for Mr. Miller to get his hands on the Old Testament. His comments merit no comment from us; the Shield commercial speaks for itself."

Leaving aside (with difficulty) that naive crack about the Bible, I point here to the exemplary suppressiveness of this seeming "trifle" in *Advertising Age*. Indeed, "the Shield commercial speaks for itself," but the guardians of the spectacle try to talk over it, permitting it no significance beyond the superficial pitch: "—so you'll feel *cleaner!*" Through managerial scorn ("no comment") and journalistic ridicule ("mind spasm . . . hallucination"), they would shut down all discussion. (J. Walter Thompson later refused to send anyone to debate the matter with me on a radio program.) Thus was a divergent reading written off as the perversity of yet another cracked "professor"—when in fact it was the ad itself that was perverse.

Although that campaign did not appeal to its TV audience (J. Walter Thompson ultimately lost the Shield account), such belligerent "common sense" does have a most receptive public. While the admakers— and others—insist that "people today are adwise" (see p. 24 above), in fact most Americans still perceive the media image as transparent, a sign that simply says what it means and means what it says. They therefore tend to dismiss any intensive explication as a case of "reading too much into it"—an objection that is philosophically dubious, albeit useful to the admakers and their allies. It is now, perhaps, one

49

obligation of the academic humanists, empowered, as they are, by critical theory, to demonstrate at large the faultiness—and the dangers—of that objection.

A HISTORICAL NOTE ON THE SHIELD COMMERCIAL'S pseudofeminism. Since 1982, the contemptuous housewife has all but vanished from the antiseptic scene of advertising; Gail was among the last of an endangered species. By now, the housewife/mother is a despised figure—most despised by actual housewife/mothers, who make up 60% of the prime-time audience. Since these viewers now prefer to see themselves represented as executives, or at least as mothers with beepers and attaché cases, the *hausfrau* of the past, whether beaming or sneering, has largely been obliterated by the advertisers. In 1985, Advertising to Women Inc., a New York advertising agency, found that, out of 250 current TV ads, only nine showed recognizable Moms.

This is a triumph not for women's liberation, but for advertising; for, now that Mom is missing from the ads, presumably off knocking heads together in the boardroom, it is the commodity that seems to warm her home and tuck her children in at night.

In any case, the Shield strategy itself has certainly outlasted the wry and/or perky Mommy-imagoes of yesteryear. Indeed, because the sexes are now at war within the scene of advertising (and elsewhere), the nasty visual metaphors have become ubiquitous. For example, note how "Amy," in the ad below (taken from *Good Housekeeping*, February 1988), appears to topple her wincing boyfriend with a shapely knee right to the tulips. ("Ohh . . . ")■

"Family Feud"

. . . .

FAMILY FEUD" MAY WELL BE THE CLEVEREST GAME show on TV. It's certainly the most absorbing. "Family Feud" has been on the air since 1975, it comes on (in most cities) twice a day, and yet it hasn't lost its fascination, and probably never will, as long as millions stare at millions of TV sets. When Mark Goodson and his associates first cooked this trifle up, they created one of TV's few abiding things, a spectacle as durable and bright as Johnny Carson, or a no-wax floor.

If you aren't a regular viewer of "Family Feud," you might enjoy a leisurely description. Of course, trying to describe a game show is a bit like trying to describe the kind of dreams you have when half-asleep with fever. Even the weirdest of fantasies, however, has its own implicit structure, and so does "Family Feud," whose generic craziness conceals a form as rigid and significant as the plan of any other public ritual.

The show starts with the usual sudden uproar. "It's time for—'Family Feud'!!" someone yells, backed by a screechy din that sounds like bluegrass music played by speed freaks. We see the title, its dark red letters rendered in mock needlepoint across a yellow oval, like an enormous sampler, and then the title turns into some surname—PFISTER, say—also lettered in mock needlepoint. The studio audience goes nuts, the music yelps and twangs, as the oval zips leftward like a sliding door, revealing a sort of mock-Victorian parlor, where the five immobile Pfisters pose in wacky imitation of some old-fashioned family portrait. After the announcer shouts their names, the Pfisters break out of this *tableau vivant* and line up, five abreast, applauding back at the applauding crowd. This rapid process then repeats itself, showing us the Pfisters' rival house—say, GRUBB—and then both little clans come bounding out onto the stage, a hectic edifice of lurid hues and tiny winking lights, and face off gaily, five abreast, each standing in a happy row behind a sort of elongated podium.

Now the music turns to brass, hiccuping and blaring in the Vegas mode, and everybody's clapping. Then, ". . . the *star* of 'Family Feud,' " whoops the announcer, *"—Richard Dawson*!!" The place goes crazier, and out strolls this aging, deeply suntanned figure, resplendent in a

51

roomy three-piece suit of glossy brown or gray, a huge carnation shining on his left lapel. He meanders downstage between the cheering Grubbs and Pfisters, as a much-loved drunk might join a raucous party thrown in his honor, and halts to do a spot of mellow shtick. We see at once that Dawson is no typical M.C., not an unctuous, chortling "host," beaming like a salesman, but rather comes on with the boozy self-possession of a weathered libertine. He seems pure show biz, a veteran of unnumbered poolside hangovers. As he glistens on the screen, his asides a little slurred, his shirt cuffs vast and blinding, you start to feel a little groggy, and your Sony starts to smell of aftershave. And yet, while Dawson thus evinces the authority of smooth decay, he also wears, incongruously, the uniform of high-paid middle management—the ample suit, the boutonniere, a glittering watch chain. He is, in short, an ingenious combination of intimidating traits. With his gray Neronian bangs, his puffy, umbered face, and his obtrusive vest, he looks like some old Roman debauchee now working as a district manager for Burger King.

The families on "Family Feud" clearly regard this wry and shiny boss, not just with something like affection, but with deep respect. At first, this seems a little strange, given the glaring contrast between him and them. For, whether the Grubbs and Pfisters claim to hail from L.A., the Bronx, or Salt Lake City, they really represent our fabled heartland. Invariably bright-eyed, cheery, vigorous, and neat, these folks all look as stolid and clean-cut as Dawson seems unwholesome. Although he's clearly not their type, however, Dawson counteracts his daunting aura with intense displays of flattering concern. He falls all over them from start to finish, with an oleaginous noblesse oblige perhaps unrivaled on TV.

After his moment downstage, he turns to do some quick preliminary schmoozing with each team's captain, usually the Dad or elder brother. Leaning forward chummily, with a familiar drawl, Dawson orders Mr. Pfister to identify the family, and the eager patriarch booms back at him, with strained heartiness: "Well, Richard," Pfister thunders, "this is my beautiful wife Adele—my lovely daughter Gina—my good lookin' son Todd," and so on, as the camera pans across this taut ménage, each Pfister greeting "Richard" with a bellow or a chirp, according to gender. There's some talk about how Pfister earns his livelihood, and then, at the chat's conclusion, the team formally presents the star of "Family Feud" with some homely offering, usually handmade, such as a bag of cookies, a necklace made of chestnuts, or an inscribed hat.

After a similar brief visit with the Grubbs, Dawson shouts, "Let's play the feud!" and swaggers over to his central place behind a smaller podium, beneath a big bright board comprised of numbered slats. A Pfister and a Grubb stand ready at his left and right, as Dawson reads a question, which he always introduces with the same revealing formula: "One hundred people surveyed, top six answers on The Board, here's the question: Name an appliance that's always plugged in." Grubb and Pfister each lunge forward, and the first to smack a massive button on Dawson's podium gets to answer first: "A vacuum cleaner!" hollers Grubb, who is not, perhaps, as quick as his right hand. Chuckling, Dawson looks up at The Board: *"Vacuum cleaner?"* he calls out, but The Board is still, and there flashes over it a coarse red "X," emphasized by a derisive honk. Dawson turns to Pfister, who, knowing her appliances, shrieks out, "A *toaster!*" Dawson addresses The Board with this wiser answer, whereupon one of the slats turns over with a ping, revealing the word "toaster" and a certain number, representing points.

The Pfisters exult, because they've won the chance to play this question out. Dawson proceeds down the line along their podium, asking each of them to name another ever-plugged-in thing. Until the schedule starts to tighten, Dawson will conduct each brief interrogation with an efficient stream of cagey banter; and he always greets each female panelist with a loud kiss on the lips, as the menfolk stand there, grinning tightly. (The kiss is Dawson's trademark.) The Pfisters keep it up until they win or lose the round. That is, they either guess every answer on The Board, thereby winning all the points available, or they come up with three "wrong" answers, whereupon the Grubbs jump in and try to guess one answer yet unchosen, stealing the round if they succeed.

The game goes on through several rounds, each devoted to another mundane question—one that refers either to the world of goods ("Name something you have two of in your bathroom"), the teachings of TV ("Name the wealthiest man in show business"), or the routines of daily life ("Name the first thing you do when you wake up in the morning"). Finally, whichever family earns three hundred points gets to play the "Lightning Round." After a show of deft commiseration with the losing Grubbs, who, no less upbeat, promptly disappear, Dawson moves down front and center, as one quivering Pfister comes to stand beside him and another prances off stage left. All is quiet; the Pfister's head, inclined, eyes closed, as if in prayer, appears in closeup—and then Dawson reads off five quick questions, the Pfister blurting out an answer to each one, as fifteen seconds tick away. When time's up, both turn around to hot applause, and face a sort of scoreboard at the rear of the stage. With one familiar arm around the Pfister's neck, Dawson repeats each question and reply, pausing as each answer shows up on the scoreboard with some number next to it. Once we get the grand subtotal, Pfister No. 2 sprints back to undergo the same ordeal. The suspense is captivating, as we wait to find out if the Pfisters have racked up two hundred points, which will win them $10,000.

If the family succeeds, the crowd once again goes berserk, and the winning Pfisters grab each other, bouncing up and down as if attempting a collective levitation. As Dawson wanders offstage, many further Pfisters, hitherto unknown, come bolting down the aisles to join their kin. We cut to a commercial. When the show comes back, the much-augmented house of Pfister stands spread out, euphorically, across the stage, and Dawson hands one of them (usually a tot or oldster) a big sheet of white cardboard, with the amount they've won inscribed in Magic Marker, in a childish scrawl. Sometimes, if there are any kids onstage, he hands out lollipops. Finally, we see the credits, and, under them, the Pfisters frolicking and clapping to the rhythm of the grating theme.

What is this all about? Why is this show so popular, why so engrossing? Unlike other game shows, "Family Feud" is never heatedly competitive, nor does the cash prize ultimately matter. Dawson tends to discourage the grim desire to score, turning faintly chilly when confronted with impatient avarice. Usually, however, he doesn't need to convey such scorn, since the players are nearly always buoyant, either good winners or good losers. In fact, both families have more or less cleaned up before the game begins, since the show pays for their trips west, puts them up in a hotel for two nights, and provides them with a car and a comfortable per diem.

If the point of "Family Feud" is not the prize, then maybe it's the emphasis on kinship. "Family Feud" would seem the most straightforward *family* show on television. Its "stars" appear to be just plain folks, exemplars of the old domestic virtues. For one thing, each household sticks together with amazing loyalty. No matter how stupid someone's answer, even if Dawson gets the giggles, the others show maniacal support, clapping hard and roaring out, "Good answer! Good answer!" Such clannishness seems out of place on television, whose impulse is to shatter families, not unite them, ceaselessly exhorting each and every "individual" to go his/her "own way," i.e., to live a "life" of nonstop buying. "Family Feud" appears a broad exception to the TV rule, from its opening title, with "family" proclaimed in scarlet letters, through its closing video portrait of the Pfisters/Grubbs/O'Rourkes/Barzinis/ Goldbergs/Jeffersons/Wongs/Romeros, each group rewarded, seemingly, for its intense togetherness.

And yet, in fact, it isn't the familial bond that wins the prize on "Family Feud," but the family's successful self-erasure. Each of Dawson's questions is a test of sameness, its answers based on tallies of "one hundred people surveyed," well ahead of time, by the show's producers. A "correct" reply is therefore not the smartest, but the *least* inventive answer, matching an alleged "consensus" expertly defined and validated by the show itself. Thus the irresistible appeal of "Family Feud" is also the attraction of TV, which tells us endlessly what "we" believe, thereby using our supposed group sentiments to reconfirm its own authority. "Family Feud" is basically a festive variant of those other forms of modern tabulation, the marketing survey and the opinion poll. And so it is precisely like TV itself—a pseudopopulist diversion based on crude statistics.

For all its seeming family pride, then, each group that plays on "Family Feud" does not come on to manifest its own discrete identity, but rather struggles to get rid of it. Victory demands the absolute suppression of any wayward thought or preference, any eccentricity that might define the family apart from TV's bland reconstruction of ourselves. If they want to win, the players must respond with ready minds of total emptiness, letting the mythic mass speak through them. Thus "Family Feud" is actually a high-speed ritual of absorption, which has its consummation only when five beings demonstrate their own ecstatic averageness. In visual terms, the real reward is not the money, which we never glimpse, nor even Dawson's cardboard token, but the climactic moment when those nameless others pour from the audience onto the stage, creating the illusion of an oceanic merger, as the separated clan now happily dissolves into the gathering flood of erstwhile watchers.

Once we recall its proper meaning, the title too suggests this terminal absorption. A "family feud" is not, in fact, a dispute between two separate houses, but one that divides a *single* family into warring factions. The show's real purpose is to celebrate, not specific households, but the encroaching, all-inclusive tribe of viewers, that unseen mass into which those households long to be reintegrated, nervously competing for acceptance like extruded siblings. In other words, all the families on "Family Feud" appear to be related to each other, seeming fundamentally alike, however various their surnames, hue, or points of origin.

THESE SUPERFICIAL DIFFERENCES MEAN QUITE A LOT TO THE show's creators, who consider "Family Feud" a tremendous example of progressive toleration. As the show's producer, Howard Felsher, told me, it is "the only game show to use interracial families," and the only one that features handicapped players (other shows preferring to exclude them, since viewers turn nasty when they see afflicted persons lose). Dawson, furthermore, meticulously kisses every female, "irrespective of age, color, or religion," a practice that inspires "a lot of hate mail."

Even if it does offend a few thousand crackpots, however, all the ostensible diversity on "Family Feud" actually amounts to nothing, because the program's many families are, in fact, impossible to tell apart. Some may be multicolored, another may include a paraplegic, but nearly all are indistinguishably blithe and peppy, displaying exactly the same "good attitude." This is the only quality that counts on "Family Feud," whose process of selection is, therefore, exquisitely exclusive, since it is intended to screen out, not any patent traits, but subtler deficiencies of mood or temper.

Of course, the show's custodians are unconscious of its real exclusiveness. Felsher's paean to the show's warmhearted liberalism was immediately followed, and subverted, by his account of just how few would-be contestants finally ever make it onto "Family Feud." "Within two or three years," he recalled, "we had milked L.A. of the cream of L.A. families," and so they set out to the north and east, in search of further families no less fresh and thick than that original Californian product. By now the producers have extracted players from every state of the union, and continue to maintain their stores with frequent and expensive junkets all around, inspecting, on each stop, about eight hundred families in four days. All in all, it costs roughly $500,000 per annum "just to keep the show good," that is, to make sure that everyone we watch will seem to certify the program's image of the ideal family. A player might sometimes play a little too intently, but there is never any bickering, no livid disappointment, no angry blame on "Family Feud," whose teams all bounce and clap alike, all cheer each other's errors and successes equally.

The families' apparent sameness must, in part, reflect an actual similarity. For instance, many of the families represent the same vague social stratum. Although we sometimes see a team whose captain is a cabbie, say, or an ophthalmologist, most of the father figures seem to inhabit that gray realm of low-to-middle management wherein Richard Dawson's vest appears to symbolize the highest power. However, the players' sameness may have less to do with any prior class identity than with the implicit pressures of the show itself, which will reward with its exposure only those contestants who can and will behave like grateful employees, or overstimulated children. And yet the presentation is more complicated still, because this TV show does not just fabricate a certain image of the happy norm, but at the same time undercuts that image, in order to enhance the dominance of TV.

For it is basically TV which Dawson stands for, TV that lends him his charisma, charging his outlandish image with its cool power. Although his suit and suntan each evince a different kind of potency, it is TV that makes him seem unassailably superior to his dim, childlike wards.

Whereas these indistinct contestants just flash by, tense and squealing, Dawson is a finished man of television, having mastered its style completely in the course of his imperceptible career: after an apprenticeship in British show biz, he became a regular on "Hogan's Heroes," and then a "permanent panelist" on "The Match Game," a frequent guest host on "The Tonight Show," and is now a quintessential TV entity, as smart, detached, and self-contradictory as the medium containing it.

Dawson approaches his provincial visitors exactly as TV regards its viewers. On the face of it, he seems to think the world of his players. He beams and coos all over each bright guest, as if, beneath his smarmy surface, there beats the doting heart of some old grandma. And yet this deft solicitude is not maternal, but commercial, the factitious "caring" of the corporate ad. Like McDonald's, Sears, American Airlines, IBM, etc., Dawson feigns a tender admiration for his subjects that actually belittles them. He always makes a beeline for the youngest or the oldest or the one on crutches, singling out, for his most ardent flatteries, those players who are most helpless. And when the captain describes his dismal job ("Well, Richard, I'm the assistant comptroller of a major hospital supply corporation!"), Dawson marvels politely, as you might treat a nine-year-old who tells you his career plans. Thus, through his pretense of esteem for these figures, Dawson genially exacts their full compliance, getting them to jump around and squeak like tots assaulting some department store Santa. Praising Dawson's fulsome tact, Howard Felsher put his finger squarely (if, again, unwittingly) on the crucial contradiction: "Dawson goes to each person, and *talks* to them, and gets to *know* them, and pats them on the *head*, and gives them a *lollipop*. He treats them like *human beings*!"

And Dawson dominates these human beings, not just by patronizing them, but also through the constant threat of his incisive ridicule. His is that televisual sangfroid that we also note in such comedians as, for instance, Johnny Carson, David Letterman, or Martin Mull, and in (again) most TV commercials—that air of laidback irony against which all enthusiasm seems contemptible. Underlying his displays of maudlin warmth, in other words, there is in Richard Dawson a relentless impulse to deride, with true aplomb, whatever is uncool or idiosyncratic, i.e., whatever is outside of, or less cool than, television. Whenever someone gives an odd or idiotic answer, Dawson devastates it swiftly with a murmured gag; and he often breaks into sudden fits of mimicry, putting on a redneck's twang when talking to the Arbs of Arkansas, doing Sessue Hayakawa in his exchanges with the Nakamuras of New York, and so on. Despite his able clucking, we always sense the abler parodist that lurks within; and so, we gather, do the families, who perceive that Dawson could, if he felt like it, utterly humiliate them, and

57

who therefore seek to mollify this witty manager through those ritual gestures of propitiation: they let him kiss their women, and they try to impress their innocence upon him with pathetic tokens of their wholesomeness.

Thus they attempt to win his, and TV's, acceptance, but the attempt must fail, because that joyful norm which they've been made to represent does not exist. The image of community on "Family Feud," and in the sunny worlds of numberless commercials, is merely a device whose function is to make TV seem like our happy home; whereas TV, in fact, only keeps us dispossessed, an extended mob of orphans with our noses pressed against the glass. The families on the screen may seem to have arrived in that bright place which we can only gape at, they may seem to have embodied that ideal which TV disingenuously proffers; and yet all they're really doing is what we do when we sit and watch: trying desperately to keep up with that low "reality" which TV and its sponsors have arranged for us. Although Dawson's questions seem simply to refer, objectively, to our bleak status quo, in fact they reinforce it. Implicitly ruling out the possibility of other ways of life, they require each player to know perfectly the consumer's trivial daily world, and nothing else. The show rewards those who, through their "right" answers, manifest a dumb acceptance of "the way it is"—the daily grind, the flood of products, the names and faces on TV.

Within this exhausting system, it becomes impossible to cling for long to any close community, although we are repeatedly enticed with images of that elusive closeness. It is therefore fitting that this apparent tribute to the family should turn out to be a shattering burlesque, as we discover once we take another look at the explosive opening of "Family Feud." The mock sampler, the mock bluegrass, the mock-Victorian mock portrait each suggest TV's familiar attitude of up-to-date contempt for the archaic family, an institution that once seemed to resist the blandishments of TV and its clientele. The opening, moreover, not only jeers at those dated symbols, but visibly subverts them, showing that TV has now replaced those emblems of familial fixity with its own endless, pointless, self-advancing change. The "sampler" slides away, the figures in the "portrait" jump into motion, the "bluegrass music," suggestive of the settled clan, turns into Richard Dawson's cue. Paradoxically, this spectacle itself has now become familiar, although it never can replace that real community which it applauds and cancels out. Absorbed by this off-putting introduction, we watch until the family that cheers together disappears together, and then we stare at something else.

Afterword

■ ■

I N 1988, LBS COMMUNICATIONS PRODUCED A NEW version of "Family Feud" for prime-time broadcast in the fall. Dawson "was never considered for the job," claimed LBS's chairman. "It's not that he didn't do an effective job, but you've got to move on." Dawson was replaced by a comedian named Ray Combs, who started his career doing warm-up routines for sitcom audiences. "Richard Dawson was great," Combs told *Advertising Age* in February 1988, "but his time for that show has passed. There are going to be people who love him, and people who love me. That's show business."

Certainly there is nothing new or interesting about such pitiless replacement—an essential feature of the market system generally, "show business" included. It is worth noting, however, that the second "Family Feud" was immediately touted as a show better than the first—better because more ironic. Thus *Advertising Age:* "Remember the osculating Richard Dawson who planted his lips on every female contestant on the old 'Family Feud'? Forget him. This new version dispenses with blandishments in favor of gibes. Host Ray Combs is a stand-up comic who trades jokes with the contestants. And it works."

The implication here is that Dawson was not also an ironist, not full of "gibes," but an old-fashioned suitor, quaintly serious with his "blandishments" and "osculations," and therefore laughable himself, in our cool eyes. Thus does the culture of TV continually sell the flattering myth of both "our" recent graduation into irony, and the comic earnestness of everyone who came before (see above, pp. 14–16).■

Off the Prigs

● ●

HILL STREET BLUES" IS NOT A HIT. OUT OF 97 REGU-
lar series in the 1980-81 season, the new police drama
ranked only 83rd in popularity. Nevertheless, Fred
Silverman, former head of NBC, claimed to like the show,
and expected it to pick up next season. In this case, he was
probably not relying on his instincts. Fred Silverman's instincts are a national disgrace, having brought us a number of emetic
divertissements whose reruns will foul the airways for the next thirty
years: "Charlie's Angels," "Fantasy Island," "The Love Boat," and too
many more. "Hill Street Blues" is in a different class, and ordinarily
would have a very short half-life, if subjected to Silverman's usual standards. For once, however, Silverman seemed to have heeded America's
television critics, who have cheered the show with an outcry of defensive praise unprecedented in the history of television.

By and large, they like it for two reasons. First of all, it strikes them
as very realistic, and so they tend, in their plaudits, to use certain ad-
jectives that suggest the cast of characters in a porno remake of *Snow
White*: "gutsy," "gritty," "racy," "raunchy," "punchy," "tough," and
"steamy." And yet they also applaud the show's correctness as a liberal
statement: the show is good because it contains little violence and no
offensive ethnic stereotypes. While its characters are ethnically diverse, enthused one columnist in a recent issue of *TV Guide*, they are
simply "a gathering of *human beings* who just happen to have widely
different last names. (You know, like real life.). . . . All [these] characters are so genuine and worthy, it's impossible not to like them."

NOW THAT'S HEARTWARMING, IF NOT VERY STEAMY. IN "REAL
life," it seems, there are no ethnic traits, nor any such things as national character, regional identity, or class consciousness. And everyone is
equally "genuine and worthy." This is gritty realism? In fact, "Hill
Street Blues" is not both true to life and idealized, because such a combination is impossible. A work might either reflect "real life" or transcend it. As it happens, "Hill Street Blues" does neither. Although
promising at first, the show soon settled down to do little more than
promulgate a tired ideology.

61

Its "realism" is largely the quick result of a few well-worn cinematic devices. A hand-held camera, for example, lends many scenes the jerky immediacy of a documentary. There is also plenty of inner-city texture. The precinct-house is credibly seedy, the producers having worked hard to see that things break down: the furnishings are dim and battered, the heat goes out, the vending machines (a running gag) have to be beaten regularly. The streets are a mess, like many of the characters, who overrun this perfect squalor in endless sleazy multitudes. Actors jam the foreground, background, middle distance, and stream across the frame from points unknown. Surely no cop show has ever seemed this crowded; this is *French Connection III*, directed by Thomas Malthus. Even the soundtrack is cluttered. The background hubbub nearly drowns out the dialogue, which is no mean feat, since the characters generally bellow as if going deaf. (You know, like real life.) Their dialogue also overlaps, charging the action with the sort of rich confusion that we notice every day, in films by Robert Altman.

Although this kind of naturalistic din has suffused many American films since the 1960s, on television it seems like a novelty. The show is also structurally unlike the usual prime-time item. Each episode is more fluid and various than the typical plot-and-subplot arrangement, sustaining at least three unrelated stories at a time. Moreover, things don't wind to a tidy close just before the final credits, but stray into subsequent episodes, as in a soap opera. Such openendedness, and the anarchic milieu, create an impression of hectic vitality. This impression is not lasting. Once we spot the gimmicks, that air of "realism" disappears, leaving a tissue of clichés, artfully modernized.

The old-fashioned cop show, best represented by Jack Webb's early productions ("Dragnet," "Adam-12"), usually would go like this: two stern half-wits drive around Los Angeles, looking for "suspicious behavior." Although technically policemen, these dank prigs seemed more like social workers from beyond the grave, always butting in and moralizing with dead faces. No one could be whiter than these guardians of the norm, who protected their necropolis from the threat of a faint diversity (creeps, crooks, punks).

SUCH WERE THE TV LAWMEN OF ANOTHER DAY, WHEN BOYS liked girls, skies were blue and blacks were Negroes. Now, of course, most (some?) of us laugh at those grim squares, preferring a groovier sort of policeman, hip, streetwise, and yet "caring," likely rebellious without losing his authoritative air, 100 percent American and still engagingly ethnic—Kojak, Baretta, Toma, Columbo. Collectively, these cops are not a force of clones, but as diverse an army as any band of bad guys, even as diverse as the very USA.

The Hill Street cops reflect this myth from the top down. The leadership is nicely varied. We have a Spanish-American lieutenant (Rene Enriquez) who runs the plainclothes division; the Polish-American sergeant Phil Esterhaus (Michael Conrad); and an Italian-American in Captain Frank Furillo (Daniel J. Travanti), the man in charge. Because this trio is acceptably motley, like the crowd in a United Way commercial, we are supposed to applaud it automatically. And just in case we miss the point, the show includes a built-in satire of the thick-witted WASP in the character of Howard Hunter (James B. Sikking), commander of a SWAT-type outfit. A large, eager buffoon with an angular jaw and blinding teeth, Hunter is accoutered like Douglas MacArthur and sounds like one of Nixon's henchmen (E. Howard Hunter?), always singing the praises of excessive force in bizarre bureaucratese.

THIS DEVALUATION OF THE STRAIGHT WHITE HUNTER would seem to place "Hill Street Blues" opposite the likes of "Dragnet," but the shows have much in common. Under the surface of his slight ethnicity, for instance, Captain Furillo is as much a pill as Jack Webb's Sergeant Joe Friday. His heritage is a great device, allowing him the authenticity of being Italian, while letting him overcome the stereotype of being Italian. At first, his looks suggest a perfect synthesis of various streetwise types. (He looks like James Caan wearing Roy Scheider's nose.) But Furillo is no warm and explosive Mediterranean, like Travolta, De Niro, et al. On the contrary, he plays so intently against that type that he seems to be turning to cement right on camera. He never moves his neck, and rarely speaks above a soft, slurred monotone, as if afraid that, if he ever lets go, he might break out into an oily tan and start touching everybody.

Furillo's stiff joints are a sign of integrity. He is, of course, much purer than everyone above him. His superiors are always inviting him out to lunch or breakfast so they can harass him with corrupt advice: he should "play ball," etc. He'll never capitulate, or have a bite, but sits and eyes their loaded plates with monkish disapproval. On the other hand, he unbends slightly among his underlings, sometimes even permitting himself a tight little smirk over their wacky ways.

Furillo's function is to seem superior to everyone around him, so that we can feel superior by identifying with him. This strategy is obvious when it refers to those in power: Frank's various bosses and counterparts in the police establishment are all smooth toadies and pompous fools, easy targets like the overdrawn Hunter. We are meant to look down on them because they are unenlightened. When it comes to the common man, however, the strategy becomes more insidious: through Furillo, we find the show's little people—civilians as well as policemen— terribly colorful and cute. Each cop is just an amalgam of certain social and psychological tics, all of them stereotypic. We can look down on these characters because their "foibles" are at once laughable and easy to define.

Belker (Bruce Weitz) is a funky maniac who likes to bite off parts of suspects, yet always phones his mother (hostile/Jewish). There is patrolman Andy Renko (Charles Haid), a loudmouthed northerner who puts on a Texas accent and always feels slighted (inferiority complex/"good ole boy"). Through this device, the show can include the obligatory cowboy without having to import a real one. J. D. LaRue (Kiel Martin) has a drinking problem and is always scheming (alcoholic/white trash). They are lovably flawed, unglamorous, and weak, presented with the same affectionate contempt that imbues those TV commercials showing "real people" in all their droll impotence.

NOT ALL THE SHOW'S CHARACTERS ARE SO CONDESCENDingly drawn. The derision, in fact, is highly selective, expressing the liberal bias that has made the show a critical success. For instance, there is nothing funny about those cops who represent, however obliquely, the Third World. There are two black officers, Hill (Michael Warren) and Washington (Taurean Blacque). One is handsome, diligent, brave, and upright, and so is the other one. (Washington is more flamboyant than Hill, and that's the only difference.) Ray, the Hispanic lieutenant, is another paragon, soft-spoken and attractive in a fatherly way.

The women are also the figments of some earnest liberal (male) imagination. Lucy (Betty Thomas) is a policewoman, not good-looking, but with a great personality: able and dedicated, yet vulnerable. On the other hand, high ratings demand a measure of tease, and so we have the well-groomed Veronica Hamel as Joyce Davenport, who spends her days in the Office of the Public Defender and her nights in the sack with the divorced Furillo. We are supposed to see Davenport as a liberated woman because she acts like an unfriendly man. In moments of postcoital repose, as Furillo lies back resting his neck, she bends grimly over some piece of homework, wearing her lover's shirt and man's glasses. She also calls him not "Frank," but "Furillo." She is supposed to be much preferable to Furillo's ex-wife Fay (Barbara Bosson), a shrill flake whose main function is to assault her ex-husband with labored quips: "Harvey is boiled beef, Frank," she complains of an erstwhile boyfriend. "I want escargot."

All the dialogue is painfully arch and overwritten, no matter who's speaking. Esterhaus's lines are all tortured circumlocution, a bad parody of Damon Runyon, and Conrad struggles mightily to make it funny.

But his verbal mannerisms, like Fay's or Hunter's, get lost in the general flood of inept repartee. Aside from rank clichés ("I need you!" "I'd hate to see you get hurt." "It's OK to cry," etc.), there are stunningly clumsy attempts at clever banter: "Lots of workaholics, of which I consider you one, break out in hives at the mere thought of a vacation." "If you want to see battle scars, I've got a whole closetful." A promotion, says Davenport, will give Frank "more time for the better things in life, namely *moi*." It's all meant to sound snappy and intriguing, like *interesting* people saying *interesting* things, but it only sounds like what you'd overhear in a singles bar for mediocre television writers.

The show tries to cover its shallowness with these inanities, and with the various naturalistic techniques. So far, the viewers haven't bought it. Silverman and the critics have blamed the bad time slot (Saturday at 10:00, 9:00 CST), assuming that a better one will make a big difference. It may not. And why? Because American viewers have such high standards, and consider "Hill Street Blues" overwritten and badly acted? That may seem unlikely. The millions who watch "Real People" or "The John Davidson Show" are probably not too finicky about dramaturgy. On the other hand, they might reject the show's unmistakable smugness, its air of liberal righteousness, its propagandistic pitch disguised as something "gutsy." This mass response could indicate a new awareness, because there are still too many shows like this, piously telling us how to think and "feel" while suggesting a subtle elitism. Such a rejection of "Hill Street Blues" would not be further evidence of any so-called "turn to the right," but simply the repudiation of something dated and offensive. As network television continues its slow decline, the failure of this show would be one more healthy sign of approaching death.

Afterword

· ·

HERE, AS WITH THE GIPPER (SEE BELOW), I MADE THE mistake of pretending to speak with the *vox populi*—a bullhorn that should be used with greater care, if at all. The new time slot did, of course, "make a big difference," propelling "HSB" toward the top of the ratings. Eventually, the show did lose most of its loyal audience, but that decline may or may not have anything to do with my own reasons for objection.

Moreover, an eternal optimist, I had no idea how bad TV could get: "Miami Vice," a show indistinguishable from the shirt ads in *Gentlemen's Quarterly*, makes any episode of "Hill Street Blues" look, in retrospect, like *Uncle Vanya*. Nevertheless (until it too lost momentum), "MV" had a following as devoted as the fans of the stone-faced Frank Furillo. (After this piece appeared, *The New Republic* received an unprecedented volley of letters—all hostile.) Within the academy, "Miami Vice" was a particular favorite among the postmodernists, who applauded its neon emptiness as a sign of (what else?) irony.

Since "HSB," the show's creator, Stephen Bochco, has gone on to better things: "LA Law," which he produces with Terry Louise Fisher, is often brilliant, as witty and engaging as the earlier show was overblown—although its writing too is sometimes flawed by the usual Bochcovian floridities. ■

Cosby Knows Best

- -

BILL COSBY IS TODAY'S QUINTESSENTIAL TV DAD—AT once the nation's best-liked sitcom character and the most successful and ubiquitous of celebrity pitchmen. Indeed, Cosby himself ascribes his huge following to his appearances in the ads: "I think my popularity came from doing solid 30-second commercials. They can cause people to love you and see more of you than in a full 30-minute show." Like its star, "The Cosby Show" must owe much of its immense success to advertising, for this sitcom is especially well attuned to the commercials, offering a full-scale confirmation of their vision.

On the face of it, the Huxtables' milieu is as upbeat and well stocked as a window display at Bloomingdale's, or any of those visions of domestic happiness that graced the billboards during the Great Depression. Everything within this spacious brownstone is luminously clean and new, as if it had all been set up by the state to make a good impression on a group of visiting foreign dignitaries. Here are all the right commodities—lots of bright sportswear, plants and paintings, gorgeous bedding, plenty of copperware, portable tape players, thick carpeting, innumerable knickknacks, and, throughout the house, big, burnished dressers, tables, couches, chairs, and cabinets (Early American yet looking factory-new). Each week, the happy Huxtables nearly vanish amid the porcelain, stainless steel, mahogany, and fabric of their lives. In every scene, each character appears in some fresh designer outfit that positively glows with newness, never to be seen a second time.

Like all this pricey clutter, the plots and subplots, the dialogue and even many of the individual shots reflect in some way on consumption as a way of life: Cliff's new juicer is the leitmotif of one episode; Cliff does a monologue on his son Theo's costly sweatshirt; Cliff kids daughter Rudy for wearing a dozen wooden necklaces. Each Huxtable, in fact, is hardly more than a mobile display case for his/her momentary possessions. In the show's first year, the credit sequence was a series of vivid stills presenting Cliff alongside a shiny Dodge Caravan, out of which the lesser Huxtables each emerged in shining playclothes, as if the van were their true parent, with Cliff serving as the genial midwife to this antiseptic birth. Each is routinely upstaged by what he/she eats or wears or lugs around: in a billowing blouse imprinted with gigantic blossoms, daughter Denise appears, carrying a tape player as big as a suitcase; Theo enters to get himself a can of Coke from the refrigerator, and we notice that he's wearing both a smart beige belt *and* a pair of lavender suspenders; Rudy munches cutely on a piece of pizza roughly twice the size of her own head.

As in the advertising vision, life among the Huxtables is not only well supplied, but remarkable for its surface harmony. Relations between these five pretty kids and their cute parents are rarely complicated by the slightest serious discord. Here affluence is magically undisturbed by the pressures that ordinarily enable it. Cliff and Clair, although both employed, somehow enjoy the leisure to devote themselves full-time to the trivial and comfortable concerns that loosely determine each episode: a funeral for Rudy's goldfish, a birthday surprise for Cliff, the kids' preparations for their first day of school. And daily life in this bright house is just as easy on the viewer as it is (apparently) for Cliff's dependents: "The Cosby Show" is devoid of any dramatic tension whatsoever. Nothing happens, nothing changes, there is no suspense or ambiguity or disappointment. In one episode, Cliff accepts a challenge to race once more against a runner who, years before, had beaten him at a major track meet. At the end, the race is run, and—it's a tie!

Of course, "The Cosby Show" is by no means the first sitcom to present us with a big, blissful family whose members never collide with one another, or with anything else; "Eight Is Enough," "The Brady Bunch," and "The Partridge Family" are just a few examples of earlier prime-time idylls. There are, however, some crucial differences between those older shows and this one. First of all, "The Cosby Show" is far more popular than any of its predecessors. It is (as of this writing) the top-rated show in the United States and elsewhere, attracting an audience that is not only vast, but often near fanatical in its devotion. Second, and stranger still, this show and its immense success are universally applauded as an exhilarating sign of progress. Newspaper columnists and telejournalists routinely deem "The Cosby Show" a "breakthrough" into an unprecedented *realism,* because it uses none of the broad plot devices or rapid-fire gags that define the standard sitcom. Despite its fantastic ambience of calm and plenty, "The Cosby Show" is widely regarded as a rare glimpse of truth, whereas "The Brady Bunch" et al., though just as cheery, were never extolled in this way. And there is a third difference between this show and its predecessors that may help explain the new show's greater popularity and peculiar reputation for progressivism: Cliff Huxtable and his dependents are not only fabulously comfortable and mild, but also noticeably black.

Cliff's blackness serves an affirmative purpose within the ad that is "The Cosby Show." At the center of his ample tableau, Cliff is himself an ad, implicitly proclaiming the fairness of the American system: "Look!" he shows us. "Even *I* can have all this!" Cliff is clearly meant to stand for Cosby himself, whose name appears in the opening credits as "Dr. William E. Cosby, Jr., Ed.D."—a testament both to Cosby's lifelong effort at self-improvement, and to his sense of brotherhood with Cliff. And, indeed, Dr. Huxtable is merely the latest version of the same statement that Dr. Cosby has been making for years as a talk show guest and stand-up comic: "I got mine!" The comic has always been quick to raise the subject of his own success. "What do I care what some ten-thousand-dollar-a-year writer says about me?" he once asked Dick Cavett. And on "The Tonight Show" a few years ago, Cosby told of how his father, years before, had warned him that he'd never make a dime in show business, "and then he walked slowly back to the projects . . . Well, I just lent him forty thousand dollars!"

That anecdote got a big hand, just like "The Cosby Show," but despite the many plaudits for Cosby's continuing tale of self-help, it is not quite convincing. Cliff's brownstone is too crammed, its contents too lustrous, to seem like his—or anyone's—own personal achievement. It suggests instead the corporate showcase which, in fact, it is. "The Cosby Show" attests to the power, not of Dr. Cosby/Huxtable, but of a consumer society that has produced such a tantalizing vision of reality. As Cosby himself admits, it was not his own Algeresque efforts that "caused people to love" him, but those ads put out by Coca-Cola, Ford, and General Foods—those ads in which he looks and acts precisely as he looks and acts in his own show.

Cosby's image is divided in a way that both facilitates the corporate project and conceals its true character. On the face of it, the Cosby style is pure impishness. Forever mugging and cavorting, throwing mock tantrums or beaming hugely to himself or doing funny little dances with his stomach pushed out, Cosby carries on a ceaseless parody of some euphoric eight-year-old. His delivery suggests the same childish spontaneity, for in the high, coy gabble of his harangues and monologues there is a disarming quality of baby talk. And yet all this artful goofiness barely conceals an intimidating hardness—the same uncompromising willfulness that we learn to tolerate in actual children (however cute they may be), but which can seem a little threatening in a grown-up. And Cosby is indeed a most imposing figure, in spite of all

71

his antics: a big man boasting of his wealth, and often handling an immense cigar.

It is a disorienting blend of affects, but it works perfectly whenever he confronts us on behalf of Ford or Coca-Cola. With a massive car or Coke machine behind him, or with a calculator at his fingertips, he hunches toward us, wearing a bright sweater and an insinuating grin, and makes his playful pitch, cajoling us to buy whichever thing he's selling, his face and words, his voice and posture all suggesting this implicit and familiar come-on: "Kitchy-koo!" It is not so much that Cosby makes his mammoth bureaucratic masters seem as nice and cuddly as himself (although such a strategy is typical of corporate advertising); rather, he implicitly assures us that *we* are nice and cuddly, like little children. At once solicitous and overbearing, he personifies the corporate force that owns him. Like it, he comes across as an easygoing parent, and yet, also like it, he cannot help betraying the impulse to coerce. We see that he is bigger than we are, better known, better off, and far more powerfully sponsored. Thus, we find ourselves ambiguously courted, just like those tots who eat up lots of Jell-O pudding under his playful supervision.

Dr. Huxtable controls his family with the same enlightened deviousness. As widely lauded for its "warmth" as for its "realism," "The Cosby Show" has frequently been dubbed "the 'Father Knows Best' of the eighties." Here again (the columnists agree) is a good strong Dad maintaining the old "family values." This equation, however, blurs a crucial difference between Cliff and the early fathers. Like them, Cliff always wins; but this modern Dad subverts his kids not by evincing the sort of calm power that once made Jim Anderson so daunting, but by seeming to subvert himself at the same time. His is the executive style, in other words, not of the small businessman as evoked in the fifties, but of the corporate manager, skilled at keeping his subordinates in line while half concealing his authority through various disarming moves: Cliff rules the roost through teasing put-downs, clever mockery, and amiable shows of helpless bafflement.* This Dad is no straightforward tyrant, then, but the playful type who strikes his children as a peach, until they realize, years later, and after lots of psychotherapy, what a subtle thug he really was.

An intrusive kidder, Cliff never fails to get his way; and yet there is more to his manipulativeness than simple egomania. Obsessively, Cliff

---

*Cliff's managerial style is, evidently, also Cosby's. According to Tempestt Bledsoe, who plays Cliff's daughter Vanessa, Cosby "can make kids behave without telling them to do so." (Quoted in *People,* 10 December 1984.)

sees to it, through his takes and teasing, that his children always keep things light. As in the corporate culture and on TV generally, so on this show there is no negativity allowed. This is a conscious policy: Dr. Alvin F. Poussaint, a professor of psychiatry at Harvard, reads through each script as a "consultant," censoring any line or bit that might somehow tarnish the show's "positive images." And the show's upscale mise-en-scène has also been deliberately contrived to glow, like a fixed smile: "When you look at the artwork [on the walls], there is a positive feeling, an up feeling," Cosby says. "You don't see downtrodden, negative, I-can't-do-I-won't-do."

Cliff's function, then, is to police the corporate playground, always on the lookout for any downbeat tendencies. In one episode, for instance, Denise sets herself up by reading Cliff some somber verses that she's written for the school choir. The mood is despairing; the refrain, "I walk alone . . . I walk alone." It is clear that the girl does not take the effort very seriously, and yet Cliff merrily overreacts against this slight and artificial plaint, as if it were a crime. First, while she recites, he wears a clownish look of deadpan bewilderment, then laughs out loud as soon as she has finished, and ends by snidely mooing the refrain in outright parody. The studio audience roars, and Denise takes the hint. At the end of the episode, she reappears with a new version, which she reads sweetly, blushingly, while Cliff and Clair, sitting side by side in their high-priced pajamas, beam with tenderness and pride on her act of self-correction:

My mother and my father are my best friends.
When I'm all alone, I don't have to be.
It's because of me that I'm all alone, you see.
Their love is real. . . .

Never have they lied to me, never connived me,
talked behind my back.
Never have they cheated me.
Their love is real, their love is real

Clair, choked up, gives the girl a big warm hug, and Cliff then takes her little face between his hands and kisses it, as the studio audience bursts into applause.

Thus, this episode ends with a paean to the show itself (for "their love" is *not* "real," but a feature of the fiction), a moment that, for all its mawkishness, attests to Cliff's managerial adeptness. Yet Cliff is hardly a mere enforcer; he is also an underling, even as he seems to run things. This subservient status is manifest in his blackness. Cosby's blackness

73

is indeed a major reason for the show's popularity, despite his frequent claims, and the journalistic consensus, that "The Cosby Show" is somehow "colorblind," simply appealing in some general "human" way. Although whitened by their status and commodities, the Huxtables are still unmistakably black. However, it would be quite inaccurate to hail their popularity as evidence of a new and rising amity between the races in America. On the contrary, "The Cosby Show" is such a hit with whites in part because whites are just as worried about blacks as they have always been—not blacks like Bill Cosby, or Lena Horne, or Eddie Murphy, but poor blacks, and the poor in general, whose existence is a well-kept secret on prime-time TV.

And yet TV betrays the very fears that it denies. In thousands of high-security buildings, and in suburbs reassuringly remote from the cities' "bad neighborhoods," whites may, unconsciously, be further reassured by watching not just Cosby, but a whole set of TV shows that negate the possibility of black violence with lunatic fantasies of containment: "Diff'rent Strokes" and "Webster," starring Gary Coleman and Emmanuel Lewis, respectively, each an overcute, miniaturized black person, each playing the adopted son of good white parents. In seeming contrast to these tabletop models, there is the oversized and growling Mr. T, complete with bangles, mohawk, and other primitivizing touches. Even this behemoth is a comforting joke, the dangerous ex-slave turned comic and therefore innocuous by campy excess; and he too is kept in line by a casual white father: Hannibal Smith, the commander of the A-Team, who employs Mr. T exclusively for his brawn.

As a willing advertisement for the system that pays him well, Cliff Huxtable also represents a threat contained. Although dark-skinned and physically imposing, he ingratiates us with his childlike mien and enviable lifestyle, a surrender that must offer some deep solace to a white public terrified that, one day, blacks might come with guns to steal the copperware, the juicer, the microwave, the VCR, even the TV itself. On "The Cosby Show," it appears as if blacks in general can have, or do have, what many whites enjoy, and that such material equality need not entail a single break-in. And there are no hard feelings, none at all, now that the old injustice has been so easily rectified. Cosby's definitive funny face, flashed at the show's opening credits and reproduced on countless magazine covers, is a strained denial of all animosity. With its little smile, the lips pursed tight, eyes opened wide, eyebrows raised high, that dark face shines toward us like the white flag of surrender—a desperate look that no suburban TV Dad of yesteryear would ever have put on, and one that millions of Americans today find indispensable.

By and large, American whites need such reassurance because they are now further removed than ever, both spatially and psychologically, from the masses of the black poor. And yet the show's appeal cannot be explained merely as a symptom of class and racial uneasiness, because there are, in our consumer culture, anxieties still more complicated and pervasive. Thus, Cliff is not just an image of the dark Other capitulating to the white establishment, but also the reflection of any constant viewer, who, whatever his/her race, must also feel like an outsider, lucky to be tolerated by the distant powers that be. There is no negativity allowed, not anywhere; and so Cliff serves both as our guide and as our double. His look of tense playfulness is more than just a sign that blacks won't hurt us; it is an expression that we too would each be wise to adopt, lest we betray some devastating sign of anger or dissatisfaction. If we stay cool and cheerful, white like him, and learn to get by with his sort of managerial acumen, we too, perhaps, can be protected from the world by a barrier of new appliances, and learn to put down others as each of us has, somehow, been put down.

Afterword

● ●

I HAVE A REASON FOR JUXTAPOSING THIS ESSAY WITH the next: Dr. Cosby has much in common with the presidential image. In 1987, Video Storyboard Tests Inc., a polling outfit, named Cosby as "the most 'believable' celebrity endorser"—the same believability that, for a term and a half, made Reagan hugely popular, against every claim of morality and reason. As Cosby could get away with fronting for a firm like E.F. Hutton, Reagan once could get away with nearly anything—and through the very medium that, its champions claim, has made the national audience very knowing.

Like the celebrants of "Hill Street Blues," of pseudo-feminist spectacle, and of TV's images of war (see pp. 61–65, 219–30, 151–65), the authors of "The Cosby Show" are incapable of seeing any difference between the real world and their own enlightened bias. Presumably fighting evil "stereotypes," they feel free to proffer, and to deem as "realism," fictions far more fantastic than the most dated depictions— more fantastic, because the newer depictions do not seem dated.

Interviewed by *Harvard Magazine* in 1987, Tom Werner, producer of "The Cosby Show," recalled that "we saw unreal things on TV—atypical families, children constantly talking back. We wanted to make a show where people watching would say, 'How did they get inside my house?'" And, interviewed in *The Christian Science Monitor* the same year, Alvin F. Poussaint, the Harvard professor of psychiatry whose job it is to censor all the "stereotypes" in each week's script, proclaims— correctly—that "television can do a lot better in more truly mirroring, or being a mirror of society in its diversity," while boasting of the show's relentless "positive images"—as if the Huxtables "truly mirror" most, or any, of the households watching them.

Perhaps Harvard's alumni and faculty can look at that preposterous scene of affluence and murmur, "How did they get inside my house?" Most people cannot, however—and that inability explains, in part, the show's success. But the point about such fantasy is not just that it is "unrealistic"—that children do "talk back," for instance, or that there is criminality among blacks, or that warfare gratifies some of its participants.

Rather, the point is, first, that TV, whose only purpose is to push consumption, should not dictate anyone's self-image, however right-minded a given program's censors. And—more important—it is surely not the case that all those "positive images" infuse the audience with the pride and vigor that you need to get ahead. "Everywhere I go," says Poussaint, "people in the black community feel proud that the show is doing so well and that it has positive role models." However, it takes far more than a spectacle of affluence to end poverty or end discrimination; and in fact such advertising-idylls do not motivate their viewers to go out and claim the world, but only make the world seem drab and disappointing by comparison. A psychiatrist writing in *TV Guide* quotes a woman who is "a devotee of 'The Cosby Show.' She told me, 'I always compare how my husband deals with a situation with what Bill Cosby would do.' When her husband is crabby or nasty, or can't defuse an argument with a warm, Cosbyesque joke, she ends up feeling angry, even cheated." It is just such unhappiness that TV and its sponsors both require and reinforce, even as they promise our fulfillment.■

Virtù, Inc.

∎∎

"**E**VERYONE SEES WHAT YOU SEEM TO BE, FEW PERceive what you are; and those few don't dare oppose the general opinion, which has the majesty of the government backing it up." Thus Machiavelli, in *The Prince,* suggests that most people put their trust in what they see, and that the would-be ruler must exploit this mass credulity by wielding his image with subtle skill. What everyone wants, above all, is a good show: "The masses are always impressed by appearances and by the outcome of an event—and in the world there are only masses. The few have no place there when the many crowd together." If he wants to stay in charge (and in health), a ruler has to please those staring and complacent multitudes with a public pose of sanctity, which will let him carry on the gruesome work of politics without losing his footing. The man who can thus remain on top, seeming good while doing necessary evil, is a figure of *virtù,* a term implying "power," "courage," "talent," "will," "strength of character," and other qualities of a heroic individualism.

Machiavelli showed considerable prescience when he wrote his bitter treatise in 1513: "The whole world is watching," *The Prince* points out, and now the networks and the satellites have translated that metaphor into literal truth. If politics has become less dangerous since the Renaissance, it has also, because of television, become a lot more superficial. In order to prevail today, the plucky office-seeker may not have to arrange clandestine stranglings, but he had better cultivate an understated manner and a level gaze, keep his statements short, and wear a light blue shirt at all times. This bland facility is now the main requirement for political success, even among those few who run for President.

And so, if Machiavelli were alive today, he would probably update his book with some reflections on how our Presidents use television, and vice versa. He was, for his era, an unusually scientific sort of theorist, basing his principles on actual cases. He based *The Prince* primarily on the example of that efficient monster, Cesare Borgia; and he would certainly base his new chapters on the career of Ronald Reagan, the smoothest surface this side of the Iron Curtain.

BOXED IN

■ ■ ■ ■ ■ ■

Reagan would seem to be the latest model in *virtù* itself. On the one hand, he approaches all the ugly tasks of his regime with the exalted ruthlessness of Frederick Barbarossa, "stout Cortez," or, to adopt a more appropriate model, Dirty Harry: Reagan "shoots straight" and "gets tough," he goes by "horse sense," he's got plenty of "guts" and "balls" and other meaty attributes. And yet, even as he earns such right-wing plaudits, Reagan still manages to come across as an easy-going, *decent* fella. It is an impressive contradiction. Here is a President who takes from the poor to give to the rich, ravages his own country-side, has supported infanticide abroad, undermines the Bill of Rights, busts unions, props up murderous dictatorships and is otherwise trying to turn the whole world into a sweat shop; and yet, whenever he appears, he has you thinking, somehow, that he's "a nice guy."

Of course, if we judge Ronald Reagan by his actions, or by his incli-nations, or even by the company he keeps, we have to conclude that he is not nice at all, if "nice" is taken to mean "kind" or "good." On the contrary, Reagan is "nice" as Iago is "honest"—that is, he is extraordi-narily adept at affecting tones and postures that people trust without thinking. In other words, Reagan is considered "nice," not because he is nice, but in part because his image answers (temporarily) the emo-tional needs of quite a few Americans, who, tired of feeling cynical about their leaders, will swallow anything. And, like a good TV com-mercial, Reagan's image goes down easy, calming his audience with sweet inversions of the truth.

First of all, the image is meant to make the viewers think that Reagan is someone "just like you and me." Although this Administration has made a public point of dragging pomp and ostentation back into the White House, Reagan himself seems like a humble janitor at heart. Even at the dressiest affairs, and on the grandest state occasions, he has us thinking that he wears white socks and carries a penknife. Aside from partly obscuring the vulgar opulence of the Reagans and their tribe, this seeming averageness has the effect of distancing the Presi-dent from his cruel strokes of policy—you wouldn't think such a *nice guy* could *do* such things, as shocked neighbors often put it on the eve-ning news.

So far, this seems like basic statecraft, of the sort that Machiavelli would have grasped at once. However, he would have had a little trou-ble understanding how anyone could believe in Reagan's pose of com-monness, which bears no clear relation to the world we commonly inhabit. In order to comprehend how Reagan can seem "just like you and me" without resembling anyone on earth, Machiavelli would have to sit through hours of bad old movies, pore over hundreds of dime novels and Horatio Alger stories, and otherwise school himself in the recurrent images of American myth. Only then would he perceive that Ronald Reagan is merely an anthology of the worst of American popular culture, edited for television. He comforts us, not by epitomizing what we are, but by reminding us of what we used to think we were, or, perhaps, of what we think we used to be. In either case, his image is an eloquent symbol of reaction, forever promising the return of an illusory past.

Reagan seems to face us from within that past; he seems never to have fallen into modern times, or even into adulthood. Despite his advanced age, he comes across as a giant child who would be father to us frightened men and women. While we struggle in the world from day to day, making less and fearing more and more, Ronald Reagan calls his wife "Mommy," and sports the same haircut that he wore when Hitler took over the Sudetenland. Although withered, he seems permanently boyish—not like an actual boy, of course, but something like a boy in an old movie: the lop-sided grin, the wavy thatch, the eyebrows impishly tilted, etc., remind us of all those scrubbed and hearty little guys in *Boys Town* and a hundred other movies of the Great Depression. Such a man, we sense, must be as sincere and innocent as anyone ever played by Mickey Rooney; and his policies, we hope, might let us live those happy days once brought to us by MGM.

OF COURSE, THE REAGAN IMAGE ALSO HAS ITS COMMANDING aspect, but it too seems anachronistic, and faintly puerile: the big old sheriff, protector of the weak, loping toward Air Force One with his little lady at his side. Although this pose demands the obligatory Western gear, it comes through more in Reagan's oratorical style than in his boots and shirts. He speaks quietly, a little hesitantly, with his eyes to the ground, as if not used to public speaking; and he often punctuates his statements with a folksy little waggle of the head and shoulders, so that we won't take his speechifying too seriously. All in all, the style suggests another complex pose of innocence—this President is a pure-hearted cowpoke, respectful to the ladies, wry and self-effacing with the boys.

Although these personae are derived from the movies, Reagan's Hollywood apprenticeship has, perhaps, been overemphasized by the casual students of his rise. His film career was undistinguished, because his celluloid image was basically too dim and vacuous to withstand the competition of more vivid presences. But this very emptiness has made him perfect for TV, which thrives on mundane types, demanding a pseudohomely style that Reagan puts on easily. While he couldn't fill the grand patterns of the silver screen, then, he has managed, with immense success, to adapt those patterns to the smaller

scale of television. Moreover, he has learned to liven up his every televised appearance with frequent shifts in expression, constant movements of the head, lots of warm chuckles and ironic shrugs and sudden
frowns of manly purpose. Such perpetual motion is a must on television, and a must for Ronald Reagan, who tends to lose his charm when
he comes to rest. At such terrifying moments of repose, all the boyish-
ness drains out of him, and he suddenly starts looking like an anacon-
da, with his beady eyes and flat lipless head.

As long as he's running smoothly, however, Reagan is unfailingly attractive, not at all like a predator, nor, in fact, like anything other than
what he seems—"a nice guy," pure and simple. However hard we try to
glimpse the man concealed within that jovial disguise, Reagan remains
impenetrable, a pleasing surface through and through. Machiavelli
would have to marvel at such a thoroughgoing facade, and we too
should appreciate the spectacle, after all the bad performances we've
suffered through for years: LBJ, abusing his dogs and exposing his belly;
Richard Nixon, hunched and glistening like a cornered toad; Gerald
Ford, forever tipping over; Jimmy Carter, with his maudlin twang and
interminable kin. While each of these men, appallingly, kept lunging at
us from behind the mask of power, Reagan's mask and face are as one.
It's been a long time since we've seen such integrity in government.
Indeed, not since John Kennedy have we had such a united front for a
chief executive.

HOW DOES REAGAN DO IT? OR RATHER, HOW IS IT DONE?
Machiavelli too would wonder about this, and would try, in his new
afterword on modern politics, to work out an explication of Reagan's
strange success. And he would find that this success is based not only
on the original tenets of *The Prince,* but on those tenets modernized for
the demands of television.

First of all, Machiavelli would try to account for the fact that Reagan,
despite his daily atrocities, continues to seem "nice." Although this
persistent air of sweetness owes much to Reagan's earnest yokelism, it
also results from the clever use of prominent patsies, a strategy which
Machiavelli recommends specifically in his treatise: "Princes should
delegate the ugly jobs to other people, and reserve the attractive functions for themselves." Reagan is kept seemingly innocent by this device: David Stockman, a mere instrument, used to take the heat for
Reagan's cuts and slashes, Al Haig often seems like the one who *really*
wants to crush the Cubans, and so on. Thus people have been able to
persist in the belief that their President is just and well intentioned, and
that any ill consequences of his rule are only the capricious doings of
his subordinates.

Although this tactic, in itself, does not depend on visual effects (it worked long before the invention of TV), it implies a corollary which has proven indispensable to this Administration, whose shrinking appeal is based entirely on appearances. In this age of television, it matters less what people do than what they look like. Therefore, the function of the President's men is not just to make his policies seem like their mistakes, but also to make the President himself look better by contrast with themselves. If Machiavelli were to update his directive in accordance with the current practice, he would say: "A president should surround himself with ugly people doing ugly jobs, in order to seem that much more attractive himself by doing no job at all."

Guided by the spirit of this precept, some unknown genius, or ingenious committee, assembled Ronald Reagan's Administration, employing that same skill and subtlety with which the President himself had been assembled. Few chief executives have gained so much from their associates; beside his aides, Reagan seems to take on warmth, authenticity, even vitality, and other alien qualities.

Everyone in this Administration has a real job, providing some of the essential contrast that makes Reagan seem credibly human. Even the qualities of the colorless serve this purpose. For instance, there are those unremarkable men, like Caspar Weinberger and Donald Regan, who simply look like Republicans, i.e., as if their one desire in life is to repossess your house. These sober corporate types serve to offset those maverick qualities that once made Reagan seem like something fresh. And then there are those solid staffers—Ed Meese, James Baker, Larry Speakes, etc.—who look something like an assortment of boiled eggs. Compared to them, Reagan seems like someone with a lot of character in his face, or at least like someone with a face.

Then there are the more important and misleading contrasts, involving Reagan and the superstars of this production. As the youth in charge of deprivations, for instance, David Stockman was, before his lapse, a perfect foil for Reagan. His was the zeal and excessive cleanness of the untried moralist, which allowed the craggy Reagan to seem (for a while) restrained and wise. General Alexander Haig has something of the same effect on Reagan's image. He is an openly belligerent cold warrior, and otherwise behaves like someone who should be watched at all times. He first made this impression during Nixon's twilight period, when he wrested sinister control over the household, like Mrs. Danvers in *Rebecca;* and then, after last year's shooting, he blurted, "I am in control!" which clearly suggested that he wasn't. Despite these hints of madness, or rather because of them, Haig stays firmly in his place, making Reagan seem moderate, and perhaps even necessary.

But the most perverse and daring stroke of contrast in this spectacle is, of course, the appointment of James Watt as Secretary of the Interior. Watt would be unbearable in any visible capacity, but placing him as guardian of our virgin spaces and small furry animals was a particularly sadistic move. Looking like something hewn from the very bedrock which he longs to disrupt, Watt has made a special talent of his loathesomeness, with his incoherent jeering and his fits of hostile piety. Reagan has suggested that forests cause lung cancer, but next to Watt he starts to look like Johnny Appleseed.

AND FINALLY, THERE IS NANCY, REAGAN'S OWN MOMMY Dearest, whose frozen presence at her husband's side suggests, paradoxically, that Reagan is a man of passion. The President can also seem mellow and outdoorsy by appearing alongside this rigid wife. Making their way in and out of distant conveyances, the two of them act out a little pageant that celebrates the contradictory values of the right, he dressed as a lumberjack or wrangler, she in some lurid swatch of *haute couture*. Reagan does not ordinarily come across as very physical, but he seems as warm and earthy as a farm animal when accompanied by Nancy who, glassy-eyed and overdressed, always looks as if she's just been struck by lightning in a limousine.

Stockman, Watt, Haig, and Mommy have served their purpose beautifully, humanizing the President in the eyes of most Americans, and, at the same time, gladdening Reagan's true believers by appearing cold and hateful, which is, among the ultraright, not a shortcoming but a sign of grace. As useful as Reagan's satellites have been, however, neither they nor Reagan's charms would have accomplished anything without the full support of our journalists, particularly those who use a camera. "While it always helps to surround the President with freaks," Machiavelli would go on to say, "it is even more important that he learn to snow the press."

WHY IS IT THAT WE THINK OF RONALD REAGAN AS "A NICE guy"? And is it "we" who think it? In fact, it is not the growing numbers of the unemployed, the desperate single mothers, the students and teachers forced to leave school, or the farmers, or the union members, or the old, or the young, or the poor, or the middle class, who keep babbling about how "nice" the President is. Those who find him "nice" are in a dwindling group, comprised of some defense contractors, a few lunatics in Orange County, and most of our TV newsmen, who persist as Reagan's biggest boosters. "He's a nice guy," Bill Moyers recently asserted. "I'm gonna admit something," Sam Donaldson has said. "He's a hard President to cover for most reporters, because he is such an amiable, warm, human being." (So much for journalistic ethics.)

Innocuous as they may seem, these mawkish tributes are deplorable. First of all, they cannot be dismissed as detached and harmless observations, because there is no such thing on television news: such "commentary" always works to half-create (at least) the phenomena which it seems merely to describe. When Sam Donaldson calls Reagan "warm" and "amiable," that opinion, casual or not, immediately takes on the pressure of a fact, and so Reagan becomes warm and amiable, even if he isn't. More importantly, the newsmen's general fondness for Reagan explains, in part, the respectfulness with which his image was broadcast throughout the campaign. The press, and TV in particular, helped immeasurably to elect Ronald Reagan by playing to his strengths, by letting him evince himself in all his "niceness," by politely avoiding any shots or revelations that might have compromised the seeming wholeness of his image. He came across as a man disinterested, natural, and pure, the innocent object of Carter's "mean campaign," which appeared, by comparison, to stink of politics.

Thus Reagan won because his image was a perfect television spectacle. Now that he's in power, however, it would seem that he might be in danger of extinction by the very medium that created him. His chummy style has created certain problems. For instance, it is still true, as Machiavelli once wrote, that "a prince must see to it that his actions bespeak greatness, courage, dignity, and strength"; and yet, evidently, a President now has to seem "nice" and approachable, everybody's pal. How can a leader seem both great and small? How does he get "closer" to television without succumbing to its equalizing tendencies? For television is, indeed, subversive, more dangerous to a President's well-being than any number of imaginary Libyans. It is an antiheroic medium, straining out charisma and amplifying little flaws; and it tends to exhaust the appeal of its stars very quickly.

It is therefore necessary for the would-be leader to cultivate a new kind of reserve. "Having encircled the President with truly odious people," Machiavelli would advise, "and having gotten him in good with the reporters, you must always take care to *keep him at a distance*." This rule is not a simple one, as the example of Reagan's image demonstrates. First of all, a President should not be allowed to get too close to the cameras. Like Reagan, he should always appear far away and in transit, waving merrily at everyone, as if going to the beach. Such brief and cheerful appearances will keep the President looking young, and will lessen the risk of his saying something that someone else will only have to rephrase later.

HOWEVER, KEEPING THE PRESIDENT FAR AWAY INVOLVES more than simply putting space between him and the minicams. One reason for this distancing is to obscure the fact that the President is mortal, and this objective sometimes demands measures other than simply physically removing him. As in Reagan's case, it can demand plastic surgery, contact lenses, the liberal use of Grecian Formula 16 and an occasional outlandish fiction, such as last year's story that the President, after getting shot, came tap dancing into the emergency room and then did shtick during surgery. As one whose actions should "bespeak greatness," furthermore, the President must never be seen to do anything patently silly, a kind of distancing which sometimes calls for a little prudent suppression. Last May, for instance, the Dick Clark Company, for a show called "TV Censored Bloopers," tried to get hold of some old movie outtakes that (according to *Variety*) "included muffed lines by Reagan and others as well as failed props." The footage was refused. Even Richard Nixon once tried to cut loose on television, grumbling "sock it to me!" on "Laugh-In"; but this President, seemingly so genial and relaxed, never appears televised without seeming carefully closed.

These are understandable and even necessary ploys, especially from Machiavelli's point of view. If leadership is to succeed at winning the devotion of a people, it can't go around exposing itself, flaunting its liver spots, its aches and pains, its flubs and stumbles. A man of *virtù* must avoid such disquieting candor; he must neither show his scars, nor tell of close calls with homicidal rabbits, but withhold himself as Ronald Reagan seems to do, remaining perfectly hidden behind an awesome mask.

However, Machiavelli, watching Reagan walk and talk, might start to get a little nervous. When he advised the deft construction of a noble public face, he assumed, of course, that someone would be there behind it. This, as we know, is no longer a necessary feature of political leadership; the phrase "Reagan's image" is redundant. With a good staff and some of the cleverest equipment money can buy, Reagan does not need to be present when he's on the air, nor, therefore, at any other time. His only job is to enact those functions devised by his programmers, and he does this in a very lifelike way. Thus the influence of the media has brought Machiavellian doctrine to bizarre fulfillment: the best way for the modern prince to keep this real self hidden is not to have one.

And the television news people continue their involvement in this fantasy. Having gotten Reagan into office, these entertainers are now trying to reverse themselves, suddenly acting leery and impartial, affecting that hardboiled skepticism that lets them feel like journalists. While this new antagonism has resulted in a few illuminating stories on the evening news, most of what passes for critical coverage is merely third-rate theater criticism. We hear about "gaffes," "embarrass-ments," "tense moments," spokesmen getting slightly riled, and are meant to take these trivial slips as somehow tantamount to major scandal.

This is partly the result of the reporters' inability, what with the many deadlines and the need for footage, to do much more than show up at the daily briefings, press conferences, and state receptions, which they scan (in vain) for something meaningful. The obsession with ap-pearances, however, is not just an isolated consequence of the report-ers' schedules: it comprises their essential orientation, which is something that they have in common with the men who run the coun-try. The press and the President's men may act like adversaries, but they're really in cahoots, working together to call attention to the Presi-dent's image, and to nothing else. Evidently the declining quality of American life is less important than what the viewers think about that image. In a paradigmatic encounter with Reagan in January 1982, Dan Rather sounded more like a publicist than an interviewer, talking about "perceptions" and "signals," at one point making this assessment: "This is going to be a continuing problem for you, *getting people to believe* that you really do know what's going on in the interior of your Administration" (emphasis added). Reagan's not knowing what's going on would seem to be *our* "continuing problem," not his, and one of disastrous proportions; but Rather, with the assumptions typical of his profession, could see the danger only as a problem of packaging.

THUS TELEVISION HAS REDUCED OUR POLITICAL CULTURE to a succession of gestures, postures, automatic faces. Machiavelli, tak-ing note of all this feeble imagery, would lay his pen down with a tired sigh. "So much for *virtù*," he would say to himself, wondering what became of those creative few whose fierce talents he had once sought to define. And, while thinking of that vanished strength, he would proba-bly contemplate this new absurdity: that *virtù*, which once enabled the startling individual to control the impressions of his image, has itself declined into an image; and this image of the mighty individual is a corporate fiction, the careful work of committees and think tanks, re-peatedly reprocessed by the television industry for daily distribution to a mass audience.

The modern prince, in other words, is entirely a creature of TV, which sets him up and breaks him down according to its own implicit schedule—he thrives only as a novelty, then turns at once into a joke or a nostalgia item. This precariousness is nothing new in the world of politics. "Let me observe," writes Machiavelli toward the conclusion of *The Prince,* "that we can see a prince flourishing today and ruined tomorrow, and yet no change has taken place in his nature or in any of his qualities." Machiavelli ascribed such reverses to the influence of the goddess Fortune, the fickle arbiter of all men's ups and downs. "The prince who relies entirely on Fortune comes to destruction the moment she changes," while the prince who counts on his own *virtù* might be able to endure.

But whereas a prince could presumably master Fortune if he made a hero's effort, no President can ever beat TV, no matter how slick and likable his image. Even the well-made Ronald Reagan is finally, and with great subtlety, being dismantled by the anchormen, who now begin to make him seem, although still "nice," a quaint and slightly ludicrous old figurehead. And if Reagan's sturdy image can be thus subverted, any politician's can as every President's is. As with Reagan, so it was with Carter, with Ted Kennedy, with Gerald Ford, etc., and so it will surely be with all the rest. Our candidates will continue to flash by between commercials, seeming to inhabit no real space, offering nothing but a short performance; and so we'll watch as we watch everything, not bothering to participate, because participation won't be needed. The show, we'll figure numbly, must go on.

VIRTU, INC.

Afterword

■ ■

"He never thinks in Machiavellian terms," said a confidant
who talks with him frequently. "He's always Sunny Jim."
—New York Times, 15 March 1987

W HAT HAS CHANGED SINCE THIS ESSAY WAS WRITTEN during Ronald Reagan's second year in office? On the one hand, nothing. As the Reagan era nears its end, our political culture is still (of course) wholly spectacular. "The economic mood music is very positive for us right now," enthused one ex-Reaganaut, a Dole adviser, in mid-January 1988. In the White House as on Madison Avenue, "perception management" is still the main domestic policy. "A senior official in the Administration," reported the *New York Times* in 1987, "said the White House had decided to 'flood the market' with legislative proposals as a way of *'making people think* that we're in charge again.' " And the telejournalists are still complicit in this p.r. enterprise: "Now the question is," Dan Rather asked Reagan just before the 1987 summit meeting, *"how can you convince Americans* that you have the command of the kind of complex information that's necessary here . . .?" (emphasis added in both cases)

And as Reagan's context has not changed, neither has he changed—since he is (as of this writing) still not there, and nothing comes from nothing. "He," furthermore, is even now generally regarded as "a nice guy," despite the many crimes that are still carried out by the regime that his sponsors and associates have put in place. The catalog of enormities needs now to be expanded, to include the resurgence of sweat shops throughout this country, the near-tripling of electronic surveillance operations by the government, the massive poisoning of our land and water, the steady increase of our homeless population, an unprecedented level of official malfeasance, the redesign of the Federal courts into an organ of reaction, and on and on. Nevertheless, many viewers still believe what Admiral John Poindexter told the Iran/contra panel: that "the President is a very humane individual," so moved by the plight of those held hostage in Iran that he would have tried anything to spring them—although there is growing evidence that his people cut a deal, in 1980, with the Iranians, to make sure that our then-hostages

89

would not be freed until after Election Day. (As of this writing, the TV news has made no mention of this too-explosive story, despite damning revelations by—among others—Barbara Honegger in *In These Times,* Christopher Hitchens in *The Nation,* and Flora Lewis in the *New York Times.*)

And yet everything did change, once the news of Col. North's secret shipments, of Bud McFarlane and his cake, etc., universalized the "perception" of Reagan's emptiness. In 1982, I was oversanguine: although it was true that the President's ratings had lately dipped, and that he was (therefore) sometimes represented, on TV, as "a quaint and slightly ludicrous old figurehead," he was about to rebound from that brief low point into an unprecedented popularity and (therefore) "Teflon" status, i.e., treated as a god by the reporters. After the Iran/contra story, however, he was jeered as widely and as energetically as he had earlier been celebrated.

Now, of course, the Democratic leadership would openly admit that they could see right through him. "The truth of the matter is," remarked ex-Speaker Tip O'Neill in January 1987, "he knows less than any President I've ever met." A few months later, Jim Wright, O'Neill's successor, observed that Reagan "is ignorant of the facts of which a President should be aware, and willfully so." And the President's old allies agreed, especially after Reagan developed his surprising crush on Mikhail Gorbachev. Now the Great Communicator, once the colossus of the right, was "a useful idiot for Soviet propaganda," according to Howard Phillips of the Conservative Caucus. And along with all the partisan jeering and sectarian resentment, the mass media began to submerge the erstwhile titan in a flood of ridicule: "Reagan Becoming Comics' Delight," proclaimed one headline in March 1987, and the newsmen themselves joined in on the fun. Now they hectored Reagan at his few press conferences, badgered him at photo opportunities, and came up with dozens of subversive stories, such as the AP item reporting an absurd mishap with a contact lens, and bearing the headline, "President Bruises His Eyelid."

It was indeed ironic that this empty President should end up as the premiere butt of TV's empty irony—for he himself, a nothing, was nothing but an ironist. Not only was he very good at mouthing the countless televisual sarcasms of his speechwriters ("How do I spell relief? V-E-T-O," etc.), but he was also skilled at "taking refuge in self-deprecatory humor," as the *New York Times* put it in 1987. Even as he triumphed through his theatricality, he would often jest about it: "They gave me a new set," he joked at one press conference before his downfall, referring to the grander room where the journalists would thenceforth query, then, later, shout at him.

The Reagan irony, however, involved much more than his "self-deprecatory humor." Indeed, his whole presidency was an ironic exercise,
since it was little more than one long and open contradiction of the
ideology that he professed so warmly. He railed for years against the
Federal deficit while swelling it enormously through military spending.
Vowing to "get the government off our backs," he and his cabal filled
every possible position with like-minded authoritarians, who worked
only to expand the power of government to listen in, to open mail, to
censor books and records, to restrict the availability of official
records—even coming up with an "emergency" plan to suspend the
Constitution, in the event of widespread public opposition to the Nicaraguan adventure; and they were just as diligent in bolstering the State
in various foreign lands. And Reagan also ironized the rightist creed
through his personal conduct—a divorcé and indifferent Dad who
preached the sacredness of Family, a champion of Christ who almost
never went to church. Finally, there was all the antidrug moralizing:
"Just say no," etc. This pitch was ironized not only by the fact that the
President's spooks were busily importing tons of narcotics even as he
spoke, but also by the subtler fact that Ronald Reagan, whose voice and
grin made everybody woozy, trusting and oblivious, was a drug himself.

The presidential joke might have lasted "right to the finish line," as
Reagan put it in his last State of the Union speech, if a Lebanese newspaper had not exposed the one self-contradiction that the public would
not tolerate: while playing the tough guy ("Make my day," etc.), Reagan
was in fact a sap, a chump, arming the very enemies whom he was
threatening to kick around. This revelation quite destroyed the credit
earned by Reagan's "victories" over those convenient despotisms in
Libya and Grenada. One good look behind that patriarchal mask, and
the whole world finally saw the void it had been watching:

> . . . the President's advisers say such poll results, which have con-
> sistently shown up for months, are deeply troubling to Mr. Rea-
> gan. Mr. Reagan is a man of vast self-confidence, they say, but
> throughout his career, as an actor and as a politician, he has
> thrived on the admiration and approval of others.
>
> The President, they say, needs the warmth of public accep-
> tance to stay healthy, and when he lacks it, he can wither into a
> mood of despondency and frustration. As one close associate put
> it, "His *sense* of integrity, of honestly dealing with people, is very
> central to his self-esteem." (*New York Times,* 12 July 1987; em-
> phasis added)

Thus, all along, that seeming iron man was only a projection of the gazes smiling on him, and so it vanished once the gazes cooled. Ostensibly a hardy relic of the good old days when men were men, etc., this withered man was just one more boring victim of the culture of narcissism, like Norma Desmond in *Sunset Boulevard,* or like any adolescent shopper, checking her looks in every passing mirror.

To call Ronald Reagan a victim, however, may seem as improper as his own infamous claim that the SS too were "victims," like the Jews they murdered: for the consequences of the Reagan irony have not been funny, but disastrous, and not for him. The derision that began in 1986, while mildly gratifying, was—like the adulation that preceded it—too heavily concentrated on the man himself to constitute a real critical perception: TV—as I suggest throughout this book—is given automatically to such extreme and trivial depictions. It is not Reagan's so-called "management style" that now requires consideration, nor his near-senility (aka "the age issue"), nor his many entertaining "gaffes," but the true murderousness of his regime.

In cataloging the various proofs of Reagan's "niceness" in 1982, I made the charge that the President "has supported infanticide abroad." This brief aside stirred up much outrage, not only among certain editors at *The New Republic,* where the essay first appeared, but among some readers, one of whom invoked Pol Pot as a vivid sort of counterargument; and no less a moral authority than Patrick Buchanan railed at the charge as "libelous." In the light of subsequent events, it is fitting that I not only explicate that ugly claim, but reinforce it, and even extend it.

What I had in mind back then, specifically, was the Administration's dogged refusal to support the global boycott of the Nestlé Corporation, whose officers had been marketing infant formula in Third World countries such as India, where the waters were (as they still are) so heavily polluted that the use of formula was fatal to the babies who drank it. Although breastfeeding was a safer (and cheaper) practice in such places, Nestlé discouraged the custom for the sake of profit. So powerful was the evidence against the Nestlé campaign that every member nation of the World Health Organization upheld the boycott—except the United States, whose delegation, headed by Reaganauts, would not thus impede the progress of free enterprise. Here, then, was a program known to cause the deaths of infants, and yet the Reagan team refused to act against it—sufficient grounds for charging that Reagan did indeed "support infanticide abroad."

That argument might seem tortuous, because the cause of death was indirect, and the infants would not have died outright. Since 1982, however, it has become all too easy to sustain the accusation of infanticide. On 15 July 1987, for instance, the Nicaraguan contras, a force created, managed, and exhorted by the Reagan apparat, attacked the village of San Jose de Bocay, killing, among others, three children and a pregnant woman. On 20 December, attacking the village of Siuna, the contras fired machine guns into a drainage pipe, killing the five children and two women who were hiding there. On 4 February 1988 the contras attacked a farm cooperative in Santa Elisa, killing Benito Calero, his wife, and two children with a mortar shell that blew their hut apart. A seven-year-old boy was also killed by crossfire. Two days later, a bus was hit by mines laid by the contras, killing seventeen people, including five children, one of whom, an infant four months old, was the war's youngest victim.

The list could go on, for each of these atrocities represented a typical day's work for that army, whose quest was so important to the President that he once proclaimed with pride, "I am a contra!" Similarly brutal operations by other of Reagan's "friends in the region" were (and, as of this writing, are) commonplace, as in El Salvador, Honduras, Guatemala, where the military, systematically terrorizing the civilian population, tends not to go easy on the very young. In their "sweep" of El Quiche in 1987, for example, Guatemalan troops forced seven-year-old boys to walk ahead of them, as a shield against guerilla fire.

Not all of Reagan's infanticidal acts were carried out by proxy or by ideological allies. The illegal bombing of Tripoli in 1986, publicized as a stern payback for Muammar Qaddafi's terrorist activities (which were in fact revealed, in 1988, to have been the work of Palestinians), claimed the lives of many innocents, including Qaddafi's baby daughter. In response to this news, Reagan thus turned ethicist, invoking other terrorist murders to excuse those planned in the White House: "It's something you regret any time children or innocent people are killed. On the other hand, I was equally sorry about a little baby that was blown out of an airplane and fell 15,000 feet to its death. I also feel badly about an 11-year-old girl that [sic] was shot down in cold blood for simply standing in the airport at Rome" (*New York Times,* 22 March 1986).

Leaving aside the moral implications of this statement, it is enough to note the recurrence of infanticide as one gross upshot of "the Reagan magic"; and the death of innocents cannot all be attributed to Third World troops, since it also took place here, and as a clear consequence of Presidential policy. In 1987, the Children's Defense Fund reported that "the nation's infant mortality rate was one of the highest in the industrialized world"—a rise coterminous with Reagan's term in office: "In contrast, in 1950, the United States had one of the lowest rates" (*New York Times,* 3 February 1987). Most of the victims were, of course, the children of the poor. The Coalition for the Homeless found, in 1986, "that of 6,527 children under the age of 1 who died [in New York City] from 1981 to 1984, almost half—3,070—were buried in the trenches in Potter's Field" (*New York Times*, 23 November 1986).

The term "infanticide," however, may be too precise a term to apply to Reagan's influence on the very young, for his policies also merely starved and/or stunted those children strong enough to have survived them. Reviewing the Census Report in 1987, Tom Wicker noted that "children, shamefully, are the poorest age group, constituting 13.6 percent of all those living in poverty. In 1986, 20.5 percent of all American children, and almost a quarter of those under 6 years of age, lived below the poverty line" (*New York Times*, 19 November 1987). In 1987, one education specialist described the "horrible conditions" in many of the nation's preschools, where "children have died as a result of neglect," or "are often emotionally damaged for life as a result of bad early childhood experiences"—a problem that was simply absent from the Reaganite agenda: "President Reagan has no interest in quality day care" (*New York Times*, 11 October 1987). As along the Ganges, so in the slums of the United States: Reagan's impulse was always to abet the forces of the market, however dangerous to the young. In 1987, researchers at the Center for Disease control reported that, because of "Government nutrition programs and the increasing popularity of breastfeeding and iron-fortified foods," the rate of anemia among poor children "had dropped by almost two-thirds from 1975 to 1985." Those Government programs, begun in 1973, had lasted only because Congress had refused the "cutbacks proposed by the Reagan Administration" (*New York Times*, 27 September 1987).

All these examples ought to justify the charge that the Great Communicator has indeed "supported infanticide abroad," and then some. And even this atrocious record has been half-hidden by the Reagan irony; for, even as he authorized—however vaguely—all that death and deprivation of the young, Reagan also hymned his praises of "the family," wept for the murdered innocents at Bergen-Belsen, decried abortion as a form of "baby-killing"—and Nancy helped out too, by arranging numerous photo opportunities with handicapped toddlers. This is perhaps the greatest irony of Ronald Reagan's long career in show business. Because of it, there are thousands who are not alive, or alert enough, to laugh at it.■

A Viewer's Campaign Diary, 1984

- -

"Art thou that traitor angel, art thou he,
Who first broke peace in heav'n and faith, till then
Unbroken, and in proud rebellious arms
Drew after him the third part of heav'n's sons
Conjured against the Highest, for which both thou
And they, outcast from God, are here condemned
To waste eternal days in woe and pain?"
                            —*Paradise Lost*, II, 689-95

1.

N 3 NOVEMBER 1983, DAN RATHER, HAVING INTRO-
duced the "CBS Evening News" and himself with a
semicordial smile, suddenly tensed up, and made the following grim announcement:

> Syria tonight appears to be making a major new move in Leba-
> non—a potentially ominous situation—with possible far-reaching
> ramifications for U.S. forces in the area, for Israel, and for peace
> in the Middle East and beyond.

Before we could leap from our chairs to bolt the windows shut, Rather
continued:

> It involves violent new fighting in northern Lebanon, within the
> Palestine Liberation Organization. The combatants are forces
> loyal to Yasser Arafat, and more radical Syrian-backed rebels,
> who believe diplomacy should be abandoned for more armed
> struggle.

We were then shown a typical filmed report from Lebanon, telling
us, basically, that Arafat was still under siege, and was asking Syria to
stop it.

Even with its lively bits of battle footage, the report had to seem anti-
climactic after Rather's nerve-racking lead-in. For there was no "major

new move" by Syria, whose responsibility for the PLO rebellion had been well known for some time. Nor was there any evidence to support Rather's tortuous implication that Syria was somehow going to get those "U.S. forces in the area," then Israel, and then the rest of us. His announcement, in fact, was little more than a series of gratuitous shockers: "ominous situation," "violent new fighting," "more radical Syrian-backed rebels," "armed struggle." With its evocation of some as-yet-unseen and spreading evil, it amounted, despite all its redundancies and polysyllables, to this simple message: *"Boo!"*

This opening move was meant to make us jump. It was therefore a typical bit of televisual rhetoric, the sort of prefatory jolt devised to make us watch programs like "Miami Vice" or "Knight Rider"—ample girl walks down deserted street (followed jerkily by the hand-held camera), hears footsteps, looks back, screams, gets stabbed/abducted/raped, and then the credits come. As Dan Rather's little fiction demonstrates, however, the anchorman knows how to zap us far more skillfully, insinuating violence rather than depicting it. Moreover, the brutal opening that hooks us into sitting through "Hunter" or "The A-Team" is usually related to the ensuing story, whereas the telejournalistic tease need not have much, if anything, to do with what it seems to introduce. Such disjointedness is rare on television. There is only one other kind of TV spectacle that worries us as slyly as Dan Rather does, evoking dreadful possibilities that don't pertain to what comes next, and that is the TV commercial—man wakes up in dead of night, sees wife is missing, calls her name, bolts out of bed, then finds wife crying on front stoop. Despite these hints of desertion and dementia, however, wife turns out to be shedding tears of absolute contentment, whereupon her easy hubby fetches her a cup of Taster's Choice.

This rhetorical congruence between the ads and newscasts on TV reveals the way in which the network newsmen actually regard us. Whether or not they would admit it, and even if they aren't aware of it, nearly all the TV newsmen think of us, not as an audience of grown-up citizens, but as a market. Thus what directs the newsmen is not that legendary "liberal bias" condemned so often by the right, nor is it any such cabal of corporate higher-ups as is frequently invoked by vulgar Marxists. Rather, the TV newsman does the bidding of those higher-ups entirely on his own and without knowing it, simply by thinking as they think; that is, by regarding us as a potential mass of buyers, inattentive, fickle and dim-witted, and who therefore need to be expertly stroked or startled or cajoled, anything to keep the ratings high.

Given this deep commercial orientation, the news machine's exceptionalist ideology, its frequent claims to be devoted to "the public

interest" and therefore better than "the rest of television," are unjustified. It is the function of the news, just as it is the function of "The Dukes
of Hazzard" or "The Price Is Right" or an ad for Pizza Hut, to sell us. And
while we might expect the news to drop its hard-sell methods at least
when it comes to our presidential contests, given what's at stake, it is in
this very coverage that the TV news now fails us most disastrously. Indeed, those contests have long since been appropriated by the newsmen.
These interventionists have displaced our electoral function, not just by
blabbering before the polls have closed, but far more subtly, and
throughout each long campaign. It is through its daily newscasts that TV
has disenfranchised its spectators, and not through such extraordinary
broadcasts as the "polispots" or the candidates' debates. Some observations on the last Democratic contest, as TV helped determine it, might
illuminate the news machine's campaign to keep itself in power.

Like the commercials that pay for it, TV's political coverage relies on
two crude rhetorical strategies to keep the viewers tuned in—titillation
and flattery. Although the news titillates more egregiously than it flat-
ters us, its flattery might actually be more ruinous in effect. For now,
we'll concentrate on the news' titillations, which arise primarily from
the continued rapid deployment of disquieting pictures.

Only the blind, of course, have not seen for themselves that TV's
political coverage, like all of TV's news, tends to favor only the most
lurid footage—spats, "gaffes," threats, hecklers. Even the captains of
the news machine sometimes complain about this sort of thing, albeit
inconclusively. And yet the full influence of the visuals remains unrec-
ognized. A typical news story does not just happen to include a series of
adventitious images, but its "story" or narrative is so thoroughly determined by those images that, without them, it may make no sense at all.
Here, for example, is much of the report delivered by CBS' Bruce Morton on 6 June, the day of the New Jersey and California primaries:

Gary Hart has called Walter Mondale the candidate of the past.
But today Mondale went riding on something both old and new,
San Francisco's cable cars, which have just started running
again. Jesse Jackson had his feet firmly on the ground in Los
Angeles. Hart got the scary ride of the day when one engine of
his chartered 707 jet caught fire just after taking off from
Philadelphia.

After this, Morton presented the results of a CBS/*New York Times* poll
showing Mondale's clear lead in New Jersey.

Now, taken as a piece of literary journalism, this is a rather incoherent narrative. In fact, it sounds less like a passage of lucid reportage

than like some weird riddle, suggesting that Bruce Morton had, by 6 June, finally taken one transcontinental flight too many: "Gary Hart may think Walter Mondale is behind the times, but Mondale took a trolley-ride today," Morton seems to be saying. "Jesse Jackson was in Los Angeles, walking on the ground. Hart's jet almost crashed." As crazy as it sounds, however, Morton's commentary was in fact an exemplary bit of TV newspeak, a wholly (as it were) visual utterance. First of all, it served perfectly to highlight the images that played along with it. As Morton spoke, there was, sure enough, some footage of the Mondales and Mayor Feinstein, grinning happily aboard a cable car, which rolled along, its bell merrily ringing, as a few bystanders cheered. Then there was a shot of Jesse Jackson greeting passers-by out on a sidewalk, and then some shots taken inside Hart's disabled jet.

Thus, the newsman automatically promotes the medium that owns him, first of all, by carefully deriving all his metaphors from whatever images we might be gaping at. By adapting his own language to the real attraction, Morton did not have to worry about boring us with any taxing information or analysis, and so he successfully exploited, and thereby reinforced, TV's mainly visual appeal. Nor did Bruce Morton have any choice in the matter, but had to write a quick gloss on the day's pictures, or else he might have had to do some thinking, read a book or two, and then he would have missed a lot of deadlines and gotten himself fired. This is why his ostensible report included, typically, no comparisons of the candidates' respective records, nothing about the various constituencies concerned, but told us only what we knew already—that Mondale, Hart, and Jackson were campaigning.

However, Bruce Morton is not quite as innocent a figure as this description makes him sound; for his account, although seemingly inane, was not at all pointless, but subtly loaded in the winner's favor. The first two sentences, for instance, sound like a non sequitur only if we fail to listen to their actual biased message: Even if Gary Hart has churlishly "called Walter Mondale a candidate of the past," Mondale is unstoppable, enjoying the inexorable forward motion of that over-hauled cable car, which is "both old and new" as he is both old-fashioned, a seasoned Democratic trooper, and yet renewed by current popularity. According to this formulation, moreover, it is Hart who has "called" Mondale names, whereas Mondale, evidently, is too blithe and self-possessed an engine to demean himself with any such political behavior. For his base slanders, Hart has been punished with a "scary ride"—a derisive way to put it, implying that Hart is childish, reckless, can't control his vehicle, while his serene opponent just "went riding."

Morton's disingenuous gloating was not the expression of his personal preference. Rather, he—like nearly all the other newsmen—thus subverted Hart and championed Mondale entirely for the sake of the TV news, which must translate all conflicts into the crudest of binary schemes. The newsman's commentary, in other words, is doubly visual. Not only are its metaphors subservient to the footage, but it creates an overall conception of events simple enough to take in with one quick mental glance. This is why all presidential contests, both for the nomination and for the office itself, are now represented by the newsmen in terms of this venerable image: the chosen one, deserving and infallible, magically above the stuff of politics, is challenged by some desperate aspirant whose heart is full of malice, and who therefore cripples himself by making lots of "gaffes."

Thus Carter lost his "mean campaign" against the kingly Reagan, just as Ted Kennedy had, a few months earlier, failed in his wretched effort to unseat the righteous Carter. So too, for that matter, was the unfortunate Eugene McCarthy thwarted every time he tried to violate the sacred schema with some foul third party. The newsmen will tolerate a third force only insofar as it creates the sort of discord that they love to amplify, but they will never take such innovation seriously. If Jesse Jackson has failed to come across on TV as a real contender, perhaps this is the prejudice that he ought to have questioned.

But, this year, it was Hart who was deliberately subverted by the newsmen, and always in the same implicit way, and on all three networks. On the day of Hart's "scary ride," ABC's Steve Shepherd began his report with that dramatic footage taken inside the stricken jet: "It was the most exciting thing to happen to Hart since he won Ohio," Shepherd began, suggesting that Hart was not only a has-been, but the type who would do anything for kicks: win an election, die in a plane crash—hey, what's the difference, Pops? This thrill-crazed punk seems convinced that heavenly forces will take care of him: "Even if he loses ground to Mondale today," Shepherd concluded in his rich baritone, "he may well fight on for the nomination, hoping for some kind of miracle victory." Such hints of mad overreaching were based on nothing but Steve Shepherd's guesswork as to what was going on inside Hart's head, a method dear to the newsmen, and especially to Shepherd, who often sounds as if he were dictating a bad historical novel. On the previous day, he had asserted, over a shot of Hart celebrating with his daughter at her graduation ceremony, that "beneath his smile, there was bitterness."

NBC's Roger Mudd also did some subtle jeering on 6 June, late in the evening, after it was clear that Hart had lost New Jersey. Like Morton, Shepherd, and the rest, Mudd used a visible object as a deprecating symbol; and he too sounded off about Hart's secret feelings, although, in doing so, he sounded less like a hack novelist than like a Grand Inquisitor. He had been scheduled to hold an interview with Hart, but

Hart had cancelled it, and so Mudd, addressing Tom Brokaw, improvised this bit of allegory: "Well, we had a chair ready for the senator, Tom, but he didn't show up. And this empty chair [Mudd pointed at it] is really symbolic of the, of the sad state of, uh, of the Hart campaign."

Mudd then proceeded, with his glacial smirk, to read Hart's mind: "It was a long trip for him this evening, from the East, but he just came and announced that he didn't want to do interviews, uh, because he wasn't sure about California. But I think he just doesn't want to talk about what's probably been the worst day of his campaign."

Given this high-handed dismissal of the candidate's excuse, it probably made little difference whether Hart showed up or not, since Mudd was bound to gloat just as smugly in Hart's face as in Hart's absence. (Mudd's previous interview with Hart had been little more than a succession of trivial accusations.) Although the stunning arrogance of Roger Mudd may well deserve extended treatment, it would lead us off the subject, since there are other network newsmen just as arrogant. What matters here is the disturbing fact that all these telejournalists work in agreement, promoting a certain vision actively—even if obliquely—and thereby participating in the race which they purport to "cover" from the sidelines.

But why was Hart made to play the necessary role of hapless loser? TV's visual imperative explains only why there must be such a role, and not why it was foisted upon him instead of Mondale. The race, after all, was very close for a few weeks. Indeed, it was so close after New Hampshire, and that unexpected surge for Hart appeared so damaging to Mondale, that, for a while, the news depicted Hart as the eagle, Mondale as the stumblebum, and it did so through precisely the same low televisual tactics later used to do Hart in. One evening, for example, at least two of the networks broadcast stories about the flailing Mondale, including, as symbolic proof of his political distress, a shot of the candidate trying to leave a building as the door closed in his face. "Things weren't going well for Mondale today," one reporter said of this irrelevant mishap; implying, idiotically, that no door would ever do that to a winner.

The race was not so close for long, however, and so Hart was soon forced to trade places with his rival, his jet and smile and "empty chair" now serving the purpose of Mondale's door. As soon as Hart *seemed* not to be "the people's choice," the newsmen chose against him, and that was that. Whether Mondale was way out ahead or close in front, or even when he and Hart were running even, Hart's campaign was thenceforth represented as an ill-advised and hopeless venture. And the newsmen always thus undercut the seeming loser, always abet the winner, however slight his lead, because their impulses are not "liberal," not "conservative," but wholly, timidly majoritarian. The newsmen's purpose, in other words, is not really to "inform the public," but to tell the public what the newsmen think the public is already thinking.

Such cautious second-guessing is a form of exploitative flattery. The newsmen play it safe by instantly applauding "us" for "our" superior judgment, however "we" may judge, since, after all, the customer is always right. Like any astute marketer, the newsman relies on the latest opinion polls, not just for the numbers that he must include in his report, but to figure out just how that whole report ought to be slanted, in order to repeat the mass consensus that the polls seem to define. And as this commercial strategy explains why it was finally Hart who had to be subverted, so does it explain the striking eagerness with which the newsmen all went after him. Because it is the newsman's business to say what people want to hear, he sees himself as one who understands the simple folk who watch him, sees himself, in fact, as their custodian; and so he doesn't like it whenever something takes him by surprise, or otherwise seems to elude his control. Although Hart's early victories were good for a few jolting stories, the newsmen seem to have resented Mondale's "upset" because they hadn't seen it coming. Hart's cool manner, furthermore, his refusal or inability to seem beholden to the newsmen, also seems to have annoyed them. They are, after all, the masters of this game, and therefore expect a certain show of self-abasement from the office-seekers who depend on them.

And yet, while they control the scene which they purport to be observing, the newsmen will not acknowledge that they wield any influence whatsoever. They believe that they are somehow cleanly removed from the reality which they revise, just as TV itself is wholly innocent, transpicuous, "our window on the world." Suggest that the coverage might be biased, and the newsman will defend himself at once, and in all sincerity, with this absurd credo. In May, Tom Brokaw, interviewing Jesse Jackson in Baltimore for the "NBC Nightly News," was briefly interviewed himself by a local TV reporter, who asked first if Brokaw thought that Jackson had been let off easy by "the media."

Sometimes, claimed Brokaw, Jackson had indeed been treated "more gently" than the two white candidates, while at other times Jackson had been "held to maybe even harsher conditions." All in all, "there's been a kind of ebb and flow." Warming to this image of the tides, the anchorman went on to suggest that Hart and Mondale had each been subjected to the same kind of evenly fluctuating coverage. Hart "had an awful lot of attention about his name change and his age confusion, and so on, along the way," and "there's been a kind of an ebb and flow for" Mondale, too: "A lot of people were pounding him about the big labor connection, and then he was on a roll again." "So,"

Brokaw summed up, with a revealing grin, "that's part of the price of being a presidential candidate."

Understandably, the reporter seemed intrigued by this invocation of transcendent rhythms. "The ebb and flow," he asked, "how do you account for that?" It was a good question. Here is Brokaw's full reply: "Well, we're not a consistent business. This is not a mathematical formula in which we're engaged. You know, journalism is a reflection of the passions of the day. It's a reflection of the change that occurs."

Now, this brief analysis of TV journalism is not very promising, since, first of all, it doesn't make any sense. Having dictated that all presidential candidates must undergo the same rigid process of intermittent hazing, Brokaw then insisted, inexplicably, that the TV news "is not a consistent business." There also seems to have been a bit of a decline in the ideology of his profession. The purpose of "an able, disinterested, public-spirited press," wrote Joseph Pulitzer some years ago, is to "preserve that public virtue without which popular government is a sham and a mockery." Such idealism may sound pretty funny nowadays, but if journalism is merely "a reflection of the passions of the day," then surely we're all screwed. You won't get anything but nervous reinforcement of the status quo from such so-called journalism, which would be about as bold and truthful as the Top 40.

But then, of course, that's exactly what we have. And yet Brokaw was not about to let himself admit that the TV news reinforces anything, since the purpose of his mystic utterance was to make it clear that the TV news has no effect at all. "There's been a kind of ebb and flow." Thus, the network news is somehow like unto the waters of the earth— a force of nature, deep, ubiquitous, and grandly uncontrollable by any mortal entity. Such a system, Brokaw was suggesting, is ultimately too big to attack or favor any mere candidate, but is as impartial as that God Who, in the beginning, made all the oceans and the minicams.

And the reason why the TV news is so supremely fair, Brokaw was implying, is that the TV news is really nothing in itself, but only an extension of the national will. "The ebb and flow," in other words, refers not to any actual ocean, nor even, it turns out, to "the media," but to our oceanic populace, of whose large and ever-shifting sentiments the TV news is only "a reflection." And that national will is also, of course, transcendently impartial, ever just, because it is a pure and natural force, eternal and autonomous, like the tides, uninfluenced by any lowly human enterprise, such as, for example, the TV news.

Brokaw's effacement of his mammoth industry was every bit as artful as any slanderous bit of "coverage." At first, in talking about Jackson's "ebb and flow," Brokaw, clearly, was referring only to the candidates' treatment by reporters; but then, by favoring only the vaguest of referents, he gave the impression that the other candidates had been subverted, not by any TV newsmen, but by everybody else. Because of "the big labor connection," Mondale received a "pounding" from "a lot of people," i.e., not TV reporters, who would never have considered calling our attention, say, to the union leaders standing next to Mondale while he gave a speech. And the claim that Hart "had an awful lot of attention about his name change and his age confusion" suggests that those pseudoissues had first inspired gigantic public rallies, which were then reported.

Although the TV news is not at all objective, its employees all solemnly subscribe to an ideology of objectivity. Or rather, it is this very creed of heavenly impartiality that allows the newsmen to be partial, as it is one purpose of an ideology to posit an ideal which you can then proceed to violate in its own name. It is through their vast pretense of uninvolvement that the newsmen implicate themselves, like so many schizophrenics, coolly describing the results of their own influence as if somehow detached from it.

Hart was, predictably, the main victim of this telejournalistic pose. For instance, just after his first successes, the newsmen began to peg their stories on this burning rhetorical question: "Will Hart be able to get his message across?" The answer was implicit in the question, and the answer was "no." So long as the TV newsmen are wondering aloud about any candidate's so-called "message," that message isn't going to come across, since it's up to them to find it out and tell us about it. Otherwise, the candidate will need a lot of dimes, because he'll have to use the telephone to fill the voters in. Through that dishonest question, the newsmen managed, in one deft stroke, both to withhold his "message" and to blame Hart for their silence, as if he'd lost his voice, or couldn't speak English.

But of course Hart does speak English, often more precisely than the other candidates. Furthermore, he does indeed have certain "new ideas," as any reader of, say, the *New York Times* could have found out for himself. But then the TV newsmen did not really want to make Hart known to us, but to make it look as if his early victories had been the sorry consequence of clever shamming, mere p.r., the sort of slick and empty advertising used to push a lousy product that stops selling once "the people" recognize its flaws. This was particularly undeserved, since Hart had won at first *without* having to be sold by the network news.

But that, perhaps, was his crime, and so the newsmen played deaf to his positions, while writing stories on his muteness. Meanwhile, they reconfirmed the legend of Hart's brilliant emptiness by taking up Mondale's brilliant, empty "Where's the beef?" They broadcast this

103

televisual riposte as much as possible, endorsing it by seeming merely to report it; and yet, incredibly, they also treated it with scorn, affecting the usual detachment: Mondale's "Where's the beef?", Brokaw commented one evening, with an expressive sneer, "got a lot of play," as if it hadn't been played endlessly on Brokaw's program.

The newsmen are adept at projecting such self-righteousness. In describing the spectacular political behaviors that they require, they act contemptuous, as if somehow above the tawdry antics that they themselves arrange for us, as hypocritical as pimps deploring fornication. Although Mondale's allusion was thus jeered at by its exploiters, Hart was the most frequent object of their scorn. On 6 June, summing up the race, Mudd claimed that Hart had blown it when he "began straining, eager and willing to go anywhere, do anything to be photographed," as if a presidential candidate has to "strain" to find himself surrounded by reporters. In Trenton, Steve Shepherd said on the same day, "Hart got himself photographed munching doughnuts." "Got himself photographed"? By whom? The disdainful tone of these put-downs suggests that no network cameraman had ever stooped to gratify Hart's loathsome appetite for coverage. Of course, Mudd's and Shepherd's comments were each accompanied by a shot of Gary Hart, but that footage must have been mailed in by Hart himself.

We are also meant to think, evidently, that Walter Mondale has been too big a man to worry about getting photographed, and wouldn't have cared if his campaign had not been televised at all. On 3 April, ABC's Peter Jennings reported that Mondale, "at a subway stop in Brooklyn," "tried to lay out the differences between himself and Gary Hart." As opposed to this earnest performance, "Gary Hart," said Jennings in the next breath, "began the day at a nursery school, not a lot of votes in there. But outside he used the backdrop to make a pitch for day-care facilities." Through such innuendo, the TV news made Hart seem guilty (and Mondale innocent) of theatricality, as if theatricality were not the very essence of campaign politics—and the very form and content of the TV news.

For his presumptuousness, then, as well as for his lesser status, Hart received a heavy punishment. By making him appear to be the loser, the newsmen made him lose. This is not to say that Hart would certainly have won if TV hadn't been involved, but that Hart—like Carter, Ford, Ted Kennedy, McCarthy—could *not* have won as TV represented him. For the newsmen create the situation which they pretend to be reporting—create it, indeed, *through* their ostensible reports. If, day after day, we see a candidate stammering and bumping into things, hear him described repeatedly as "struggling," "lashing out," and so on, we must soon regard him as incompetent, unlucky, and unpopular, and so he has indeed become unpopular, which means, of course, that he must also be unlucky and incompetent—not "presidential," because the TV newsmen have not chosen him to represent "the people's choice."

2.

ON THE SECOND NIGHT OF THE DEMOCRATIC NATIONAL CON-vention, some viewers got mad when ABC suddenly pre-empted the Jennings/Brinkley coverage with an old episode of "Hart to Hart." Their pique was understandable, but then so was ABC's decision. After all, that convention was monopolizing prime time, whose every minute is worth a lot more in advertising fees than Peter Jennings' entire collection of shirts. Whatever got televised, therefore, had to be sensational enough to keep us all tuned in for the commercials; and if an event lacked the necessary impact, it would have to be punched up somehow by the anchorman, or by one of his roving henchpersons. Unfortunately, there was, on that night, a brief period when the convention goings-on were largely uneventful and complex, so mundane that no TV newsman could inflate them. It was then that the top dogs at ABC decided to broadcast a car chase; and for this they blamed the Democrats. "Hart to Hart" ran for twenty minutes, and it would have gone on even longer, if the Democrats, said one network manager, "had not sped things up."

NBC and CBS, however, also meant business. In replacing their coverage with a third-rate rerun, ABC did not depart from the standard practice, but pushed it to extremes, since all three networks did their best to turn the convention into a spectacle as lurid, trite, and fast-paced as any other prime-time thriller. This effort was under way even before the convention started. On the regular evening newscasts early in the week, there were prominent stories highlighting the assemblage, all around Moscone Convention Center, of many gung ho deviants—crusading potsmokers, a pallid clown named Zippy the Pinhead, hookers, punks, and tree worshippers. Ostensibly a chuckling evocation of American diversity, each of these stories was in fact calculated to heat the audience up with glimpses of wild weirdos about to go berserk. It was no coincidence that the actor most visible in these reports was also the one most likely to gross out the majority of viewers: Sister Boom Boom, a transvestite who camped it up in a nun's habit. Thus, in advance, the convention was subtly advertised as a grotesque and shameless rampage, just the sort of orgy you expect whenever Democrats convene, and especially in San Francisco.

As it happened, of course, there was never any such uprising. But if we wanted to see a bunch of freaks trash the convention, all we had to do was watch the network newsmen on the job. While the Democrats managed to stage a show of unity, the newsmen tried, all week, to stage a coup: TV's documentary spectacle is *their* turf, and so they struggled to proclaim their own control of the event. Of course, we were asked to see this offensive, not as a bid for power, but as the search for truth. According to this myth, the newsmen, savvy and detached, were carefully penetrating the Democrats' facade, in order to find the hidden facts and let us learn them. "One of the things we want to do with our coverage all week long," Dan Rather seemed to believe, "is to differentiate between the essence of the reality, and the agreed-upon appearance of things."

And yet, if we ever did glimpse "the essence of the reality," we had to do so despite the intervention of the TV news, which took two forms. On the one hand, the newsmen tried to flatter us by condescending broadly to the whole procedure, as if to wink at us and say, "*We* know this is all pretty stupid, don't we?" At the same time, however, they never stopped trying to titillate us with promises of an immense disaster, fatal for the Democrats, thrilling for the audience. To this end they tried to blow up every minor bit of discord, every seeming blunder, sometimes even starting fights, in order to keep each of us locked in a posture of pop-eyed anxiety.

Thus we learned that the art of convention coverage demands an exquisite sense of decorum: When should the newsman smirk? When should he forecast doom? Each network sabotaged the proceedings in its own peculiar way. In the ABC anchorbooth, condescension was the device favored by the two co-anchors, David Brinkley in particular. Sneering, it seemed, with his whole body, Brinkley was a veritable fount of condescending epithets: he called the final balloting "a wonderful little ritual," predicted that the platform debates would be "nice, neat, quiet, peaceful, like a garden club sitting around eating watercress sandwiches," and so on. Meanwhile, the overdressed Peter Jennings slouched and chortled at his side, like a headwaiter idling with his boss near the cloakroom of some pretentious restaurant. Jennings, however, provided more than his diverting haberdashery. He would also interject the necessary hints of doom whenever Brinkley went too far belittling the occasion.

On NBC, Tom Brokaw managed all by himself both to sensationalize and to jeer. On Tuesday night, for instance, he reported grimly on "the booing of Andrew Young," who had angered many in the hall that day with a speech defending runoff primaries. Young, Brokaw said redundantly, had been "in the embarrassing, awkward position of being booed by other black delegates." After some footage of the booing, Brokaw tried to depict that intense agreement as a national catastrophe:

"That was *totally* unexpected, that's some of the *worst booing* that we've seen at a Democratic National Convention, and some of the *worst booing* that we've seen at a convention in, what, twenty years or so, when Rockefeller appeared before the Republicans in 1964 in the same city." While clearly very good at exaggeration, Brokaw also proved himself an expert at gratuitous condescension. On the final night, as we watched Geraldine Ferraro facing the exultant delegates, Brokaw remarked, over the images, "Geraldine Ferraro . . . The first woman to be nominated for vice-president . . . Size six!"

At times, CBS's Dan Rather, too, belittled the occasion, usually by attempting to convey its all-American flavor—"part oratory, part grand opera, part hog calling," was how he described it early on. Of course, if anyone else had referred to the convention as a "hog calling," we would have to regard it not just as a condescending vulgarism, but as a grievous insult to the candidates. However, it was only Dan Rather talking, and so no one ought to mind, since it is never clear that Rather knows exactly what he's saying. His words are usually intended not to signify, but to beat against your consciousness like so many mental baseball bats: "The keynote speaker, New York Governor Mario Cuomo," he announced at one point, eyes bulging dangerously, "has given the Democrats their first, big, opening, exciting moment of this convention!"

When Rather strained, however, it was often not to condescend or to capture first big opening moments. Throughout the week, his main concern was to foretell enormous damage to the Democratic ticket. More than Jennings or Brokaw, and with far more evident relish, Rather amplified dissensions and invoked dire consequences, thereby playing repeatedly on fear, which has always been his favorite rhetorical device. There was, indeed, no point to his ramblings other than their obsessive sensationalism. It is worth noting that CBS won the highest ratings of the week, and that Rather, furthermore, "was generally considered," reports the *New York Times*, "to have provided an intelligent, comprehensive center to his network's coverage." In fact, Rather was appallingly inarticulate, seemed to know almost nothing about politics, and kept spouting "facts" that were dead wrong. The only datum in his mind, and the only thing he managed to convey, was this assumption: *Whatever happens means disaster for the Democrats*.

Rather aired this conviction in several uneasy chats, some with Bill Moyers, some with Walter Cronkite, both of whom appeared to be keenly embarrassed by the anchorman's automatic fatalism. Whenever something had gone well for the ticket, Rather would dismiss it, offering instead a tortured argument to prove that Walter Mondale was a goner. On Monday night, Bruce Morton reported on Geraldine Ferraro's great popularity among the delegates. With Moyers wincing across from him,

BOXED IN

■ ■ ■ ■ ■ ■

Rather countered with this supposition: "You said that the big winner so far at this convention is Geraldine Ferraro. But I wonder—and this is only a wonder—if the big winner isn't Ronald Reagan, with a convention that begins with former vice-president, uh, former president Jimmy Carter." The Carter speech, Rather argued, was probably "another Mondale mistake," since it would allow the Republicans to stigmatize the candidate with his predecessor's record (as if they couldn't do this in any case).

Here Rather was suggesting that Carter's prime-time appearance was already a big issue, and that it would remain a hot item right up until Election Day, overshadowing even Geraldine Ferraro's candidacy. Later that night, Rather became even more desperate in his attempt to fabricate bad news. Cuomo had spoken, and Cronkite had just praised the speech. Here is how Rather struggled to minimize the value of the keynote address:

> We both agree, I think the hall, certainly, with its thunderous applause for Cuomo, to—agree that this was a—one of the better keynote addresses.
>
> However, Mario Cuomo will not be at the top of the ticket. Walter Mondale will be. And early in the race Cuomo himself said that Mondale reminded his mother of *polenta*—a kind of bland Italian mush.
>
> Now with Mondale at the top of the ticket—and again, to repeat parenthesis it's Mondale at the top of the ticket, not Ferraro—Given this keynote address—never *mind* the keynote address. What you have is a ticket made up of Northern liberals with the union label. And can it win?

"Yes," Cronkite replied, with a flash of annoyance, "it *can* win. The question is, *will* it win?" The ex-anchorman seemed to catch, and to resent, the sensationalistic drift of his ex-subordinate's ravings. "Can it win?" is a question that must reduce all subsequent discussion to the sort of breathless dramatizing that is Rather's specialty. Indeed, Rather had turned completely incoherent under the pressure to coarsen everything into cliché. His only concern was to evoke a thrilling image of doomed effort, and so he blurted out whatever disparate damning factors he could think of—Mondale's blandness, no Southerner on the ticket, the labor stigma. "Given this keynote address—never *mind* the keynote address." While Carter's speech would stick to Mondale for all time, Cuomo's speech was evidently not going to handicap the candidate, and so Rather veered clumsily away from it.

In constructing his dark vision, however, Rather went beyond the mere suppression of all promising developments, to the outright revision of historical reality. He asserted, for instance, that "no Democratic ticket has been elected in this century without a Southerner on the ticket." This would be true if it weren't false, since no Southerner ran with FDR and Henry A. Wallace in 1940. And Rather later reinforced the myth of Mondale's perfect unelectability with a larger and more preposterous fiction. After Jesse Jackson's speech, Cronkite remarked that Jackson "is probably considerably to the left of the great bulk of the party." This obvious point was news to Dan Rather, who immediately used the revelation to corroborate his *idée fixe*:

> You have Walter Mondale, who's staked his whole political career on the liberal Democratic position. Not only has he not apologized for it, he's proud of it. Geraldine Ferraro is in the top 1% of the House of Representatives when it comes to voting for liberal programs.
>
> Jesse Jackson—if it is true, I'm not sure—I'm going to think about that—I'm not sure I agree with you that he's staked out a strictly liberal position. If that's true, then, *what you're suggesting is,* it may play into Ronald Reagan and the Republicans' hands, in that they can now say, "Listen. We have the right and the middle of the road. The Democrats have only the liberal left." (emphasis added)

Cronkite, of course, had suggested no such thing. Trying to stay calm, he protested that "Jackson hasn't prevailed," and then went on to explain very carefully that Walter Mondale is not a leftist. This, however, seemed to make no impression on Dan Rather, for whom "left" and "liberal," "Mondale," "Jackson," and "Ferraro," all meant the same thing: "loser."

Rather was not alone in his obsession with danger for the Democrats. The same obsession motivated those newsmen who were roaming the convention floor, wearing headsets and brandishing long microphones. They used the format of the interview as Rather used the mode of off-the-cuff analysis—to represent every possible development as a fatal blow. Whereas Rather harped exclusively on Mondale's problems, however, the interviewers jabbed whomever they were talking to. They clearly wanted to depict the convention as a brawl with no survivors, and so, in nearly every confrontation, they labored to extract confessions of failure and/or elicit cries of disappointed rage, using "questions" as a torturer might use a cattle prod.

On Tuesday night, after the platform had been adopted, there was an exemplary series of encounters on NBC. First, Roger Mudd nabbed

Eliot Cutler of the Mondale campaign. "Why," Mudd asked, "if Walter Mondale has control of this convention, [did] he [have] to yield on two of the five disputed platform planks?" Cutler replied that "the objective has been to unify the party," so that it didn't matter much how certain "minor disagreements" had been settled. Mudd seemed not to be listening. "But," he asked again, "if one of the things Walter Mondale must do is exhibit *control* and *decisive leadership*, wouldn't he do that saying, 'This is what I want, and I'll take no less'?" Cutler then repeated his original answer.

Typically, Mudd's question was unanswerable: "Mondale's a real wimp, isn't he?" was what he was asking Mondale's aide. The question was meant, all at once, to make Cutler jump, make Mondale look weak, imply that the Democrats were still ruinously divided, and set Mudd up as a wise observer gazing down serenely on all that interesting discord. Mudd's insinuation was itself entirely arbitrary: in the next interview, Mondale now figured as a big bully, and for the very same reason that Mudd had cast him as a little sissy. "Does Jackson look *squeezed* in all of this?" Don Oliver was asking Paul Tully, another Mondale aide. "How can he go to his people and say that they won much, when they lost the major ones?"

Like Cutler, Tully kept his cool: "Always the concern was, that there was full and fair hearing, and respect." Now it was Connie Chung's turn to do some needling. Standing beside a Jackson delegate named Al Vann, she said: "All the Mondale people are saying is that you wanted— Jackson's people wanted just a little respect so that you could air your feelings, but how do *you* feel about having three of your most *important* planks go down and having to *cave in* on a fourth?"

Not only had Chung distorted Tully's cautious statement in order to make it sound as scornful as possible, but she asked the question in a voice oozing with solicitude, as if Vann were three years old and had a boo-boo on his knee. Nevertheless, Vann refused to give her what she wanted, although he was understandably much angrier than Tully or Cutler. It was "shame on the Democratic Party," he said, deploring the general neglect of his constituency, and then Chung tried repeatedly to translate his unhappiness into a headline: "You really believe that Jackson delegates, black votes will not go to Walter Mondale because of this," she prompted him. "I didn't say that," he replied, and so the struggle wore on, until Chung finally had to quit.

Clearly, NBC was getting nowhere. As if to goose things up, Brokaw interceded with his bit about "the worst booing" he had "seen" in twenty years. Then Ken Bode appeared, and made one last heroic effort to force a scream out of an interviewee. Standing beside a Jackson delegate and erstwhile booer named Paul Valteau, Bode started out by

110

dwelling on the rudeness of the booing. Valteau, however, was the coolest subject yet. He insisted on explaining, and with impressive clarity, *why* Young had been booed. He went on to make a lucid case against Young's position, delivering the sort of basic information that we perhaps should have learned from Tom Brokaw or Ken Bode, who changed the subject once he saw that Valteau wasn't going to break. Bringing up the platform struggle, he went Mudd, Oliver, and Chung one better, by simply wiping out the only victory the Jackson forces had achieved: "What will happen here with Jackson delegates," he asked, "who haven't had a victory in the convention at all?" Even this reckless overstatement failed, however: Valteau reminded Bode of the affirmative action plank, and so the grilling ended.

Thus a complex situation did not just go unexplained, but vanished behind a succession of jangling and incongruous images: Mondale's a weakling! No, *Jackson* looks weak! *Mondale's a tyrant!! NO BLACKS WILL VOTE FOR MONDALE*!!! JACKSON WON NOTHING!!! Here the telejournalists' strain was obvious, and so these interviews, like most that took place during the week, were comic. There was another, however, less amusing episode, in which the telejournalist prevailed.

On Wednesday night, Ed Bradley of CBS confronted Mayor Harold Washington of Chicago. "Your city," Bradley began, "is a good example where there have been problems in Democrats sitting down and working with each other." He then asked if the Democrats in Cook County can "work together," adding enigmatically that "you and the man standing behind me here don't even deal with each other." As Washington could see, and as we would soon find out, Bradley's mystery guest was none other than Alderman Edward Vrdolyak, aka "Fast Eddie," the mayor's archenemy on the Chicago City Council.

Washington, his face gone hard at the mention of Vrdolyak, answered Bradley with a careful statement, the gist of which was, "No, we can't deal with each other. But maybe our two factions can work separately for Mondale." Bradley, however, wasn't listening. As if Washington had not spoken, Bradley suddenly tried to pull Vrdolyak into the picture, whereupon the mayor pulled back angrily. "Now wait, now wait, now wait—I didn't want to get into a discussion!" he protested, and then completely lost his temper when Vrdolyak started talking into Bradley's microphone: "Turn that camera off me!" the mayor snapped. "And don't ever do that again!" He turned away and sat down among the delegates, with his back turned to Bradley, who, all the while, kept repeating, "But can the two of you work together? Can the two of you work together?"

Now Vrdolyak emerged, tanned and glistening and all smiles, to take the mayor's place as Bradley's subject. He seemed relaxed and unassailable, a master of that sly jocularity once used so winningly by his equally devious prototype, Richard J. Daley. "Can the two of you work together?" Bradley asked yet again. "Certainly!" Vrdolyak insisted. "But you don't even talk to each other here!" scolded the reporter. "I talk to him all the time!" kidded the alderman, his cunning eyes atwinkle. "I say, 'Hello, Mr. Mayor,' and he says hello to me." As Vrdolyak laughed to himself, Bradley turned and said, with a somber gaze into the camera, "I think what we have here is an example of the kind of problem that the ticket faces. We have two Democrats who can't work together!"

Washington then spoke up from his chair, without turning around:

The problem is the press, which has no respect for people at all. And you think you can intrude upon people, just to get a few lines in the—in the press. That is totally and completely bad, and I am stunned that a man of your high caliber, and moral/ethical standards, would stoop to such a thing.

That prompted this remarkable exchange:

EB: Mr. Mayor, I'm asking you if two Democrats can work together.
HW: Don't ask me anything else. You are one of the lowest possible individuals I've seen! How dare you call yourself a pressman?
EB: Well, Mr. Mayor, I work with my colleagues.
HW: You're an insult to common sense!
EB: I work with my colleagues.

Bradley looked, again, into the camera, to call this scene, again, "a perfect example" of the Democrats' grave problems. Fast Eddie now dropped his grin and put on a look of deep concern, shrewdly using his moment on TV to represent himself as the one who's been the victim in Chicago. "It's not a good situation," he said sadly. "But I think we'll all be together for the ticket in November," he summed up heartily, then added, with one last simulation of regret: "But it's been a tough fourteen months!"

Finally, Ed Bradley directed one last tragic gaze into our living rooms, and drew the moral for the third time: "Dan, I think you see an example of the problems the Democratic Party has!" And then there was Rather, who now made the previous uproar seem even more obscure by laughing it off as just another instance of old-fashioned Democratic shenanigans: "Well, Ed, Mark Twain's line, uh, always comes to mind in circumstances such as that. It was Twain who said, 'I belong to no organized political party, I'm a Democrat.' "

From the shared standpoint of most network newsmen, those action-packed three minutes of TV time were a huge success. There was a grizzled pol spewing insults and demanding, like a gangster, that the camera be turned off, just the sort of irate blustering that we like to watch on "Sixty Minutes." Moreover, here we had a vivid "example," as Bradley said several times, "of the problems the Democratic Party has." It looked like a revelation. With that outburst, Harold Washington seemed to blow the Party's cover, giving us a glimpse of the raw reality that was seething just beneath the collective pose of "party unity."

And yet, although Washington did come off badly, the fact remains that everything he said was true. "The press," without a doubt, "has no respect for people at all," and it was clearly the case that Bradley wanted nothing other than "a few lines in the press," or the televisual equivalent: a bit of uproar, as pointless and unilluminating as any three minutes of "Airwolf." What we learned from all the fuss was only what we knew already, the same fact that prompted Bradley to approach the mayor in the first place—that Chicago's Democrats don't get along. For that matter, even Rather's coy afterword was of dubious value, since the author of that famous joke was not Mark Twain, but Will Rogers.

More than merely empty, however, the spectacle actually concealed the political reality that Bradley was purporting to make known to us. At no point during or after this event did anyone explain the situation in Chicago. Neither Bradley nor Rather seemed at all concerned, or qualified, to let the viewers know about Washington's efforts to dismantle the old Democratic machine, or Vrdolyak's efforts to dismantle Washington. To the uninformed viewer, that ugly rift, fraught with racism and involving many vested interests, appeared as nothing more than a little misunderstanding, easy to resolve, if only both parties would just sit down and "work together." And, as Bradley played the scene, Washington appeared to be the one impeding such a sweet conciliation: "Well, Mr. Mayor," the reporter reprimanded him, "*I* work with *my* colleagues." Despite his feigned concern for the welfare of all involved, Bradley was indifferent to the mayor's dilemma. Because Washington had thus far been the loser in Chicago, failing to break the deadlock calculated by his enemies, he could not, even as a gesture, join hands with Vrdolyak on TV, since, by thus embracing the man who had been shafting him, he would have seemed, to his constituents, to be giving in. And yet he could not diplomatically refrain from that embrace, because Bradley and the camera forced it on him.

At this moment, then, Harold Washington couldn't win; and so Ed Bradley couldn't lose. If Washington had proven docile, Bradley

113

could have stood between the two old foes like the noblest of peace-makers. On the other hand, the furor was even better—because it was exciting—and yet Bradley could appear to be deploring it, even though he'd caused it. Thus the moment's true political struggle was being fought between the mayor and the newsman, whose every utterance was actually a deft assertion of control. Three times he gazed regretful-ly into the camera, to define this gripping tumult as an "example" of some larger problem, which he never clarified—a move whereby he managed to establish his own normative function as the chorus to this scene. And the question that he asked no fewer than twelve times—"Can the two of you work together?"—was answered by the very fact that he kept having to ask it, and yet he kept on asking it, because it both reemphasized the thrilling discord that he'd provided for us, and at the same time allowed him to appear as a disinterested observer, detached from, and high above, all such ugly bickering.

Bradley's subversion of the hapless Washington, however, did not affect the image of the party. Although the newsmen worked like de-mons to blow the whole event to smithereens, it remained intact. The big speeches were so powerful, most of the delegates so resolute and eventempered, that the convention projected a grand integrity that kept the telejournalists excluded. For all their veiled put-downs, loaded questions, and disaster-mongering, the newsmen failed to undo the Democrats, who came out ahead when their show was over. At the end, all Dan Rather could do was try to keep us in suspense with ominous closing questions, as after some old-fashioned soap opera: "The Demo-crats have their ticket," he said, goggling portentously. "But *will it be a ticket to ride?*"

While it was not clear what Rather meant by this allusion to the Beatles, there was no mistaking his implicit tease: *"Tune in tomorrow and find out!"* And therein lies the secret of the news machine's true power: everyone will go on tuning in to the TV news. While the conven-tion, therefore, may have thwarted them, the telejournalists were cer-tainly not beaten, since, in their daily newscasts, they were free to represent reality in whatever way they deemed most saleable. And, however sure and unified the Democrats seemed in San Francisco, the national memory of that week would not withstand three months of the usual spectacle: footage of "gaffes," minor spats, meaningless acci-dents, and other such suasive trivia. In fact, no true politics—whether we term it democratic or republican—could survive such "political cov-erage." Through its marketing techniques, what the TV news has acci-dentally fostered is the perfection of a party mechanism that cannot be dented by the very TV news that inspired it—a campaigning entity so smooth, believable and gratifying that there is no lens or telejournalist capable, apparently, of penetrating it.

Thus was our president elected.

Afterword

■ ■

IN 1987 GARY HART WAS ONCE AGAIN SUBVERTED BY the media—not for handling Donna Rice, but for mishandling the media. Hart's sin, or error, was twofold. First, he expected the journalists tailing him to wink (so to speak) at his amours, as if he were Wendell Willkie, or JFK—that is, as if this were not the culture of TV. This expectation made Hart careless. Then, having been "found out" (his affairs were no big secret), Hart compounded his mistake by trying to get tough with the media, in the manner of the GOP, circa 1972. In a speech at the National Press Club he lashed back at the *Miami Herald*, heatedly denying everything—a move that got him nowhere, although it did inspire a friendly letter of condolence from that old stonewaller and seasoned press resenter, Richard Nixon. Hart ought rather to have emulated Gerry Studds, the Representative from Massachusetts who, having been discovered seeking congress (as it were) with several Senate pages (male), went all humble and apologetic on TV, and was thereby exonerated, even though his crime was, in American eyes, a lot ickier than straight philandering.

There are several points to make about Hart's second downfall (and, surely, about his unexpected comeback moments later). Certainly it suggests a complex double standard operating behind or through the political spectacle. Having knocked the press for questioning his probity, Hart was made to look so bad that he was finally forced to quit the race—whereas, nine months later, George Bush won a big boost for his campaign by doing exactly the same thing. On 25 January 1988, appearing on the "CBS Evening News" for a prearranged interview, Bush feigned sudden, towering indignation when asked about his true role in the Iran/contra plot, and engaged Dan Rather in an astonishing ten-minute shouting match. Here—for a change—the reporter's line of questioning was, or would have been, quite legitimate, since it pertained to the candidate's official conduct, not to his sex life; and yet Bush's broad evasive tactic earned him not suspicion but wild praises for his toughness, and so his faltering campaign was born again. This difference between the fates of Hart and Bush reminds us that, when it comes to exploiting popular resentments (of the press, in this case),

117

rightists are usually more adept than liberals (see below, pp. 125–28); and the difference also suggests that Americans make too big a deal out of sexual (mis)behavior, while underestimating acts of true corruption: clandestine warfare, illegal arms sales, perjury, drug dealing—just to name a few.

This last point needs to be refined, however, for it seems not to be "Americans" in general who are thus obsessed with the genital lives of (certain) politicians, but the reporters. Polls provide a dubious reflection of public attitudes, but they are surely accurate in revealing that most voters do not care how or with whom a candidate delights himself; and Hart's easy reentry (so to speak) into the race confirms those statistics. Because the journalists are always looking for new ways to "tell the people what the people are already thinking," and because they think "the people" are as prudish and dull-witted as advertising and the right imply, they harp on sex, to the exclusion of important matters. Thus they boxed Hart in: "I can't get out," he told his friends the night before he quit the race; and thus they help to box us in. ■

Sickness on TV

- -

I COULD WATCH JERRY LEWIS FOR HOURS, AND that's what I did over Labor Day weekend 1981, when he hosted the sixteenth annual Muscular Dystrophy Telethon. Just what is it that makes him such a riveting spectacle? It isn't talent, although Jerry Lewis is exceptionally talented, a master of filmmaking and stand-up improvisation. Rather, his particular appeal reflects an attribute that is both simpler and more complex than talent: "He's crazy," said Robert DeNiro, in a taped appearance that was both a tribute to Lewis and a plea for donations. Of course, De Niro probably meant "irrepressible" rather than "clinically insane," but the primary meaning is too appropriate to be ruled out.

Watching Jerry Lewis run his telethon is a nerve-racking thrill, like watching an agitated schizophrenic conduct a heated group discussion in an empty room. He is many men in one, all of them demented. Much of the time he acts like a sort of hoodlum priest—the Sage of Vegas. With a mike in one hand and a smoke in the other, hair resplendent with well-greased comb marks, he saunters up and down the stage at the Sahara, philosophizing in a language all his own: "Mankind is an interesting and very, very complicated issue. . . ." "The corporate picture has had a dirty deal for a long time. . . ." "If more people cried, we wouldn't have as many wars. . . ." Then, in the middle of all this solemnity, he'll suddenly fly into his usual routine, jumping around and quacking.

This year, Lewis seemed even crazier than usual. Not only did he keep interrupting his own weird orations with automatic bursts of shtick, but he babbled about "love" with the unsettling fervor of a pious tramp who'd finally lost his mind. This show, he kept saying, was a "love-in," on the "Love Network," and he and his guests did everything but post the banns: "Jerry, we love ya," yelled José Feliciano. "I love ya, Lorna," Jerry called to Lorna Luft; "I love *you*, Jerry," Lorna cooed. "I love ya, Joey," Jerry quacked at Joey Heatherton; "You're very special, Jerry," Joey croaked. Of course, you can always expect these types to behave that way; Lewis had managed to recruit the cream of show biz, or at least that slightly rancid portion that sticks to Las Vegas—Charo, Sammy Davis, Frank Sinatra, Pearl Bailey, Jack Jones, Bill Cosby, Tony

119

Orlando, etc., the kind of people who always fondle each other on national television. But there was something unusually forced and desperate about the fond show at the Sahara, where all the talk of "love" was only a device to hide other, less comfortable feelings.

For instance, Jerry Lewis, the much-loved *primum mobile* of the "Love Network," is a man barely able to contain his rage. All his mugging, wheedling, weeping, and pontificating seem only the expression of a vast, unquenchable resentment. He is a figure of immense self-pity, obviously seeing himself as a pathetic little schnook, despite his imposing presence, his years of success, the grateful millions. In other words, his role as friend to the sick is simply another version of the maudlin role he played in most of his films: the hapless jerk, well meaning but unloved. While he poses as a father figure to the afflicted, calling them "Jerry's kids" (although some are over 21), he clearly identifies with them, sharing in their wretchedness, because they are so much more genuinely pitiable than he could ever be.

His hostility demands many outlets, and finds them on the telethon. As a celebrated clown, for instance, he felt free to ridicule some of his supporters, making funny faces behind their backs while they struggled with their presentations (which *was* hilarious, if disconcerting). Moreover, he conducted this "love-in" with the sort of paranoid rancor that you'd expect from a Moonie congress rather than a charitable fundraiser. He kept referring to imagined enemies, and railed against "the negative people, who don't know the meaning of joy." Those nay-sayers will eventually get theirs, if this loving man has anything to say about it. "If you do not respond," he threatened his viewers, "then one day we will have a telethon for people who we will hopefully inject feelings *into*!"

In short, he acted like those psychopaths who appear on fundamentalist talk shows, weeping with love for Jesus Christ while longing to kill somebody. Like Lewis himself, the whole telethon reflected some of the darker aspects of today's American scene. The show was charged with that hollow "revival spirit" that is supposed to demonstrate our national regeneration, and which never does. The inspirational bits were not uplifting. Lola Falana, who usually performs as if she wants to love the whole world, or at least a couple of platoons, introduced her act with this uncharacteristic bleat of piety: "I believe in God, and I believe in Christ, and I believe that He lives when we shine." The headache-inducing Ben Vereen also got religious, belting out several Christian showstoppers. And Wayne Newton, looking like one of those evil lawyers who try to bilk the Three Stooges out of their inheritance, closed the telethon with an orgy of bad faith.

Although Lewis celebrated their altruism, these performers were using muscular dystrophy as an occasion to demonstrate their own fervent devotion to the will of the majority. It's a great way to win applause, as the corporate sector has also discovered: McDonald's, Seven-Up, Anheuser-Busch, Sara Lee, United Airlines, and many others sent representatives onto the show to hand Lewis hefty checks and gain some favorable p.r. They took pains to be as visible as possible, appearing time and time again, and yet Lewis could not stoop low enough in sentimentalizing their motives, turning his show into one long testimonial to the cuddliness of Big Business: "They are *friends*, on a very *emotional* and very *caring* level," he said of those corporate officers, most of whom would probably do anything to bar him from their country clubs. "How do you not hug and kiss people like that?"

OF COURSE, WHAT JERRY LEWIS DOES—CONSIDERED APART from why or how he does it—is entirely admirable, and the same is true of those corporate gifts. People with muscular dystrophy are in distress, and if it takes an ugly circus like the telethon to raise the money for their treatment, then such a circus must take place. Nevertheless, we ought to consider the more sinister effects of such a show, and its real significance, particularly if we care about the sick.

Whatever good they may accomplish in the short run, these television shows dehumanize the sick, reducing them to pitiable objects. Early on, Lewis showed a taped encounter between ABC's David Hartman and an ailing man named Nelson Rodriguez, who had already lost one brother to muscular dystrophy, and who faces death himself. Hartman fished for grief with the usual pointed, morbid questions ("How did you feel when your brother died?"), at one point asking, "What does 'humanness' mean to you?" Rodriguez answered that it means being considered a person, not just someone diseased. Ignoring this answer, Hartman continued his interrogation, finally hitting pay dirt as Rodriguez began to cry.

The sick man suddenly stopped moving. It was not actual death, or further paralysis, but a freeze-frame; and then that image of the immobilized Rodriguez appeared on a huge video screen onstage at the Sahara, with Jerry Lewis, his back to the camera, standing motionless, looking at the image, broadly "moved," yet unmoving. The stasis lasted for about ten seconds, offering—as television always does—a perfect visual metaphor for the futility of pity—the victim, forever sad and damaged; the "caring person," fixed in his concern; ourselves, still and staring, with our mouths hanging open.

The telethon is not unusual in its use of the afflicted. For the past few years, the shattered human being has appeared variously on television, on the stage, in the movies: *The Elephant Man, Children of a Lesser*

121

God, Best Boy, Whose Life Is It Anyway?, Coming Home, etc. We might like to believe that this sudden prevalence of afflicted heroes suggests that ours is a highly compassionate society, but there is no justification for this belief, especially not now. Our obsession with the broken and dependent man, in fact, may reflect our sense that *we* are somehow crippled, somehow incomplete, having let our feelings, thoughts, and other vital functions slip out of our control. We have television to do our perceiving and emoting for us, and those benevolent corporations make a promise that they mean to keep: "We do it *all* for you." In other words, our public "caring" for the handicapped may only be a form of self-obsession, a grieving for a victim who is still alive.

WHEN YOU'RE LOOKING FOR A VCR, GO WITH YOUR EARS WIDE OPEN.

Afterword

■ ■

SINCE THIS PIECE WAS WRITTEN, THE SPECTACLE'S routine celebration of "the shattered human being" has taken on a new dimension. The impaired are, of course, still heavily sentimentalized, as in the "Special Olympics" and other TV dramas of the retarded. Now, however, TV also presents the broken person in a suitably ironic guise: as "Max Headroom," the limbless commentator, compulsively wisecracking, with no existence off TV: a literal "talking head" that at once jeers TV and sells TV's products. (The rise of this effigy relates to the post-Sixties cult of the robotic: see below, pp. 285–303.)■

Patriotism Without Tears

■ ■

LIBERALS ARE NOT VERY GOOD AT SOUNDING PATRI-otic. They may have performed wonders for the American Way, but as soon as they start trying to get emotional about Old Glory and the fruited plain, it's time to look for the nearest exit, because this is an act that never works. Those fits of fervor always seem to be missing something, whereas the nasty raptures of the ultraright are usually pretty convincing. Right-wingers have just what it takes for a compelling show of patriot-ism: they long to unite in order to face off against an enemy. These folks know, or sense, that the deep joy of patriotism arises from the wish to jump up and down, with a good conscience, on some alien face. When they salute our flag or hum our anthem, therefore, they do it with the credible passion of the semicivilized. Liberals, on the other hand, are much too finicky and dishonest to admit to so gross an appetite, and so their flag waving seems forced, evasive, moralistic. Rather than express a love of country, in fact, the liberal show of "patriotism" expresses mostly fear of what patriotism really means, its unpleasant origins, its cruel necessity.

We will never have a better example of such repression than we had on the evening of Sunday, 22 March 1982, when ABC broadcast a great big mess called "I Love Liberty," produced by Norman Lear and featur-ing scads of the famous and quasi-famous, all enacting moments that supposedly hailed America, "warts and all." There was Rod Steiger as "an angry gay," Burt Lancaster as Learned Hand, Mary Tyler Moore as Mrs. Stephen Douglas, Judd Hirsch as a prewar immigrant, and so on. Ostensibly a celebration of George Washington's birthday, although aired weeks later, this two-hour hodgepodge of songs and skits was ac-tually meant as an upbeat rebuke to the American right: "liberals can be patriots too!" the show insisted, perversely using right-wing de-vices—marching bands and marching songs, sermons, an enormous flag, the word "America" much abused—to push liberal values, as if those devices have no historical connotations, and can simply be used to any end by anyone. Rather than symbolize the particular impulses of our national past, in other words, these images were emptied of all their

125

disconcerting meanings and reduced to ornament—colorful bits of "Americana" used to liven up a liberal pep rally.

For instance, toward the beginning of the show, Barry Goldwater, a colorful bit of Americana if there ever was one, appeared on one of the stages in the midst of a packed and cavernous amphitheater to introduce a certain production number. Looking a little dazed, he explained that, while *he'd* wanted the number to be very grand and showy, his associates had wanted something "subtle," and so they'd had to do what Americans do best: "we compromised." There then took place a spectacle of such colossal incoherence and vulgarity that words must fail to do it justice. Three actors made up like the Spirit of '76 came limping rhythmically on stage to fife and drum and wild applause, and then all hell broke loose. It was our national heritage as Hieronymus Bosch might have dreamt it up after a night of too many Cheezits and reruns. There was a black marching band, a yellow marching band, a piebald marching band, all rushing nowhere in different directions and blaring out completely disjunct semitunes; a black youth heaving a baton in one place, a little Oriental girl flailing one somewhere else, and a whole platoon of Indian cheerleaders; four doughboys cavorting, a group of Western settlers skipping in a ring, three women dressed like Betsy Ross flying their flag like a kite, a bunch of Confederate officers casually waving, Uncle Sam on stilts, some busty suffragettes, an obscure trio of unicyclists wearing bright blue shirts with stars all over them, everyone jerking around within an echoing din of drum beats, roars, screams, and tinny snatches of martial melody. This chaos went on until a giant flag unfurled and several thousand balloons fell out of the ceiling, and then there was silence. "Well," said the haggard Goldwater, trying to look arch, "that was a compromise!"

In fact, it was a nightmare, and therefore quite revealing. Although intended to evoke America's heritage, those hectic moments suggested nothing about our history except our total alienation from it. The spectacle reduced our past to an illegible jumble of clichés; and one function of that unlikely collage was to obscure the violence of patriotism beneath the consoling fictions of the liberal world view. The scene's general anarchy served to conceal the martial implications of all those varsity images. The rigid formation of each marching band, suggestive of the well-run phalanx, was impossible to notice in that disorderly mass; and none of the tunes was allowed to dominate the action with its stirring rhythms, but all were broken into harmless fragments by the incessant cutting. Moreover, what was most remarkable about the scene, aside from its confusion, was its pervasively, schematically multiracial character, which also functioned to drown out the call to arms. The show attempted to redeem the threatening icons of the past simply by tinting them: take the drum major, the majorette, the marching musicians, etc., and make them yellow, black, brown, white, red, so that they stand for Brotherhood instead of glorifying combat. Thus the chilling homogeneity of the tight-knit clan of warriors—at once the end and basis of the patriotic impulse—disappears into a heartwarming image of diversity, of men too various to find the solidarity that leads to, depends on, arises from, war.

This motley and peaceable "America" seemed, paradoxically, to be no nation at all, but a vague constellation that includes, and thereby cancels out, all the lesser, more definite nations of the earth. Martin Sheen functioned as the show's chorus, and in that capacity paid tribute to the grand nullity of such a national ideal. He appeared early on, pacing the stage and addressing the spirit of George Washington in a self-righteous, hectoring bark: "Mr. President, I'm willing to bet you that right *here* in this *hall, right here tonight*, there are people representative of *every nation on earth!* Let's find out!" So saying, he began a sort of global roll call, his epithets eliciting an evergrowing wave of mob approval: "First of all, how many people here are native Americans? Lemme hear from ya! Native Americans! How many Hispanics? How many Hispanics here? How many blacks?" Having suggested that all blacks, Hispanics, and Indians have come here from three countries, Sheen went on to catalog the rest of the world: "How many Irish? Italians?! Poles! Germans! Swedes! How many Israelis?! Arabs! C'mon! Let's hear it! How many Russians?! Chinese! Vietnamese! Portuguese! Dutch! French! Even British!" Finally, the applause had grown into a narcissistic self-ovation of awesome magnitude, which Sheen brought to a climax with the ultimate show biz rallying cry: *"C'mon, let's hear it for us!"*

This moment betrayed the suicidal inclination that is implicit in the liberal ideal of a pacific diversity. "Every nation on earth," each with its own longstanding character, disappears into "America," which itself remains amorphous, absorbing everything and therefore ending up as nothing. The nations ultimately mattered less than the mere fact of their membership in this blank federation; Sheen's ethnic chant soon became inaudible under the roar of that American applause. Thus, again, the show denied the very impulse which it seemed to be indulging. While patriotism has, over the centuries, served to harden the identities of peoples in their bloody oppositions, this "America" undoes the results of all that painful definition, reducing the nations to so many multicolored specks in its own indistinct self-portrait.

It was indeed a featureless portrait which was televised throughout the broadcast of "I Love Liberty"; and the same national image continues to appear on television every hour, every day. Lear's "America" recalled that variegated and good-natured herd which we see in ads for Pepsi, Coke, Dr Pepper, Replay gum, etc.—a mass of happy shoppers, apparently defined by superficial differences, but fundamentally united in their urge to purchase things no more distinctive than themselves. We are meant to see these shoppers as our models; and television would, ultimately, have us do no more than look at what it tells us that we are, and then go out and buy whatever it takes to resemble that prescribed image. The process must (or does) lead to a deadlock of eternal self-obsession, which was all that "I Love Liberty" could offer as the end of "patriotism." There was Sheen's brash invitation to self-love; and, later in the show, Robin Williams ended a stand-up bit as the American flag with this fond sign-off: "Don't look at it as saluting *me*— look at it as saluting your*selves*, . . . If I may say so from here, long may *you* wave." (Vast applause).

For all its strain and hoopla, then, the show presented us with an America that is not really worth much, an America that conforms entirely to the feeble wishes of contemporary liberalism: it is a nation of good feelings and easy acquiescence, risking nothing, making no demands, inspiring neither trust nor passion. "I Love Liberty." The title is subtly antipatriotic, denying all community in favor of a pseudopersonal preference, as if freedom were a Big Mac or a Seven-Up, a pleasure for the individual consumer. Moreover, like the show itself, and like the ideology the show expressed, the title deletes from patriotism anything that might seem negative about it, any suggestion of hatred, intolerance, bigotry, the desire for conquest or revenge. These things are unattractive; and yet they have been the essential determinants of culture, helping to create all that is best even while threatening it. Although liberals deny the crucial value of compulsion—of hierarchy, principle, force, repression, conflict, tragedy—they themselves become most passionate when faced with the very things which they would extirpate: "I Love Liberty" was itself the result of such antagonism, although the show lacked the spirit to name its enemies openly. It could have been a masterpiece of patriotism if it had tried somehow to face and include those enemies, who are also very much Americans, and who also hate as well as love.

"The air of expectancy was bursting at the seams"

ERE IT IS, DAYS AFTER THE EXCHANGE OF VOWS, AND I'm still groggy from having watched television's coverage of the royal wedding. I thought the sun would never set on it. First there were all those preliminary "specials," and then the day itself went on forever, a seeming eternity of coverage. From the dead of night into the afternoon, the stalwarts of the news stayed on the job, really *covering* the whole occasion, like soot. "You want something very, sort of, stirring," Prince Charles had said (referring to the wedding music), and that's exactly what the networks gave us: London, teeming and jubilant, half-appeared behind the networks' correspondents, who would not shut up, or get out of the way, but worked for hours to replace or adorn the images with their own dead commentary. They were as tiresome as those other creatures of television, people who talk behind you at the movies.

The pageantry *was* splendid, what you could see or hear of it, and there were, as if by accident, several moments of exquisite spectacle: Lady Diana's slow emergence from the glass coach, her bridesmaids unfurling her vast train; the choirboys, in their cassocks and thin ruffs; the congregation's magnificent closing chorus of "God Save the Queen." It was all pure gold for the cameras, but our reporters missed it because they couldn't stop babbling about it. Dan Rather, Peter Jennings, Barbara Walters, David Hartman, and their henchmen seemed intent on convincing us that this occasion was not trivial, but grand, handsome, "historic." They could have made the point by keeping quiet. (These impressions, incidentally, refer only to ABC and CBS. If I had tried to cover NBC as well, I might have lapsed into a coma.)

They couldn't keep quiet because their purpose was not to show us the royal wedding, but to show us that they were showing it to us. This is typical of television news. Supposedly "our window on the world," television ought to be the perfect medium for events such as this. "One

129

of the things television does best," boasted Rather, "the thing we *do* best, is to *take you there*." It was half-true once, but today it's almost never true at all. Back when television was younger and more modest, it could approach the world with a certain self-effacement; the camera often showed events as if it were a mere onlooker, like ourselves. But now that this medium is older, more successful, and aware of its huge influence, it has itself become the story, half-creating whatever it purports to reveal and calling it "news."

This was the case with the major issue of the week before the wedding: Lady Diana's crumbling nerves. The crisis of this nonstory occurred when the young bride-to-be, trying to watch her fiancé play polo, finally cracked under the pressure of all those journalists goggling at her. And there it was on television: Lady Diana slowly sinking into herself, then getting up and leaving in the middle of the game. This clip was accompanied by the usual bland exposition ("tears in her eyes . . . tension building for weeks," etc.) which presented the scene as if it were a natural occurrence, like an earthquake, which the cameras had just picked up by chance. The reporters were pretending that it had nothing to do with them, when it was, in fact, their doing.

In other words, the medium is itself the most insidious of boors, worse than any loudmouthed tourist or staggering gate-crasher; and those reporters covering the wedding did their jobs with suitable discourtesy. Conducting the blitz for CBS, the clenched and unctuous Dan Rather seemed unsure of his pose. Was he just a country boy, trying to fathom all this trumpery for the other sons of freedom back home? Or was he the CBS superjournalist, wearing the mantle of Edward R. Murrow and therefore obliged to cover this royal event with all possible savoir faire? Not knowing which to choose, he tried them both by turns, going back and forth from mechanical awe to aggressive expertise.

HE KEPT CROWING ABOUT HOW GREAT THE WHOLE THING was, clearly convinced that no American would stand for it. The effort taxed his eloquence. He raved about a "wonderful procession," "a wonderful view of St. Paul's Cathedral," "a wonderful portrait" of the royal family, and on and on, showing off a critical vocabulary he must have learned from Lawrence Welk. He was also given to pushy outbursts of amazement ("What a picture of a bride!" "What a scene through that doorway of Westminster [sic] Cathedral!" "What an honor to be able to see this!"), and at one point went completely nuts, trying to put the whole thing into words: "Costumes, drama, music, animals, mysticism—*spectacular*!"

He was assisted in his anchor spot by Lady Antonia Fraser, who provided bits of monarchical biography, and David Frost, who did some general clarifying. It soon turned into a comedy of (bad) manners. Rather asked her ladyship to tell the little people ("the truck driver, the steelworker") just why this occasion wasn't completely empty. Her answer was gracious, although she looked like someone who'd just swallowed something sickening but was too polite to mention it. Frost was not that tactful. In fact, he was often downright snide. "Any minute now," Rather said at one point, "we'll be looking for our first sight, our first glimpse, of Lady Diana." "Any minute now," snickered Frost, "we'll see our glimpse."

If Rather had to play the part of the tormented bumpkin, he managed to strike back at his hosts, first with a show of belligerent pedantry, then with some plain arrogance. Frost mentioned that Charles was the first Prince of Wales to qualify for a university degree, which casual revelation sent Rather tearing through his index cards: "First Prince of Wales educated at a regular school, the first to earn a university degree, the first to ride a steeplechase, the first to jump from an airplane, the first to have flown jets and a helicopter—" He paused, then added, "The list is long," as if to say, "*That*'ll show you! Now shut up or I'll keep reading!" And soon after this, Rather carried on an interminable analysis with fellow correspondent Tom Fenton, pointing out how nice it was that this "show" (the wedding) allowed the British to say, " 'We *like* each other! We *like* being British!' "—a remarkable fact, Rather went on, considering the high unemployment, the riots, the end of the empire, the national paralysis, etc., etc. His two cohosts were conspicuously silent, and Murrow was turning over in his grave.

If Rather seemed too garrulous, he was restraint itself compared to the gang at ABC, who jabbered as if afraid of losing consciousness. At least Rather piped down during the ceremony proper; ABC's Peter Jennings hardly seemed to take a breath, his every comment obscuring what it was supposed to explain: "It's worth listening to the organ, it's one of the finest in the world, it's German-built, Handel has played on it, and so has Mendelssohn"—and on he rattled, drowning out the organ with this recitation of its pedigree.

This is, of course, the sort of prattle that we get from sportscasters, and so it was perfectly in keeping with the Super Sunday spirit of the network's coverage. True to the background of its president, Roone Arledge, ABC's news division treated this event like a mammoth football game—the Wedding Bowl. Not only did Jennings do the usual nonstop play-by-play, but lists of "facts" were often superimposed on the action, as if this were the Olympics: "The Choir / Youngest member age 10 / Practice time 14 hours per week / Each member plays at least one instrument."

BOXED IN

■ ■ ■ ■ ■ ■

ABC's anchorfolk were as rude as Rather, although it was not their native cohost whom they mistreated (the merry Robert Morley), but the much put-upon royal bride, who made a slight mistake in reciting her vows. Peter Jennings's cohort at the anchor desk was Barbara Walters, whose function, as the networks' resident yenta, was, as ever, to talk about the clothes and tribulations of the rich. During the ceremony she was oddly silent (perhaps taking a short nap), until the end, when the couple were on their way to sign the register. "And you know, Barbara," Jennings suddenly said in midyammer, "I thought, earlier on, I detected a touch of nervousness in the Princess of Wales."

This call to dissection brought Walters snapping back to life. "You know," she meowed, "she seems to just do everything *right*, and perhaps this is why the people love her *so* much. *Even* the mistake that she made when she said—uh—her now husband's name backwards—she said 'Philip Charles' instead of 'Charles Philip'—" "Barbara," Jennings answered, all compassion, "we look back just at that moment, and, as you point out, the Princess of Wales did make a minor, and totally *forgivable*, fluff." Minor, forgivable, and too good to pass up: right after this simpering duet, they actually *played back* the audio part of the tape so we could savor that "forgivable fluff" once more, even drowning out the beginning of a Handel oratorio to amplify that little slip.

This was not nobly done. Moreover, these people are in no position to judge anyone's flubbed lines, since they committed more than their own share. Jennings referred to somebody named "Pope John the Paul," mentioned "a very waving Prince Andrew," and told us that the wedding party ate a "sumptuous, simple lunch." In the course of a news update, he informed us that Bani-Sadr of Iran had just "asked for political exile" in France. And at one point he referred excitedly to "the open carriage, the footmen resplendent in their gold and scarlet behind," which is a sight that I believe I missed.

Some of his historical asides were equally startling. He referred to one of Henry Purcell's works as "a 7th-century hymn," claimed that Charles I was beheaded in 1625 (the year of his coronation), and, in reading his own list of firsts for the present Charles, came up with one that was as farfetched as it was baffling: "The first Prince of Wales to reach the age of 30 unmarried since James Stuart back in the 18th century, in 1718." Even with all these errors, Jennings, a resident of England, still appeared to know a lot more about the place than did the fast-paced Rather, who restricted himself to bizarre utterances like this one: "Is the air of expectancy just literally bursting at the seams out there as it is here? It must be!"

The greatest rudeness was committed toward us, the viewers, who were forced to look around those talking heads, to try not to hear those self-assured voices, to look for that vivid and immediate marvel which television always promises, never delivers. We looked for beauty, and were given numbers. The newscasters may not have learned much about British culture in preparing for this event, and they may have been ill-schooled in the national tongue, but they had been diligent in jotting down as many dates and weights and lengths and sizes as their files would hold, giving us history according to the *Guinness Book of World Records*: St. Paul's has the second-highest dome in Europe, has seventeen bells, weighing from 300 pounds to two and a half tons, that would ring 4,000 changes of music on the wedding day; the nave is 652 feet long; the yacht *Britannia* has a crew of 276, is as long as four football fields; the wedding cake is five feet high, weighs 250 pounds, contains fifty pounds of marzipan, etc., etc.

These are the sorts of facts with which the networks crowded out the modest glories of that day. Wandering around outside the cathedral, Tom Fenton, an incredulous chuckle in his voice, asked people why they put up with all the mobs and waiting, why they didn't stay home and watch the wedding on television. "I know all that," one woman said, "but you wouldn't have the atmosphere, you know?" The fact that he would even have to ask the question is almost as appalling as the "coverage" itself.

Afterword

· ·

T O ACCUSE A NEWSMAN OF *IMPOLITESSE* MAY BE TO flatter him, since boorishness is an old sign of journalistic integrity, like the cigar butt or the crumpled fedora. This kind of guy takes no baloney from the Big Shots: the city bosses, the corrupt tycoons, or—as in this case—a bunch of fancy-pants English aristocrats.

This pose is especially ludicrous among the telejournalists, who are themselves too smooth and highly paid to pull it off; and their discourtesy, moreover, no longer bears the whiff of egalitarianism, since they inflict it on all classes—the lower classes most of all. In these pages I have noted telejournalistic rudeness at a royal wedding and a political convention (see above, pp. 105–15), but the reporter needs no such grand occasion in order to start misbehaving, for he does it routinely in the homes and neighborhoods of the workers and the poor, usually when they are grieving.

Such callousness is, of course, not new, but it has become far more flagrant in the culture of TV—at times so outrageous as to provoke resistance. In April 1987 an apartment building under construction in Bridgeport, Connecticut, suddenly collapsed, trapping dozens of laborers in heavy rubble. Their co-workers tried for days to dig them out, and had to contend with even more than the natural agony of such a situation:

> Hundreds of reporters, photographers and radio and television crews have crowded the site since the accident, and the press, competitive as is often the case at incidents of wide interest, has behaved with an aggressiveness that has piqued the anger of families, searchers and officials alike.
>
> On occasion, members of the press have pushed and shoved one another to get pictures and interviews, thrust microphones or cameras into the faces of unwilling people and peppered volunteers, officials, relatives of victims and others with questions.
>
> A television crew Saturday night got into a confrontation with the police after being ordered off an upper floor of a nearby apartment building where it was seeking an overview. Another crew

135

was barred from the roof of a building after a camera fell, nearly striking someone below. (*New York Times*, 27 April 1987)

There were also "three psychiatrists at the scene," furnishing the press with brisk appraisals of the workers' psychic health: " 'They're moving from denial and hard work to anger and great sadness,' " one of them observed learnedly, as if that "anger" were not directed at the surrounding mob of journalists—including the one interviewing him. So angry were the workers by the fourth day of the search that "a series of sometimes ugly incidents" broke out, requiring that the area be closed to the reporters and those bearing their impediments.

The rising popular resentment of the press has less to do with a protofascist animus against the Fourth Estate than with such episodes as these; and, of course, the TV news will frequently take stock of its own excesses, discuss them on "Nightline," for instance, suggesting inconclusively that reporters should be nicer, maybe. It is not merely the unconstraint of certain individuals that is the problem, however, but the totality in which they function.

Forced to be "competitive," the newsman must—like any other employee—perform with due "aggressiveness," whether covering a wedding, a convention, or a gruesome accident: an "aggressiveness" that is all show. He must commodify the feelings of the participants or victims, and therefore tries to goad them into pithy utterance by assaulting them with blunt and idiotic queries: "How do you feel, knowing that your friends might be dead?" And the telejournalist is automatically hardened for this task by the hard apparatus that he serves and represents: "Technology is making gestures precise and brutal, and with them men," wrote T.W. Adorno in 1944. "It expels from movements all hesitation, deliberation, civility. . . . The new human type cannot be properly understood without awareness of what he is continuously exposed to from the world of things about him, even in his most secret innervations"—a perception that applies not only to the newsman's incivilities, but to the viewer inured to them.■

Black and White

. . . .

THE WORD "RACISM" OUGHT TO BE AS COMPLEX AS the tangled thing which it denotes; and so it should be handled carefully, as a delicate gauge to help assess an old and varied problem. All too often, however, the word is used as a blunt instrument, cutting conversations short and making people circumspect. Thus wielded, it is not an analytic or descriptive term, but a mere accusation, based on a limited conception of racism. It is, first of all, a reduction of the whole range and history of our interracial struggles to the crude oppression of one side by the other. And this "racism" is as abstract as it is one-sided. It is not a social or historical phenomenon but merely a dark impulse, atavistic and irrational, lurking in every white heart and nowhere else.

Although the charge of "racism" is ostensibly intended to expose the secret thoughts and deeds of bigotry, it is actually a means of concealment. It inhibits frank discussion of what really happens between blacks and whites today; it demands the suppression of any experience that might contradict the sentimental myth of simple, unilateral persecution. The charge of "racism," in other words, forces us to ignore the very conflicts that have kept racism going: it demands not that we resolve our differences, but that we repress them, and this insistence on repression has perverted all our thinking about race. What we often consider "racist" nowadays is not the mistreatment of one race by another, but the mere acknowledgment of differences between blacks and whites—different histories, different cultures, unequal origins within these borders.

There are more middle-class blacks than there used to be, and whites often act very tolerant. There are other important improvements besides. But old conflicts remain. By repressing those realities, we have not simply failed to eliminate them—we have actually made them worse, maintaining the old inequities under an up-to-date disguise. In trying to escape the uneasy deadlock of slaves and masters, we have stereotyped ourselves back into it, thanks to that simplistic "racism" which we all abhor. Many blacks now present themselves as angry victims of (white) racism, and as nothing more; and many whites, guilt-ridden and uncertain, eagerly defer to that black self-image,

137

taking all responsibility, as masters must. This national psychodrama may seem like a sign of progress, but it perpetuates the worst aspects of a racist society—all blacks as victims, all whites as victimizers, the two neurotically united forever.

Strong contrasts, lots of pathos, easy distinctions between weak (good) and strong (bad)—this is the stuff of television, which reflects (and half creates) these crude impressions. Television illuminates our racial woes, just as it illuminates our other social problems: inadvertently, by exemplifying (and so prolonging) the very flaws which it purports to analyze.

Take "America—Black and White," a ninety-minute documentary on our racial problems produced by NBC and broadcast on 9 September 1981. The title couldn't have been more fitting. For one thing, it summed up the program's conclusion that "America still remains, in many ways, two nations," that blacks are still outcasts in this free country. And, unfortunately, the title also provides an apt critical judgment of the show itself, which turned the recent history of race relations into prime-time melodrama, reducing complexities to black and white.

"Reported by Garrick Utley, with Emery King," the show swept far and wide across American society, moving from the suburbs of New York to Harvard University, from the rural South to Watts and Detroit, and elsewhere. And yet, despite its travels, the show got nowhere. Its conclusion was a simple one: that America's blacks are still suffering because of "racial attitudes—prejudice, racism."

Although this doesn't explain much (at the end of ninety minutes, we might expect something a bit more challenging), this evocation of a vague "racism" does have a certain aesthetic advantage for the purposes of video. Like many other shows, "America—Black and White" used "racism" as the basis for a series of contrived dramatic situations, featuring blacks and whites as two crude opponents: villains and victims. It was social criticism at the low level of "Roots." Although the program told us little about racism in our society, it revealed a lot about the subtle sort of racism that pervades television news. The program, in fact, was typical of television (news and "entertainment" shows alike), which usually belittles blacks in the very act of taking their side, while dismissing whites entirely. It may be the most dangerous sort of racism, because it is subtle, seems benevolent, and is often expressed in shows that come across as true reflections of "the way it is."

This sentimental racism works through dual caricature. All of America's whites, we infer, are equally devious, heartless, and remote, united in their groundless "prejudice." White students at Harvard, white parents in New York were not to be distinguished from the likes of Strom Thurmond and the Ku Klux Klan. And while the whites came across as a pitiless horde, the blacks were, time and again, embodied in some single pitiable figure—The Black, an eternal victim who suffers beautifully.

Of course, this broad device demanded that the whites be utterly dehumanized. The show began with a report on Rosedale, New York, a once "all-white community" whose original residents now feel themselves hemmed in by a growing black population. First we saw the bad guys. "These are some of the white voices of Rosedale," Utley said, introducing some grainy footage of several tense, middle-aged whites sitting around and complaining about affirmative action. Utley provided the background. In 1977, he said, the local school "had three black students for every white one. White parents said the school was over-crowded, that their children were being harassed by blacks." The whites kept trying to start another school, with a black enrollment of only forty percent, and the blacks, assisted by the federal government, defeated all those efforts. With implicit disapproval, the program showed a few more snippets of white discontent. "I won't send my child into a school where he's going to be a token white," one woman protested. "Why? I don't feel it's a healthy atmosphere."

This is, obviously, a case of "prejudice." Isn't it? Consider Utley's formulation of the whites' grievances: *White parents said* the school was overcrowded, that their children were being harassed by blacks." By compressing the charges into a sort of list, the sentence implies that the whites were coming up with a lot of desperate excuses. Its emphasis is not on the atmosphere at school, but on the white parents' claim that the atmosphere was bad; such emphasis has the effect of making the claim seem dishonest. And was it? Were the children being harassed? It would seem to be a crucial question, one that a good reporter would pursue, and yet the makers of this documentary (who can afford to send their children off to private schools) did not bother to address it.

"In the past," Utley hurried on, the whites "would have moved out," but today "they can't afford to. Since they cannot escape blacks, they have to face them—face David Fleming." Cut to Fleming, a youngish and attractive black man, talking in his living room: "I call them the Archie Bunker Syndrome group," he smiles. "They are afraid of any change."

Fleming is an obvious success—"a salesman of surgical instruments," Utley said, who came to Rosedale "looking for a larger home for his growing family." With Fleming as its momentary hero, the show began cross-cutting from Fleming as he talked about Rosedale to Fleming as he drove his son to Little League, coaching all the way (". . . and *never* take your eye off the ball!"). After this fancy bit of montage, the program took us to "the graduation ceremony at a school for gifted

139

children," where Fleming's daughter gave the valedictory: "We should set our goals high and strive to meet them," etc.

So these were some of the blacks whom Rosedale's whites "cannot escape"! Now why should anyone want to "escape" such people? Is it possible that David Fleming and his gifted daughter like to roam the school grounds, wielding surgical instruments? Obviously not. What we were meant to think, however, is equally absurd, and much more destructive.

Fleming was used as Sidney Poitier was used in *Guess Who's Coming to Dinner?*, and as so many blacks have been used in films and on television: not as a sterling character who might make racists feel ashamed, but as a means to deny what whites find most terrifying about blacks. The image of Fleming was meant as reassurance that blacks are never violent, that the black underclass is not dangerous, because blacks and whites are exactly the same, "under the skin." Fleming seemed, in fact, whiter than the whites—peppy entrepreneur, family man, owner of a house and car, etc.; a solid citizen, as opposed to those "white voices" that refuse to vanish. If it weren't for "racism," in other words, Our Way of Life could contain all differences, by painlessly erasing them. And yet, in fact, it is not our System that erases differences, but television, with its constant repressions of the unpleasant.

IN SHOWS LIKE THIS, TELEVISION REPRESSES THE REAL EF-fects of slavery, even while purporting to lament that institution. By insisting that blacks and whites are entirely alike, television denies the cultural barriers that slavery necessarily created; barriers that have hardened over years and years, and that still exist, exacerbating all those complicated hatreds that must endure between masters and slaves. These hatreds have never been more intense and debilitating than they are now, as blacks and whites commingle in our cities, many whites discovering what it feels like to be openly menaced by hostile people of an alien color. In other words, both races suffer. Television, meanwhile, constantly simplifies these hatreds, calling them "racism" and blaming them all on one side: "America—Black and White" presented whites as the detached authors of black suffering, as if this country were no different from South Africa; and all that's needed, the show implied, is for whites to have a change of heart, as in some old Frank Capra movie. It is not a useful message, or a timely one. While many of yesterday's white liberals are now edgy and disillusioned, feeling they have learned a bitter lesson, this "documentary" merely retailed these misconceptions: that blacks are the only ones in pain, that whites are the only ones who hate.

The real crime of Rosedale's whites, then, was that they called

140

attention to those differences which television labors to repress. They had the gall to feel menaced by a black majority, when we all know, from watching television, that blacks are incapable of the sort of resentment that can turn violent; that blacks, in other words, aren't really human. For this inconvenient behavior, the whites were appropriately punished by the program, which presented them as irrelevant, ludicrous, "prejudiced," "the Archie Bunker Syndrome group," "afraid of any change." If "racism," as we often hear, entails the demotion of some ethnic group to the status of nonpersons, then this program was racist in its presentation of the whites.

And yet, as broadly "problack" as the program seemed, its depiction of the blacks was entirely offensive, and far more damaging than the dismissal of those dim "white voices." The show offered us a series of black protagonists, each one a sort of tragic hero, slightly overplayed. Fleming was the first of these noble underdogs. He emerged as the star of Rosedale in the opening report's last scene, a bitter school board hearing where the whites tried, once again, to regain the *status quo ante*. The show's partisanship was now unmistakable, the cameras following the proceedings from the blacks' point of view, and clearly lionizing David Fleming. He was shot from a very low angle, so that he seemed gigantic, overpoweringly righteous, as he orated to his allies in the familiar pulpit-thumping style: "You will walk," he intoned, with biblical passion and unclarity, "and you will serve as juggernauts! And no Dolores Grant, or poor other ignorant, bigoted racists, whether they be on this school board, or whether they be walking with white sheets in dark alleys!" After finishing, to wild applause, Fleming sprang up to the table at the front of the room, where the school board members were sitting, and got into a shouting match with one of them, as the camera followed close behind him, catching all the fuss. And then the meeting broke up acrimoniously, blacks and whites exchanging jeers and shrill charges.

Who won? It is another crucial question. The images suggested black defeat—black people shouting at those dour whites up on the dais, blacks leaving the room, bitterly denouncing their apparent persecutors—and, more importantly, David Fleming, the blacks' representative, was acting like a loser. Clearly egged on by the presence of the camera at his stomach, he struck the familiar pose of noble struggle; and when he leapt to confront his oppressors, he appeared to be acting from a sense of uncontrollable frustration. It seemed a familiar spectacle: the blacks going down in glorious defeat, as usual. It was therefore downright jarring, and almost incredible, to hear Utley say that the blacks had won, that the whites had lost—because television teaches us that blacks don't know how to win.

141

BOXED IN

■ ■ ■ ■ ■

The other reports were similarly cast. At Harvard, we learned, most of the 502 black students were recently angered by the release of a document called the Klitgaard Report, drafted by a special assistant to the president: "Blacks and women scored high on entrance exams," the report concluded, "but did not perform well once admitted to the university." Harvard should therefore "not compete so heavily for blacks," who might do better at "slightly lesser institutions."

The release of this report was represented as another act of cruel racism, and, here again, the point was made through strokes of drama. Was the Klitgaard Report inaccurate? Or just impolitic? And does it have to mean that blacks and women are dumber than white males? Rather than deal with such questions, our reporters simply found themselves another personable underdog: a pretty coed named Rosalynn Roos, who spoke at length of her depression. Of course, her lonely sorrow had to appear against the backdrop of a cold white multitude, and so there were shots of various white undergraduates—more "white voices"—questioning the wisdom of racial quotas; these were "conservative whites," said Emery King, without explaining what that meant. The report ended with a group of black students singing dolefully on some steps.

The show's final segment was the strangest. We saw some trogs at a Klan rally in Connecticut, and then we saw what was presumably a corrective to such viciousness: Dr. Charles King, "president of the Urban Crisis Center in Atlanta," goes around "conducting sensitivity seminars on race," and we saw some of his work. King, a towering boor with a voice like the blast of a hostile tuba, stood before a mixed group of college students, provoking the whites with theatrical explosions of self-pity. "What do you mean by 'oppressing'?" asked one crabby white type. "Am I oppressing black people?" "Yes, because you asked, 'What is oppression?'" King bellowed illogically. "Since you *know* what oppression is, *you* are one of the persons *do*ing it through your damn *ig*norance, *fool*!" King's purpose, Utley chimed in, is "to get whites and blacks to face their own racial attitudes," which is one way of putting it, although it looked like just another est-type scam, with King mooing belligerently at his shifty white viewers: "If *you* would *feel* the problem, then *we* would not *have* a problem as a *race*!"

BETWEEN THE DRAMAS OF FLEMING, ROOS, AND KING, THERE were other, sadder moments, as various destitute persons came and went, none of them star material—young men who seemed old and broken, people who can't learn to read. The show punctuated these appearances with shots of nasty-looking politicians (Strom Thurmond, Ronald Reagan, Orrin Hatch), which made the villains/victims thesis

seem pretty accurate. All the show's blacks, in other words, were meant
to come across as *poignant* figures, whether charismatic or pathetic,
whether well-to-do or on the brink.

Although contrived with the best intentions, this sort of presentation can only work against black progress. Watching such shows, we
begin to assume that blacks can't ever make it, that their plight is eternal, a fact of nature. Apparently, David Fleming and Rosalynn Roos, for
all their personal successes, still inhabit that nether region of shanties
and welfare. And, conversely, the black poor are not remarkable for
their poverty, their membership in a certain social class—a condition
which could, presumably, be changed—but for their blackness, a condition of permanent woe.

As presented in this and other programs, the blacks seem unlikely to
improve their lot because they seem to take to suffering with such soul-
ful gusto. The show consistently aestheticized the black plight: the Harvard students sang, in their unhappiness; B.B. King sang "There's Got
to Be a Better World"; and there were those rousing theatrical moments
when King and Fleming hammed it up. This kind of thing may be inevitable on television, which will always use the best (i.e., broadest) shots;
and, to their credit, the makers of such programs surely want to make a
strong impression. But whatever the reasons, it must be recognized
that television has impaired the black movement by turning the various
black styles—behavioral, rhetorical, musical—into stereotypic signs of
authenticity. Television seems "right on" for bringing us, say, shows
like "Good Times" or the ranting of a Dr. Charles King. Such hopped-up
displays give the false impression that progress has occurred simply
because blacks appear on television.

No one is innocent in this process. If television has transformed
black politics into a stale docudrama, it is because blacks have enjoyed
the opportunity, and whites have enjoyed the show. Indeed, to explain
it any differently—to say that blacks have simply been "oppressed" by
the medium—would be inexcusably racist, suggesting that blacks are
too passive and too feeble to be held accountable for their behavior. It is
an odious assumption, and a familar one; and it was the guiding assumption of this show.

"If *you* would *feel* the problem, then *we* would not *have* a problem as
a *race*!" Not only is this formula naive, implying that one's emotional
response can overcome political and cultural realities; but it is profoundly slavish. It suggests that blacks are obsessed by whites, the weak
waiting angrily for the strong to do something; and so it bespeaks the
surrender of all responsibility in an outburst of blame and self-pity: "All
my problems are your fault!"

The program did not just provide a forum for these sentiments, but

143

actively encouraged them in its quest for the pathetic. However, the program exploited these displays of bitterness for more than merely sensational purposes. These images helped to convey the show's real message, which was that blacks are weak and need to be protected—by the white viewer, by the television industry, by the government. If the villains/victims structure places all the blame on the villains' side, it looks there too for all effective action. Blacks are like unto little children, the show implied throughout; they can't do right, and so, of course, they can't do wrong.

"Meet Augustus Williams's family," said Utley somberly over footage of some children in a squalid shack. "He and Betty, the woman he lives with, have ten children." "This is the home of Carrie Washington," he said at another such point. "She is 31 years old, has nine children, and no husband." These reports on black poverty in Mississippi made very clear that these people are in real distress; but Utley seemed to exploit those sufferers to make a condescending point. He simply took for granted the existence of all those hungry children, never asking the parents why they had so many little ones under such circumstances, never bothering to analyze those circumstances. He implied in short that these people were absolutely helpless, so lame that it was pointless to suggest that they try to help themselves, even a little. Such reports were meant as a pitch for further government assistance, but they went too far, depicting the poor as gentle, feeble animals.

THUS UTLEY, ALL UNKNOWING, HELPED TO PERPETUATE THE very misery which he was trying to redress, by endorsing, perhaps even celebrating, that helplessness which is the basic problem. The show itself was implicated in the same contradiction. It actually exalted itself as the protector of those huddled masses, who, it appeared, would have curled up and died if it weren't for the intercession of the news people; the show, in other words, seemed to be standing in for the reluctant government. This was the general sense of the documentary, with its eagerness to champion the blacks, and at times it became explicit. We followed an illiterate youth named Cortez Walker as he looked despondently for work. "On this day," said Emery King, Walker "was turned away from two other locations before he tried a Burger King downtown."

"What kind of trouble do you have?" asked King. "I have trouble, like, pronouncing some of the words on the application," Walker answered. Then, in voice-over, King made this heartrending revelation: "His only experience—some culinary training in reform school. But, had we not been there, the management would never have known about it," because Walker couldn't read the word "culinary." Then,

144

under the camera's watchful eye, Walker turned in his application, albeit halfheartedly.

It was a sad scene, and it was very decent of the crew to step in and help; but this was small compensation for the general destruction which television has helped to bring about among its young black viewers. If they can't read, it may have something to do with their having grown up watching hours and hours of television, which, "Sesame Street" to the contrary, does not do much for literacy. If they feel powerless and bitter, it may have something to do with that flood of bright commercials, which tempts them endlessly with visions of a million things which they can't hope to buy. If they feel that their anger is meaningless, it may have something to do with that television world that shines on forever, without showing the slightest trace of their unbearable rage. And if they feel isolated, and have no feeling of community outside the gangs, it could have something to do with the general disappearance of all community into our gray-lit living rooms, and with the hastening disintegration of the black movements, which television has helped to bring about. In short, the subtlest unpleasantness which television has repressed in its years of "covering" the racial issue may be television itself, which makes slaves of those who entrust it with their freedom.

Afterword
■ ■

AFTER THIS ESSAY WAS WRITTEN, SEVERAL BLACK performers reached superstardom in the culture of TV: on the box proper, Bill Cosby; in the movies and in concert, Eddie Murphy; on CD, Whitney Houston, Michael Jackson, Prince. The spectacle was integrated further by the successes of playwright August Wilson and filmmakers Robert Townsend and Spike Lee. And other black artists gained new renown through the adaptation of their work by white musicians and directors: Joseph Shabalala and the group Ladysmith Black Mambazo through their inclusion on Paul Simon's "Graceland" album, Alice Walker through Steven Spielberg's film version of her book *The Color Purple*, and so on.

This new and (literally) spectacular success by certain blacks has moved many liberal observers to proclaim a utopian breakthrough in race relations—the same myth that surrounds "The Cosby Show" (see above, pp. 71–78). In 1987 Dr. Alvin Poussaint, Cosby's censor, asserted that "despite the remaining conservatism [of whites] and the resurgence of some racial incidents, there's greater acceptance of blacks being in all aspects of American life." At the same time, the anthropologist Alexander Moore sought to explain the new black superstardom with the hopeful claim that "we whites collectively regret the decades of enjoying [blacks'] performances while discriminating against the individuals."

What is socially remarkable about the new black superstardom, however, is not that it reflects an improved reality: on the contrary. To say, in 1988, that "old problems remain" would be to understate the problem drastically. While Whitney Houston smiles down from the highest heavens of celebrity, and while the glittering Michael Jackson does his billion-dollar moonwalk all around the world, real life for most American blacks is a nightmare rarely publicized: "It is worse, not better," as the Rev. H. V. Savage, founder of Toledo's Kitchen for the Poor, put it in 1987. Far from evincing any "collective regret," whites—or those whites who feel exposed to economic hardship and (therefore) the threat of violence—have shown, in the Eighties, hostility above all. Such has been the case out in the streets, where atrocities like the

Howard Beach incident and the Goetz explosion (only the best-known of such attacks) suggest not "greater acceptance of blacks," but something like a war between the races. The campuses too have been rocked by the new racist animus—and not only Southern schools like the Citadel, the University of Texas, and the University of Alabama, but schools like Mount Holyoke, Brown, the University of Massachusetts, the University of Michigan, the University of Chicago, and on and on.

And aside from these examples, there is statistical evidence that— while not as bloody and dramatic (i.e., televisual) as a fatal beating or a case of persecution in some dorm—betrays a situation even more appalling than any random violence. In 1987, it was reported that, while the population of the cities has declined since 1970, and with it the number of poor whites, the numbers of the black poor have increased, their percentage of the cities' population has increased, and so the ghettos where they live have gotten denser, shabbier, more dangerous. Whether they inhabit housing projects like Chicago's Cabrini-Green, or welfare hotels like New York's infamous Martinique (where whites and Hispanics are also forced to stay), they live no better than those crammed into the shanties of Soweto or the units in the Gaza Strip.

It is precisely this general misery that enables the black stars to shine so lustrously: for, in order to appeal, the spectacle requires the very unhappiness which it seems to have banished from its own bright scenes (see p. 78 above). For the poor black, the image of Whitney Houston or Cliff Huxtable is a narcotic representation of wealth and power and quasi whiteness; and for the nervous white, each black superstar appears implicitly as a capitulator, reassuringly preoccupied with Coke or Pepsi, and/or with his/her own success—even Eddie Murphy, for all his devastating parodies of Cosby, is no less openly obsessed with his own princely income. (Murphy's case is further complicated by the scapegoating that is a central feature of his "raw" stand-up routines: as whites like Earl Butz once jested about lazy niggers, so does Eddie Murphy gratify his angry audience with put-downs of fags and bitches.) Unlike many of the black celebrities of yore—Redd Foxx, James Brown, Moms Mabley, Wilson Pickett, the early Richard Pryor— these commercial icons bear no funky traces of the world they left behind them.

Thus the culture of TV acts as a retardant on social progress; and the spectacle is regressive in another way. By emphasizing only the most visible events, TV, first of all, conceals social and economic reality in pious rituals that have upstaged the very struggle which produced them, and which they were meant, presumably, to maintain. The image of Martin Luther King has been used in just this way. His official cult, of course, is depoliticized: "It seems to focus almost exclusively on

148

Martin Luther King the dreamer," Julian Bond observed in 1986, "and not on Martin Luther King the antiwar activist, not on Martin King the challenger of the economic order, not on Martin King the opponent of apartheid, not on the complete Martin Luther King."

And while it thus offers a sanitized memorial of the civil rights movement, TV in its latest phase disables precisely the sort of extraordinary gesture through which the civil rights activists could once promote their cause on television. In a culture saturated by empty "media events" like Liberty Day and Hands Across America, among too many others, such plain happenings as a protest march can no longer (as the admen might put it) "break through the clutter." "The chief barriers to racial justice today," commented Kenneth B. Clark in 1987, "are more subtle and much less conducive to media coverage." "I don't think the marches in [Howard Beach and Forsyth County, Ga.] are going to remedy the fundamental problems of black poverty, black unemployment, or teenage pregnancies," said Roger Wilkins at the same time.

In the culture of TV, what it might take to rectify those "fundamental problems," or even to address them, might finally prove unbearable to watch.■

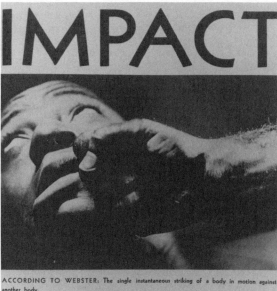

ACCORDING TO WEBSTER: The single instantaneous striking of a body in motion against another body.

ACCORDING TO YOUNG & RUBICAM: That quality in an advertisement which strikes suddenly against the reader's indifference and enlivens his mind to receive a sales message.

YOUNG & RUBICAM, INCORPORATED · ADVERTISING

NEW YORK · PHILADELPHIA

· 81 ·

How TV Covers War

N ITS LATEST TV AD CAMPAIGN, DEVISED TO AT-tract recruits, the U.S. Army offers us a potent jingle, the impression of fast action, and an unintended glimpse of truth. We hear the usual piercing voices pipe the following refrain: "Be—all that you can be!—in the Army!" Mean-while, we see a series of young soldiers, each confidently doing his crucial job: one mans a tank, one sits in a jet, one charts a course, etc. The stirring pitch suggests that Army life is not just fun—it's an adventure in self-fulfillment. Once we tune out its stimulants, however, the ad presents us with a prospect both more accurate and less exciting. What it shows, in fact, is not an assortment of young men "being all they can be," but a succession of intricate machines, each one tended by a placid figure in a uniform. The hardware is imposing; the soldiers are completely blank, wearing headphones, starting en-gines, staring into computer terminals.

For all its high-pitched jubilance, the ad depicts a grim situation: the dead end of the history of modern war. Five hundred years of techno-logical advance have reduced the soldier to a minor implement, fixed and simple, like a spark plug, used to fire off those spirited engines that now do nearly all the slaughtering. This demotion of the warrior seems to have begun in the fifteenth century, when the first guns were used to shatter the preening cavalries of Europe. "The musket is a weapon in-vented in Germany in our time,'" wrote Pius II in the early 1460s. "Powder made of charcoal from the fig or willow, mixed with sulphur and nitre, is poured into it; then a small ball of lead, the size of a filbert, is inserted in the front end." This new device could easily dispatch the bravest man on horse or foot, as the pope suggests in a tone of indignant wonder: "No armor can withstand the force of this engine, and it also pierces wood."

Thenceforth, as the West proceeded slowly to industrialize, war moved ever further from the grasp of its participants, becoming more autonomous, not so much a human conflict as a gross conjunction of victims and machines. By the early nineteenth century, this process seemed to have become complete, eliciting applause from those who

151

considered it a sign of progress. Hegel, for example, saw this mechanization as a step that purified warfare of its savagery:

> Only through this instrumentality [i.e., the use of guns] could that superior order of valor be called forth, that valor in which the heat of personal feeling has no share; for the discharge of firearms is directed against a body of men—an abstract enemy, not individual combatants.

Others were less idealistic, more nostalgic. "The new way of fighting, the variation of weapons, the artillery, have robbed military life of that which is most attractive about it," wrote Benjamin Constant in 1813.

> One no longer tastes that keen delight in the will, in action, in the strengthening of mind and body, which made the ancient heroes and medieval knights love hand-to-hand combat.

If *l'artillerie* were enough to degrade the craft of war in 1813, how can we begin to appreciate the soldier's insignificance in 1915, when machine guns, fragmentation bombs, poison gas, and depth charges first began to express themselves in force? What of the impact of such later innovations as the land mine, radar, automatic rifle, guided missile, napalm, nerve gas, Agent Orange? Since the Great War, "the new superfluity of killing agents," John Keegan tells us, has transformed "the very environment of the battlefield into one almost wholly—and indiscriminately—hostile to man."

In such a killing zone, there is not much need for prowess or practiced abilities. Crack marksmanship, for instance, is no longer a desideratum at the front, where the atmosphere itself is so explosive that the meticulous blasts of the sharpshooter have become redundant. "Hitting the target," Keegan writes, "for centuries the principal military skill, is henceforth to be left to the law of averages." For that matter, the sudden use of a nuclear "device" would quickly invalidate all the special talents of the battlefield, along with "the battlefield" itself.

Nor is it only in time of war that arms displace the man. Even now, reports James Fallows, our soldiers are actually kept idle by their weaponry, most of which is too fragile and expensive to be used much. The army's gunners stationed in Europe and Korea, "where they would presumably be charged with stopping the Soviet tanks with TOW missiles, get to fire at most once a year with a live round," because "the rounds now cost $6,000 apiece." And in the Air Force, "the main barrier to the formation of a cadre of experienced pilots is that so many of them quit" because they don't do much flying, since their temperamental jets are usually out of commission.

Along with this progressive degradation of the soldier there has been a new kind of estrangement, enforced by the technology of war. Since World War I, the enormous scale of mass combat has forced even the ablest general off the field and into the armchair, to be guided by mere reports of the violence raging somewhere else. Throughout this century, this distance has been growing, as the representation becomes more precise. In the Great War, the "front" was, for the first time, far too big and vague to be overseen by the individual leaders, who therefore had to stay behind the lines, studying maps and messages. And now, those who supervise the next catastrophe will be able, theoretically, to follow every development as it occurs, with the help of satellites that can track missiles and warships, locate nuclear explosions, forecast inconvenient weather, and photograph in clear detail any visible area, however tiny or remote.

All these mediating gadgets, however sensitive, must blunt the sense of war in those who use them. Translated into so many blips and telecasts, the fact of war becomes no more than a pressing abstraction, charged with suspense but not noticeably bloody. The same effect obtains for many individual soldiers, those elite technicians encased in the finest jets and tanks, which are built to devastate a countryside and its inhabitants without themselves sustaining any damage. Raised above the crawling infantry, these men are accoutred to approach a battle as their superiors are equipped to gauge it—in a mood of perfect equilibrium and snug detachment. Suspended in this state of artificial infancy—the same state that attracts us all to the promise of advanced technology—the soldier would seem to become psychologically incapable of spoiling for a fight, of closing with some tough opponent, but wants instead to search and destroy without risk, to translate his belligerence into his buttons and extensions, and simply let his fingers do the warring.

In short, it is the intended function of our weaponry to keep war at a distance, even while sustaining it. The overestimation of our hardware, for example, makes the human enemy seem alien, a freak of nature. Our jets and tanks become the indisputable proof of our superiority, things of supreme, self-evident value, so that any destructive counterattack strikes us, not as a worthy challenge, but as downright effrontery, a gross insult to the sacred weapons carrying "our boys." Those guerrillas who fight in person, on the ground, showing their teeth and hacking away in the old-fashioned manner, now seem uncanny, either subhuman or superhuman, as they threaten our machinery with atavistic skills; while the Soviets, more fitting

153

adversaries, are utterly nonhuman, a nation of secret sites and proliferating warheads.

And, as it seems to cancel out the breathing enemy, so does our hardware seem to distance us from what wars really do, to friend and foe alike. Long immersion in technology can make war seem as safe for those who enter it as it looks to those who plan or conduct it from afar. The concept of warfare in outer space, which our military now prepares to realize at vast expense, represents the absolute fulfillment of the technocratic vision. Herman Kahn, the *New York Times* reports, "foresee[s] the day when 'clean wars' could be fought in outer space," with "intense light rays," "space mines and decoys," and "robot warrior craft." Inspired by (among others) Daniel O. Graham and Lyndon LaRouche, the Reagan Administration finds this Atari program irresistible. In outer space, that great playground for bureaucratic speculation, there will apparently be none of the "petty circumstances which cannot be properly described on paper," none of those "difficulties" which, Clausewitz reminds us, "accumulate and produce a friction which no man can imagine exactly who has not seen war." Apparently beyond the reach of chance, outer space offers the deft consultant a realm where, yes, it finally will be possible to deploy machines that enable a kind of war "in which the heat of personal feelings has no share," a place where battle can flash silently, decisively, without leaving any bloody mess.

Up, up, and away—and yet the higher we soar above the scene of battle, trying to transcend the pangs of war in and through the very weapons used to fight it, the more gruesome, more protracted, more extensive war becomes.* Since warfare first became pervasively industrialized, no major war has been either brief or "clean"—quite the contrary. The place-names of premodern military history—Thermopylae, Issus, Philippi, Hastings, Agincourt, Pavia, Yorktown, Waterloo—exert a fascination that is essentially dramatic, evoking the key moments of reversal, recognition, and climax in what we still nostalgically interpret as a global story; whereas the great place-names of modern war often generate a different order of association, each denoting an event of such prodigious and explosive horror that it defeats all impositions of narrative, all spectatorial projection, all attempts at evocation, which

---

* A few years after this essay was written, Ronald Reagan gave succinct expression to this fantasy of universal rescue by some final supramilitary mechanism: "Advancing technology, which originally gave us nuclear weapons, may one day make them obsolete," he told an audience of high school students. "The currents of progress are sweeping us to safety." (Quoted in "Reagan Sees More Teachers in Space," *New York Times*, 8 February 1986)

can never seem to say as much as the mere word "Passchendaele," or "Ypres Salient," "Stalingrad," "Dresden," "Hiroshima."

Thus, through a dark kind of synecdoche peculiar to this era, some proper nouns are now taken to memorialize remote atrocities. But at the times when those atrocities took place, language was used, not to convey the horrors of war, but to put them at a distance: official words were issued as just one more type of authorized materiel. Like submachine guns, or gas, or atomic bombs, certain misleading terms and phrases have been devised and mass-produced by warring governments, in order to conceal the novel agonies of battle from civilian populations ill-equipped to tolerate them. Here again, the Great War marks a starting point: the first extensive, systematic use of propaganda by a government (the British, whose achievement in this area made a big impression on young Adolf Hitler); and the gray dawn of official euphemism, which now imbues our fragmentary culture like polluted air. "Public euphemism as the special rhetorical sound of life in the latter third of the twentieth century," suggests Paul Fussell, "can be said to originate in the years 1914–18," the years that inaugurated an age of apocalyptic violence whose outcome we are still awaiting, at a distance.

Are we helpless to survive within this process? After all this, is it possible to break down these distances? The outlook is bleak; and yet, perhaps, our salvation may be in our midst already, unnoticed until now. Technology, which has made war both invisible and all-consuming, has also blessed us, many think, with the means to remember what's at stake, by giving us television.

IS TV IN FACT A POTENT FORCE FOR PEACE? IT WOULD APpear to rediscover precisely what those long-range weapons do, what those euphemisms actually refer to. It reminds the man who's dropped the bomb just what that bomb is meant to do to men and women, children, neighborhoods; and it deftly undercuts the pose of objectivity implicit in a government's bureaucratese: "incursion," "protective reaction strike," "limited nuclear exchange," "political infrastructure," etc. When such unsuggestive language fills the newspapers, George Orwell wrote in 1946, "a mass of Latin words falls upon the facts like snow"; that snow doesn't stick on television, which always homes in on the dead, allowing no excuses.

Modern war clearly demands this kind of plainness, as we learn from the recent history of literary style: our machinery has helped us to commit atrocities, yet has simultaneously enforced the sort of diction needed to describe them. The Civil War and "the mechanical age," Edmund Wilson points out, combined to simplify American prose, demanding "lucidity, precision, terseness"; and the later, larger wars honed down still more the language of those many writers—journalists as well as novelists and poets—who have struggled to convey the horror, paradoxically, by understating it, rendering it with photographic coolness and exactitude. Through such unflinching reporting, it might be argued, the best war correspondents, and writers like Hemingway, Remarqué, Céline, and Mailer, have aspired, *avant l'image*, to replicate in words the bleak and graphic vision of TV.

The TV coverage of the war in Lebanon seems to have persuaded some that the medium, with its direct and unadorned depictions, may someday usher in an Age of Peace. Confronted with the image of the dead, the viewer can only see and sorrow, and never stand for war again. That, at any rate, is the conclusion drawn by some well-known commentators, who agree about the fact, but differ on the question of its value. A war usually has a purpose, writes George F. Will, of greater moment than the suffering of its victims. Will therefore distrusts TV's inherent pacifism, suggesting that, "had there been television at Antietam on America's bloodiest day (September 17, 1862), this would be two nations," since Americans "might have preferred disunion at the price of union, had they seen the price, in color in their homes in the evening." Ellen Goodman, on the other hand, sees this "price" as all important, and so asserts that TV, "intrinsically anti-war," "brings home what war is all about: killing, wounding, destroying. It doesn't film ideas, but realities," and "this is our greatest hope."

Both of these responses take for granted the idea that television does indeed, as the cliché has it, "bring war into our living rooms." We often hear the same assertion from the figureheads of television, who venerate their medium for having pulled us out of Vietnam. "For the first time," writes Dan Rather, "war was coming into our homes," and William S. Paley too recalls that "television news brought the war into American living rooms almost every night." These observers are only speaking metaphorically, but they present the metaphor as fact: they identify war footage with war itself, as if, after watching each night's newscast in the 1960s, the average viewer had to count his dead, and vacuum the shrapnel out of his couch.

It is, in fact, the great myth of television that the medium somehow gives us an immediate impression, conveying not images, but actualities; and its coverage of war is supposedly the most compelling example of such supreme truthfulness. This pretense of objectivity makes TV's many actual distortions—whether inherent or imposed—all the more insidious, because their camouflage is perfect, fooling not only the viewer, but even most of those who work within the medium, naively claiming to reveal "the way it is."

But what do we see when we sit at home and watch a war? Do we experience an actual event? In fact, that "experience" is fundamentally absurd. Most obviously, there is the incongruity of scale, the radical disjunction of locations. While a war is among the biggest things that can ever happen to a nation or people, devastating families, blasting away the roofs and walls, we see it compressed and miniaturized on a sturdy little piece of furniture, which stands and shines at the very center of our household. And TV contains warfare in subtler ways. While it may confront us with the facts of death, bereavement, mutilation, it immediately cancels out the memory of that suffering, replacing its own pictures of despair with a commercial, upbeat and inexhaustibly bright.

WHILE IT THUS SURROUNDS ITS PAINFUL IMAGES WITH buffers, TV also mitigates them from within. The medium may pose as the purveyor of raw history, but if war weren't suitably processed for the domestic market, if each disaster didn't have its anchorman and correspondent to introduce it, gloss it, and pronounce its simple moral, we wouldn't stand for it, any more than we could take those football games that played in 1981 without the usual commentary. The TV newsman comforts us as John Wayne comforted our grandparents, by seeming to have the whole affair in hand. This hero functions as the guardian of our enclosed spectatorship. Therefore, when we see a newsman shot to death, as happened in Guyana and El Salvador, we react with an especial horror, because we realize that TV is not, in fact, immune to the events which it observes, but that the protective apparatus can be shattered; and if the medium does not confer invincibility on those who manage it, it surely can't safeguard its helpless viewers.

It is only this kind of violence—extraordinary, unexpected, fully visible, and inflicted on the viewer's alter ego—which can make a strong (if brief) impression on TV. For, despite all we have heard about the harrowing plainness of the footage, we simply can't and don't respond to televised violence as intensely as we would if we were right there on the scene. If we did away with all the ads and newsmen, in other words, the experience would still, necessarily, be mediated, and its impact ultimately slight. Even in extreme close-up, the medium maintains a subtle distance between viewer and victim, presenting every pang and ruin with an ineradicable coolness. Over the years we have seen, not only wars, but assassinations, executions, drownings, beatings, shoot-outs, fatal brawls, and nearly every other kind of cruelty—but how much of this do we remember vividly? If we had actually been present at the many horrible events that we have seen take place on television, we

157

would all be as hard and wise as the Wandering Jew, or a nation of quivering shut-ins.

Because the TV image is intrinsically restrained, then, it is not the newsman's purpose to take the edge off an unbearable confrontation. His illusory control performs a different function, necessitated not by the nastiness of actual events, but by TV itself. What upsets us most about those images of aftermath is not so much their painfulness as their apparent randomness; we suddenly arrive upon this unexpected scene and ask ourselves, *"Why this?"* Watching the news, we come to feel, not only that the world is blowing up, but that it does so for no reason, that its ongoing history is nothing more than a series of eruptions, each without cause or context. The news creates this vision of mere anarchy through its erasure of the past, and its simultaneous tendency to atomize the present into so many unrelated happenings, each recounted through a sequence of dramatic, unintelligible pictures.

In short, the TV news adapts the world to its own commercial needs, translating history into several mad occurrences, just the sort of "story" that might pique the viewer's morbid curiosity. Thus political events appear as lurid crimes: the wars in Lebanon, El Salvador, Guatemala come to seem as chilling and mysterious as the Manson killings, Patty Hearst's kidnapping, and the Tylenol affair. *Everything* begins to seem the work of chance, so that "chance" begins to lose its meaning; and the news itself, while fostering this impression, at the same time purports to comprehend the chaos. And so we have the correspondent, solemnly nattering among the ruins, offering crude "analysis" and "background," as if to compensate us for the deep bewilderment that his medium created in the first place.

While TV confuses us precisely through its efforts to inform us, so it only numbs us through its mechanical attempts to work us up. If it can't convey some sense of a war's origins or purposes, then perhaps, as Ellen Goodman thinks, it must at least enable us to apprehend war's personal results—"killing, wounding, destroying." But the medium's immanent remoteness won't permit such revelation; and so TV's custodians struggle desperately to overcome this reserve, trying to find a technical method of arousing the very sympathy that their technology inhibits to begin with. They invariably zoom in tight on the mourner's face, as if we can feel more intensely for another by looking deep inside his nose; and they cut hectically from one appalling image to another, trying to force revulsion through a sort of photographic overkill.

And while television keeps us unenlightened and unmoved, it fails to evoke the conflicts that it covers. As a means of conveying the realities of war, TV is all but useless, precisely because of that very quality which, some think, makes TV the perfect instrument for just such communication: its uninflected vision. For war is, above all, intense, whereas television is too detached to convey intensities. Passion, for instance, rarely registers on television except as something comical or suspect. The medium therefore undercuts the warrior's ardor: crusaders, patriots, and revolutionaries all seem equally insane on television, and the will to power seems nothing but an aberration, a recrudescence of "machismo" or a burst of "deviance." This, according to the liberal argument, is all to the good, since all "aggression" is unnatural and ought to be exposed as such. But TV also strains out the intensity of suffering, flattening the martyr as it ridicules the persecutor, trivializing both victim and tormentor. "Television especially is supposed to reveal the real tragedy of war," Peter Jennings complained from West Beirut last August, "but the camera has not adequately captured the misery this battle between ideologies has produced."

But that camera can't record "real tragedy," because death has no finality, no poignancy, on television. Because the medium cancels out the living presence of its figures, homogenizing all identity, whether individual or collective, it can't restore the impact of a single loss, or express the decimation of a people. Since no one seems to live on television, no one seems to die there. And the medium's temporal facility deprives all terminal moments of their weight.

THE UNIFORMITY OF TV'S VIEW INCLUDES NOT JUST WAR'S victims, but wars themselves. As the medium subverts all overpowering commitment, all keen belief and pain, so it equates jihad, class struggle, imperialist assault, blood feud, and border strife, never capturing whatever is peculiar to specific conflicts, and thereby reducing all wars to a vague abstraction known as War. The medium gave us a "keyhole view" of Vietnam, writes Michael Arlen, reducing that war to a mere handful of unilluminating images, rarely gruesome, never evocative. Similarly, the war in Lebanon was nothing but a lot of sunny rubble, explosions amid tall white buildings, dark women railing at the camera; the wars in Central America, nothing more than rumpled guerrillas doing push-ups in the woods. In short, TV expresses War largely through a few aesthetic images; and even these impressions are unsuggestive. The medium's eye is too jaundiced, its on-the-scene equipment much too cumbrous, its scope too limited, to permit the full delivery of the particular atmosphere—frightening, unique, and fatally arresting—of a given war at a certain time and place.

WHILE THE WRITER OR FILMMAKER CAN RECREATE THE AMBI-ence of a war long finished, the correspondent can't evoke the war that's going on around him. Here again, some presumed advantages of

159

television turn out to be mere hindrances. TV's celebrated presence-on-the-scene only prevents its commentators from arriving at a larger sense, a more informed impression, the sort of grasp that viewers need in order to be moved themselves. Perhaps we can't expect a working journalist thus to transcend his own assignment, when he has a daily deadline; but there is one kind of detachment that doesn't necessitate long reflection, and that is the ex post facto reconstruction that the writing journalist must perform. However, even this achievement is beyond the TV newsman, whose expressive faculties have been supplanted by his footage: if he can show you what he sees, then he needn't labor to express it, and so his eloquence recedes, his perceptions coarsen, as all he has to do is make authoritative noises for the soundtrack, and stand there for the visual cadence, mike in hand. In covering modern war, the newsman is no less reduced by his equipment than the soldiers flying overhead, or rumbling past in tanks. Thus diminished, the newsman is not only incapable of sounding like Hemingway, but can't even reach the descriptive level of earlier war correspondents like Philip Gibbs, Herbert Matthews, Webb Miller, or Edward R. Murrow.

Unable to evoke or analyze, the TV newsman, we would think, ought at least to live up to the claims of his medium, and tell us what he knows (if anything) objectively. But TV may be the least objective medium, because it makes its loaded points from behind an apparently neutral mask: "The camera doesn't lie." While the news report is more or less devoid of atmosphere or telling information, that seeming vacuum is in fact filled up with expressions of the televisual world view, which is the intellectual equivalent of the broadest, coarsest visual image. This world view is a heavy distillation of our general ideological assumptions, which are often dangerously simple to begin with. Further simplified to make a bold impression on the little screen, our ideology comes back to us in especially crude, delusive hunks, disguised, of course, as straightforward reportage.

According to this televisual reality, in a war there are no issues, and only two sides: the bullies and the little guys. Since TV brings us conflicts ahistorically, an attack must necessarily be unjustified and unexpected, its victims innocent, its authors brutal. The purpose of this melodrama is not to "awaken public opinion"—TV can't properly be said to awaken anything—as to treat the viewer to an easy dose of rage and pity. This kind of manipulation may seem quite noble, a cry of honest indignation meant to halt a heinous crime, but it is actually expressive of the subtlest bigotry, the most self-serving moralism.

For the TV news loves a good victim; and while this attitude suggests a most enlightened, charitable impulse, it is not conducive to an activist response, because this love is fatally possessive of its broken object: "Stay as you are!" it tells the oppressed. "Your battered face has earned you our esteem!" Within this schema, the worst thing that can happen to the underdog is not to die or go on suffering, but to become unpitiable, to stand up strong. Because the news allows no categories between those of the noble weakling and the ugly victor, any group that does attempt to shed its lowly status zips straight from subjugation into villainy. Whenever this occurs, the journalists turn indignant; yet they wouldn't have it otherwise, as long as the new configuration yields fresh victims for the sympathetic camera.

THIS SENTIMENTAL STRATEGY RELIES ON AND PERPETUATES the oldest stereotypes, and is therefore the expression of mere bigotry, largely unconscious, frequently well meaning, and therefore worse than any overt hatred. Blacks and Jews, the most despised of peoples, have been the major objects in this scheme, shifting from handsome victim to pariah, from one debased status to the other, according to how autonomous they seem to those who work on television. As long as blacks abided by the principles of King and Gandhi, they were aestheticized as Eternal Losers, eyes soulfully pitched upward; but as soon as they acted on their anger, whether as rioters or Black Panthers, the news took back that holy glow and cast them as an unexpected menace, only to reinstate their wings and halos in these quiescent times. And now the Jews of Israel have forfeited their saintliness by acting as Americans used to, expropriating land that isn't theirs, teaching their enemies an atrocious lesson, and doing some harm to innocents as well.

According to the news, the real crime of the Israelis was not their invasion per se, but their willful abandonment of the Jew's historic role as martyr. This was the dominant theme of TV's coverage of the war in Lebanon. Israel, said Richard Threlkeld from Beirut, "has confounded its enemies and . . . commanded fear and respect, but it is not the Israel that its first Prime Minister, Ben-Gurion, always imagined it would be. That Israel, that light unto the nations." Despite the denials of the networks' presidents, it was indeed the case that the coverage of that war was heavily biased against Israel, although not in a way that ought to comfort the Palestinians. The news did consistently inflate the casualty figures, dwell on atrocities, stress heavily the fact of censorship, and otherwise depict Israel as the only guilty party. The Palestinians have also suffered at others' hands—for example, King Hussein's—but the TV news never trumpeted that outrage.

This is hardly meant to justify what Israel did in Lebanon, but merely to define the real animus behind TV's characterization of that war. For the Palestinians too have been diminished by the coverage. As

161

Israel was excoriated for having shed her crown of thorns, the Palestinians were suddenly ennobled, playing the erstwhile Jewish role of victim. As such, they were translated into total helplessness, mere bleeding figures with no grievance, no threatening aims, no voice other than the networks' voices. "In the news," writes Ellen Goodman in approval of the TV coverage, "the sides are not divided into good guys and bad guys, but aggressors and victims." This nondistinction actually equates the "victims" with the "good guys" and thereby cancels out the complicated history in Lebanon, along with the PLO, which doesn't really fit in either TV category.

This omission preserves the simple-minded opposition that the medium imposed upon that conflict. And which side benefits from this reduction? Certainly not the Israelis, who, once the PLO have been erased, appear to have invaded Lebanon simply for the fun of killing Lebanese civilians; and the Palestinians too have been distorted by the TV fiction, which presents them as disorganized, unrepresented, politically unconscious, and therefore fit for pity, in dire need of the medium's own illusory protection. As in El Salvador and Northern Ireland, so here TV created a beleaguered and pathetic mass, "caught in the middle," completely apolitical, and therefore in no shape to strike back later: TV, in short, will only champion those groups whom it can sentimentalize. It has no interest in a stoic people, or in a population that takes careful steps toward self-possession. For when the Palestinians fight again, their belligerence will, as usual, appear as unexpected; and if they eventually find that they too "command fear and respect," they may also find themselves portrayed, therefore, as evil.

WHAT CAN TELEVISION TELL US, THEN, ABOUT A WAR? HERE is a rich example of the medium's expressiveness, chosen at random from last summer's coverage. On the "NBC Nightly News" on 2 August 1982 Roger Mudd delivered the following introduction: "Watching the shelling and the panic and the smoke and the death in Beirut on television night after night can have a powerful impact. But, as John Chancellor's commentary tonight reveals, seeing it in person is of quite a different magnitude." Chancellor then appeared from overseas, and gave us this:

> What will stick in the mind about yesterday's savage Israeli attack on Beirut is its size and its scope. This is one of the world's big cities. The area under attack is the length of Manhattan Island below Central Park. Five hundred thousand people live here. One in a hundred is a PLO fighter. And it went on for such a long time: before dawn [sic] until five in the afternoon. Systematic,

sophisticated warfare. The Israeli planes just never stopped coming. For an entire day, Beirut rocked and swayed to the rhythm of the Israeli attack. The Israelis say they were going after military targets with precision. There was also the stench of terror all across the city.

Nothing like it has ever happened in this part of the world. I kept thinking yesterday of the bombing of Madrid during the Spanish Civil War. What in the world is going on? Israel's security problem on its border is fifty miles to the south. What's an Israeli Army doing here in Beirut? The answer is that we are now dealing with an imperial Israel which is solving its problems in someone else's country, world opinion be damned. Nobody knows how the battle of Beirut is going to end. But we do know one thing. The Israel we saw here yesterday is not the Israel we have seen in the past.

Chancellor clearly wanted to convey his own experience of bombardment, but his language is dead, its function having long since been usurped by videotape. What was it like? Well, "it went on for such a long time," the "planes just never stopped coming"; and these colorless phrases culminate in an image both impersonal and feebly aesthetic: "Beirut rocked and swayed to the rhythm of the Israeli attack." This image, which reduces the bombardment to a sort of urban jitterbug, does not convey a strong impression of the citizens' fear, as Murrow's London broadcasts did so well. All that the clause does, in fact, is reproduce the viewer's detached perspective; Chancellor might just as well have watched the bombing on TV, which is equally incapable of expressing others' fears and sorrows. The report's one reference to the vivid human presence is a mere cliché, thrown in as an afterthought: "There was also the stench of terror all across the city."

"What in the world is going on?" Chancellor asks. "What's an Israeli Army doing here in Beirut?" These are good questions, but he's supposed to answer them, not pose them. Rather than provide some history, he merely bolsters our incomprehension with his own, thereby turning the event into a mystery, which, like a priest, he can seem to grasp and solve by uttering a well-known moral formula: "The Israel we saw here yesterday is not the Israel we have seen in the past."

Thus, into the descriptive void of the report there drops the familiar clod of ideology, disguised as an objective fact: "But we do know one thing." At once "savage" and "imperial," Chancellor's Israel has undergone a sudden, terrifying metamorphosis. "I kept thinking of the bombing of Madrid during the Spanish Civil War." Why? Was little Johnny Chancellor, age nine, in Madrid when it was bombed in 1936? Probably

163

not. Then is the Spanish Civil War in any way comparable to "the battle of Beirut"? Not noticeably. What Chancellor actually means by comparing this war to one he's only read about is that Israel has indeed become its opposite, has jumped straight into that other category, since Madrid was bombed, for Franco's sake, by the Junkers 52 of Hilter's Condor Legion.

As this report is typical of television, we must conclude that the medium does not "bring home what war is all about," but rather what TV is all about. Television's seeming transparency is in fact the medium's cleverest fiction, offering what seems a clear view of the world, yet in a way that only makes us more familiar with, more dependent on, TV.

BUT LET'S SET ASIDE ALL THESE DISTORTIONS—THE shrinkage, the implicit distancing, the illusory containment, the imperceptible mist of ideology—and grant that TV does tend to present, as Goodman puts it, "less glory and more gore." Does this also mean that TV is "intrinsically anti-war"? There is no reason to think so; and this belief in television's salutary bias is not only unfounded, but intolerant, positing only one morally acceptable response. To assert, with Ellen Goodman, that on TV "the sides are not divided into good guys and bad guys, but aggressors and victims," is to say that the viewer, when he sits down to watch TV, is suddenly cleansed of all personal identity, all preconception, and can now apprehend the conflicts of the world from an exalted, unimpeachable standpoint, seeing reality through God's own eyes, or Ellen Goodman's. Far from conducive to a world of peace, such "objective" certainty is probably more dangerous than any archaic faith, because it reflects, and has at its disposal, the most enormous system of technology that has ever choked the world.

For not even the most sophisticated Sony has a perfect moral faculty built into it. We usually see what we want to see on television; and TV complicates this tendency by helping to determine that original desire. If it thinks that we want war, it sells us war. The medium can easily circumvent the pacific influence (if any) of its graphic images. Like radio or the yellow press, TV too can beat the drum. "Granted, television helped get us out of Vietnam," writes Michael Arlen, "but it also helped march us in."

And even if the medium weren't influential, the images per se dictate no automatic pacifism. Confronted with those pictures of the slaughtered Palestinians, a Phalangist viewer, or a member of Gush Emunim, would surely smile at the sight of all those dead "aggressors"; nor would the televised corpses of Israelis draw tears from any fervent anti-Zionist. And it isn't only foreigners who take sides. Had there been television at Antietam on America's bloodiest day, this country might indeed still be two nations; but not necessarily, as George Will supposes, two nations frightened into peace, but two nations still at war, each side still watching every battle, and still finding, on the screen, excuses for refusing to negotiate.

And, had the Civil War been thus prolonged by television, the newsmen would, of course, continue to lament it, crying automatically for peace while shooting everything in sight. Truth is indeed the first casualty in any war, and our journalists have never been less honest than in this sentimental era. In his memoirs, published in 1946, Herbert Matthews wrote this sentence:

> The urge to go out and fight, to pit one's strength and wits against the forces of nature, to seek adventure, risk life and take joy in comradeship and danger—these are deep feelings, so deep that even I who love life and family and luxury and books have yielded to them.

And, of course, that stirring list of hard inducements implies another, which Matthews took for granted: "the urge for a terrific story." No TV newsman would make such a frank avowal: Matthews's "deep feelings" have become, not only difficult to gratify, but entirely taboo; and the old craving for a scoop now comes concealed in journalistic pieties about "the public's right to know." In a recent *TV Guide,* Dan Rather, asked what event he'd most like to report in the year 2000, came up with this: "Good evening, from CBS News. Peace and good will toward all living things prevails [sic] everywhere on earth and throughout the cosmos."

Now what would Dan Rather do, deprived of war and ill will in the cosmos? His utopian pronouncement, as frightening as it is disingenuous, does not reflect the sentiments of a living human being, but the contradictory longings of the medium that has consumed him. TV has us automatically deplore or ridicule all anger, fear, political commitment, deep belief, keen pleasure, exalted self-esteem, tremendous love; and yet, while making all these passions seem unnatural, the medium persistently dwells on their darkest consequences, teasing the housebound spectator with hints of that intensity that it has helped to kill. In fact, despite its pleas for universal calm, what TV depends upon is something else: brutal wars abroad, and an anxious peace in every living room.

Afterword

▪ ▪

ARGUING THAT TV's "IMAGES PER SE DICTATE NO AU-tomatic pacifism," I used a number of hypothetical examples: Phalangist, anti-Zionist; Yankee or Rebel. It is now possible to point to actual cases—for, after 1982, TV became the primary rhetorical medium of the ultraright, whose militarism was in no way softened by that experience. Indeed, TV accommodates their paranoia, for while its visual coolness tends to subvert the passion of their fanaticism, its melodramatic bias suits their motivating vision of a world divided between Us and Them.

Thus Ronald Reagan, although a product of TV, displayed a medieval fondness for the Apocalyptic face-off. In 1984, the *New York Times* observed that "he usually refers to Christians as 'we' and the adherents of all other religious faiths as 'they' "—a verbal tic made poignant by his frequent references to Armageddon. Such bellicose piety is, of course, common among Reagan's natural constituents: "Sometimes," Mrs. Oliver L. North told *Life* in August 1987, "I feel like 'they're' up there, they've got all the guns—and then there's 'us.' It's very comforting to know there will be an ultimate judgment." Col. North himself promoted the same dichotomous worldview: not only as an anticommunist zealot, but as a gifted TV actor, playing the earnest David overcoming the Congressional Goliath—a spectacle that sent his partisans into Manichaean raptures: "It's absolutely classic," exulted G. Gordon Liddy, having watched the hostilities between North and House counsel John Nields: "A lean, hard, strong, battle-ready Marine Corps officer locked in mortal combat with a 60's residue with long hair. The hard jaw versus the soft jaw."

Despite such bloodlust (or lust, perhaps, in Liddy's case), TV is not a rabble-rousing medium (see p. 324)—unless the rabble (like those above) are already eager to be roused. "TV," it is true, "can beat the drum," but it tends not to, because its only purpose is to keep us watching, buying, watching—a point that bears reemphasizing, and updating, through the analysis of another, later bit of TV's coverage of the Middle Eastern conflict:

167

BOXED IN

■ ■ ■ ■ ■ ■

Good evening. This is the "CBS Evening News," Dan Rather reporting. First: amazement. Then: outrage. Tonight: above all, confusion. Who—if anyone—has custody of the four Achille Lauro hijack/murderers, those young men who took partly paralyzed 69-year-old American Leon Klinghoffer from his wheelchair, shot him, killed him, and tossed him overboard? Who—if anyone—will bring the murderers to justice?

This opening performs in no way like the first paragraph of a standard newspaper article, which—however biased—would still affect to orient the reader. On the contrary: Rather's purpose here was wholly televisual—i.e., to *disorient* the viewers, and to react on their behalf. At first a mere sequence of explosive nouns, followed by a question so long, garbled, and repetitious that its precise point finally disappears, Rather's lead-in functions only to spread darkness, and fear within that darkness. The plaintive phrase "Who—if anyone?" reveals nothing, but was meant to lead us in a cry of pain; Rather spoke it twice, giving us nothing but anaphora. And the subsequent catalog of atrocities merely amplifies the murder, making the account as hideous as possible in a few seconds. Ignoring what little evidence was then available, Rather referred to all four suspects as active "hijack/murderers," and then further hyped the crime by absurdly multiplying it: "those young men" first "took" the victim "from his wheelchair," then "shot him" and "killed him" and "tossed him overboard." It was as if the killing of "partly paralyzed 69-year-old American Leon Klinghoffer" might not have seemed quite horrible enough if it had happened only once.

Whereas, in 1982, TV cast the Israelis as the Nazis, now—three years later—it was some of Israel's enemies who were apparently acting out of motiveless malignity. Now there was no mention of the earlier atrocity—the invasion of Lebanon—which was, at least in part, the reason for this new one. And so, again, the crime seemed pointless, baseless: its facts misrepresented, its history suppressed, and only for TV's sake.

The real point of the anchorman's lurid rhetoric, then, is to frighten us into depending on the apparatus of the newscast, himself included—and this aim points us toward the actual focus, the secret content, of the TV news. Backed by a map of the seven continents, and—it is implied—in constant contact with dozens of reporters flying in and out of every hot spot, the anchorman sits before us as if exquisitely attuned to the whole world; and yet he is in fact attuned exclusively to us, uses his reporters' data only to promote our continual discomposure as we sit before him. His prefaces need not be accurate, therefore, because their

168

■ ■ ■ ■ ■ ■ ■ ■ ■ ■ ■ ■ ■

true referent is not the day's events but we who must be made to keep on sitting, keep on sweating:

"First, amazement. Then: outrage." Thus the "report" began as if by slapping us across the face, and then proceeded to disturb us even further with the hint that *we* were all in danger, because "the four Achille Lauro hijack/murderers" were still at large. This alarmist strategy surely explains why Rather chose automatically to say that Leon Klinghoffer had first been taken "from his wheelchair" and then shot, despite the evidence that the victim had been shot while sitting: Rather's image of someone forced out of a chair before being murdered makes it easier for us to fear, deep down, for our own lives, since we too, as we watch TV, are chairbound Americans (and "partly paralyzed" at that).

Such terrorism makes us grateful to the terrorist—grateful, finally, for our ostensible release at newscast's end, when the anchor suddenly grins us through some little item cute or quaint, to leave us chuckling optimistically after all that pointless torment.■

Rock Music: A Success Story

Where All the Flowers Went

SOME OF US USED TO THINK THAT ROCK WOULD DIE with its beads on, gunned down in the street by agents of the law. This thrill of paranoia was the bequest of rock's abrasive history. As the Great Domestic Annoyance of the Fifties, in the days of Elvis Presley, rock and roll played with sinister jubilance off in the distance, breaking the jowly slumbers of the burghers and their wives, and sometimes it exploded right upstairs, in one of the kids' bedrooms. Dad, paunchy and balding, gripping the evening paper in one angry fist, hammers against the bedroom door, and yells hoarsely into the hypnotic din: "WILL YOU TURN THAT DAMNED THING DOWN!" Downstairs in the kitchen, Mom clucks to herself fretfully.

The uproar began when Colonel Tom Parker bought Elvis Presley from Sun Records in 1955. In 1958, the momentum was fatally interrupted when Presley was drafted, which seemed to inspire a massacre: scandal ruined Jerry Lee Lewis's career, Buddy Holly and Richie Valens were killed in a plane crash, and Chuck Berry was arrested for violating the Mann Act. (Little Richard had escaped this visitation by embracing religion in 1957.) Rock was suddenly leaderless, much to the benefit of promoters like Dick Clark, who oversaw the manufacture of an unthreatening new generation of "teen idols." Singers like Bobby Vinton, Bobby Vee, Bobby Rydell ("There was nothing but Bobbies on the radio," Jerry Lee Lewis grumbled) wooed the American teenager and won Dad's heart. There was no need to break down the door and stomp on the phonograph, because rock's threat had exhausted itself.

Although the music's spirit died in 1958, the Fifties lasted until late 1963, when the Beatles released "I Want to Hold Your Hand" in America. The Beatles made rock and roll outrageous again, reminding their young listeners that rock was not just music but the vindication of a possible community. The Beatles defined "straight" by presenting themselves as its unsettling alternative. Confronted by Elvis's lean sneer and snaking hips, Dad swelled with indignation. But when he saw the Beatles wagging their shaggy heads at the microphones, and saw the hordes of girls in heat ("What do they *see* in those guys?"), he was incredulous.

173

BOXED IN

■ ■ ■ ■ ■ ■

DURING THE SIXTIES, THE LUDICROUS IMAGE OF DAD POUND-
ing on his daughter's bedroom door evolved into a terrifying fantasy:
the State would smash the tubes and cut the wires. It did not seem
farfetched for the Blue Meanies in *Yellow Submarine*, steeped in the
hue of law enforcement, to savage every form of musical expression.
The rock star's droogish image had taken on a revolutionary glow; his
music rang like a call to insurrection: "Got to revolution!" shouted the
Jefferson Airplane; "We want the world and we want it now!"
threatened the Doors. We feared that Dad, encouraged by S. I.
Hayakawa, would pull the plug, a strategy pursued by Richard Nixon,
whose diligent harassment of John Lennon suggests that the President
saw *Yellow Submarine* between viewings of *Patton*, and decided that
the Meanies had a strong game plan.

This fantasy was not unfounded, for the wielders of power distrusted
the energy of rock and roll. Politicians and Bible thumpers would proclaim that rock was a communist device, while the Kremlin condemned
that ungovernable beat with equal vehemence. Rock, having evolved
among the poor, and appealing to the young before they learned to co-
operate, seemed the music of those who could not or would not take
part in the orderly business of society. It flowed through the air,
straight to the nerves, immune to the settling influence of any status
quo. It appeared to have great liberating potential: all those people,
moving in bliss to the same beat, might accomplish anything.

Woodstock made it clear that rock would spark no revolutions. Because that gathering took place without bloodshed, journalists wrote
happily that the kids were okay after all. But Woodstock was peaceful
because most of its 300,000 participants were too stoned to stand up,
let alone make a fist. Rock fans are hedonists; they want to luxuriate in
fine blasts of sound. They may curse and break chairs if the concert
doesn't start on time, but they do not run outside and embrace wild
dogmas. Woodstock's (and rock's) definitive moment came when Abbie
Hoffman clambered onstage to address the woozy multitudes and Pete
Townshend of the Who, the act in progress, stepped up behind him and
kicked him off.

The festival marked the beginning of an end, as Elvis's induction
had. While the "counterculture" was trying to keep its eyes open at
Woodstock, John Lennon was agonizing over his disenchantment with
the Beatles, whose dissolution was made public in April 1970. Five
months later, Jimi Hendrix choked to death in his drugged sleep, and
two weeks after that, Janis Joplin died of a heroin overdose. The following year, Jim Morrison suffered a fatal heart attack and Duane Allman
died in a motorcycle accident. Eric Clapton, a victim of drug addiction,
went into seclusion for three years.

174

The "community" was stricken, but the music didn't stop. More and more records came out, and concerts went on, much amplified, but rock had lost the keen joy of something fresh and illicit. Its body went on dancing but it had lost its soul.

The difference shows in little things, especially on television, which has incorporated rock and roll and all its faded symbols. When Presley first appeared on Ed Sullivan's show in 1956, his furious groin was blocked from sight. Now we can watch a performer called Alan impersonate Presley on "Don Kirshner's Rock Concert." He gyrates assiduously and makes worshipful speeches about his idol, who is reportedly too depressed to leave the house. Dean Martin used to get big laughs on television deriding rock musicians' looks. Sonny and Cher, who once sang about how the grown-ups mocked their penniless love, now get big laughs on television deriding each other. Drugs, once the rock world's forbidden pleasure and the cause of so many infamous deaths, are as popular as police dramas, and therefore just as interesting. Sammy Davis's jewelry collection includes a solid-gold cocaine blade; a president's son "admits" that he has "experimented" with marijuana. It might seem time to start looking for new taboos, but the so-called youth culture makes it hard to be outrageous. Unfortunately, the time is right for a history of rock and roll.

THE ROLLING STONE ILLUSTRATED HISTORY OF ROCK & ROLL is thorough and melancholy. Appropriately, this big red slab of a book, with its solemn title registered in tall white characters, looks like a pop tombstone. Its seventy essays tell of one burnt-out case after another; most of those musicians who have not succumbed to an appalling death have slipped into unseemly decrepitude. Death by overdose or gunshot wounds is horrible, but woe to him who's left behind, surrounded by tone-deaf promoters. "When he died," said Eric Clapton of Jimi Hendrix, "I went out in the garden and cried all day . . . not because he'd gone, but because he hadn't taken me with him."

Equally wistful are the twenty-six contributors to the *History*, but this mood is probably not new to them. Feeling left out is an occupational hazard of rock criticism, which struggles to interpret something that requires no interpretation: "Rock 'n' roll music gets right through to you without having to go through your brain," says John Lennon, invalidating volumes of rock criticism. Although rock musicians may consider themselves artists, theirs is the least cerebral of the arts, and the sleaziest. The rock critic tries to appraise and explicate a music whose artists and listeners are anti-intellectual and usually stoned, and whose producers want more than anything to own several cars.

And now the rock critic is an old-timer as well as an outsider. A pop

175

journalist whose reviews could be forgotten along with the music, he has become a historian in spite of himself. Like rock, his work was meant for consumption, not preservation, and yet he must now look back on the development of his evanescent subject and establish its official record.

The musicologists of tomorrow will find rock's history somewhat bewildering, for the currents of rock's development are unclear, and less relevant than its momentary impact. Rock's growth has been disorderly: it never adopted a home, but gathered speed in brothels, back yards, garages, and gyms. Furthermore, it is fast and sensual, ill-suited for a chronicle. It does not want to last; it wants to explode.

A history of explosions might give us the survivors' points of view, but it would tell us little about the way the blasts felt. This is the case with the *History*, which does not convey the exuberance of rock so much as it expresses the gloom of rock's critical establishment. The book tries to be groovy and monumental at the same time. The editor, Jim Miller, betrays this ambivalence in his introduction. He concedes that "a history of rock cannot help but violate the music's essence," but then hopes "that rock really does represent a lasting cultural statement, a popular expression that will survive its moment, either as artifact or artwork."

It may be, but "a lasting cultural statement" does not need books like the *History*, which is most successful when least authoritative. Because rock's "significance" is entirely a matter of one generation's response at a certain time, the book's best essays are frankly reminiscent: the critic dispenses with the fiction of detachment and tries to recall the music's lost effect. However, the critic is older and smarter than he was when first smitten by the sound, which he knows has always been carefully exploited by a vulgar industry, so he will avoid romanticizing his memories, and will write with a sense of humor. And he should not shrink from telling a few good stories, because rock is a candid personal music, inextricably involved with such sensational concerns as brief encounters, professional difficulties, and illegal habits. The *History*'s best critics (Greil Marcus, Lester Bangs, Barry Hansen, among others) have a sense of their subject's limits, and so their clever essays play against the book's archival pretensions.

THE *HISTORY* ASPIRES TO COMPREHENSIVENSS: ONLY A FEW small-to-medium acts (such as the Fugs, Spirit, Sha Na Na) are never mentioned, and these are forgivable omissions. Errors of fact are few and small: for instance, a picture of Chad and Jeremy is captioned "Peter and Gordon." It is only when the book's contributors look for rock equivalents to the discovery of the wheel that the material becomes questionable. Buddy Holly, writes Jonathan Cott, "was the first to use strings on a rock and roll record," but then Ken Emerson reports that Roy Orbison "helped pioneer the use of strings." Maybe the two musicians worked together: Holly set up the music stands while Orbison got the violins out of the truck. Charles Perry credits the rock musicians of San Francisco with "the deliberate introduction of feedback," whereas Dave Marsh asserts that feedback was Pete Townshend's "primary technique" as early as 1966 (just before "the San Francisco sound" caught on), and then John Morthland tells us that Jimi Hendrix "was already beginning to experiment with feedback" in "late 1965 or early 1966."

Rock has evolved too chaotically to yield the chronicler a series of noteworthy turning points. And rock does not stand still for intimations of its supposed immortality. The moment of rock, like the moment of lovemaking from which it took its name, is sweet because fleeting, valuable because short-lived. Like sex, it literally plays itself out. Pete Townshend expressed rock's self-destructiveness when he used to batter his guitar to splinters, and Jimi Hendrix did the same when he set his moaning instrument on fire. The critic thinking of marble and gilded monuments is in the wrong business. Dave Marsh intones that "My Generation" "earned the Who an eternal place in rock history," a contradiction in terms. Langdon Winner insists that Little Richard's name belongs on "any list of rock immortals."

Eager to justify rock's place among the more respectable arts, some critics try to convey an impression of great learning, as if there were Departments of Rock Studies competing with the other disciplines at every big university.* Discussing Buddy Holly, whose style is most memorable for its simplicity, Jonathan Cott drops the names of Picasso and Petrarch, alludes to *Peter Pan* and *Lolita*, quotes Shakespeare's Sonnet 116, and claims that Chuck Berry "took on and extended Walt Whitman's visionary embrace of American geography." "It is tempting to view all of Holly's recordings as a synchronic rather than a diachronic structure," he muses, although nothing could be less tempting, or less appropriate to rock & roll.

The *History*'s hundreds of photographs, selected and arranged by Robert Kingsbury, convey rock's outlandishness and will relieve the reader when he tires of Cott's posturing and the other contributors' woe.

WHAT MAKES THESE CRITICS SAD MAKES TONY PALMER FURIous. *All You Need Is Love* is an ironic title for this "story of popular

---

* Ten years later, this sounds more like prophecy than satire.

177

music," for Palmer's thesis is bitterly fatalistic: every genre of this century's popular music has been commercialized into extinction by greedy white men. Furthermore, Palmer considers the Beatles' "All You Need Is Love" "a compelling example of the worst in 'popular' music," which makes his book's title seem strange at first, until it becomes clear that Palmer likes popular music only because he enjoys hating it so much. Aside from sneering at the eponymous song, Palmer knocks the Mills Brothers, the Supremes, and the Drifters, slights Bob Dylan as the purveyor of "a middle-class music," snarls that Nashville "strangled" country music, describes Johnny Ray's act as "clumsy and tuneless," refers to Glenn Miller's sound as "the antithesis of jazz or swing," and calls Bill Haley "a clod."

Palmer treats every popular musical idiom of this century as if it were entirely discrete, and even invents a few categories for the sake of heated attacks on "the music industry," which Palmer sees at work in every cranny, turning black funk into white pap. He considers greed a Caucasian trait which certain blacks have adopted to the detriment of their music: "Berry Gordy was once a production line worker in Detroit. Now he is boss of a multimillion-dollar black show business organization, which proves that to escape the ghetto it is necessary to beat the white man at his own game." Palmer also thinks that all commercial music is bad. Gordy's Motown became successful "at considerable risk to the black man and his music," seethes Palmer, losing control of himself completely as he lights into Diana Ross and the Supremes: ". . . out of her spindly, predatory body crackled hit after hit. In their neat little trouser suits, the Supremes oohed and aahed with immaculate togetherness. They pouted and hitched up their breasts. With lacquered wigs and blasted smiles. . . ."

The Supremes made good records, and their enormous audience included whites and blacks, rich and poor. Would Palmer have the Supremes shouting spirituals around the washtub in some shanty, far beyond the walls of Gordy's Hitsville, USA? Like most purists, Palmer seems to think that black musicians were funky by choice, that they played makeshift instruments and lacked teeth because they preferred it that way.*

Palmer takes rock's defiant gestures literally, waiting for the music to effect a revolution. Elvis Presley "had cut loose a whole generation. He had united white and black. He had brought sex into the open and

---

*Palmer's sort of reverse-racist purism has no place in the culture of TV, whose black superstars appear perfectly—sometimes fantastically—deracinated (see above, pp. 147–49). This shift reflects less on an ideal of whiteness than on the cultural primacy of the commodity.

demonstrated the possible." Palmer is the ultimate fan, reminding us of that word's derivation from "fanatic." He craves the vicarious thrill of someone else's rebelliousness, and jeers when the idol turns out to be human. Although he has no ear, he is an exacting judge of ideological purity.

While posing as a serious critic, Palmer works like a saboteur. He edits some of John Lennon's remarks to construct an insider's confession of how the Beatles used every available kind of drug (whereas the statement he quotes about heroin, for instance, refers only to John and Yoko), and merges the misquoted lines of two different Stones songs to present what is supposed to be a representative verse of decadent lyrics.

But *All You Need Is Love* is dishonest in a subtler way. Janis Joplin "swaggered around like the nigger-loving whore that Port Arthur thought she was, her parchment arms flailing like a berserk windmill. . . . She paraded the stage like a debauched Carnival Queen, or King Kong in drag." This is meant to "expose" rock's decadence, but none of Palmer's targets is as tasteless as his own prose, which exploits Joplin's misery to give the glossy book a little more spice. Palmer's disgust with commercialism is also disingenuous: *All You Need Is Love* contains twelve exquisite full-color reproductions of early sheet music covers, supposedly intended to "demonstrate the nature of the sell—sentiment, racism, star appeal, patriotism—as well as the importance of illustrative skills." That sounds scholarly, but not very convincing: lavish reproductions are just the thing for a slick gift book. For fifteen dollars, *All You Need Is Love* will harangue you on the evils of commercialism.

Rock itself is paralyzed by the same contradiction. Even as it sang of new worlds, rock was always on its way to selling out. One rock chronicler happily points out that the music has been commercial from the beginning. Discussing "the early success of phenomenons like Elvis Presley" in *Rock, Roll & Remember*, Dick Clark sums up the mood of rock's first phase: "It was a pioneering era. Young, swinging capitalists went into the record business to satisfy the demand for rock 'n' roll." This chirp of avarice ought to send the whole *Rolling Stone* staff right through the window. Nevertheless, off-putting though his attitude may be, Clark might be expected to have some thoughts about co-optation, for he supervised the softening process that took nothings like Frankie Avalon, Fabian, and Bobby Rydell and turned them, virtually overnight, into rich nothings.

But if Clark has any interesting thoughts at all, he has apparently decided to keep them to himself. He recounts trivial conversations verbatim ("I'll order you a ham and Swiss cheese on a hard roll and a

179

Coke," somebody told him in 1957), and describes non-events in great detail. Clark has not noticed any decline in the music, and had no ear for possible hits (he thought that "She Loves You" sounded "kind of hollow"), perhaps because he owned no records: he stocked his house with empty album jackets for his appearance on "Person to Person," whereupon "my record collection became famous." His two divorces make him sad because his domestic life did not look as good as his record collection: "I'd find a woman, marry her, raise kids, own a house and car, and we'd grow old gracefully together. It's a source of deep-seated disappointment to me that that didn't happen."

Clark cares for nothing but appearances and the money they require. He was perfect as architect of the cover-up that followed the grease and violence of the Presley years. After all the hollering, it was time for the reaffirmation of familiar virtues: sexual restraint, hard work, good grooming. Clark looked the part, and learned to be convincing. After his traumatic involvement in the payola investigations, he resolved on nothing more than increased self-protectiveness: "I learned not just to make money, but to protect my ass at all times."

SUCH WHOLESOMENESS BECAME OLD-FASHIONED IN THE mid-sixties, a time when Mick Jagger projected a style more appealing to the rock fan. Roy Carr's *The Rolling Stones: An Illustrated Record* is a pictorial history of the Stones' everthickening image, and the ultimate expression of the rock fan's self-abasing antihero worship. Carr brags about the Stones' toughness like a short kid who hangs out with the school bully: the Stones "have consistently refused to be sat on," Carr slavers, agreeing with Palmer's claim that the Stones were "outlaws from the start." Jagger should be pleased by this response to his pose of gritty independence, which has made him as rich as Dick Clark became protecting his ass at all times. Despite their wicked reputation, the Stones are young, swinging capitalists who have always dogged the Beatles' steps, and who were in such a hurry to cash in on the success of Woodstock that their concert at Altamont was scandalously botched. Jagger's fans are mostly high school students, because nobody else (except Carr and Palmer) could continue to believe that the Stones are menacing.

Most of us now know that rock is a cry of revolt underwritten by major corporations, and that it can no longer defy the business establishment that pays for it. The music is too successful: "The logic of profit," writes Robert Christgau, "has created a market too big for the genre." And rock is too successful in another way. The appeal of its rhetoric has been answered; the dream of Woodstock Nation has come true. "Everybody clap your hands!" rock's most common exhortation, has been literally obeyed, much to the critics' chagrin. The man on-stage didn't really mean *everybody*; he meant everybody in that young audience, everybody who believed in the vague freedoms which (we thought) Dad longed to crush. We clapped joyfully because it was *our* music, and we would play the damned thing as loud as we wanted. But Dad did something worse than break down the doors and cut off our speakers. He ran in and danced beside us.

THE ROMANCE OF PERSECUTION HAS ENDED. ROCK SOUNDS feeble without the proud illusion of defiance. It may have been "co-opted" all along, handled by shrewd promoters from the beginning, but it was exciting as long as nobody knew this depressing fact. The music sang out for feelings of community, however loosely defined, and Dad's business partners made sure that the music would get what it wanted. This inevitable taming process was improved by technology. Like cinema, rock has become dependent on fine gadgetry. Producers, who often have more to do with an album's sound than the musicians, are called in to contrive a certain style, like interior decorators or the Avon Lady. Records cost more to produce, but the effects are too nice to reject: "It pains me to make albums that are so expensive," says producer Peter Asher, "but when the technology exists to improve something, it seems wrong not to do it."

This "technology" is a pervasive neutralizing medium. "The Ballad of John and Yoko," censored on AM radio in 1969, wafts transformed through high-rise elevators, dentists' lobbies, and airport terminals. "It seems wrong not to do it": once the first guitar was amplified, there was no turning back. All rock aspires to the condition of Muzak.

THE PHRASE "ROCK STAR" CONNOTES IMMOBILITY AND heaviness, and the status it describes is, literally, a drag. No artist is more encumbered. And in the midst of all the sound equipment, costumes, cars, and hangers-on, the rock star himself is a product in demand, grabbed in every way by everyone. "One has to completely humiliate oneself to be what the Beatles were, and that's what I resent," John Lennon has said. But, according to the musicians interviewed in *What's That Sound?*, an anthology of excellent pieces from the last seven years of *Rolling Stone*, the greatest pressure comes from the audience.

Having once broken his guitar "by complete accident," Pete Townshend finds himself unable to stop: "The actual performance has always been bigger than my own patterns of thought." Performing on his own, George Harrison priggishly refuses to play his Beatle songs as they had first sounded: "The image of my choice is not Beatle George." Paul Simon claims that the dissolution of Simon and Garfunkel is a relief, because "it becomes harder to break out of what people expect you to do."

"Just keep moving around and changing clothes is the best," says John Lennon. "That's all that goes on: *change.*" The formulation of this blunt credo is the subject of Anthony Fawcett's *John Lennon: One Day at a Time*, which describes the sufferings of an artist who was trapped in the part of countercultural hero. As Lennon broke with the Beatles and moved through a series of other frustrating commitments, Fawcett was a sympathetic observer, and has successfully conveyed a sense of Lennon's genuine creativity and resilience. Lennon was miserable for years because he tended to go where he was pointed even if his instincts rebelled, and they often did.

Fawcett concludes that "vulnerability to outside influences lies at the core of John's personality," but that after every disheartening involvement Lennon "would come back to the philosophy that it's in your own head, the answers are within yourself." The thesis illuminates our memories of Lennon's Beatle years. Rock stardom must have been a long spell of bewildering pressure for someone as sensitive as Lennon, who changed his looks repeatedly with different beards and haircuts, as if to protect himself from those who would freeze him into the image of Beatle John. He was ambivalent about the fuss he had helped to create: "And now my life has changed in oh so many ways, / My independence seems to vanish in the haze," he sang at the height of it all. Behind the wordplay and gruesome comedy of his two books, there seems to be a shy man hiding, teasing the world with nonsense. While Paul would always pull a cute face at the camera, Lennon seemed to distrust the universal scrutiny. His mugging seemed defensive, and he would stare straight back at the lens only with Yoko at his side, as if to taunt his old audience with a non-Beatle association.

Even after he broke with the group and sang "I don't believe in Beatles," Lennon moved from cause to cause as zealously as one of his own most volatile fans. The story has a happy ending. Fawcett's book and Pete Hamill's interview in *What's That Sound?* present a contented artist who has neither died nor sold out. Rock's moment has passed, and John Lennon can continue to do his best in whatever way he wants.

GREIL MARCUS IS CONFIDENT THAT LENNON WILL HELP KEEP rock alive. Marcus's fine essay on the Beatles in the *History* ends optimistically: the ex-Beatles, "who saved the game close to fifteen years ago, have no alternative but to work to keep it going." Marcus's other essays in the *History* are unsettling amid the other critics' lamentations, like cheerleaders in a funeral procession. His spirits are bright because he assumes that rock will always bounce back.

Mystery Train is an impressive book, well-informed and frequently hilarious. Marcus begins by establishing two "ancestors," Harmonica Frank and Robert Johnson, "as metaphors more than musical influences." In the early Fifties, Frank expressed rock's irreverent joy; in the Thirties, Johnson foreshadowed rock's violence and fear. Against the "backdrop" of these early chapters, Marcus discusses more recent performers, discerning in their careers conflicts which he sees at the heart of American culture. However, the book's basic opposition is not between happy Frank and Gothic Johnson, but between Dick Clark and Mick Jagger, the good citizen and the disruptive rebel: rock suddenly takes everything by storm, then settles into respectability; when things get dull, rock bursts forth anew, just when Dad begins to feel comfortable.

Marcus mentions Tocqueville, D. H. Lawrence, and Leslie Fiedler, but he is too intelligent to impose critical order on rock's mixed bag. He knows that his subject resists magisterial treatment, although he probably knows more about rock's crazy, trivial history than anyone else. He attacks the crabby purism of critics like Palmer (see the discussion of "Hound Dog" and "Louie Louie"), and with his lively, anecdotal style he puts certain pretentious critics to shame. In fact, there is more of rock's spirit in this book than there is in rock music.

Marcus's light touch befits an inspired piece of pop journalism, but his assumptions are murky. He describes a bland American "mainstream" which "provides such a perfect antithesis to the realities of American life that inevitable discrepancies come out of the woodwork, come with enormous force . . . and with them come the resentment and the humor that keep the soul of the place hanging onto life." Rock expresses these "discrepancies" and will always reassert itself against sameness and complacency. But what if rock has no surprises left? What if its most shocking gestures become detached from its rebellious spirit and become part of the "mainstream" it opposes? Rock seems to need an enemy who will disapprove; it needs to dream of Big Brother, of Dad at the door with an axe. But this implicit argument has become confused since Woodstock, which evoked Huxley's dystopia, not Orwell's. If permissiveness itself becomes complacent, how could rock ever be startling? Because Marcus assumes that complacency must be inhibiting, he overlooks a disquieting possibility: a nation mellowed half to death under the banner of self-discovery.

Ironically, John Lennon still defines the pop culture mentality: "the philosophy that it's in your own head" appeals to millions. This disavowal of public movements has itself become a public movement. The old maxims of the Sixties, "Do your own thing" and "Let it all hang out," guide Dad as he raises his consciousness, studies est, smokes dope, and haunts singles bars (Dad has been divorced for years). Rock may never recover from this widespread liberation.

ROCK TOOK US BY SURPRISE, THEN BECAME FAMILIAR AND imitable. Marcus rightly sees this process as inevitable, but, unlike such musicians as Lennon, he pays little attention to its personal destructiveness. "Elvis: Presliad," his final chapter, is a brilliant reading of Presley's image, but it treats Presley himself as if he *were* his image. There is no mention of Presley's recent reclusiveness and eccentricity, behavior that hints of some deep misery within the walls of Graceland. "These days, Elvis is always singing," Marcus concludes, projecting an image of Presley that resembles Marcus's image of indefatigable rock. Although Marcus's treatment of "myth" in rock music is often rewarding (the chapter on Sly Stone is especially good), "myth" is never distinguished from other exalted terms like "persona," or from terms more appropriate to the rock industry, such as "gimmick" or "pose".

If Marcus were to examine such words, he might not be so sure of rock's good health. In the first flush of rock's excitement, we were amazed and delighted, eager to soar into rock & roll heaven, from whose heights we would look down at Dad, and laugh. There was something happening there, something unworldly and indefinable, as our superlatives suggested: out of sight, far out, too much. Now there is nothing left but after-images, which the critic tries to sort and measure. Having drifted back to earth, rock has been entombed in texts. *Mystery Train*, like these other retrospectives, attempts to tell the continuing story of a finished thing.

Carr, Roy. *The Rolling Stones: An Illustrated Record*. New York: Harmony Books, 1976.

Clark, Dick and Richard Robinson. *Rock, Roll and Remember*. New York: Crowell, 1976.

Fawcett, Anthony. *John Lennon: One Day at a Time*. New York: Grove, 1976.

Fong-Torres, Ben, ed. *What's That Sound?* New York: Doubleday/Anchor, 1976.

Marcus, Greil. *Mystery Train: Images of America in Rock 'n' Roll Music*. New York: Dutton, 1976.

Miller, Jim, ed. *The Rolling Stone Illustrated History of Rock & Roll*. New York: Random House/Rolling Stone, 1976.

Palmer, Tony. *All You Need Is Love: The Story of Popular Music*. New York: Viking, 1976.

The King

∎∎

IN THE FIFTIES, ELVIS PRESLEY APPALLED HIS ELDERS and delighted his fans by singing about sex with obvious pleasure. No matter what the lyrics said, Presley seemed to change them as he sang them. His vast success depended equally on the adulation of teenagers and the revulsion of their parents, for it was Elvis's seeming promise of forbidden things that began all the excitement. This violent national ambivalence was inspired largely by television, because Elvis had to be seen to be believed, or believed in. After gaining a big following, mostly in the South, on the strength of concert tours through 1954 and 1955, he appeared on several television programs in 1956, just after the release of "Heartbreak Hotel," his first million-seller. (He might have appeared the previous year, on Arthur Godfrey's "Talent Scouts," but failed his audition.) Thousands of young viewers were ecstatic, having discovered someone who could tap and reciprocate their own energy. On the other hand, various clergymen and columnists made outraged statements about the imminent decline of American culture.

TODAY IT IS DIFFICULT TO UNDERSTAND THE REACTIONS OF the righteous, who hadn't seen anything yet. A later generation of rock stars would do everything but pull their own heads off onstage; Elvis just got worked up. His act was uncomplicated. He was backed by drums, string bass, and lead guitar, and haphazardly slapped out a sort of rhythm accompaniment on his own guitar, which he used primarily as a prop. Wearing baggy pants and what looked like a very fat person's sportcoat, he wriggled and jerked as if trying to undress without using his hands. He made teasing faces; his smile had a leer built into it. Ed Sullivan tried to mitigate the erotic impact by televising Presley from the waist up (which naturally made the area from the waist down seem doubly intriguing), but this made little difference: the girls in the studio audience screamed, nearly drowning out Presley's voice, a collective display of pubescent desire that made a lot of viewers nervous.

As Elvis drew bigger and more demonstrative adolescent audiences over the three-year period of his stardom in the Fifties, the nervousness also increased, finding a good deal of incoherent expression: Elvis was "morally insane," "a whirling dervish of sex," his music "a sort of nightmare of rhythm." What Elvis's shrill detractors failed to understand, aside from the English language, was the fundamentally symbolic character of those hysterical concerts. Elvis sang and shook all over, the girls wept and squealed, then everybody went home. The libido was getting a lot of bad press (if any) in the Fifties, a situation which Elvis's fans seemed to intuit. It has become a cliché of rock criticism that Elvis was a liberating figure, a pop Henry Miller, who allowed his fans to express themselves sexually. It would be more accurate to say that Elvis provided a lot of young people with an opportunity for vicarious release. If he had really effected a sexual revolution, those legions of girls might have done something more than scream.

In fact, Elvis never acted like a "sex fiend" (to use that quaint expression of the Fifties), but rather like the girls whose fantasies he inspired. Like Marlon Brando, with whom he was often compared, and like James Dean, another contemporary, Presley projected an aggressive vulnerability, a strength that was not so much forceful as passive. He did not strut and glower like a potential rapist, as, say, Jerry Lee Lewis did; it was only in the late Sixties that Elvis began to toughen his image with broad hints of machismo, in songs like "US Male." Elvis was an imploring figure in the Fifties, as many of his biggest hits suggest: "Don't Be Cruel," "I Want You, I Need You, I Love You," "Love Me Tender," "Teddy Bear" ("Baby let me be your lovin' teddy bear, / Put a chain around my neck and lead me anywhere"), and others. Although American pop idols did not become epicene until the Sixties, Elvis, like Dean, Brando, and Montgomery Clift, projected a new masculine type, unlike such frankly virile figures as Clark Gable and John Wayne.

There was also an element of racial novelty in Elvis's appeal, which surely had something to do with the reaction against him, as racism and the fear of uncontrollable sexual appetites have much in common. Elvis's first five singles, recorded for the Sun label in Memphis in 1954 and 1955, suggest a great debt to such black blues singers as Arthur Crudup and Wynonie Harris. Elvis loved black music just as he loved country and western music. Although his hagiographers are surely mistaken in suggesting that he meant his career to improve race relations, it is certainly true that he was the first person in America to get a hysterical white mob to approach a black phenomenon without violating the Bill of Rights.

He sang so convincingly like a black man that his earliest promoter, interviewing him for a Memphis radio station, made sure that Elvis announced to the listening audience that he had attended Humes High School, a discreet way of assuring everyone that the kid was nice and white (one characteristic implying the other). Elvis's appropriation of blackness was not restricted to his music. Again like Brando, he did not look entirely white (a statement that might have annoyed him), but seemed a curious amalgam of the races: with his full lips, broad nose, and jet-black hair (dyed), he was a new kind of idol, looking ahead to such Sixties celebrities as Mick Jagger and Malcolm McDowell. The sleek, aquiline look of Fred Astaire or Leslie Howard was becoming old-fashioned. Is it possible that the heroes of the young are often marked by features that evoke the dispossessed?*

All these faintly subversive traits lost their poignancy when Elvis started taking the advice of Colonel Tom Parker, who became his manager in 1955. For a few years Parker exploited Elvis's image of the essentially good-hearted outlaw: in the films *Love Me Tender* (1956), *Jailhouse Rock* (1957), and *King Creole* (1958), Elvis was variously victimized, killed, or flogged as Brando was often killed or flogged in his definitive films. However, Parker knew that there was far more money to be made than the nation's children could afford to pay, and set about legitimizing Elvis's image. He supervised Elvis's induction, figuring (correctly) that if his charismatic client could serve his country rather than offend it, the conversion would result in fun for the whole family.

Having livened things up for three years, then, Elvis joined the army in 1958 ("It's a duty I've got to fill and I'm gonna do it," he said dutifully), and then, after returning to civilian life in 1960, spent the last seventeen years of his life gaining weight. He tended to corpulence and gorged himself with junk food, but his real weight problem was not physiological. Throughout the Sixties and Seventies, Elvis took on fleets of Cadillacs, dune buggies, snowmobiles, and jets, giving away as many as he kept. He expanded Graceland, his Memphis mansion, where he surrounded himself with expensive gadgets and hired attendants. He bought other estates, including a ranch in Mississippi. He wore rings and pistols and capes and massive gold buckles. He collected badges and trophies and rifles. He would not leave the house by himself.

THE COLONEL HAD PROMISED TO MAKE ELVIS RICH, AND kept that promise, but exacted complete trust in return. He was a shrewd entrepreneur, but his guidance of Elvis's career does not

---

* Not any more. Today "the heroes of the young" are reminiscent not of the underclass, but of the "past"—i.e., old movies, old TV shows, dated fashions—which they revive in the all-pervasive spirit of parody. This shows, obliquely, the influence of TV. While Elvis's mien and music, or Mick Jagger's, could arouse the dancers with an illusion of solidarity, the hippest acts today—Madonna, Prince, David Bowie—seek rather to gratify the sense of spectatorial irony.

suggest much sensitivity. He worked out an agreement with the producer Hal Wallis, who acquired Elvis for a series of idiotic low-budget films that corroborated the comforting new image which the Colonel had chosen: in most of them, Elvis plays a swell guy who's a big hit with several large-breasted women, leading to romantic entanglements and the occasional fistfight. These films all made huge profits, and bored Elvis, who turned out an average of three a year from 1960 to 1969. He was bitter about having to work with "lousy scripts," and resented the fact that Wallis used the profits from *Blue Hawaii*, which, like every other Presley film, was a critical disaster, to make *Becket*, a critical success. A few years before he died, Elvis was offered the male lead opposite Barbra Streisand in *A Star Is Born*. This might have provided him with an opportunity to do something interesting for a change. He liked the idea, but the Colonel told him that he wouldn't get enough money.

Perhaps the Colonel had to ignore Elvis's potential talents in order to keep his original promise. Certainly, he knew how to keep Elvis timely long after the initial blaze of fame had cooled considerably. In 1968 Elvis released "If I Can Dream," and released "In the Ghetto" the following year: both songs (one hopeful, one somber) are socially conscious, and both sold well after a three-year period of flops. What is more remarkable than Elvis's sudden use of fashionable material, however, is the fact of his professional longevity, which was the result of a peculiar aspect of his charisma. The Colonel did not create this quality, but knew how to enhance and preserve it.

Although Elvis remained for twenty years the world's highest-paid performer, his fans, throughout the Sixties and Seventies, were cultists, indulging a fondness that had become eccentric. Those who pledged allegiance to "the King" were, by and large, not likely to enjoy the irreverent poses of the idols of the Sixties. For all the ebullience of their music, the Beatles seemed somewhat too cool and impudent; Bob Dylan, rasping out jeremiads, was too much of a beatnik to please Presley's more conservative worshipers: for worshipers they were, having come to regard their idol as a god. While Dylan and the Beatles, attuned to the times, treated their stardom with irony, Elvis remained inaccessible.

Celebrities of the Sixties replaced the pose of deity with a pose of casual sincerity. We watched Dylan throw tantrums in *Don't Look Back*, and witnessed the dissolution of the Beatles in *Let It Be*. Elvis's last two films, *Elvis . . . That's the Way It Is* (1970) and *Elvis on Tour* (1972) were also documentaries, but conveyed no sense of having found a private person. Dylan's songs, ostensibly dealing with social injustice, were actually bits of autobiography; the Beatles squabbled and got divorced with much publicity, whereupon John Lennon sang laments about his mother, and George Harrison described the scenery on his spiritual pilgrimage. Elvis never wrote his own songs (although the Colonel often managed to wrangle coauthorship royalties for his client), and never made any obvious personal statement.

HE WAS PROCLAIMED "THE KING" NOT BECAUSE HE WAS THE first great rock star, nor because he outsold and outlasted every other contender for the crown; that crown was not available to successors, for Elvis's magnificent voice is inimitable (as his dozens of professional imitators make very clear), and the peculiar circumstances of his initial stardom unrepeatable. Elvis's aura of regality evolved from a special quality of his personal style, an air of impenetrable self-possession. He was an iconic figure, ever ready for the adoring public eye, in other words, ever like a king. Until the early Seventies, when he began to go onstage sick, bloated, truculent, and heavy with contempt (he would practice karate kicks between songs, and sometimes read lyrics from a piece of paper), there seemed to be no disjunction between the public and the private man. In thousands of photographs he appears confident, magnetic, essentially reserved, and without any distinct personality whatever.

He projected an inwardness without introspection, at once offering and withholding himself, and was therefore the perfect object of mass worship. Unattainable, he was an entity of inscrutable surface upon which his fans could easily project their desires. To those who aged and fattened along with him, he was still the daring hero of the Fifties; to those who wished to believe in someone quintessentially American, he was a saint. When Elvis lurched tubbily through his concerts during the past few years, forcing out fragments of his old hits over an extra chin, his devotees reacted with the usual enthusiasm, seeing not a bored and ailing man but the King himself rocking down Memory Lane. His opaque, impersonal veneer allowed his fans to believe that he evinced whatever qualities they most admired: he was generous, courteous, wholesome, manly, reverent but good-humored, gentle but, if pushed too far, a tough guy. He was everything the Sixties seemed to discredit. In the eyes of the faithful the King was a regular prince.

Some of the recent books on Elvis provide us with similarly happy impressions. *The Private Elvis* is an exercise in wishful thinking by a reporter who would like very much for us to believe that she and Elvis were friends. They first met, May Mann claims, in 1957 on the set of *King Creole* (which began production in 1958), where Elvis was supposedly going through a scene that bored him, until he noticed the author sitting nearby, whereupon: "The music seemed to ripple from his body in the sheath of shimmering sex that no one has ever been able to emulate."

What was "the private Elvis" like, under the sheath? Mann mentions "his shining, wholesome character, honesty, integrity, and the real human, kind, compassionate side of his nature," and makes similar statements for nearly 300 pages, at one point asserting that "from the inception of his career, Elvis Presley has been the most bombastic and controversial figure in show business." The book also contains several pictures of "Elvis with the author," who stares worshipfully into his right ear while he looks intently elsewhere. These pictures, at least, have the ring of truth.

My Life with Elvis, "The Fond Memories of a Fan Who Became Elvis's Private Secretary," is a bit misleading: Becky Yancey was one of two women who worked for Elvis's father Vernon at Graceland. Yancey did not exactly have a "life with Elvis," since she went home at five every day, about two hours after Elvis climbed out of bed. Furthermore, Elvis was in Los Angeles and elsewhere at least as often as he was in Memphis during Yancey's tenure. In fact, she knows so little about Elvis that her publisher has seen fit to make a paragraph out of nearly every sentence, and to separate the chapters with title pages, methods that have added about thirty pages to this slight book. Yancey discusses how much Elvis's wife Priscilla liked tuna fish, mentions the time that Elvis's chimpanzee tried to pull off her skirt, and discusses Grandma Presley's fierce temper. When Yancey first met Elvis in 1961, she threw up on him. No subsequent encounter was as memorable as that.

Nevertheless, Yancey is sure that Elvis "remembered the Golden Rule and treated others as he hoped to be treated. Certainly, there were times when his temper flared, but Elvis always tried to do what was right." Yancey and her collaborator Cliff Linedecker (a writer whose speciality is "the unknown") were evidently in a big hurry to let the world know what a good person Elvis was. *My Life with Elvis* was begun before Presley died, and was not very carefully revised or proofread before it was rushed into publication three months early to cash in on his death. Many of the references to his tastes and habits are still in the present tense, and the reader who does not pass out before page 50 will come across such sentences as "Priscilla like hair pieces" and "In return, Linda turn Elvis on to 'Whammies.'"

These two books are well padded with chatter and trivia because Elvis never seems to have broken through his aura to provide these observers with material. It was not likely, moreover, that a competent writer would have gotten close to Elvis, who preferred the company of hired toadies willing to surrender themselves to his will and largesse. The outsider has only the inadequate reports of these insiders to work with. Even Jerry Hopkins's thorough and dispassionate *Elvis: A Biography* (which ends in 1971, leaving Elvis still married and supposedly happy), as good, perhaps, as an outsider's book can be, devotes several pages to the history of Tupelo, Mississippi (Presley's birthplace), and other ancillary matters.

THE MOST REVEALING OF THESE BOOKS, AND SURELY THE most sensationalist, is *Elvis: What Happened?*, a horrifying collection of the reminiscences of three men who worked for years as part of Elvis's toady collective. Steve Dunleavy (one of Rupert Murdoch's toadies) has reworked the men's impressions into a lurid, scattered narrative that owes something to the works of Mickey Spillane and several episodes of "Starsky and Hutch." The three men, Red West, Sonny West, and Dave Hebler, were suddenly dumped after twenty, sixteen, and three years of service respectively, and it would therefore be easy to dismiss their stories as the highly colored tattlings of disgruntled employees.

Despite the book's tawdriness, however, and despite the strong possibility that the motives of the tale-tellers were not admirable, *Elvis: What Happened?* is convincing, and certainly not padded. If we are to believe what we read, Elvis gradually became an explosive megalomaniac as his wealth and boredom increased over the years. His body was ravaged by pills. He loved guns, and regularly shot out television sets and light fixtures, sometimes nearly killing various acquaintances. He was obsessed with law enforcement, tagged along on narcotics investigations in Memphis, and was so intent on getting himself a real narc's badge (an honorary one wouldn't do) that he finally went to see another maniac, then this country's president, and got what he wanted. He was cruel to his "friends" (it is hard to find an accurate word for hired companions), intolerant of other performers, anti-Semitic, anti-Catholic, and contemptuous of women, causing at least three of them serious physical injury. If he believed in the Golden Rule, he must have been a masochist.

The men frequently interrupt these stories to grieve over the transformation of good old Elvis into an unpredictable monster. Time and again they express disgust or embarrassment over Elvis's deeds, raising an obvious question: Why did they stay? ("He certainly had a power over us," admits Red West in an understatement.) And what was it about good old Elvis that was so good? The men chuckle over the hours of wacky horseplay Elvis initiated: team fights with Roman candles, chasing a runaway tractor, knocking down a three-bedroom house with bulldozers. As long as Elvis was such a fun-loving, open-handed guy, he was "beautiful," but when he exploited the master's prerogative, giving

191

orders, bursting into vituperation, treating his underlings with contempt, he was no fun any more. Whichever way he struck his friends, he never seems to have managed to grow up. The most depressing thing about *Elvis: What Happened?* is that its authors, who knew Elvis as well as anyone did, seem not to have known him at all. They knew his moods, appreciated his maniacal generosity, but were finally unable to discover him.

IT SEEMS THAT NO ONE COULD DISCOVER HIM, FOR HE BOLstered his reclusiveness, weighing himself down, walling himself in. The King led a monarch's life of opulent seclusion; circumstances, both within and beyond his control, made impossible his lone entry into the world of commoners. He adored his mother, who walked him to school every day until he was fifteen. She protected him from many of the painful things that attend a life of poverty; according to Red West, she once pelted a boy with groceries for threatening her son. Upon her death in 1958, Elvis was already an international celebrity, just beginning his army stint. After his return to civilian life, he started putting on all that glittering protective weight.

His construction of a microcosm evokes the image of a Snopes family in the Space Age. Graceland, the home of the organization that was himself, was tended by a large vague clan of Presleys and deputy Presleys, each squandering the vast gratuities which Elvis used to keep his whole world smiling. Vernon Presley had a swimming pool in his bedroom. Elvis's stepmother had her breasts lifted. Priscilla had her ears flattened. Elvis had his face lifted. Peacocks ran about the grounds, and one once attacked its reflection in the hood of a Rolls Royce. There was a jukebox next to the swimming pool, containing Elvis's favorite records. What did the "whirling dervish of sex," once called "the Hillbilly Cat" and "the King of Western Bop," play on that bright machine? His favorite songs were "Gigi," "What Now My Love?" and "Autumn Leaves." Even his music had gotten fat.

Elvis carefully tended his little world with such costly cosmetic touches, living as the retired spectator of his own things. He would spend hours in his bedroom, watching his property on a closed-circuit television. "He lives in a shell but he's comfortable," said Nancy Sinatra in the late Sixties, raising questions about the meaning of "comfort." Elvis seems to have wanted to bedeck himself into oblivion; his career was a long process of accretion, at home and onstage. Shortly before he died, he started carpeting the ceilings.

ELVIS'S DEATH HAS TRANSFORMED THE STUFF OF SCANDAL sheets into expressions of something like polemical controversy: Who was the "real" Elvis? Was this King no more than a Great Pretender? May Mann's book, originally called *Elvis and the Colonel*, was tellingly retitled to cash in on the vanished mystery; *Elvis: What Happened?* was intended, says Sonny West, "to present Elvis with a challenge," but Elvis's death has changed the title's emphasis. The book is now a challenge to the faithful.

It will probably make no more difference to them than the discovery of the Dead Sea Scrolls made to the Fundamentalists. Elvis's fans were never interested in the possibility of a human Elvis, but worshiped him for reflecting their own wishes. The search for the real person will end without success. The King is gone, but the aura remains, making a lot of people very rich. "The Colonel's plans are the same today as if Elvis were still here," said Elvis's road manager just after the funeral. What used to be sold as "souvenirs" at every concert are now advertised as precious relics on late-night television commercials and in the back pages of cheap magazines: wristwatches, medallions, idealized portraits (Elvis as a rock Jesus), t-shirts, hideous macrocephalic dolls, special albums, memorial books. The Colonel gets a piece of the action. Does Elvis symbolize less for his fans merely because he happens to have died? The very quality that made his fans adore him has made his death seem like an afterthought.

———

Hopkins, Jerry. *Elvis: A Biography*. New York: Simon and Schuster, 1977.

Mann, May. *The Private Elvis*. New York: Pocket Books, 1977.

West, Red, Sonny West, and Dave Hebler, as told to Steve Dunleavy. *Elvis: What Happened?* New York: Ballantine Books, 1977.

Yancey, Becky and Cliff Linedecker. *My Life with Elvis: The Fond Memories of a Fan Who Became Elvis's Private Secretary*. New York: St. Martin's, 1977.

Dead captain steers old ghost ship into port

WEEKLY WORLD
NEWS
55¢

May 24, 1988   30587   VOL. 9, Issue 33

CUPID'S CALLING!
Man's wrong number gets him a bride

Sneak preview of blockbuster new book!

ELVIS IS ALIVE!

Horror movie scares dog to death!

The King admits his funeral was faked and tells of secret life in Michigan!

ARTIST'S CONCEPTION of how Elvis Presley looks today at the age of 53. The King is living a quiet life — far from his millions of adoring fans.

Sex-change mom begs doc: 'Turn me back into a man'

Teen marries boyfriend's grandfather

Bug-size UFO found on playground!

ROCK MUSIC: A SUCCESS STORY
Afterword

■ ■

IN EARLY 1977, I WAS WRONG TO CALL ROCK MUSIC "a finished thing," because it was then just coming up for the third time. After the Age of Elvis and then the Sixties, there was now an unexpected coda, a (roughly) five-year period remarkable not only for its sudden musical inventiveness, but for its somber tone. This period of "New Wave rock" (entailing punk and other fleeting subgenres) had none of that innocent exhilaration, that sense of generational awakening, which had twice before infused the music. In this post- and anti-Woodstock phase, rather, the mood was one of bitterness and disenchantment. Now the most distinctive singers—Debbie Harry, Johnny Rotten, Joe Strummer, Graham Parker, Nick Lowe, and the brilliant Elvis Costello, among others—sang without trying to sound like Southern blacks, thereby making the Jaggerian drawl and twang sound a little silly; and in their plain accents—whether British or American—they tended to sing not about love or any other affirmative experience, but about death by overdose, abortion, goon squads, colonial occupation, TV news, the wrecking ball.

In the Sixties too, rock had, of course, reflected on some ugly subjects, but even its darkest numbers then were (for the most part) laced with a romantic sweetness, and often further pastoralized by the vocal Southernisms. Eleven years after "the Summer of Love," rock—at its best—was all but purified of that earlier transcendent impulse; and rock at its worst was similarly pure. Whereas the ornate and hypnotic riffs of Cream, the Doors, and Jimi Hendrix (to name a few) had, in the Sixties, countered the expansionist status quo with an ideal of narcotic inwardness, their loudest emulators in the Seventies—the practitioners of "Heavy Metal"—offered mere pounding fantasies of might, guitars and singers frankly screaming.

The disenchantment of rock did seem finally to clear the air of a lot of pious jive left over from the Sixties. Unfortunately, that fading jive was all that stood between the music and the advertisers. "Even as it sang of new worlds," I wrote in 1977, "rock was always on its way to selling out." In retrospect, one might reword it this way: "As long as it kept singing of new worlds, rock could not sell out completely." Once

195

disabused of all the old utopian notions, rock's makers, listeners, and promoters were free to see the music as a mere sales device—or rather, free to *watch* the music making sales: for rock and roll, once too wild for television, became, after c. 1981, a necessary adjunct of TV's all-pervasive ad.

In other words, right after rock's third wave, or last gasp, TV absorbed the music absolutely, going far beyond the mere domestication that I observed in 1977. By the mid-Eighties, TV had not just "incorporated rock and roll and all its faded symbols," but had actually transformed the music, turning the experience of rock into a televisual experience. Of course there were, in the Eighties, still good albums coming out, but nowhere near as many, and almost none as good, as what had been available ten, twenty, thirty years before. The point here, however, is not just the comparative dullness of rock in the Eighties—an arguable matter, after all—but the reason for that dullness: TV had blunted rock's kinetic impact for the sake of the commodity.

Commercial from the beginning, rock now became a mere commercial means—the new soundtrack for TV's commercials. In the mid-Eighties, advertisers started grabbing every serviceable oldie in the rock and roll canon, hoping that each vivid tag might jump-start the nostalgic yearnings of the aging viewer. This was, and is, a deliberate project. "This music was once the most important thing in the lives of the people we're trying to sell cars to now," said a senior v-p and "music director" at Young & Rubicam in 1987, referring, indirectly, to Ford's Mercury account. "This music creates a good feeling. People start remembering some of the best times in their lives, when they were carefree." Similarly, William M. Backer, President of Backer & Spielvogel, noted the "tremendous nostalgia in the over-35 group for songs of the late 50s and early 60s. They're less heavy and less serious than today's, and they say a lot of things that automotive advertisers want to say."

It might come as news to many in "the over-35 group" that when, say, the Ronettes sang, "I'll make you happy, baby, just wait and see,/ For every kiss you give me, I'll give you three," what they actually meant was something like, "6-YEAR/60,000-MILE POWERTRAIN WARRANTY!" Such a translation would not surprise the ad people, however, since their only aim in life is to displace all your desires onto the client's product, whatever it may be. Thus they can see nothing wrong with revising an old love song so that it seems to woo a hatchback or a cheeseburger, a bowl of cereal or a chicken snack, as they have done, for example, by using "Ain't No Mountain High Enough" to pitch Fords, by redoing the Platters' "Only You" as "Only Wendy's," by using the Turtles' "Happy Together" to sell General Mills' Golden Grahams, and by using the Diamonds' "Little Darlin'" to push the "Chicken Little" sandwich for Kentucky Fried Chicken Corp. Obsessed with the account, they have no qualms about distorting some great "jump side" of the past, so that a song once meant to get you up and dancing now has you sitting there and humming about "breakfast bagels" or drain cleaners or granola bars, as was the case, in 1987, with Bobby Darin's "Splish Splash," used to sell Drano, and with Jerry Lee Lewis's "Whole Lotta Shakin' Goin' On," redone for Burger King as "Whole Lotta Breakfast Goin' On," and with Danny and the Juniors' "At the Hop," now better known as "Let's Go Take a Dipp," i.e., a Granola Dipp from Quaker Oats.

Formerly, rock would often make fun of its high-cultural antecedents, as a way to celebrate itself: "Roll over, Beethoven!" sang one old master in his early manhood. Now the best rock songs are themselves routinely ironized, as another way to celebrate the commodity. (And that irony itself expresses the commodity: see above, pp. 15–16.) Songs once passionate are now a joke; to try remembering their intensity is only to replay a subversive jingle in your head, now that "Hurt So Bad" is a song about disposable razors from Gillette, and "I Can't Help Myself" is a song about a brownie mix from Duncan Hines. Now, viewer, try to listen to "I Heard It Through the Grapevine" without thinking about raisins. And try now to recall the utopian dimension of those songs that once suggested bettering the world, but that have since become mere ads within it: the Beatles' ambivalent "Revolution" from 1968, used to sell running shoes in 1987, which was also the year that "The Age of Aquarius" stopped referring to the dawn of the Millennium, and became instead an ad for the Ford Aerostar van.

It was not Dad, then, who finally did the music in, but certain of its own devoted fans: "The people in decision-making positions nowadays," observed rock critic Robert Palmer in 1987, "are the people who grew up with rock and roll." It would be wrong, however, to blame the great commercial tie-in only on the youngish members of the marketing establishment, because the musicians too have done their part. When Dave Clark refused, in 1985, to let Union Carbide have "Glad All Over" (to sell Glad Bags), he was behaving strangely for a rock composer. Paul McCartney, another of the few holdouts, was said to be livid over the corporate use of "Revolution" and some other Beatle hits, which had been sold by Michael Jackson, now owner of the rights: McCartney, along with George Harrison and Ringo Starr, sued Nike over the song's appropriation. (McCartney is less protective of the works of others. The owner of many songs, he sold, in 1987, Buddy Holly's "Oh Boy!", which thenceforth went like this: "All my life, I've been waiting,/ Today there'll be no hesitating—/ Oh Buick!")

Rock musicians have not only sold the songs that make the whole

197

BOXED IN

■ ■ ■ ■ ■ ■

world sing, but have even personally sung them. Linda Ronstadt, who would not redo her hit "Get Closer" for J. Walter Thompson's Close-Up toothpaste campaign, "is clearly the exception," *The Wall Street Journal* noted in 1987. "When you hold up a lot of money," observed one Thompson manager, "there are few people today who stand on principle." (Chubby Checker refused to do "The Twist" to sell a power screwdriver, but only because Skil Corp. would not pay him enough.) Rod Stewart, Phil Collins, Roberta Flack, Fats Domino, Aretha Franklin, Stevie Wonder, and Chuck Berry, to name just a few, have all covered earlier hits for the advertisers, while others have actually performed in the commercials, either kicking out the jams, like (for example) Michael Jackson, Lionel Richie, David Bowie and Tina Turner for Pepsi, or just doing a hip walk-on, like (for example) Lou Reed and Grace Jones for Honda.

Thus has rock past been retroactively translated into advertising. In the culture of TV, however, it is not just the oldies that are put to this commercial use, for a rock song today might be converted to a jingle at the moment it becomes a hit. And if the rights are too pricey, there are "stock-music houses" that specialize in counterfeits: "If you say you want [Madonna's] 'Like a Virgin,'" said a producer at Ted Bates Advertising in 1986, "these guys can pull out a piece of music that is so close, it's almost unbelievable—but it's different enough to be legally okay." On the other hand, if an advertiser can afford the song but not the singer, there are ways to fake that special voice: "With the sophisticated electronic equipment in recording studios today, companies can come very close to duplicating a popular singer's voice," remarked one promoter in 1987. While not always "legally okay," this use of "sound-alikes" has enabled, for instance, "Arlo Guthrie" to sing "The City of New Orleans" for Oldsmobile, "Tom Petty" to sing "Mary's New Car" for B.F. Goodrich, "Nancy Sinatra" to sing "These Boots Are Made for Walking" for Goodyear, and "the Beatles" to sing "Help!" for Ford's Lincoln-Mercury division. ("Former Beatles producer George Martin," reported *Advertising Age* in 1985, "helped recreate the sound of 'Help' in London's Air Studios and assisted in selecting U.K. singers who sounded like the original Beatles.")

Whether using originals or fakes, the advertisers have—through TV—de-eroticized the music. They have done this, first of all, by making rock refer not to the happy body of another, but to a Coke, a candy bar, a Honda, Drano, Schlitz, Sony: "Do you want to dance, under the moonlight, / Thrill me all through the night?" sings the imploring voice of "Bette Midler" to (evidently) a dark Ford zooming elliptically across a twilit beach.

And as TV has transformed rock into a new vehicle for the commodity fetish, so has TV denatured the music by turning it into spectacle. The all-important beat, once meant to get you moving, is now a mere hypnotic complement to the hypnotic images of TV advertising, requiring you to stare instead of boogie. Thus rock has been turned into its opposite—a means of keeping everybody separated, sitting still and buying everything. "Go to the jungle and they have the rhythm and it goes throughout the world and it's as simple as that," said John Lennon in 1970. "You get the rhythm going, everybody gets into it." This hopeful invocation of (literal) collective movement has taken on a grim new meaning since the rise of "music marketing." Now "everybody gets into it," but it is TV, not "the jungle," that sets the beat—and so the music is no threat: "I think the [rock] videos have gone a long way in demonstrating to advertisers and agencies that these artists are very presentable," noted BBDO's Philip Dusenberry in 1984.

Rock critics, who have a job to do, tend to scoff at the suggestion that the music turned boring in the Eighties: "Nostalgia!" they hoot predictably, and then list a dozen "hot" new albums, as if such a catalog might prove that rock is still "alive and well." But if rock is a drag in concert, its well-being is at risk, however many CD's sold last week—and TV, unmistakably, has deadened the atmosphere of rock's live shows. "For a certain class of performer," observed Jon Pareles in September 1985, in a remarkable "Critic's Notebook" in the *New York Times*, "young girls happily play the roles that they've seen other young girls enact in video clips, screaming and rushing for the stage. More often, however, the response is at the other extreme. . . . At concerts by bands whose careers were spurred by video exposure, audiences are likely just to sit there."

They don't tap their toes. They don't shout along with lyrics, or react when a singer slips a local reference into a song. They hardly reply when a performer addresses them directly; they have to be urged, "Say yeah!" When Madonna performed at Radio City Music Hall, her dress-alike fans dutifully stood up on their chairs and, barely moving a muscle, watched. And Madonna sings dance music.

Bruce Springsteen, for probably the first time in his career, had something similar happen when he played Giants Stadium. For a decade, Mr. Springsteen has drawn hugely devoted, eager fans who know every song by heart. In the past year, however, his commercial fortunes—and video exposure—have skyrocketed, and at Giants Stadium his core audience was diluted. For every sing-along, stomp-along fan, there were two or three silent watchers.

199

"Like any music with African roots," Pareles concluded, "rock calls for participation; something is missing without it. The kick of unpredictability is essential to live music—assuming an audience is willing to notice it."

Thus rock itself has been boxed in, despite its early promise of a way out—out of this world, or at least out of the house for some fun tonight. Rock's pleasurable basis now is not the dancing body, or bodies making love, or even the delicious yawn and stretch of the body stoned. On the contrary: rock's fading thrill today arises from our very disembodiment, for rock is now the music of technological enclosure. Boxed in, we enjoy the music all the more, although that boxing-in has helped to make the music joyless: " 'It's an entirely different ball game for advertisers because music has become a bigger part of people's lives,' " an executive v-p at Grey Advertising told the *Wall Street Journal* in 1985. "He notes the large following that music-video programs have attracted and the legions of people plugged into radio ear phones"—and, he might have added, the millions en route to and from the job, sedentarily bopping to the gorgeous rhythms of the car stereo.

Here, then, is a music that is no longer strummed, blown, and banged, but programmed, and then received in solitude by immobile millions watching TV, or driving to work, or "plugged into" Walkmans, or sitting through live performances as "silent watchers" lost in memory of the video. Here is a music whose players and composers now collude overtly with the multinationals, helping to pitch a thousand products, and, on TV, appearing "very presentable" to the "advertisers and agencies." Here, moreover, is a music that is now acceptable to many on the right, and that is in no way at odds with what some used to call "the power structure": Jacques Chirac, wearing blue jeans and a Walkman, went eagerly to hear Madonna's Paris concert in the fall of 1987; and in January 1988, the *Christian Science Monitor*, in a report on "the American debut of Avtograf, one of the Soviet Union's better-known rock bands," included this suggestive passage: " 'I thought it would be a gas to watch Reagan do the State of the Union, then check this out,' said a short, pudgy fellow who, in his daytime incarnation, works as an analyst for the State Department. 'They aren't bad.' "

And yet, despite all such evidence to the contrary, rock is still automatically applauded as a heroic force of freedom and dissent, forever rising up against authority—so applauded by the authorities who have destroyed it. "It's the voice of rebellion," commented an MTV spokesman in 1987. Evidently, "the romance of persecution" dies hard. In films like *Footloose, The Buddy Holly Story,* and *Dirty Dancing,* among others, and in countless rock videos, and in almost as many regular TV commercials, the spectacle solicits the allegiance of the viewer by

200

showing rock defiant, challenging and overcoming the repressive Dad of old: "Yes, we *will* dance!" the scene cries out heroically, as if this were 1956—and as if the scene itself were not requiring us to sit still for it.

Now that rock has become a force to reckon with behind the Iron Curtain, it may well have rediscovered, in Moscow, Warsaw, Budapest, the intensity and drive of its early years in the United States and Britain. Over there, its antiauthoritarianism is convincing (or will be, until the authorities have learned how to kill it with kindness). Over here, its implications of "rebellion" are a corporate joke, like the hundreds of songs sold out to advertising. "The same bastards are in control, the same people are runnin' everything, it's exactly the same. They hyped the kids and the generation." So said John Lennon in 1970, when asked what difference rock had made since 1963. Unbearably, he is not around to say it now.■

The Promise of Cinema

The Lives of the Stars

W E MAY HAVE A LOT TO LEARN ABOUT WATCHING movies, but we're very good at seeing through them. People know how to jeer at the old-fashioned propaganda turned out by Hollywood for nearly half a century, from D. W. Griffith's (racist) *Birth of a Nation* in 1915 to Doris Day's (sexist) comedies of the early 1960s. "It is, generally, a bad time for illusions," writes Mickey Rooney, brooding over the disappearance of "nice clean movies" and "the illusion of the great star." Most would agree, but not mournfully. Having had our consciousness raised over the past fifteen years, we are proud enough of our awakening to shrug off all our naive dreams.

For example, it is now doubted that a lot of wishing and a little struggling invariably pay off. (The success of *Rocky* is only a fluke.) According to the old movies, success always comes to the peppy and the resolute. Those kids in the chorus get that bilious entrepreneur to lighten up and tap his feet, and so it's on to Broadway! That earnest lawyer-fella touches the hearts of decent folks all over, and so it's on to the White House! While artists usually succumb to the agonies of Genius, inventors, athletes, scientists, and businessmen, people with a Great Gift or a Great Idea, end up quickly vindicated and beloved, looking benevolent in powdered hair.

At the same time, many movies dramatized the sorrows of the wealthy, as if to assure us that we were better off as we were—with the sun in the morning and the moon at night and a diet of Spam. Throughout the Depression, the movies implied that money was poison, that only regular folks knew how to have fun, that the rich and their lackeys seemed faintly European, or worse. And in later films like *Caught, Humoresque, Young Man with a Horn,* and *A Place in the Sun*, among others, a humble person's romance with someone wealthier leads straight to disaster. Although the travails of the rich continue to provide Americans with a vindictive thrill, class conflict is no longer part of the story. When we see a bunch of stuffed shirts vexed by some happy-go-lucky man of the people, we sense that the moment is old-fashioned, as in *Heaven Can Wait* (based on *Here Comes Mr. Jordan*, 1941) or

Hair (which alludes heavily to *Hallelujah I'm a Bum*, 1933). (The success of these recent films is probably a fluke.)

From the 1940s through the early 1960s, the movies taught that women who worked in office buildings were always sad. Whether boss or secretary, the working woman continually fought the melancholy of life without a man. The secretary was a little better off, since she at least could serve the guy of her dreams, concealing her adoration under brisk efficiency. The female executive was far more wretched. She had to strain to seem commanding, like an adolescent knowing that his voice might crack at any moment. Her employees were always handsome men, strolling into her office, leaning on her desk, every suave phrase really meaning: "How about it?" After fighting these assaults for a while with clipped retorts and starchy looks, she would finally give in, loosen her collar, let down her hair, and murmur "Darling!" in the arms of her rightful master.

The same dilemma was frequently played out "backstage," as *chanteuses* and actresses slowly went to pieces over the lure of the spotlight. These movies all told cautionary tales, drawn from "real life," of girls gone wrong: in *Jeanne Eagels, The Helen Morgan Story, Where Love Has Gone* (about Lana Turner), *Funny Girl* and *Rose of Washington Square* (Fanny Brice), *Love Me or Leave Me* (Ruth Etting), *Too Much Too Soon* (Diana Barrymore) and *Lady Sings the Blues* (Billie Holiday), women who perform for a living end up painfully attached to various creeps and hoodlums, presumably because the nice guys go to those sensible girls who turn in their greasepaint or stay home from the office. In these sad stories, the only alternative to wedded bliss is self-destruction through drugs, alcohol, bad company, or all three. The suspicion that female performers lead wicked lives is apparently, after nearly 400 years, a thing of the past. (The success of *Lady Sings the Blues* is surely a fluke. And if *The Rose*, a forthcoming movie based on Janis Joplin's life, becomes a hit, that too will be a fluke.*)

While American women vainly fought their biological imperative, their European sisters knew better. The European heroine would never button up her femininity in man-tailored tweed (unless, like Dietrich, she meant to be outrageous), nor could she be led astray by her passion for the limelight. Occasionally some "Russian" woman, played by Greta Garbo *(Ninotchka)* or Hedy Lamarr *(Comrade X)*, might forget her tender feelings and spout a lot of commie hogwash, but such ideological corruption was unusual (and short-lived). The European woman Lived for Love. The insouciant Parisian whore, the Italian earth mother, the

---

The Rose was a hit.

Hispanic she-devil: all lived to grimace in a man's embrace, and to pick up, in loving wonderment, an occasional baby.

In order to perpetuate these and other myths, Hollywood needed a myth of its own, as thrilling as the best American movies. "That land, called Hollywood," writes Raoul Walsh, "was a mythical abstraction without geographical boundaries." If we have outgrown the myths reflected in the movies, we have also outgrown that "mythical abstraction," in which so many of America's ideals found subtle expression.

"Hollywood" was the golden terminus of westward expansion, epitomizing all the wonders of the New World: a soft climate, unprecedented freedom, ubiquitous gold. Gold sweetened the oranges, burnished the sunny leaves, covered the hillsides with a reddish haze. For decades, thousands traveled west in a second Gold Rush, to test the words of Horatio Alger and the Word of God; for Divine Providence seemed to do its most spectacular work in Hollywood. Any John Doe might suddenly find himself with an elegant new name and hundreds of shoes.

Even as it attested to God's bounty and Manifest Destiny, Hollywood was known to be a city of sin: its skies were not cloudy all day, its nights were delicious. Despite this fabled lewdness, however, the biggest stars seemed immune to scandal. "All the big names," writes Eddie Cantor, "were sober, earnest people who lived on diets and answered fan mail." Those who gave Hollywood a bad name couched (so to speak) far from the limelight: ambitious extras, shopgirls on the make, unscrupulous Jews with "connections." In other words, while Hollywood's climbers and middlemen merged in coital frenzy, Crawford, Gable, Grant, Power, Wayne, Davis, et al. spent their evenings at the hearth, reading from the Bible between sips of Ovaltine.

It was not just some lingering Victorian bias that made this myth so popular, but a widespread longing to believe that the stars were as strong in real life as they seemed in the movies. Scandal, the disquieting revelation of physical need, was too suggestive of mortality. As Hollywood's elect, the stars were expected, whether on or off the screen, to deny the inevitability of death: their movies had happy endings, their lives had none. Their divorces never seemed like terminal rifts, but good things for all concerned. Every time they married, it was for keeps. Their funerals were often like premieres, their crypts like theater lobbies. And those who met disaster with a bang—Arbuckle, Garfield, Frances Farmer—were officially forgotten.

Now Hollywood is merely an industrial district with a colorful past, and its myth has dwindled into anecdotes and camp. As we have put the movies' myths behind us, so are we indifferent to the glory that was MGM, the grandeur that was Romanoff's. The stars, we now realize, were just everyday people in stellar disguise. Like life itself, they were "improved" by the studios.

There is no more vivid treatment of Hollywood's expert deceptions than Penny Stallings's *Flesh and Fantasy,* "a sort of catalogue of movie related gossip" filled with remarkable stills, many "never-before-published." Stallings's pictorial assemblage is as clever as her prose, taking the stars from the Hollywood firmament, showing them on the job and on the make. There are early portraits of the yet-to-be-remodeled (the young Garbo looking plump and woozy, the aspiring Hayworth without much forehead), pictures demonstrating how entire careers were based on vague resemblance (Cary Grant begat Gig Young, Grace Kelly begat Dina Merrill and Tippi Hedren), and publicity photos with the retouching taken out, showing, among other flaws, Van Johnson's scars, Adolphe Menjou's hairy fingers, and Claudette Colbert's lack of neck. This book seems to document every noteworthy instance of baldness, shortness, crossed eyes, false teeth, protruding ears, excess hair, and excess nose.

Stallings wittily subverts the myth of Hollywood in all its forms. She tells us what it really takes to win an Oscar. For instance, "Be deserving the year before" (Joan Fontaine, Glenda Jackson), "Wear a funny nose" (José Ferrer as Cyrano, Lee Marvin in *Cat Ballou*), or "Expire" (Peter Finch). She commemorates, with pages of stills, some of Hollywood's least convincing versions of humankind, such as the "oriental" (taped eyes, heavy lipstick, embalmed smile), the "old" (head tilted, gummy pout, frosted eyebrows), and the "legendary" (silly clothes). Stallings further deglamorizes the movies by pointing out their shared ingredients. Ever cutting costs, the moguls would dust off an old script or an old set, take a costume out of mothballs, use a tune repeatedly.

The book's most entertaining sections are Stallings's catalog of persistent rumors ("Shirley Temple is a midget"), her account of certain first choices for famous roles (Gable to play Tarzan), and her chronicle of the stars' various clashes and attractions on the set. Hollywood teaches us, of course, that what's entertaining is not necessarily true. Some of the anecdotes belong among the rumors. For instance, Stallings claims that, shortly before his death, "Errol Flynn had made tentative plans to star in the film version of *Lolita*," with the teenage Beverly Aadland, "his own Lolita," in the title role. According to the latest (and most trustworthy) biography, these "plans" were only a joke. Similarly, Stallings repeats the story about Bette Davis nearly knocking Flynn cold during the filming of *The Private Lives of Elizabeth and Essex*. Davis had wanted Olivier for her costar, and allegedly expressed her displeasure by turning a stage slap into a mighty right hook. Flynn loved a good tale. This one, which Davis denies, comes from his autobiography. We are also told that Dirk Bogarde had so looked forward to working "with one of his longtime idols, Judy Garland," in *I Could Go On Singing*, that he agreed to the project despite "the flaws in the script," but that after several weeks of Garland's temperament, "Dirk ended up referring to her as 'it.' " In fact, the two had been close friends for years. As Bogarde tells it, the producers allowed him to revise the script (which bothered Garland more than him); and he claims to have felt, when all was over, that "working with her, loving her as I did, had made me the most privileged of men."

And yet *Flesh and Fantasy* is essentially accurate. While it may sometimes twist the facts for the sake of a good story, its evocation of Hollywood rings true. Stallings has honored the spirit of her subject with this imaginative and very funny book, whose time has come. For we no longer need the myth of Hollywood, or the movies' various myths. We know that the stars were not gods, but products, and that the movies were primarily business gambits. We are no longer obsessed with that infinite wealth, those ageless faces.

Before we congratulate ourselves for being so clear-sighted and mature, however, we ought to study some of Hollywood's newest and most popular creations. Geographically, of course, the autobiographies of the stars originate not in Hollywood but in Manhattan, where the books come from. But the myths in these books were first made famous by Hollywood. As memoirists, the stars continue to sell the illusions once peddled by the studios. The biggest hits of Hollywood's current literary season tell "true stories" that sound suspiciously alike: women of uncompromising pluck fight their way upward, only to find that, without Mr. Right, it's lonely at the top, and that beauty, wealth, and fame ensure a life of misery.

Moreover, the popularity of these books suggests that the myth of Hollywood itself may not be dated after all, even if the style of its delivery has changed. Now that the studios have foundered, their erstwhile stars come forward without jewels or makeup, reminiscing in the light of day. They chat about the *amours* and nose jobs on Olympus, then shake their heads and chuckle with the rest of us. But we wouldn't find such trivia so wonderful if we were not still star-struck. No privileged coterie in the world, past or present, exerts the same fascination that still clings to the old movie colony. While we choose to forget the ones who end up waiting tables, we applaud those who have their bank accounts and brain cells still intact. We call them "survivors," as if they had spent their lives in Auschwitz rather than Bel Air. For all its connotations of rotten luck and narrow escapes, "survivor" now sounds as glamorous as "star." The star transcends mortality, the survivor eludes it. Hollywood still promises eternal life.

BOXED IN

■ ■ ■ ■ ■ ■

As its title suggests, Lauren Bacall's *By Myself* is the tale of a "survivor." Bacall is staying on alone, having been widowed (Bogart), jilted (Sinatra), divorced (Robards), orphaned, and otherwise abandoned by various lovers, friends, and dogs. The book's title also implies Bacall's emergence from behind the siren's mask, which lingered in the public memory for years: here is Betty Bacall without the mask, "by herself," telling all.

Bacall's story is full of news, and often very moving. Her evocation of Bogart and her account of his final days make *By Myself* a worthwhile memoir. But the book's "real story" is only part of its appeal. All of Bacall's straight talk is worked into a familiar scenario: as a fresh kid with plenty of guts, Betty studies acting ("No stopping me now"), makes it to Broadway (where she sees "what terrific people professionals are"), and then it's on to Hollywood! Just as her train leaves Grand Central Station, she looks into a mirror and says: "Well, Betty Bacall, this is it. This train is taking you on a new adventure, totally different from anything you've ever known. Take a deep breath."

Having exhaled, she goes to work out West, falls for Bogart in a big way ("No one has ever written a romance better than we lived it"), and sees her name in lights. But it all disappears, and Bacall is left surviving, with nothing but her memories, her children, her two-and-a-half-year run in *Applause*, her appearance in *Murder on the Orient Express*, her contract with Knopf, and her self-esteem ("I have learned that I am a valuable person"). At the end, Bacall vows to fight her old image vigorously: "It's been a losing battle so far, it may always be, but I won't give up. Not then—not now—not tomorrow." As "honest" as it seems, *By Myself*, with its doomed love affair and its plucky heroine, wealthy but lonely, is a version of *Gone with the Wind* for the "Me Decade."

Never one to be outdone, Joan Crawford has sent a long press release from the grave, and Bob Thomas has obligingly shaped it into something like a biography. Based on what the actress told Thomas throughout his years as a reporter of show biz gossip, *Joan Crawford* is Hollywood myth in its most dated form. Joan (we read) was born on the wrong side of the tracks, began backbreaking work at eleven, was treated like dirt by the rich kids at school, dropped out for Bigger Things ("I want to be a *dancer*"), impressed an agent with her spunk, was spotted in the chorus by J. J. Shubert, etc., etc. To corroborate the fairy tales he heard at Crawford's knee, Thomas invents highly dubious conversations between people who aren't alive to deny them, and quotes extensively from books and articles which Crawford "wrote." After the rags-to-riches story starts to pall, Thomas takes up Crawford's "increasingly eccentric and unpredictable behavior," but apologetically, using the myth of the rich-but-wretched actress to get his subject off the hook.

210

Crawford's eyes, Thomas bathetically concludes, "had known . . . the endless, unrealized pursuit of love."

Mommie Dearest is a lurid corrective to Thomas's hagiography, with its notorious revelations of alcoholism, joyless promiscuity with members of either sex, drunk driving, maniacal scrubbing, and, above all, an evil genius for child abuse. While Thomas at one point has the gall to liken Crawford to Mildred Pierce, Christina Crawford describes a woman who could have played the title role in *Trog*. "She was totally without prejudice," writes Thomas of the woman who, according to *Mommie Dearest*, hated fat people, and tried to keep a little black girl from attending Christina's fourth birthday party. Thomas claims that Al Steele, the Pepsi executive, "had been accepted by the Crawford children" before deciding to become Joan's fourth husband. "I heard about the marriage for the first time over a radio news broadcast," writes Christina, who had not yet met or even heard of this "man by the name of Alfred N. Steele." And we have two death scenes. In Thomas's version, St. Joan "called to the two women [who cared for her] to make sure they were eating the breakfast she had prepared. Then she died." According to Christina, the dying Joan heard the prayers of her attendant, and rallied: "My mother raised her head. The last coherent words from her mouth were, 'Damn it . . . don't you *dare* ask God to help me!' A few minutes later, Mother was dead."

Although Christina's account seems more trustworthy, her version of Joan Crawford is essentially the same as Thomas's. The determined trouper with the lovelorn eyes and the explosive sadist with the bloodshot eyes embody the same myths: misery in the midst of plenty; lots of fans, but no man of her own. (According to Christina, "poor Mommie," who "had an insatiable need for love," could never marry the men who might have satisfied her, since both of them—Clark Gable and an "Uncle Charlie"—already had wives.) And yet, while *Mommie Dearest* confirms these clichés, it also blackens the myth of uncompromising pluck. Even after winning global adulation, Christina's mother never quit striving. She was Crawford Agonistes, ever working toward the Big Break or the Comeback, thriving on ostracism and betrayals. Such gumption may seem heroic in the annals of show biz, but it isn't much fun around the house.

Books like *Mommie Dearest* and *By Myself* succeed through compromise, telling small truths to preserve the large fictions. Moreover, they recite exquisite memories in a context of atonement, like a sinner bragging in the confessional. The reader enjoys a vicarious holiday, never forgetting that privilege has its price. Bacall pays heavily for early fame and perfect marriage; Christina is tortured for her status and occasional bouts of costly fun (fantastic birthday parties, a luxurious trip to

211

Europe). In *Self-Portrait*, Gene Tierney describes another illustrious life grievously punished: "I had fame, a face people seemed to admire, friends I could count on, and an income of six figures a year. Why wasn't I happy?" Tierney's woes (years of crippling insanity, a daughter born deaf and retarded) are severe enough to compensate for all those glamorous benefits, which included the attentions of Oleg Cassini, Aly Khan, Howard Hughes, the omnivorous John Kennedy. Even the story's happy ending (she finally traded the playboys for an oilman) has its comforting catch: "I consider myself well now, but I know I have to make an effort to stay that way." Because Tierney's understated story is in perfect balance, it is, like *Mommie Dearest* and *By Myself*, a best seller.

If the joys outweigh the woes, or vice versa, the survivor formula fails. In *No Bed of Roses*, Joan Fontaine tries to pass herself off as a survivor, like a millionaire dressed in a barrel to fool the IRS. "There is much in my life that might make me the envy of many," she sighs, lamenting that she has "found no lasting romance, no marriage" that didn't jeopardize "my own happiness or freedom." Bearing up well under the agony, Fontaine proceeds to tell a story that is eloquent, light-hearted, and mistitled, describing a life of uninterrupted luxury. She hung out with Aly Khan, Howard Hughes, the omnivorous Joe Kennedy; "I invested in oil drilling, bought citrus groves in Florida, an apartment building in Beverly Hills." Too much of this book is taken up with moonlit strolls in exotic places to leave much room for the heartaches, so *No Bed of Roses* has had only middling success.

The opposite problem confronts Lena Pepitone and William Stadiem, whose *Marilyn Monroe Confidential* tries feebly to make a casualty sound like a champion. As Monroe's maid for six years, Pepitone had a chance to observe her mistress's most revolting habits, which she describes (through Stadiem) in a tone of loving reminiscence. "Marilyn was my friend," she pretends, and then natters on about Monroe's raucous self-pity, her tantrums, her colossal vanity, her "incessant belching and farting," her disinclination to bathe, her multicolored sheets (used as two kinds of napkin) and her conscription of various employees for hours of erotic service, which would often "take place on a table in Mr. Miller's old study." Of course, such an odious slob could never be considered a "survivor," and so Pepitone/Stadiem utterly contradict their sordid characterization, to make Monroe seem like yet another Little Engine That Could: "She was always a trouper, regardless of the circumstances," with "a very special determination to succeed and a will to survive," etc. By doing herself in at an early age, Monroe has made such tributes seem a bit misplaced. "To this day, her death has remained a mystery to me," Pepitone confesses predictably.

Whatever Monroe was really like (and this book won't tell us), her myth shares with the stories of Crawford, Tierney, Bacall, and Fontaine the old opposition between love and success: "I wasn't sure which mattered more to her," Pepitone muses, "a family or a career." These pushy American broads have something to learn from the tranquil Sophia Loren, whose "own story" confirms the myth of the European woman as perpetuated by Henry Miller, Ernest Hemingway, and Darryl F. Zanuck, among others. "If, at seventeen," Sophie declares, Monroe "had found a father, as I found Carlo, I think that would have been her salvation."

Sophia Living and Loving is a long encomium pieced together from many hours of conversation with Sophia and her relatives, all of whom adore Sophia. A. E. Hotchner did the cutting and pasting, mixed some metaphors and purpled the prose, but his real contribution was to sit still for Sophia's endless self-congratulation, and to buy it. Thousands of equally credulous Americans have also bought it, allured by the myth of *la femme éternelle*. As a European woman, Sophia is evidently licensed to hold forth on the mysteries of life and the wonders of herself. Certainly no American actress could get away with it.

"Born wise," Sophia struggled like any other rising star ("I was a survivor"), but, once successful, never forgot her obligations as a primal force: "The actress part of me was happy and fulfilled, but the . . . Neapolitan, childbearing Mother Earth [sic] half of me was fiercely unsatisfied." After a few miscarriages, Sophia finally satisfied the other half, and is now the Total Woman: "a good cook," "open and trusting," "very romantic and vulnerable," of "a giving nature." "I love to be considered a dish," she admits, and warns feminists not to "forsake their natural qualities," since "the love of a little child is a greater reward for a woman than any job can bring her" (which bromide would have tickled Joan Crawford).

Tierney, Bacall, Fontaine, et al. seem to apologize for selling out their femininity; Sophia, in touch with her ovaries, has "few regrets." Her wealth brings her no sorrow, because she is womanly enough to take it for granted: "I don't care about money, I never have." While her husband minds the store, Sophia looks after the kids, gives advice, does saintly favors: teaching a nasty Cary Grant "about simple humanity," teaching a guarded Carlo Ponti "to be open and honest and direct," functioning as "psychiatrist, comforter, ego masseuse" to a broken Richard Burton. She arranges for a dying woman to be flown to a hospital and revived, and has Christiaan Barnard save a child's life (and claims that she wanted "no mention of my name in connection with this project"). Her perfect femininity seems somehow dictatorial, as if she were singing "I Enjoy Being a Girl" while annexing Poland. It seems fitting that she ends this book "showing President Tito of Yugoslavia how to make spaghetti sauces."

Sophia seems utterly unlike her hapless American sisters, and yet their myths tell the same story: Sophia's struggle pays off because she is a wife and mommy first, an actress second; the Americans fall apart because they dare to try the opposite. And all Americans, regardless of gender, must appear to pay for the privileges of stardom. While the women are punished with bereavement, the men suffer from premature decreptitude. Michael Freedland's unsympathetic biography of Errol Flynn, while full of revelations (Flynn was "the subject of an anti-Nazi investigation," and once tried, with Bogart, to burn down the Warner Brothers studio), neglects Flynn's own writings, which reveal a deeper man than Freedland leeringly evokes, stressing the tawdriest details of a fast life and ugly death. Beverly Linet's dismal *Ladd*, a standard fan-magazine effusion, never seems to leave the crypt: in a "Preface," a "Prologue," and "A Note to the Reader," Linet makes it abundantly clear that Alan Ladd died young, "his once-beautiful face and strong athlete's body . . . ravaged by age, time, freak accidents, and a losing battle against alcoholism," which is basically all that Linet seems to know.

There are far better books with similar stories: *The Secret Life of Tyrone Power* ("The Drama of a Bisexual in the Spotlight") deals with yet another short-lived matinee idol, but Hector Arce treats Power's career and its pressures with unusual tact, avoiding the tone of ghoulish fascination so common among the stars' biographers. And Arce demonstrates the right kind of erudition, making Power's milieu (Twentieth Century-Fox into the 1950s) at least as interesting as Power's proclivities.

This, after all, is what such books should do: teach us something about cinema. And while certain autobiographies—by Mary Astor, David Niven, Evelyn Keyes, Hildegarde Knef, Charlie Chaplin, Lilli Palmer, and others—give credible accounts of life and labor in the film industry, Hollywood memoirs usually lapse into the comforting (and lucrative) formulas of myth. All autobiographers do some creative misremembering, but the truth is more elusive in Hollywood than in most places. Moreover, the Hollywood memoirist usually takes pen in hand because his agent has run out of encouraging things to say. Superannuated, he might misrepresent the past out of bitterness, since there is no such thing as demotion recollected in tranquillity.

The most edifying memoirs are therefore documentary, recording, on the spot, all the false starts, idiotic demands, weird accidents, and crushing disappointments of daily life in Hollywood. There are few such books. *Memo From: David O. Selznick*, edited by Rudy Behlmer, is worth any number of biographies and reminiscences. And Charlton Heston's *The Actor's Life*, a volume of diary entries covering two decades, is more direct, informative, and entertaining than any of the aforementioned best sellers.

What with his image as Defender of the Faith, Heston is not known for his gaiety. In his definitive portrayals, he is frequently presented sneering down at people from atop various mountains and horses. He has played the same role in public life, especially during the war in Vietnam, which he would frequently defend by going on talk shows to jeer haughtily at anyone who might have been against it.

The Actor's Life does not so much contradict this image as give it depth. Heston is deeply romantic in a stern, old-fashioned way, intrigued by self-sacrifice, transcendent heroism, and battles long ago. This conservatism seems to motivate Heston's powers as a stylist, and gives him a wry perspective on the film industry and its excesses. He is a keen and even likable observer, able to convey a sense of what it feels like to make movies: the laborious readying of script and cast, the problems on the set, the final reckoning of profits and reviews. Heston is especially good at describing the disorientations and brief ecstasies of filmmaking; and he has also made sure (with the help of editor Hollis Alpert) to leave in the doldrums, the interminable waiting and reluctant trips abroad to do research, hold conferences, be interviewed. Moreover, *The Actor's Life* is a valuable record of film history, recounting the various methods of William Wyler, George Stevens, Sam Peckinpah, Anthony Mann, Richard Lester, Carol Reed. Heston receives Olivier's advice, praises Orson Welles's bold techniques in shooting *Touch of Evil*, and witnesses the sad collapse of the late Nicholas Ray, in the middle of production on *55 Days at Peking*.

And yet *The Actor's Life* has not sold well, probably because it does not cohere into familiar myth. If Heston could have posed as a survivor (and the shifts in his career and family life would have accommodated such a self-portrayal), he might have won the critics' praise and a lot of money. Instead, he has written something accurate and unsentimental.

For years, the stars were seen but not heard from. They were discouraged from extemporaneous public speaking, since a burst of resentment or a four-letter word might have spoiled that illusion of superior calm. To prevent such recklessness, publicity crews kept the stars under heavy surveillance, like squads of ventriloquists hired to suppress a revolt of dummies. All public appearances were scripted. Interviews were invented outright, and those magazine articles with stellar bylines were the products of studio hackwork. Everyone in Hollywood "wrote" or "spoke" with the same stilted correctness and exaggerated tact, as if they had all learned English from condolence cards.

Now the stars can speak in their own voices. For example: "If I hadn't been so consumed by Bogie, the thrusting of me onto the national scene with such a vengeance would have been uncopable with." This sentence by Lauren Bacall may sound like a very bad translation from the Spanish, but it is certainly authentic. Authenticity per se, however, may not mean much. The stars (and their celebrants) have replaced the chilly self-absorption of yesterday's idols with the warm "honest" self-absorption of the 1970s: they have "survived" into a decade hospitable to narcissism. And this change in style helps make old foolishness seem hip. Rattling on with amiable post-1960s candor, the stars remind us that it's swell to be poor, that we'll always make it if we try, that hormones are a girl's best friend. We may be leaving these myths behind, but not wholeheartedly. They linger on into the present, making money and causing trouble, like old mobsters. And if they ever disappear entirely, it will probably be a fluke.

Arce, Hector. *The Secret Life of Tyrone Power*. New York: Morrow, 1979.

Bacall, Lauren. *By Myself*. New York: Knopf, 1978.

Crawford, Christina. *Mommie Dearest*. New York: Morrow, 1978.

Fontaine, Joan. *No Bed of Roses*. New York: Morrow, 1978.

Freedland, Michael. *The Two Lives of Errol Flynn*. New York: Morrow, 1978.

Heston, Charlton. *The Actor's Life: Journals 1956-1976*. New York: Dutton, 1978.

Hotchner, A. E. *Sophia Living and Loving: Her Own Story*. New York: Morrow, 1978.

Linet, Beverly. *Ladd*. New York: Arbor House, 1979.

Pepitone, Lena and William Stadiem. *Marilyn Monroe Confidential*. New York: Simon & Schuster, 1979.

Stallings, Penny and Howard Mandelbaum. *Flesh and Fantasy*. New York: St. Martin's, 1978.

Thomas, Bob. *Joan Crawford*. New York: Simon & Schuster, 1978.

Tierney, Gene with Mickey Herskowitz. *Self-Portrait*. New York: Wyden Books, 1979.

Tom Mix Was a Softie

· ·

THIS BOOK,"* WRITES JOAN MELLEN, "IS ABOUT THE fabrication in American films of a male superior to women, defiant, assertive, and utterly fearless." However, Hollywood's "fabrication" is nothing compared to Mellen's, which would assess "the damage done to males who cannot live up to destructive and impossible ideals" invented by a warped, reactionary film industry. "Hollywood," supposedly a single-minded entity, is the baddest wolf of all, having spent its years dictating a ruinous misconception of masculinity: "Repeatedly through the decades, Hollywood has demanded that we admire and imitate males who dominate others," begins *Big Bad Wolves*, which proceeds to huff and puff around the same point for well over 300 pages.

What we have here is a failure to discriminate. Something like a feminist critical method has been hastily applied to something like a survey of American film. As film criticism and feminist interpretation are both relatively young, it is still easy for their would-be exponents to feign great expertise without much work. Because such pretense does disservice to film and feminism alike, it demands meticulous inspection.

Mellen promotes the conspiracy theory of popular culture, insisting that movies dictate attitudes dreamt up by evil tycoons. According to this notion, Hollywood does not reflect widespread feelings, but manufactures concepts for consumption by the ignorant, who then suffer. Rather than seek to determine the cultural foundation of extant preconceptions, Mellen looks for somebody to blame them on. Although she occasionally claims in passing that Hollywood plays upon its audience's prejudices, the guiding assumption of *Big Bad Wolves* is that Hollywood simply invented "the stereotype of the self-controlled, invulnerable, stoical hero" out of thin air, to suit its own dastardly purposes.

Aside from representing sexism as a very simple matter, this argument depends upon a multiple distortion of film history. Mellen contrives a case for the movies' "cruel and impossible demand that

---

*Big Bad Wolves: Masculinity in the American Film. New York: Pantheon Books, 1980.

real-life men live up to a super-*macho* image or fail" by misconstruing plots, quoting actors out of context and generally throwing logic to the winds. Crucial details of *Shane, The Wild Bunch, Dog Day Afternoon* and other films are altered or neglected. We are told that Sam Peckinpah would find it "repellent . . . that a society could exist where the rape of a woman by a man would be unthinkable." Peckinpah may have his problems, but this is not one of them. In *Ride the High Country, Straw Dogs, Bring Me the Head of Alfredo Garcia,* and *Cross of Iron,* those who force themselves on women are the most depraved and vicious characters. "Actors," we learn, "refuse roles which allow even a hint of male vulnerability": Clark Gable "refused to affect a Southern accent for *Gone with the Wind* because he considered it effeminate," and Robert Redford "brings to the screen the same sensibility," since he "insisted on changes for the scene in which he . . . fails to make love successfully" to Barbra Streisand in *The Way We Were.* Mellen merely infers such motivation to prove a dubious thesis. According to George Cukor, Gable "did not have a great deal of confidence in himself as an actor," and so his refusal to drawl did not necessarily reflect a belief that Southerners are fruity. And the insinuation about Redford is more unfair, since he played a homosexual in *Inside Daisy Clover,* and even wanted to make his characterization more explicit than the powers at Warner Brothers would allow.

Big Bad Wolves is full of such mistaken inferences. The mainstay of Mellen's survey, however, is her convenient unawareness of the facts. "The Depression male hero" was "fiercely competitive, domineering, and stridently aggressive," "undeterred by sentimentality for those who falter in a harsh world," and so on. Like Fredric March in *Les Misérables* (1935)? Like those heroes played throughout the 1930s by Robert Donat? Ronald Colman? Melvyn Douglas? Robert Montgomery? "The Depression led to a plethora of films which insisted that only total freedom from women . . . permits a man to be truly masculine." What about William Powell and Myrna Loy in *The Thin Man* series (1934-47)? Cary Grant and Katharine Hepburn in *Bringing Up Baby* (1938)? Grant and Irene Dunne in *The Awful Truth* (1937)? James Stewart and Simone Simon in *Seventh Heaven* (1937)? Walter Huston and Mary Astor in *Dodsworth* (1936)? Laurence Olivier and Merle Oberon in *Wuthering Heights* (1939)? If the "Depression male hero" was such a gorilla, why were Leslie Howard, Herbert Marshall and Freddie Bartholomew each so popular in the 1930s?

By ignoring many films and misreading a few, Mellen implies that King Kong could have played nearly every leading role in Hollywood's history, and then some: "The popular arts have been single-minded in their repeated demand that males in America conform to a cave-man model of masculinity," an indictment that obviously includes television. Does "The Mary Tyler Moore Show" make such a "demand"? "All in the Family?" "Lou Grant?" "The Odd Couple?" "The Honeymooners?" "The popular arts" have been no more "single-minded" than the movies, which have offered a variety of masculine types. Glenn Ford, Burt Lancaster, and Henry Fonda, for instance, have often played weak or gentle heroes or, more to the point, characters too complex for vulgar classification.

In fact, the brutal, threatening male who abuses his authority has usually been the bad guy, not a "model": Edward G. Robinson in *The Sea Wolf,* Laird Cregar in *I Wake Up Screaming*, Orson Welles in *Touch of Evil*, and Robert Mitchum in *Night of the Hunter* and *Cape Fear* offer a few examples. The frequent adaptation of the Jekyll and Hyde story provides further disproof of Mellen's generalization, which also fails to apply to those characters whose heroism involves some kind of martyrdom, like Leslie Howard in *The Petrified Forest*, Kirk Douglas in *Spartacus* and *Lonely Are the Brave*, Alan Ladd in *Shane*, and Marlon Brando (a sucker for punishment) in *Viva Zapata!, The Fugitive Kind*, and *Mutiny on the Bounty*. There was considerable diversity among Hollywood's heroes until the late 1960s, when the cruel, cold-blooded protector with a phallic firearm suddenly became popular.

The movies have also conveyed many different kinds of sexism. A good feminist survey of American film would discriminate among them, as Molly Haskell does so well in *From Reverence to Rape*. Tracking down Neanderthals, Mellen overemphasizes hulking cruelty: "At worst, the male in American movies has brutalized women, his violence incomplete unless it is reflected in his sexuality." Not many heroes have done so. The kind of sexism reflected in movies is, by and large, characterized not by brutality but by protective condescension, which has manifested itself as amused contempt, unamused contempt, simple neglect, or chivalrous exaltation. These attitudes can be far more damaging than simple physical bullying, for they work subtly, sometimes appealingly, undermining self-respect. Mellen ignores the most corrosive kind of sexism in favor of the most violent, and so evades the whole issue.

Moreover, by attributing the rise of "misogyny" to a certain kind of film hero, she underestimates the extent to which sexism inheres in our culture. The causes of sexism are old and complex, most of them predating the development of cinema. In order to examine modern conceptions of masculinity with any success, it would be wise at least to begin with an intensive study of American culture. A careful perusal of nineteenth-century popular fiction might illuminate the assumptions

221

of De Mille, Griffith, Hawks, or Huston, whose preconceptions did not originate in this century. Unfortunately, Mellen has not bothered to consider anything other than a few films, and so can claim, for instance, that the villains in *The Great Train Robbery* (1903) "are clad in black shirts, the association of blackness and evil being conscious and soon to become standard," a revelation to anyone familiar with, say, *Paradise Lost* or the Bible, not to mention anyone who's afraid of the dark.

This unawareness of texts is detrimental in other ways. The film *All Quiet on the Western Front*, "surely an anomaly for 1930," was so unfashionably pacifist that its action "had to be transported to a foreign country, and [Lewis] Milestone chose a German setting, just as Dorothy Arzner, in her 1933 film *Christopher Strong*, had to exile her liberated heroine . . . by making her an English aristocrat." Mellen's point is that American society was too militaristic and too sexist to accept such stories in American settings. But *All Quiet on the Western Front* was surely not "an anomaly for 1930," since two other antiwar films, *Journey's End* and *The Case of Sergeant Grischa*, were released the same year. And, more importantly, that film's action is set in Germany because Erich Maria Remarque's *All Quiet on the Western Front* is about Germans, just as Gilbert Frankau's *Christopher Strong* is about English people. Thus inattentive to texts that bear direct relevance to her discussion, Mellen is obviously not ready to interpret much of American culture, a task demanding an acquaintance with many books, even some that were never made into movies.

MELLEN OUGHT TO HAVE ASKED HERSELF JUST WHAT "MASculinity" means. Not once in *Big Bad Wolves* is this term subjected to scrutiny, although it is used to signify, among other things, attractiveness, moral stature, energy, dissidence, and sensuality. In *Paths of Glory*, for instance, masculinity is "the recognition that all rational men are ambivalent about danger and are subject to terror." Just why this should have anything to do with gender is a question that strikes at the heart of Mellen's book. Left undefined, the book's subject constantly slides out of focus: *Detective Story* "presented maleness in terms of action derived from felt emotion," whereas Brando's "raw masculinity" sometimes "prevented the tender aspects of his personality from surfacing."

Mellen may not know much about masculinity, but she knows what she likes. "The self-controlled, invulnerable, stoical hero" acts out of "false" masculinity, while the man who is "in touch with his feelings" or "in touch with himself" is one whose masculinity is "honest." By "in touch with his feelings" Mellen seems to mean "'highly emotional,'" if not "wet." She likes characters who cry a lot. John Barrymore, who offered "a large and unrestricted definition of masculinity," has "huge tears escaping from his eyes" in the middle of *Tempest*, and, toward the end, "large tears flow from his eyes." (Evidently, men out of touch with themselves have their tear ducts located in some special place.) Tom Mix, celebrated for "the ease with which [his films] approached the whole question of masculinity," is described as "crying unashamedly and profusely" in *Dick Turpin*. James Dean, "in touch with himself," "sobs from the depths of his being" in *East of Eden,* and Paul Newman, "in touch with his feelings," "gives himself uninhibitedly to tears" in *The Left-Handed Gun*. Dustin Hoffman goes them all one better. In *Midnight Cowboy*, he "wets his pants." "When in the entire history of American film has a principal male character done such a thing?" Mellen exults. Presumably, a "masculine" man is one who leaks.

Phrases like "in touch with his feelings," although meaningless, clearly date this book, as do the epithets "Fascist" and "reactionary," which Mellen throws around with mad abandon. Such rhetoric recalls a few sorry aspects of the 1960s: fierce indignation and a cozy faith in mere emotion. The vision of the film industry informing *Big Bad Wolves* also recalls Sixties rhetoric, suggesting that the pigs are alive and well and grunting in Los Angeles, oppressing "the people," or the sensitive filmgoers, represented by Joan Mellen. This gentle audience, we learn, abhorred with equal fervor the war in Vietnam, straight society, and the films on the Mellen blacklist; the James Bond films, on the other hand, appealed "to young men involved neither in the counterculture nor antiwar activity," and Clint Eastwood's fans were "young men in the sixties who remained unaffected by any of the protest movements," and also "the disenchanted student young," although "not perhaps the more conscious." "To many at the time [i.e., J. Mellen and friends], newly introduced to the . . . works of Antonioni, Truffaut, Bergman, Buñuel and Fellini which many felt were the only films worth seeing, Bond was grotesque, a cartoon parody of maleness." So, Mellen's taste in films is the expression of a keen political sense which matured in the Sixties, while thugs and rednecks and a few dimwitted activists slavered their way through viewings of *Dr. No*.

As its main purpose is the advertisement of Joan Mellen's political correctness, *Big Bad Wolves* is entirely humorless. *Some Like It Hot* "seems daring" with its male stars "prancing through the film in drag," but "the disguise is so obvious that their masculinity is never in question." "The ideal" male in *Pillow Talk* "is the fabricated [Rock] Hudson, a bionic, plastic toy no less than his contemporary Sean Connery, as James Bond, that mini-Hugh Hefner [sic]." *Shampoo* "was made solely as a narcissist [sic] exercise for Warren Beatty as the white Shaft, a superstud," a pose which "finally appears to be a mask for distaste for women."

These incredible misreadings of some very clever films betray a profound impatience with all conflict. Without conflict there are no laughs. Tearful men with weak bladders make poor comic heroes, but then Mellen is not interested in humor. Thus liberated, she fails to see that without a belief in the fruitful conflict of the sexes, a belief that men and women are different but equal, we could not enjoy Shakespearean comedy, or *The Way of the World,* or *Pride and Prejudice,* or *Private Lives,* or *The Thin Man,* or *Pat and Mike*, or any other satisfying story of sexual rivalry.

Both the responsible feminist and the astute critic would attempt to keep certain realities in mind. Many of the phenomena which Mellen considers "sexist" have an actual basis in what most of us call "real life." In search of masculinity, she devotes her attention to Westerns, crime dramas, and war stories, which generally exclude women, since most gangsters, cowpokes, and soldiers have not been female, a fact of history and not a sexist fiction. Nevertheless, Mellen notes with disapproval that the exclusively male world of *Dawn Patrol* (1930), set at the German front during World War I, is exclusively male: "There is not a single woman in the film." Mellen also detects in "the masculine ethos" of the gangster film "sadism toward women, their fixed role as slavelike possessions, and the eroticism of violent sexuality," things which are also noticeable among real gangsters, who have never been much given to feminism. This is not Hollywood's fault, even if some films have glamorized criminals.

Mellen's intolerance becomes clearest when she dismisses the very personalities of real people as "images" attributable to the rise of film. "Dustin Hoffman and Robert Redford in *All the President's Men*" are "unburdened by family life," and so can "delve into the mysteries of Watergate free of all those family responsibilities, mortgages, dental bills, school fees and summer-camp selections which tie down nominally less masculine men." We are reminded that "John Wayne often played such a male." Since Woodward and Bernstein happened to be single and childless as they devoted themselves to "the mysteries of Watergate," this objection to a film based closely on their lives seems rather strange. Maybe there should have been a scene in which Woodward packs Bernstein's lunchbox. As "freedom from domestic commitments" is a feature of Hollywood's "false" masculinity, so is "the guise of silence," and therefore Gary "Cooper's silence derived from a rationale expressed by [William S.] Hart in his autobiography." Those who knew Cooper, an ex-cowboy, claim that he just happened to be a quiet person, but then they lack the benefit of Mellen's wide reading. "To grant their roles authenticity, actors personally become caricatures of their screen personae. 'It's just that I don't like to talk much,' Charles Bronson has said." If Bronson was telling the truth, his straightforward remark does not corroborate Mellen's argument, but disproves it.

Mellen spends many pages laboriously deriding the propagandistic war films of the forties *(Back to Bataan* [1945] contains "no criticism of America's colonial role in Asia"), but only because they aren't her kind of propaganda. A film, as she sees it, has a "thesis" or a "moral," "insisting" this or "saying" that. She would have films "say" the things she likes to hear, regardless of how improbable; she does not want art but sociology, which would faithfully reflect the conditions of life as she imagines them.

"*The Graduate,* cowardly and hypocritical at its root, fails to allow Benjamin the intelligence or imagination to define his discontent or articulate how he perceives the society he rejects, let alone how he would alter it." In other words, *The Graduate* should not present an inarticulate, apolitical young man briefly distressed about his arid prospects, but a bold rebel, in touch with his feelings. Since Dustin Hoffman played the part, there was a great opportunity missed: Benjamin could have delivered a ringing indictment of capitalism, and then wet his pants. But there are other problems: Benjamin "finds that lovemaking with an aggressive woman who likes sex holds no pleasure for the male," "a device used to keep women in their old inferior social place." Another generalization. Mrs. Robinson's self-hate and contempt for Benjamin apparently have nothing to do with the unhappiness of that affair (which never permits us to conclude that Mrs. Robinson "likes sex"). Mellen would have Benjamin looking for Ms. Goodbar, and finding her.

IT IS TRUE THAT WE ARE MANIPULATED BY WHAT WE WATCH. The commercials that pervade daily life influence us incessantly; the countless subtle messages of billboards, magazine ads, and television screens, more difficult to notice or resist than the propagandism of movies, distort our values as they help detach us from our money. This manipulation is far subtler than the overt promotion of some crude stereotype. It is dangerous precisely because it is often hard to discern, and so it will not fail until we learn how to perceive it, and how to perceive our own preconceptions making it possible.

And as far as movies are concerned, we cannot begin to analyze their political intentions or effects until a number of hard questions have been answered. Who is responsible for the content of a film, or the public personality of a star? The answers will vary from era to era, studio to studio, movie to movie. Mellen usually refers to films as the personal expressions of their directors, and tends to describe an actor as if his screen persona were all his own creation. She mentions "Mervyn Le Roy's *Little Caesar*," and claims that "What is truly male, De Mille tells us [in *Male and Female*], transcends social class or wealth." *Little Caesar* was also the work of producers Darryl Zanuck and Hal Wallis, and screenwriter Francis Faragoh, and is very faithful to W. R. Burnett's best-selling novel. What "De Mille tells us" in *Male and Female* comes directly from J. M. Barrie's *The Admirable Crichton*, on which it is based. It is therefore misleading to ascribe these movies' "statements" (if any) to their directors. "Unlike Hart, [Tom Mix] would never play a gangster or an outlaw, nor would he kill his enemies." Mix was easygoing in his films only because the mogul William Fox fashioned his image with great care, figuring that the time was right for a cheerful cowboy.

How did Fox know that his star would succeed? Does Hollywood invent public needs, or exploit them? It is not likely that the film industry would have remained solvent unless its product appealed to its audience. Does the presentation of a character imply endorsement of his behavior? Mellen insists that "we must approve the viciousness of the gangster [in *Little Caesar*] because . . . it is both successful and an acceptable route to survival." Those who have seen the film may decide for themselves if this makes any sense. Finally, has Hollywood been forcing a single masculine stereotype on the American public for more than seventy years? No. Nearly every chapter in this book brings to mind dozens of counter-examples. As propaganda, it can only convince those who already agree with it. *Big Bad Wolves* is for people who have been too busy nursing prejudices to spend much time at the movies.

Afterword

. . . .

LTHOUGH A THUGGISH PIECE OF WORK, MELLEN'S book shares a certain bias, or presumption, with later and more sophisticated feminist studies. Like *Big Bad Wolves*, many of today's feminists assume that the problem of domination derives simply from a gross authority embodied and enforced by certain unenlightened males. Some feminists perceive mass culture as a source of liberation from such personal bullying, while others, like Mellen, assume that TV and the movies simply compound the problem, by propagating the "gender roles" of the Victorian era: submissive femininity, omnicompetent manliness. (It is surely a fact of some ideological import that the majority of academic feminists concentrate on nineteenth-century literature, wherein the sexual battlelines seem clear.)

The actual situation is, however, far too insidious to be explained in such schematic terms. On the one hand, it is indeed the case that the spectacle promotes many horrific images of male dominance: not only in the revenge fantasies of Sylvester Stallone and Chuck Norris, and not only in the grisly "slasher" movies available in countless video rental stores (and savored largely by the young and the poor)—but in much mainstream advertising, which often depicts female subjugation in images no less gruesome for their indirectness. Those radical feminists who have joined forces with the ultraright in a call for censorship have recognized a real incitement to brutality, and so their response is understandable, even if their efforts pose a threat to civil liberties.

While it is true, however, that the images of *Rambo* and of certain ads extol machismo, in no way does the spectacle promote a complementary old-fashioned meekness in its female viewers. On the contrary: whether appealing to the threatened male or to the threatened female, the spectacle is calculated to bring out the beast. In this compensatory enterprise, there is no sex discrimination. "There are no woman doormats on this series," said producer Esther Shapiro of "Dynasty" in 1984. "The women are not victims. They can have the same villainy as the men."

What the culture of TV purveys to *all* its viewers, in other words, is a fantasy of power—much the same fantasy that (for instance) Lever

227

BOXED IN

■ ■ ■ ■ ■ ■

Bros. sold to its audience of housewives in 1982 (see above, pp. 43–50). Now, however, the media paragon-of-all-her-sex is no longer, like Gail, a wry homemaker, but a hard commodity and ruthless media marketeer, devastatingly sexy yet untouchable—Rupert Murdoch operating from inside Victoria Principal's body. On the cover of *People*, 25 January 1988 (for example), the beauteous Cher confronts us, ethereal gaze offset by a Pre-Raphaelite mass of raven tresses, and with huge silver trinkets gleaming at her throat and ears: "THE ULTIMATE LIBERATED WOMAN," proclaims the copy, screaming white against her midnight coif: "SHE'S MADE *MOONSTRUCK* A HIT, HER LOVER IS 23 & SHE'S TOUGH ENOUGH TO SAY: 'MESS WITH ME AND I'LL KILL YOU.' "

If it had been, say, Donald Trump or Frank Sinatra on the cover, with the appropriate pronominal revisions, that promo would have been taken—rightly—as a paean to hooliganism, not to "liberation." What the *People* cover betrays is not simply a double standard, but the utter degradation of feminism by the values of the market. In this masculinized "feminism" there is no revolutionary possibility. Such female tough guys—real or fictitious—reinforce the (sexist) status quo, by promoting the kill-or-be-killed credo that underlies it, and by offering a mere dream of potency to the working female millions who are thereby made to feel refreshed enough to go back to the job, where they are still—for the most part—pushed around and underpaid.

In February 1988 a journalist writing in *TV Guide* reported that "some TV advertisers now see two tiers of [female] viewers," typified by, on top, "the career woman," and, on the bottom, "the woman with a job." While the successful women generally tune in to the most flattering self-reflections (one p.r. woman claimed to prefer "a character I can identify with or be inspired by"), the lower-paid workers, after hours, get high on TV's flattering totality: "Lacking, perhaps, a real sense of power," one Hartford factory worker, who makes $6.85 an hour, "watches TV in general more than any specific program. And she seems to demand so little of it that she feels generally satisfied by it, even if not enthused."

The spectacle has always had this somatic value for the American work force. Certainly the distractions of vicarious pleasure have long been urged on employees: "An intelligent observer often wastes his pity on a worker whose task seems fearfully deadening to the former but full of variety to the latter," claimed an industrial psychologist in 1931. "One girl in a British factory spent a few minutes in the morning preparing her machine and materials for the day's job. After that 'she married a Duke, took a trip to the Riviera, rented a mansion in West End' and had a thoroughly delightful time while she worked." Today such

228

escapism seems dated. In the culture of TV, we feel somehow superior to the gaping drudges of the past: that anonymous "girl" with her dime novel reveries, or the Depression-era heroine of Woody Allen's film *The Purple Rose of Cairo*, who, having lost everything, consoles herself by getting lost in yet another movie. And yet little has really changed within the culture of TV: "I watch 'Dynasty' and 'Knots Landing' just so I can dream," says the Hartford factory worker in 1987. "It's, gosh, I'm through for the day," says one secretary of her TV-centered evenings, "and I can wipe out my mind."

Despite the persistence of the Rambovian ideal, and contrary to the Mellen thesis, the culture of TV is now largely woman-oriented—a marketing strategy and not a feminist development. While the old inequities remain in place, women are titillated endlessly by tales and images of the female triumphant, whether in the narratives of *Life* and *Newsweek, Time* and *People*, in films like *Heartburn, Terms of Endearment,* and *Broadcast News*—and in virtually all TV and advertising. This feminization of the spectacle represents a shift away from (and yet in fact a continuation of) the pervasive masculinism of the spectacle after World War II. From the late Forties into the Sixties, the Westerns, detective shows, and sitcoms, and many of the ads and movies, were contrived to boost the depressed morale of America's suburban males, who were now—as C. Wright Mills made clear in *White Collar*—the captives of bureaucracy, and otherwise subverted by the larger forces of the consumption system, TV included. The spectacle was their factitious compensation, offering them the same illusion of empowerment that now distracts their daughters.

And yet those daughters are now more oppressed than their exhausted Dads were in the Fifties—and oppressed by the very spectacle that now appears to take their side. For while it seems to back them up against the world of men, the spectacle in fact requires them to be everything that men have always wanted them to be: slim, smooth, poised, beautiful, albeit aggressive employees instead of dedicated Mommies. Through the spectacle, the corporation poses as the woman's ally against men, but only to become itself her lord and master. Not only does she have to work for it full-time, but she must keep buying from it, staying as if young and bright before its omnipresent eye.

Thus the spectacle belittles men, not to build up the self-esteem of women, but only to sabotage it more effectively than any mere man could ever do. One example: According to a study published in the journal *Pediatrics* in February 1988, children internalize the adult world's standard of attractiveness by age seven, or even earlier—a standard that relates directly to the rising incidence of eating disorders among the young. "I've been seeing 5- and 6-year-old girls who were

229

preoccupied with their weight," Dr. William Feldman, one of the study's authors, told the *New York Times*. "One young girl broke into tears when her mother asked her to go for a swim. The girl said she'd look fat in a swimsuit, when in fact her weight was normal for her height." TV, the report concludes, is a preeminent cause of such anxiety. "The female leads on the most popular television shows are thin, like Joan Collins on 'Dynasty,' " Dr. Feldman pointed out. "Even on 'The Cosby Show,' the women are lean, like his daughter Denise. Bill Cosby is the only one who's chunky."*

Thus even those shows full of so-called "positive images" actually subvert the confidence of their female viewers: "Dynasty," wherein "the women are not victims," and "The Cosby Show," despite its censor's vigilance against the dreaded "stereotypes" (see above, p. 77).

Here, then, is the eternal triangle, which the spectacle replays endlessly: man, woman, corporation—and as the ad below suggests, the logo always gets the girl. (Note the homunculus in the background.)■

SHERATON AND AMERICAN EXPRESS

PERFECT VACATION PARTNERS

---

*Joan Collins is, of course, not "thin." What is striking here is the fact that Dr. Feldman and his patients *see* her as thin because she is a TV star.

In Memoriam–A.J.H. (1899–1980)

OR YEARS, ALFRED HITCHCOCK WAS WRITTEN OFF as "the master of suspense," and now the late Sir Alfred has been eulogized in the same terms. The epithet is rich with slighting implications. It suggests, first of all, that Hitchcock was stuck in a rut, playing with kid stuff: he made "thrillers" (as John Ford made "Westerns"), while Welles and Bergman created Films. "Master of suspense" also connotes the technician's narrow expertise. Knowing all the tricks of the trade, that "master" could work his audience adroitly. Such a talent seems manipulative as well as limited; a "master of suspense" is, literally, a puppeteer.

Of course the epithet has always been used with affection by those ardent consumers who call themselves "film buffs." These people have a ready fondness for all the standard "great touches" and/or "classic scenes": Cary Grant on his way upstairs with the Fatal Glass of Milk, Cary Grant running away from the crop dusting plane, Cary Grant on his way downstairs with Ingrid Bergman, Janet Leigh taking her shower. By celebrating only a few thrills, these enthusiasts perpetuate the notion that Hitchcock was simply a gifted sensationalist, which is just what his detractors like to claim: "a dealer in shock, as another might go in for dry goods" (Dwight Macdonald), "a pop cynic, cinematically ingenious" (Stanley Kauffmann), "a masterly builder of mousetraps," whose techniques "have more to do with gamesmanship than with art" (Pauline Kael), etc. He has been both dismissed and idolized for the same wrong reason. Certain of his fans implicitly agree with his detractors that Alfred Hitchcock will loom large in the annals of mass titillation, along with P. T. Barnum, Josef Goebbels, and the roller coaster.

Hitchcock himself helped, inadvertently, to foster this impression. Although a voluble interviewee, he always shied away from exegesis. He would hastily explain things in the simplest terms, or frustrate questions of interpretation with genial acquiescence. Asked if a certain

231

scene might have this or that significance, Hitchcock would agree that it was possible, and the subject would be closed: "Isn't it a fascinating design? One could study it forever." Rather than play the critic, he would tell anecdotes, formulate rules on narrative strategy, and boast about his technical inventions: "By the way, did you like the scene with the glass of milk?" he asked Truffaut: "I put a light right inside the glass because I wanted it to be luminous." He would pretend not to have thought about the most important things, dwelling instead on how he got the glass to glow, the merry-go-round to run wild, the plane to crash at sea.

This apparent fascination with mechanics was sometimes taken as proof that Hitchcock was only after neat effects and crude responses. In fact, the opposite is true. He considered those effects amusing, but not all that important, since he seemed downright eager to spoil their impact by carefully explaining them. (Even while *The Birds* was still in production, he was already telling interviewers how he managed the illusion of a bird attack.) Moreover, by talking mostly about the nuts and bolts of spectacle, Hitchcock could avoid making authorial pronouncements that might have limited the meanings of his films. He would not struggle to describe what he wanted his viewers to see for themselves.

This was his implicit purpose, and the secret of his inexhaustible cinema: he wanted his viewers to learn for themselves how to see for themselves. He would have us discover our vision, and then distrust it. "You expect quite a lot of your audience," suggested one interviewer. "For those who want it," he replied: "I don't think films should be looked at *once.*" "For those who want it": although Hitchcock was adept at providing his one-shot viewers with a good ninety-minute jolt, he was uneasy about so mechanical an exercise, and worked, ever more subtly, to draw the viewer toward an awareness of visual nuance that would surpass the immediate pleasures of the one-night stand. And he could do this because he had mastered every aspect of his art.

He was a great screenwriter. Although he took a writer's credit only once after 1932 (for *Dial M for Murder*), his was the guiding intelligence behind nearly all his scripts, and "quite a bit" (he said) of the actual dialogue was his own: "You see I used to be a writer myself years ago," he once remarked, with his usual nonchalance. His narrative abilities, his sense of plot and pacing, remain unequaled. Moreover, he had a genius for colloquialism. Although largely noted for some macabre *double entendres* ("Mother—what is the phrase?—isn't quite herself today"), Hitchcock's dialogue is, in fact, exemplary in every way—witty, succinct, evocative, and full of meaning, as simple conversations, "innocent remarks," work tellingly against the visual event. This kind of irony depends on several gifts: Hitchcock was as skillful a dramatic poet as a *metteur-en-scène*. He would claim not to care about the wording of the lines, but his deft scripts and careful working habits belie this pretense of indifference. He approached his writers not as a taskmaster, but as a scrupulous collaborator, able to draw the best from Charles Bennett, Ernest Lehman, Thornton Wilder, Evan Hunter, John Michael Hayes, and many others, including his wife, Alma Reville, who was his right hand from 1922 until the end.

He also worked effectively with actors, inspiring dozens of the most memorable portrayals in cinema, and countless vivid bits from hundreds of supporting players. We are often told that his actors merely posed for the camera, but that judgment is absurd. Hitchcock's dramas of ambivalence demanded that his actors project the most complex of characterizations: Teresa Wright's Charlie, passing from blitheness into uneasy resignation in *Shadow of a Doubt*; Claude Rains's Alex Sebastian in *Notorious*, charming and miserable, then savagely resentful, and, in the same film, Ingrid Bergman as Alicia Huberman, as reckless in rejection as in love; Herbert Marshall's guiltridden ironist in *Foreign Correspondent*; Oscar Homolka's petit bourgeois subversive, sly and thoughtless, in *Sabotage*; Jessica Tandy as Mrs. Brenner in *The Birds*, struggling to preserve her household and her sanity; and many more, including Hitchcock's three great monsters: Joseph Cotten as Uncle Charlie, the dapper nihilist in *Shadow of a Doubt*; Robert Walker in *Strangers on a Train*, as the feline and dissipated Bruno Anthony; and, in *Psycho*, Anthony Perkins as Norman Bates, the boyish mass murderer and malaprop. Hitchcock displayed Cary Grant's great flexibility in *Notorious, Suspicion, North by Northwest*, and *To Catch a Thief*, showed something of James Stewart's range in *Rear Window, Vertigo, Rope*, and the remake of *The Man Who Knew Too Much*, and proved that Grace Kelly was more than just a chilly face.

"I have never worked with anyone who was more considerate, more helpful, more understanding of actors than Hitchcock," says James Stewart, who ought to know, and Ingrid Bergman once suggested that "every actor who has ever worked with Hitchcock would like to work with him again." There were a few who might have disagreed. Because he never improvised and liked to do things amicably, Hitchcock did not work well with temperamental types (Charles Laughton in *Jamaica Inn*, Kim Novak in *Vertigo*), and was impatient with those Method actors (Montgomery Clift in *I Confess*, Paul Newman in *Torn Curtain*) who asked a lot of questions. Nevertheless, his experience with actors was, by and large, a happy one, as those two tributes and many fine performances attest. That celebrated crack about actors and cattle had nothing to do with Hitchcock's practice (and is, moreover, untraceable, although Hitchcock liked to provoke people by repeating it).

It was, above all, in his use of technique that Hitchcock most obviously surpassed his peers and guided his successors. The buffs are too restrained in their praises. Since by "technique" they actually mean "ingenious bits," their little list of Hitchcock's great effects—shower, crop duster, glass of milk—is much too short. Those better-known moments represent only a handful of Hitchcock's many master strokes: in *Blackmail*, a chase through the British Museum, all done with mirrors, in the studio; in *Spellbound*, a shot, from the suicidal gunman's point of view, of a hand holding a pistol, which slowly turns and fires into the camera ("I wound up using a giant hand," Hitchcock explained, "and a gun four times the natural size"); the dizzying subjective shot in *Vertigo*; the "score" of *The Birds*, all electronic sound effects (even the climactic "silence"); the dolly back down the stairs and out into the street in *Frenzy*; and so on. As a craftsman, Hitchcock was, indeed, unparalleled, so well acquainted with his tools that he never had to look into the camera, because he always knew how any given shot would come out.

Technique, however, involves much more than virtuosity. The buffs not only ignore most of Hitchcock's technical feats, but further belittle his achievement by extolling those feats only as triumphs of engineering: they marvel that he could work his gadgets and his audience with equal dexterity, thus praising his films as just the kind of empty *tours de force* we would expect from a "master of suspense." But why, if Hitchcock was such a skillful manipulator, were his attempts at drumbeating (*Lifeboat, Saboteur, Foreign Correspondent*) too equivocal to do the job? A "master of suspense" ought to have excelled at propaganda, along with Ford and Capra, but Hitchcock's vision was not unambiguous enough. And why did Hitchcock insist that "most films should be seen through more than once," if all he wanted from his viewers was a certain number of shrieks and shudders? Did Hitchcock ever rely on gimmickry, or use his technique as a behaviorist might use electrodes? On the contrary, that technique, while always startling, was always more than that: "I am against virtuosity for its own sake," he told Truffaut: "Technique should enrich the action." That dictum was the fruit of long experience. The more carefully we study Hitchcock's technique, the more exciting it becomes, for it is always apt, suggestive, multiply significant, its images meticulously conceived and conjoined. It is, in short, the work of a man who ought simply to be honored as "the Master."

How, then, do we explode that other epithet? We might consider the other modes that Hitchcock had "mastered," and point out that he was also adept at comedy, and that he had a fine eye for the glow and shadows of romance, and that he was an able satirist. Lists, however, are no more useful than labels. Anyone can simply catalog an artist's capabilities (as I have been doing here), but that is the sport of buffs and columnists: Hitchcock's genius demands a more expansive kind of appraisal. No easy categories can do him justice, just as his would-be mimics have missed the point. His style, supposedly all lurid tricks and broad contrivances, has proved inimitable. Among the dozens of *hommages* and parodies—attempts by Truffaut, Claude Chabrol, Stanley Donen, Mel Brooks, Brian de Palma, and others—not one successfully evokes the source. No other director has been able to attain that peculiar intensity, that mood of ambiguous discovery, which gives Hitchcock's best films an emotional power that only increases with familiarity.

Hitchcock sustained this power through half a century because he never lost his thorough understanding of the viewer: "I always take the audience into account," he insisted, expressing something subtler than the cunning of a seasoned showman. He never condescended to his audience, never failed to honor their presence, and yet he never trusted them. He felt this deep ambivalence almost from the start of his career, at which time it was something new. Earlier filmmakers, such as Porter, Griffith, Murnau, and Eisenstein, had expected to uplift their eager viewers, hoping that film would put an end to war and ignorance. As a young viewer, then as an apprentice screenwriter and art director, and finally as a director, Hitchcock saw that film could have different, more sinister, effects.

Once inside the theater, individuals would meld into a wide-eyed herd. Film could bring out the worst in those huddled spectators, who might now enjoy, vicariously, the vices they would ordinarily denounce. Moreover, they appeared to be fickle as well as hypocritical and timid, taking sides according to the fimmaker's whim. Deft editing could overwhelm all ethical distinctions. If a character was nice-looking and endangered, the audience would automatically take his side: show a dashing burglar on the job, then cut to someone coming to surprise him, and suddenly the thief becomes your hero.

Since the viewers put their faith in visual conventions, moreover, "goodness" and "evil" were simply the impressions made by angle, lighting, setting, composition. The viewer would cherish the bright smile in the sunny doorway, condemn the half-lit scowl around the corner. He was, it turned out, no earnest pupil, ripe for betterment, but a thoughtless bigot, making facile judgments in the dark.

Whereas men like Griffith and Eisenstein saw themselves as the custodians of a beneficent new force, Hitchcock distrusted the new medium, with its coercive images and credulous crowds. The process of

235

spectacle—plays, concerts, circuses, games, court trials, public speeches—is always charged with menace in his films: gunmen take aim from theater boxes, murderers try to disappear into their roles, with audiences watching. Film seems especially dangerous in Hitchcock's films. In *Saboteur*, a comic shoot-out in a movie coincides with (and conceals) a real shoot-out in the movie theater, and in *Sabotage* a little boy rides a bus, carrying a time bomb (unwittingly) and two reels of film. The explosion kills everyone on board. The film ends with the explosion of a movie theater.

The uneasiness implicit in these sequences led Hitchcock to perfect a brilliant adversary style. While apparently gratifying the viewer's wish for adventure and "suspense," Hitchcock actually encourages the viewer to go beyond these vivid first impressions. Unlike his predecessors, who strained to have us see the simple truth, Hitchcock would have us see ourselves straining to see. He never allowed his audience the somnolent comforts of the dark, the soft chair, the warm buttered popcorn, but blocked that sweet escape with troubling reminders of the viewer's habits and desires. His films seem to point back at us, so that our presence and short-sightedness become a part of the story on the screen.

A famous sequence in *The Thirty-Nine Steps* provides a good example of this reflective strategy. The film begins with a legend on a marquee: "MUSIC HALL," the words lighting up, one letter at a time, to the rhythm of a merry overture. An anonymous figure appears at the ticket booth ("Stalls, please"), then inside, handing his ticket to the usher, then taking his seat: Richard Hannay (Robert Donat), a visitor from Canada, and, so far, no more remarkable than any other spectator in his (or our) midst. He watches the performance of Mr. Memory, an expert at recalling trivia, and offers, as a colorless viewer, a colorless question ("How far is Winnipeg from Montreal?"). A few minutes later a brawl breaks out, someone fires a pistol, and in the stampede for the exits Hannay finds himself embracing a frightened woman (Lucie Mannheim) who, once outside, asks him to take her home.

She behaves mysteriously upon entering his flat, avoiding the windows, asking that he turn out the lights, ignore the phone, turn his mirror to the wall. They go into the kitchen for a late supper. As Hannay, still wearing his heavy overcoat, cuts the bread and fries the haddock, "Miss Smith" sits at the table, seductively casual, slowly removing her gloves. She claims to be a spy on a mission, and says that there are two men lingering across the street, waiting to kill her. Hannay sees the men through the window, but responds coldly to her exotic story, muttering about "persecution mania" and keeping on that overcoat, as if fearing for his virtue; "You're welcome to my bed," he says, adding that he'll sleep out on the couch.

236

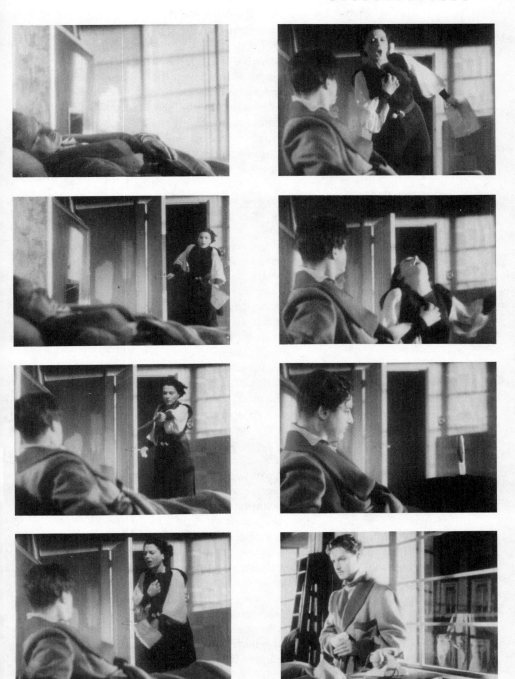

237

Late in the night, "Miss Smith" staggers into the room where Hannay lies sleeping: "Clear out—Hannay! Or they'll get you too!" She waves a piece of paper toward him, then throws her head back, chokes melodramatically, and falls. So far Hannay, sitting up on the couch, watches this unexpected death scene at a protective distance: Hitchcock shoots the woman's final agony as if it were a floor show, with Hannay as detached as any audience, his prostrate form defining the lower border of the frame, and his face turned toward the spectacle, away from us, as if he were someone sitting one seat ahead. But now Hannay's career as a spectator comes to an end. The woman falls startlingly across his lap, like a ballerina diving into the front row; and with the shock of this transgression comes the shocking revelation of a huge knife stuck in the woman's back.

Although we and Hannay see it simultaneously, Hannay ceases merely to watch. In looking down at the knife, he turns his face toward the camera, thereby giving up the viewer's sheltering anonymity and taking on the burdens of the actor. He is now vulnerable (shown for the first time without his overcoat), thrust into the very action which he had denied, and oddly guilty: Hitchcock cuts to a close-up of the telephone as it begins to ring again, then to a shot of Hannay backing toward the window, wiping his hands while staring uneasily off at the dead woman, exactly as if he himself had murdered her. The conjunction suggests that Hannay has discovered something fearful within himself: he is no innocent bystander, but capable of murder, like the men outside, or capable of being murdered, like the dead woman before him. He now assumes her obligations and her furtiveness, as if to acknowledge this realization.

The sequence is charged with more significance than can be fully treated here, but we ought to note this crucial strategy: Hannay at first regards his world as if he were not part of it, that is, just as we regard the film; and he can only become effective once he is surprised out of this attitude. Thus Hitchcock's main characters often first appear as emissaries from the realm of viewers. Carefully dressed and too sure of themselves, each apprehends his world like a bored spectator, killing time until the house lights come up. They presume themselves superior to what they watch; and we share that assumption, until coming to perceive the deeper resemblance between "hero" and "villain," the interdependence of "good" and "bad," and, by extension, the disturbing bonds between ourselves and those characters who had at first seemed evil, mad, ridiculous. Many of Hitchcock's strongest sequences are centered on a shot of recognition, in which some blithe viewer suddenly discerns himself: these shots become more powerful with time, the more we see them not as quick portraits of some "reaction" necessary to the plot, but as reflections.

Each of Hitchcock's masterpieces reflects upon its viewers differently. *Suspicion* plays on the distortions of subjective vision, showing how "suspicion" can imbue neutral images with a sense of menace: Lina suspects that her easygoing Johnnie is a murderer at heart, but only because Lina's heart is full of murder. In *Shadow of a Doubt*, satanic Uncle Charlie descends upon his sister's family in Santa Rosa, and threatens Charlie, his adoring niece, with disillusionment and death. This looks like a confrontation between good and evil, until we realize that the girl's "goodness" is merely our invention: in fact, she has called her uncle forth, and finds herself endangered by their similarity.

In *Notorious*, Alicia Huberman is repeatedly misjudged by Devlin and Sebastian, but the imperceptiveness of these two men is only a reflection of our own: Alicia is "notorious" because of us, the staring multitudes that take mean pleasure in a scandal. *Psycho* is unfailingly horrific because it suggests a deep complicity between Norman and his victims, between Norman and his viewers. And there are many more— *The Lodger, Sabotage, Secret Agent, Strangers on a Train, Vertigo, North by Northwest, The Birds*, and others—whose subtleties demand repeated viewings, whose meanings are neglected in every patronizing tribute to "the master of suspense."

These films suggest far more than any single eulogy can honor; and until they become the subject of an intensive criticism meant not only for academic readers, Hitchcock's place in cultural history will remain unappreciated. He may have been the most accomplished of modernists ("The fact is I practice absurdity quite religiously!"). As early as the 1920s, he was already working cleverly in the self-reflexive mode, and continued to do so with increasing sophistication: *North by Northwest*, for example, is a modernist masterpiece, centered on nothing at all, and repeatedly referring to itself with an inventiveness and wit unknown in our graduate seminars on literary theory. At the same time, Hitchcock's films display an exquisite sense of psychological nuance. They may be the most compelling works of this Freudian era, continually sifting "normal behavior" for its ambiguities and unspoken motives. Hitchcock may have presented more of the unconscious life than any other modern artist, from the telling quirks of everyday experience to the terrifying spells of madness. And Hitchcock's films are profoundly political. His stories of "ordinary people in bizarre situations" contain a vision as appalling as it is familiar: all of a sudden, determined agents come looking for the wrong man. This chilling situation conveys something of the panic that we sense in novels like *The Trial, Darkness at Noon*, and *1984*. But even more politically significant is Hitchcock's relentless method, available only to the filmmaker: his works encourage us to see anew, to purge our vision of official images and easy preconception. Surrounded by television, we may need Hitchcock's guidance more than ever.

Hitchcock's uneven reputation tells us something about the current state of film criticism, and also suggests that the Romantic myth of the artist is still causing confusion. If Hitchcock had been a haunted outcast, throwing up at fancy dinners and dying of cirrhosis in his forties, the reviewers would be calling him a genius. This myth is especially comforting to journalists. The success of Hollywood's great professionals—Hitchcock, Ford, Hawks—tends to rankle some reviewers, who would rather not be reminded that their judgments have no public effect whatsoever, and who therefore prefer directors who seem to need as many champions as possible: foreigners with slight domestic appeal and self-destructive or erratic types like Orson Welles and Erich von Stroheim. Many critics fail to hide a twinge of satisfaction when lamenting these abortive careers. Hitchcock, on the other hand, was too wry, too successful, too rotund to be hailed as a serious artist. He seemed, in fact, to use his public image to contradict that myth deliberately: with his pear shape, his sober clothes, his profile with its mock *hauteur*, he looked like an Edwardian greengrocer. His detractors missed the joke, taking it as evidence that Hitchcock lacked imagination, like any other stolid burgher.

That judgment was based on the most superficial of impressions, like all those glib celebrations and dismissals of his work. His great career should now be reconsidered. To refer to Alfred Hitchcock as "the master of suspense" makes as much sense as calling J. M. W. Turner "the seascape whiz," or calling James Joyce an "ace punster." He was the greatest of filmmakers, and among the greatest artists of this century. No other director has made films at once so popular and so profound; no other modern artist has moved so many different audiences for so long. For over fifty years, he tried to tease the viewer awake with films of astonishing complexity and power. Now that he is dead, we ought to look at them again.

Hitchcock's Suspicions and *Suspicion*

∎∎∎∎∎∎∎∎∎∎∎∎∎∎∎∎∎∎∎∎∎∎∎∎∎∎∎∎∎∎∎∎∎∎∎∎

The reason why a work of genius is not easily admired from the first is that the man who has created it is extraordinary, that few other men resemble him. It is his work itself that, by fertilising the rare minds capable of understanding it, will make them increase and multiply. It was Beethoven's quartets themselves (the Twelfth, Thirteenth, Fourteenth and Fifteenth) that devoted half a century to forming, fashioning and enlarging the audience for Beethoven's quartets, thus marking, like every great work of art, an advance if not in the quality of artists at least in the community of minds, largely composed to-day of what was not to be found when the work first appeared, that is to say of persons capable of appreciating it. What is called posterity is the posterity of the work of art.

Marcel Proust, *Within a Budding Grove*

FIRST IMPRESSIONS

The opening credits of Hitchcock's *Suspicion* assure us that the film we are about to see is going to be a "woman's picture." A slow orchestral overture begins to hum and tremble, and we see a few picturesque acres of well-tended countryside, receding beneath an expanse of afternoon sky—those clouds and leaves entirely motionless because sketched in crayon, the whole static prospect suggesting not a place outdoors but the execution of a "scene" imagined or remembered, an execution meant, perhaps, to fill in hours of tranquil boredom in a quiet house; and then we see, superimposed over this picture, the film's title, rendered in a stylized feminine hand, whereupon the other credits follow, as Franz Waxman's theme continues its luxuriant rise and fall, evoking the intoxicant and morbid atmosphere of a "Hollywood romance."

The picturesque backdrop, feminine script, and dulcet, quivering overture are obvious conventions of the "woman's film," a cinematic genre at the peak of its popularity when *Suspicion* was released in 1941.[1] Although broadly applied, however, these devices are apparent-

241

ly betrayed as soon as the film begins its story. Just after the credits end, the screen abruptly goes black, so that it looks as if the film has not actually started; although we hear the strident uproar of a speeding train, and, over it, a door banging shut, and then this suave apology, uttered by an unmistakable voice: "Oh, I beg your pardon. Was that your leg?" After a slight pause and no reply, the voice continues—"I had no idea we were going into a tunnel; I thought the compartment was empty"—as light flickers belatedly, then floods into the screen, and we see that this light comes from the window of a train compartment [fig. 1], which Cary Grant has just entered and where, as he settles in across from her, he now continues talking to a silent woman in the opposite seat.

"I'm so sorry," he says. "I hope I didn't hurt you." He complains about "a man in the next compartment, smoking a *vile* cigar," then asks her if she smokes, and she says, "No, I don't." "Oh, thank heaven for that," he rattles on, wincing with hangover. "After last night my head couldn't stand it. You understand, don't—?" And as if to see whether she's the type who'd "understand," he takes a closer look at her, which Hitchcock conveys with two slow tilts up her still figure, first showing her "sensible shoes," then the open book—*Child Psychology*, by Henrietta Wright M.A., M.D."—gripped firmly across her lap, and then her striped woolen coat of "mannish" cut, and finally [fig. 2] her disdainful, staring face, those eyes protectively surmounted by a low-brimmed hat, and overglazed by the wide, bright lenses of her spectacles, across which a dense and luminous reflection of the passing landscape streams like water overflowing the cold gaze of a virgin who has drowned herself to save her chastity. Confronted with this austere, well-guarded look, Cary Grant's own eyes respond with a flicker of dismay, and he imperceptibly shakes his head, as if to say, "No, I don't suppose you would."

After the credit sequence, with its implicit promise of "romance," here is a situation charged with unexpected comedy. The abrupt shift in mood entails, we now see, more than a merely sensational contrast, since the film is at once generically dislocated, or sidetracked, by the intrusion of Cary Grant, well-established, by 1941, as a comedian (albeit often in romantic situations), and essentially a presence neither somber nor cooperative enough to provide the occasion for a straight "love story."[2] Disconcertingly, *Suspicion* already seems to be *his* film. Charming, forward, slightly dissolute, he invades the story with an openness that invites and sustains our empathy; whereas, because of his reaction to her, his silent traveling companion seems not just forbidding but ridiculous. And yet this vehicle will soon be sidetracked once again.

Just as Cary Grant has withdrawn from their one-sided chat, a conductor enters the compartment to inspect their tickets. Looking efficient and severe in his quasi-military cap and uniform, the severity augmented by his graying cavalry moustache and hooded eyes, he stands between them, first taking her ticket, whose characters appear in an intrusive and apparently unnecessary tight shot: "Waterloo to Hazledene//First Class Fare." He then takes and pauses over Cary Grant's ticket, and initiates, with bland politeness, this exchange:

> Conductor
> I'm afraid you're in the wrong compartment, sir.

> Cary Grant
> (imperious)
> This is a first-class compartment, isn't it?

> Conductor
> Yes, sir.

> Cary Grant
> (with calm hauteur)
> Well then I'm all right.

> Conductor
> This is a third-class ticket, sir.

> Cary Grant
> (mildly taken aback)
> Hm?

He leans forward to take a look, and we too see his ticket in another gratuitous close-up: "HAZLEDENE THIRD CLASS THIRD CLASS"

> Cary Grant
> (indignant)
> Well, what sort of line is this, selling third-class tickets at first-class prices?

She, meanwhile, watches this intriguing comedy with a fascination almost hidden by her pretense at absorption in her book. [fig. 3]

> Conductor
> I'm very sorry, sir. That will be five-and-fourpence extra, sir.

243

      Cary Grant
      (haughty again)
You haven't change for a fiver, have you?

      Conductor
Yes, sir.
      Cary Grant
      (out of tricks)
Well then don't bother, because I haven't got one.

As he thinks things over, then starts going through his pockets, she still watches, peering furtively through her lenses, and between book and hat brim, eager to see what he'll try next.

      Cary Grant
      (counting his spare change)
Here's the best I can do.

He extends his handful of coins toward the conductor.

      Cary Grant
There. Now do you suppose the line could settle for five-and-two-pence-halfpenny?

The conductor stares back immobile; Cary Grant, also immobile, arm outstretched, returns the stare, then imperceptibly shakes his head.

      Cary Grant
No, I don't suppose they would.

He worries briefly, then lights up at the sight of his silent traveling companion, and leans towards her, that is, toward the camera, facing both her and us.

      Cary Grant
I hate to presume on our short acquaintance, but have you any change?

As if she has not been observing his dilemma, she pretends to be slightly startled by the question, then fishes hesitantly through her purse.

      Cary Grant
There! That stamp!

244

He reaches forward, toward the bottom of the frame, and plucks a stamp out of her hand; and as we hear him triumphantly counting out the whole amount in coins and postage, she stares at him with cold fury, clutching her purse shut with both hands. [fig. 4]

His imperious deference now replaced by a resentful glare, the conductor storms out.

> Cary Grant
> (flippant)
> Write to your mother!

The conductor slams the compartment doors together behind him, and Cary Grant flinches at the sound, then shoots us/her a look that says, "What a tiresome ass *he* was!" He then squints painfully into the sunlight glaring on him through the window, and shuts his eyes, covers them protectively with one hand, attempting, now that the fare's been taken care of, to sleep off the discomforts of the morning after.

She is now absorbed in a copy of the *Illustrated London News*, wherein she discovers his photograph. He is shown standing next to an elegantly dressed woman, the picture bearing this caption: "Mr. John (Johnny) Aysgarth with Mrs. Helen Newsham, Seen at Merchester."

Quietly astonished, she looks from the photograph up at him, and then we see, from her point of view, the same two images: first the photograph, and then the man, as he blinks again into the offending daylight, shakes his head once more, and settles down to sleep. [figs. 5-7]

At the scene's end, the narrative reverts to its original generic context, as this silent woman undergoes her sudden transition from the margins of a comedy to the center of a romance; and, in undergoing this shift, she appropriates the narrative, which will henceforth be determined by her own vision of her circumstances. In other words, when this woman finally both beholds and holds his picture, it is not just his photograph that she simultaneously sees and seizes, but also his vehicle—*Suspicion*—that now becomes *her* picture.

Just who is this woman, seemingly inert, and yet somehow powerful enough to dominate the narrative? When we first look closely at this guarded traveler, her most obvious and daunting characteristic is not her coldness, or her silence, or her angularity, but the general attitude that subsumes these traits: her manifest detachment. She is reading on a train. Although hurtling forward at inhuman speed, and in a public place where others can (and do) approach her, she reads as if alone and motionless, setting up an undeclared barrier against her fellow passengers. This air of privileged separateness, we can infer, reflects a sense of superiority based on the conviction of absolute innocence.[3] This reader sees herself as an exemplar of perfect mental health and/or moral probity, a self-image that is expressed first by her visible primness as she sits and reads, and then, more subtly, by the presumption of infallible objectivity advertised by her particular book—*Child Psychology*, "by Henrietta Wright." Like her whole posture, this manifest interest in child psychology betrays her powerful belief that she is fundamentally detached. She presumes herself entirely innocent of those unaccountable drives that madden children, innocent enough to look on at such unruliness and manage it, always in the right (or "Wright").

And yet this manifest detachment, apparently her definitive feature when the scene begins, is soon subverted by the scene itself, which demonstrates the self-contradiction implicit in her pose as an objective onlooker. When the conductor interrupts their abortive conversation, he subtly alters the configuration in the scene by allowing her to change from a staring object to a staring subject. What was for her a social, physical encounter, threatening in its potential intimacy, has now become a comic spectacle that comfortably excludes her. Her look of surreptitious fascination suggests her sudden sense of freedom, as, no longer forced to defend herself against the intruder's gaze, she now feels herself liberated to peek thrillingly through the screen constituted by her glasses, book, and hat brim, as if invisible herself in viewing the altercation between intruder and conductor.

Although the conductor plays the butt in the vaudevillian conflict that so furtively amuses her, he is in fact her substitute and double. She permits herself to abandon her original suspicion of Cary Grant only because the conductor now evinces it on her behalf, thereby becoming, in her eyes, a derisible walk-on such as she had seemed, just before, to us. And, in thus taking over her suspicion for her, the conductor causes, and becomes entangled in, a repetition of the previous confrontation. In waiting for the payment, he directs at Cary Grant the same off-putting stare [fig. 8], manifests precisely the same distaste for a dissolute and untrustworthy playboy, with which she had just fended off her future husband. And, just as the conductor has reenacted her previous distrust, so does Cary Grant deflate this substitute antagonist exactly as he had just turned her frigidity into a joke: "After last night my head couldn't stand it. You understand, don't—?" But she clearly did not "understand," as his dubious glance and slight shake of the head made comically obvious; and now he asks this second adversary a second such question, also intended to get an unavailing stranger to see things his way—"Now do you suppose the line could settle for five-and-twopence-halfpenny?"—and likewise subverts the second cold starer with a second comic gesture of mock concurrence.

Thus far, the scene has imaged forth a partial critique of that unspoken doctrine of detachment that the reader on the train attempts to realize. First, and most obviously, the critique refers to the heroine's revealing gaze. In watching this recurrence of the previous moment, she is now evidently as pleased as she has just felt menaced; for the man who has just assailed her with his direct attentions now seems comfortably removed from her, discomfiting a substitute victim within the apparent borders of a spectacle. In short, she imperceptibly betrays herself, taking pleasure in the sheltered observation of improprieties that would offend her if she were actually subjected to them. This evident pleasure suggests that she is, in fact, empathically involved, partaking eagerly of the vicarious experience of domination; and so she unwittingly contradicts the uninvolvement that she advertises through her glacial attitude.

At this moment in *Suspicion*, however, this fictitious woman is not the only spectator who pretends to a complete detachment that itself enables a complete absorption. She is in fact *our* substitute, the double of each viewer who sits and looks at her. When she first appears in close-up, her image displays back down to us our own positions in the audience: her quiescence, her ostensible aloofness, her passivity, her wide eyes staring into a reflective field of moving images, are the very features of the attitude in which we watch her. And yet it is not her mere physical resemblance to ourselves wherein the crucial similarity consists, but in our immediate assumption that there is no similarity. Just as her book and demeanor signify her belief that she is fundamentally exceptional, so does our first response to her appearance betray our own identical assumption, when, influenced by Cary Grant's uneasy look, we laugh at her as if exempt from her peculiar situation, just as, a moment later, she will laugh at the conductor's dilemma as if not stuck in it herself. In short, we are, quite literally, in no position to endorse and share in Cary Grant's quick assessment of her character, because we are in her position.

Her picture, in other words, turns out to be our picture, too. All her responses in this scene, however idiosyncratic they appear at first, repeat our own responses as we watch her. (And/or vice versa: we are her reflection, as she is ours.) Like her, Hitchcock implies, we presume ourselves to be detached, and yet it is through this presumption that we actually absorb ourselves. And, as she does (Hitchcock implies further), we thus disingenuously keep our distance in order to take vicarious pleasure in a spectacle of behavior that, in actuality, would frighten us.

247

But what is it that we fear? What is it that has driven us to take this cinematic refuge? Hitchcock implies an answer to these questions by using, then by pointedly subverting, the conventional credit sequence of the woman's film. With its lush strains and artificial "scene," that sequence appeared to answer our desire for a perfectly hermetic fantasy, one that might enable the illusion of escape from the very weakness that impelled us to attend this movie in the first place. We have come here, paradoxically, to surrender to a vicarious experience of power, to know empathically the feeling of omnipotence, yet without any of the risks that must jeopardize any actual self-exaltation. The credit sequence implicitly assures us that *Suspicion* will be, as it were, a private vehicle, and one safe, comfortable, and grand enough to carry each of us away from the gross pressures and keen disappointments of real intercourse.

To put it sociologically, we would say that the credit sequence was clearly intended to reassure those female viewers who came hoping to escape into a woman's film. While this was undoubtedly the case, we need not therefore assume that no male viewer could have warmed to the film's ostensible appeal. Whether it allures the female devotees of its apparent genre, or those male viewers whose expectations it has subtly feminized, *Suspicion* starts out by addressing an audience of desperate fantasists. Thus it would seem that, as implied by this opening scene, the similarity between ourselves and the movie's heroine is inexact, since we each long to be the center of a dreamworld, whereas she, with her gleaming spectacles and somber academic manual, appears to be no romantic, but a cold-eyed clinician. And yet, despite this superficial difference, there is a deeper similarity between this ruthless positivist and us devout daydreamers, for she strives to attain, through her presumed objectivity, to precisely the same sense of perfect dominance that we viewers hope to experience through empathy with some fictitious hero. It is her constant aim to occupy the invulnerable standpoint of an omniscient and immaculate observer, a position identical, in its apparent strength, to that safe, central place into which we intend to project ourselves, and which, the credit sequence tells us, is now ready for us.

No sooner is this promise made, however, than it is jarringly denied, as the screen suddenly reverts to blackness, out of which that voice apologizes for an unexpected collision with an unknown body: "I beg your pardon. Was that your leg?" The moment constitutes a rude retraction of the previous offer of escape by referring us back to these dark aisles, where actual others wander past, sit next to us, bump into us. This oblique reference to our real presence in the theater momentarily betrays to us our own escapist motivation by reminding us of the particular reality which we have come into this theater to escape—the reality *of* this theater, in which each of us is not a lone and disembodied gaze, but part of a crowd, and a being as visible as any filmed persona, and far more vulnerable because corporeal, mortal and desirous.

Such is the profound weakness of the spectator's seemingly masterful position, which she strives relentlessly to occupy throughout this opening scene (and throughout the film), always reflecting back to us our own identical, equally futile effort. She, like us, was sitting, waiting in the darkness when the film began; and she, like us, absorbed in the unfolding spectacle, resents any too-palpable interruption of her fantasizing, resists any actual contact that might threaten to supplant its antiseptic visual substitute. For us, the substitute is, in this case, *Suspicion*, or that banal *Suspicion* which the credit sequence promised us. For her, the substitute is the spectacle that she continually tries to construct out of her circumstances, a spectacle from which she assumes herself to be dissociated, and yet in which she also sees herself as central.

Originally discomposed by his physical invasion, she completely recovers her fragile equanimity, indeed, as we have seen, utterly reverses her prior mood, once she can regard his disruptiveness as a purely spectacular event, and one, therefore, from which (she thinks) she can remain exempt. However, her relationship to this spectacle is still unsatisfying, still too clearly compromised to enable the illusion of perfect mastery. The inadequacy of her position relates directly to the film's generic dislocation. Although she has now temporarily discovered the spectator's easy sense of perfect might, that sense is, in this case, entirely contingent on his imposing masculine image. Unexpectedly included in what appears to be a screwball comedy, she must experience the sense of dominance by identifying with his greater recklessness, resourcefulness, and stature—qualities that, paradoxically, only offset her blatant, sedentary weakness as she sits admiring them.

It is this actual weakness that Cary Grant temporarily exposes when, in need of extra funds, he turns toward her (and us), unexpectedly asking for "change." Now he offends her much more deeply than he had at first, sabotaging all her contradictory assumptions. First, he has deprived her of her safety, has reached across the intervening space, touching her hand and taking something from her, reminding her that she is neither absent nor invisible but both physically present and as visible as he, a transgression that returns him, once again, to the status of a "masher" who prowls movie theaters, looking for unescorted ladies like herself: "I beg your pardon. Was that your leg?" Moreover, his action points to her complicity in his performance, for, by taking her stamp to make up his needed payment, he has made her an accomplice in an instance of chicanery that she preferred to regard as a self-enclosed and distant "scene"—an accomplice, and a mere walk-on at that, a demotion unforgivable in her eyes, for in her eyes *she* is the main character in the film which she imagines, a woman's film, *this* woman's film, and not the comedy in which he clearly stars, and into which he has so easily allured her. For these contradictory reasons, she reacts with a rage as unselfconscious as it is subdued, feeling herself at once robbed, belittled, violated, and exposed, clutching her purse shut after the fact as the victim of a rape will try to hold her torn clothes together, as if to return to the time when they and she were still intact.

And yet her response to this rude exposure of her pose is not indignantly to disavow her spectatorship, but, perversely, to throw herself more ardently into her viewing. Bitterly offended, she now absorbs herself in her copy of the *Illustrated London News* as if to hide herself and blot him out, for the magazine's capacious format provides, as it were, better cover than the smaller *Child Psychology*. She flees into her magazine just as the devotee of woman's films, appalled by the risks of human intercourse—appalled, that is, by her desire to run them—will try to overcome the threat by losing herself in the colossal glow and fashionable components of the fantasy up on the screen. And yet, in both cases, the escapist flees toward images that do not annihilate the gross, importunate reality that motivated her to flee, but only revise it. Such "escape" is no escape, since it only seeks the object that inspired it, seeking it, of course, in a form that is both more manageable and more exalted. Thus it is that, when she tries to forget him by taking up the magazine, the first thing she discovers in its pages is his image, which reminds her of his erstwhile pleasurable status as the object of her self-effacing scrutiny, and with which she falls in love at once, tearing it out (as we soon learn) to cherish it in secret.

Her strong attraction to this smart portrait of the man who has just affronted her is not, then, as odd a reaction as it might seem at first, because this preference for the picture over its unpredictable referent, who sits trying to doze off in the opposite seat, repeats our preference for the motion picture over the relationships that it both supplants and idealizes. Thus the ambiguity implicit in the opening moment—"I beg your pardon. Was that your leg?"—has been fantastically resolved, the presence of the threat neurotically denied, as she reasserts the promised context of the woman's film by retreating into just the sort of fantasy desired by those who would have wanted such a movie. Twice jolted out of her absorption, she now makes a third attempt to occupy a standpoint that is permanently unassailable; and although the effort proves to be impossible, since she struggles to maintain that tenuous position in her own mind, she does succeed in capturing the narrative, taking us with her into her waking dream. Because of her influence, our narcissism now overcomes our craving for a hero. At first, we thought ourselves detached from her and allied with him, siding with the superior charm of a likable would-be seducer; whereas in fact it is she with whom we finally and (as yet) unknowingly ally ourselves, perfectly seduced, not by his aristocratic casualness and marvelous good looks, but by her ceaseless watchfulness, wherein consists an irresistible resemblance to ourselves.

THE LADY VANQUISHES

There now immediately follows a short scene that also seems to take his point of view, yet which serves, in fact, to tell us that his point of view is doomed. On the morning of a hunt, in the midst of a patrician crowd preparing to mount up, John Aysgarth appears between two middle-aged ladies, the three of them dressed with equal masculinity for the occasion. A photographer approaches and obsequiously asks to take his picture, requesting "a little bit more of your smile." Aysgarth complies mechanically, whereupon the photographer twice tries, and fails, to record the hero's image. First, three women rush brightly in on Aysgarth, flirting vigorously and impeding the photographer's view. And then, once they have bustled off, the photographer takes aim a second time, but Aysgarth, distracted by the sounds of a struggling horse, suddenly looks off to his left, and the photographer, balked again, looks off too.

What they see is a female rider reining in her fractious mount, surrounded by an immobile group of staring men. There is a dolly-in on Aysgarth's rapt expression, and then a close-up of the rider's face, its transformation the cause of his uncharacteristic wonderment: "I can hardly believe it," he murmurs. "Can't be the same girl!" But it is indeed the same woman who had glared at him back on the train, her face now as radiant, commanding, and serene as it had appeared pallid, tense, and guarded. Having regained his worldly air, Aysgarth asks one of his companions for an introduction, which she refuses, claiming that this woman is "not up your alley." He resolves to meet the rider on his own, and then the three of them turn to leave; whereupon we see the forgotten photographer slowly turn to leave as well, looking back in resentful disappointment at his elusive subject.

What this brief event accomplishes is not just to advance the lovers' relationship (a function, of course, necessary to the plot), but also to suggest that this relationship is static. For what attracts him to her is her air of narcissistic dominance, her manifest sense of being in command in her own eyes, a visible quality that, paradoxically, will prevent him—has already prevented him—from approaching her as the

251

quiescent, merely decorative figure that such a will as hers must have within its province. It is his desire for her control that makes him uncontrollable. As engrossed in her image as she is, he becomes too distracted to be photographed, is jarred into a keen desirousness that makes him something other than the public image that consoled her on the train. What she wants is not this man whom she has inadvertently surprised into life, but that diminutive, unchanging image that she can keep in mind, or pressed between the pages of her book: the same image coveted by the photographer, whose parting bitterness prefigures her own murderous unhappiness at Johnny's actual, ungovernable behavior.

As this scene suggests that they must remain estranged by the very forces that have mutually attracted them, moreover, so does it foretell the imminent extinction of his point of view. Because of her commanding image, his picture never does get taken. The photographer's deprivation thus anticipates our own, for Cary Grant, presumably the costar of *Suspicion*, is about to slip into obscurity (an abrupt reduction as surprising, in its quiet way, as the notorious cutting-off of Janet Leigh in *Psycho*). Absorbed into the tableau which she will henceforth impose on her reality—a tableau in which the only well-lit figure is her own—he will quickly dwindle from the leading man into an object even more marginal, opaque, and sinister than she had seemed initially.

Conversely, it is she who will now—in a dual sense—take the lead; and yet, while she will remain continually visible, she will actually be hiding underneath that lustrous self-projection. From this moment, she will not merely dominate the story, but will actually invent it, creating a conventional fiction out of desires and circumstances far more complex—desires and circumstances whose traces we must try to find within the very story that she uses to conceal them.

THE GENTLE READER

The action now shifts into her domain. An establishing shot presents the exterior of her father's estate: a Tudor country house fronted by meticulously tended grounds, the quiet and seclusion of the setting accentuated by the measured tolling of distant church bells, and the beginnings of an orchestral overture as peaceful as a lullaby (the aural serenity all the more pronounced by contrast with the din of hunting horns and barking dogs that closed the previous scene). These sounds ease us indoors, into the vast, elegant front room, which we see in a master shot [fig. 9] composed like a weighty and expensive stage set, or a full-page magazine ad meant to represent manorial luxury: a grand piano topped by a vase of flowers, a formidable armchair, a credenza and other such massy furnishings appear carefully arranged across the frame; and in the midst of this tableau, in the center of a window seat located at the vertex of the triangle composed by two fixed, trapezoidal sunbeams that highlight sections of the carpet, she lounges pensively, head resting on one hand, an open book lying across her lap.

Through two cuts we move in on her unmoving figure, first to a medium shot in which she shares the frame with an enameled lamp, then into a medium close-up that has her posed against the cushions and bay window; and yet we learn nothing more from this approach, because in all three shots her expression is equally illegible, her head inclined so as to make it unclear whether her eyes are closed (which would mean that she has drifted off while reading) or open (which would mean that she is reading still).

This cautious approach, which constitutes the real beginning of the romantic film proclaimed by the credit sequence, evinces the tactful hesitancy of a vistor, as if we, unbeknownst to her, have simply found her here; whereas this implicit deference actually reflects her own regard for her own image as she conceives it in the placid context of the woman's film. The approach is measured, gradual, without surprises, and therefore in marked contrast to the story's opening, when Aysgarth seemed to turn up out of nowhere. (Virtually all of his first appearances are disconcertingly abrupt.) This gradualness, and the set's imposing theatricality, do not just visually flatter her, then, but also implicitly rule out all possibility of comedy, in favor of the more sedate generic atmosphere in which she feels at home.

In short, what we now see is both the contents of a fantasy, and the fantasist herself, both dream and dreamer simultaneously depicted. And, in this attitude (and still unnamed), she is again reflective of the (anonymous) viewers who watch her in the same escapist mood in which she thus depicts herself. The ambiguity of her appearance is therefore fitting: does she wake or sleep? As we soon learn, she is not really reading even if awake, because it is not the book itself that occupies her, but Johnny's picture which she now admires, either dreaming of, daydreaming about or looking at his image. Whether or not her eyes are closed thus makes no difference, since, in either case, she is presently absorbed in fantasy, just like those who look both at and with her, albeit with their eyes unquestionably open.

In its essential similarity to the absorption of the viewers watching her, her own absorption in her picture/book suggests a certain self-image that is bolstered both by the woman's film and by its literary parent and analogue, the Gothic romance, a self-image that is a specific variant, generically determined, of the viewer's basic self-conception as Hitchcock reflects on it throughout his films. The romantic "reader," typified by the heroine of *Suspicion* as she reflects her audience, presumes herself not merely innocent, but passive, ever-to-be-victimized, thrillingly beset by the figments of the fantasy that she herself admits or generates. Moreover, this passivity is subtly sentimentalized both by the fantasy—whether filmed or written—that celebrates it, and by the inert consumer who at once admires and evinces it. Spellbound over Aysgarth's picture, this daydreamer manifests the sentimental process through her air of maiden wistfulness (an air that she continues often to affect until the final scene), as well as through the various touches—the church bells, flowers, lulling strings, etc.—that further soften her self-presentation.

Hitchcock, however, is not concerned to devise the sort of commonplace narcotic demanded by such fantasists, but rather to examine that demand. In *Suspicion*, he evokes romantic fantasy only to expose or trace the unconscious drives to which it actually appeals even as it carefully denies them. His interest, then, is not in the objective plight of some pure victim, but in the impulse to imagine such a plight, an impulse shared by both the heroine of *Suspicion* and its surrendering viewers. Thus the film is an oblique revision of *Rebecca* (1940), Hitchcock's first American production, and one whose literary source—Daphne du Maurier's best-seller—is a straightforward exercise in Gothic fantasy. Although constrained by its producer, David O. Selznick, to adapt *Rebecca* with meticulous fidelity,[4] in the later film Hitchcock retroactively subverts the premise of du Maurier's novel and his own adaptation. Like *Rebecca*, *Suspicion* is set among the rural gentry of prewar England, and stars Joan Fontaine as an inexperienced young woman who finds herself trapped in a sinister marriage with a handsome, threatening man. Despite this general similarity, however, there is one crucial difference. A perfect innocent, the nameless heroine of *Rebecca* at first seems menaced by a supernatural force (Rebecca's ghost or influence) that eventually turns out to have a rational explanation; whereas *Suspicion* inverts this Gothic pattern by presenting a heroine who is not the victim but the unconscious authoress of the evil that she fears, and which thus turns out to have, as it were, an irrational explanation.

In order to subjectivize the dark romantic plot—or, rather, to demonstrate that the appetite for such a plot is itself the fearful mystery that motivates the plot—Hitchcock chose to adapt another contemporary novel exactly as he would have wanted to adapt *Rebecca*. *Before the Fact*, by "Francis Iles" (A. B. Cox), tells the story of a woman who comes not merely to suspect, but to discover that her husband is a murderer, among other things.[5] Like Hitchcock's Aysgarth, Cox's is an irresistible charmer; but beneath that superficial charm, or because of it, the literary character is utterly satanic. Not only is he a liar and embezzler (as is Hitchcock's character), but he seduces every woman of his wife's acquaintance (including her maid), steals from his own houseguests, and murders Beaky, his best friend, as well as the heroine's father and, finally, the heroine herself. Like Iago, or Lovelace, this Aysgarth is relentlessly at work behind the scenes, the sole author of every disaster that befalls his uncomprehending partner.

Although Hitchcock later told Truffaut that he had wanted to end *Suspicion* with the husband's really murdering the wife (and then unwittingly triggering his own capture),[6] this account tells us less about Hitchcock's real intentions as director than it reveals of his inventiveness as a raconteur, since there is no such ending written into any of the screenplay's several drafts, although there does survive an early memo succinctly formulating Hitchcock's contrary design: "He will follow the novel as to story, persons, locale and sets, excepting only that he would tell the story as through the eyes of the woman and have the husband be villainous in her imagination only."[7] The crimes that the novel's Aysgarth actually commits are the imaginary crimes that obsess the film's heroine. Thus the novel's subject has become the movie's subtext: the passive and endangered heroine, of the sort whose thorough innocence the woman's film and Gothic novel function to confirm, is here exposed as the real source of the animus that so terrifies her, and which she ceaselessly imputes to the very one whom she, in fact, would like to kill.

Despite her initial pose of clinical detachment, then, she can actually see nothing clearly; but we cannot yet discern her blindness. Here at the beginning of her self-depiction, she so flatteringly reflects us as she sits and reads that we cannot suspect (unless we choose to be unlike her) that she has gained her sudden centrality at the expense of that objective vision to which she had pretended on the train. Her stardom is the proof of her delusion, which, from this moment, will continue to intensify: as soon as she is roused from her absorption on the window seat, she merely sinks, although physically awake, more deeply into her dream.

Her reverie is ostensibly interrupted by the intrusion behind her, outside the window, of a middle-aged woman, who simultaneously raps on the glass and speaks the heroine's name (now heard for the first time): "Lina!" she calls. "May we come in?" [fig. 10] As Lina rises, the woman enters an adjacent door, followed by her two grown daughters. (They are the Byrums, the trio who had mobbed Aysgarth at the hunt.) They have come to introduce someone, they say, glancing eagerly toward the empty doorway in their midst, creating suspense, and in suspense themselves, like chorus girls poised around the archway, center

255

stage, through which some famous song-and-dance man is about to make his entrance: Aysgarth then steps, beaming, through that entranceway, and is introduced to this woman who has just been thinking of him, and who receives him with a smile after hastily removing her glasses.

Mrs. Byrum's arrival would appear to constitute a call to leave the realm of fantasy and reenter the "real world." Her rapping on the glass and thereby rousing Lina out of her flattering position within her own tableau suggests the interruption, by a mundane outsider, of the movie in which Lina stars herself, and which Lina is herself projecting; for the window that separates Lina from her present visitor metaphorically suggests the screen that separates Lina from her present viewers. Moreover, by naming Lina as she awakens her, Mrs. Byrum finally dispels that anonymity which has been one feature of the general likeness between Lina and the viewers on whose behalf, and in whose image, the heroine sits there dreaming so attractively. And yet the similarity persists, since Lina keeps on dreaming even after this intrusion, which, in fact, is merely the inauguration of the dream's sweet climax. Whereas the lovers' first encounter had ended with Lina's flight from the real Aysgarth into a fantasy inspired by his image, now she "awakens" from that dream, and finds him real: this second apprehension does not reverse the prior movement into reverie, but continues it, the fantastic bias of her perception implied by both the miraculous timeliness and the marked theatricality of his entrance, as well as by her immediate abandonment of her glasses (a gesture whereby she simultaneously prettifies herself and blurs her situation).

Her romantic vision now appears to have imposed itself completely on her circumstances: all unsuspecting, and in a fetching pose, she has been sought out by—quite literally—the man of her dreams. And yet at this very moment of its apparent realization, her vision begins to crack apart against the actual object that provoked it. While expecting to maintain her place in his affections, she also struggles to enforce his place within her spectacle. Thus we see her romantic vision under stress, rent by the contradictory impulses that have created it, and betraying those realities that she intends it to suppress. Although she has apparently progressed beyond the moment of her initial vulnerability, and actively controls this vehicle as capably as she had reined in her horse, she betrays her actual entrapment through her persistent efforts to sustain, in her real life, the viewer's sense of perfect strength, efforts that repeatedly return her, paradoxically, to her status as a helpless passenger sitting in that same first-class compartment.

Aysgarth having so conveniently materialized, her circumstances and her dream appear inseparable, but then he immediately frustrates her by demoting her, again, to a subsidiary role. He invites her to join the Byrums and himself on their excursion to church. (As soon as she leaves the room to get ready, he finds his photograph between the pages of her book.) We then see all five stroll down a winding country lane as picturesque as RKO could make it—bent trees, frisking dogs, rural folks chatting beside the stile, etc.—and the score turns light and frolicsome; but this idyllic picture obviously displeases her because she has lost control of it. As Aysgarth leads the way with Mrs. Byrum at his side, Lina, ignored and looking vexed, brings up the rear between the daughters; and, as if enjoying his ability to flaw her depiction, Aysgarth actually whistles along with the merry background score, jarringly off-key.

Whereas, at this moment, it is her insignificance that bothers her, the next moment it is the direct attention of an Aysgarth far too palpable that frightens her. At the church gate, Aysgarth lets the others go on ahead and, grabbing Lina by the arm, tells her that the two of them are going for a walk. She protests, whereupon we see the Byrums pause at the church door and turn, then look bewildered, their two companions having vanished. Hitchcock then cuts from the empty gateway, seen from the Byrums' point of view, to a long shot of a remote and windy cliffside, as the playful music shifts into an ominous and plaintive minor chord, and we see Lina fighting desperately to free herself from Aysgarth's grip.

In a two-shot, as the music turns more subdued, the action proceeds less melodramatically: "What did you think I was trying to do? Kill you?" Aysgarth asks ironically. "Nothing less than murder could justify such violent self-defense! Look at you!" "Let me go!" she says, trembling. "Oh, I'm just beginning to understand. You thought I was going to kiss you, didn't you?" "Weren't you?" she asks. But he claims that he was merely trying to rearrange her hair, which is "all wrong"; and as they continue their revealing conversation, Aysgarth stands behind her and starts "fiddling" (as she puts it) with her hair. This treatment, however, is, in Lina's eyes, hardly less offensive than the assault which she had just imagined, since his behavior as "a passionate hairdresser" (as he has just jokingly described himself) reminds her of her vulnerability no less forcibly than an attempted rape or murder: *he* is now attempting to control *her* image, and so again has exerted his own mastery by emphasizing her visibility ("Look at you!").

But she must remain the supervisor of any picture in which Aysgarth appears romantically involved, an anxiety that she betrays in what sounds like an attempt to let him know that *she* has been keeping *him* under surveillance: "I must be quite a novelty by contrast with the women that you're photographed with." And then he too gives himself away: "What do you think of me—by contrast with your horse?"

"I think that if I got the bit between your teeth," she answers, now smiling to herself, "I'd have no trouble in handling you at all." Thus again she gives herself away, expressing the desire to subjugate him, the desire which she now continues to express by physically eluding him, in order to put back between them the necessary distance between herself-as-viewer and the spectacle in which she simultaneously stars: he bends forward to kiss her, and she pulls away ("I think you've done enough fiddling with my hair"), stands opposite him, takes a mirror from her purse and starts tensely studying her reflection.

For the first time, he seems frankly irritated, as if he has now sensed that the same self-absorption that originally attracted him could also exclude him. "You don't look very good like that," he says, his humor turning sour. "You look more like a monkey with a bit of mirror. What does your family call you—'Monkey-face'?" This epithet, hereafter his affectionate nickname for her, implies not only Aysgarth's accurate perception of Lina's narcissism, but also that essential similarity between Lina and her viewers (on) which the film continually reflects: "a monkey with a bit of mirror," eternally mimicking its own expression, constitutes an incisive metaphor for Lina's audience, herself included. (In Cox's novel, Johnny calls Lina "Monkey-face" because she grimaces when she eats.) Lina says nothing in reply to Aysgarth's question, but demonstrates the truth of his remarks by once more pulling back as he bends down once more to kiss her, pulling back, moreover, temporally as well as physically. Just as their lips are about to meet, she snaps her purse shut pointedly between them (an action revealed in an inserted tight shot of her hands), then rears back and gazes coldly at him. Aside from whatever this image might suggest about Lina's associating her virginity with her financial assets, the gesture represents specifically her effort to return to, and revise, that disturbing moment when he had taken the postage stamp from that same purse; and her gaze also returns them to that earlier moment on the train, when she first fended off his garrulous overtures with the same frozen stare.

And yet, as on the train, her very effort to preserve her uninvolvement eventuates in her becoming inextricably involved. Coolly gathering up her things, she starts off toward home, jesting sardonically that "if my father saw me coming home both late *and* beautiful, he might have a stroke." The two of them then approach her house; Aysgarth tells her that he will return to take her out again that afternoon, and she takes umbrage at his forwardness. As she approaches the front door, she overhears her father (Cedric Hardwicke) discussing her future. "Lina will never marry, she's not the marrying sort," he says to her mother, insisting that "the 'old maid' is a respectable institution. Besides, Lina has intellect, and a fine, solid character." With a stricken look,

Lina turns away, horrified at hearing herself thus described as precisely the sort of "solid," sexless, and permanently detached figure as she had appeared back on the train, and as she had attempted to appear again, just now, with Aysgarth, who is now standing right behind her, chuckling. And as if to deny that eternal posture of spectatorship that her father has approvingly predicted for her, Lina once again contradicts her own erstwhile cold pose by embracing Aysgarth's image; for, at this moment, all that Aysgarth represents in her eyes is a symbol of that recklessness and glamour which her father has forbidden her. Suddenly and violently, she stops his laughter with a kiss—a kiss that is not erotic but spectacular, a kiss that puts a stop, not just to Aysgarth's laughter at this moment but to his comic influence entirely; puts a stop, indeed, to *him*. For that angry kiss expresses, not her interest in him, but her impulsive resolution to inhabit as well as dominate the spectacle, a move that she will try to make at the expense of Aysgarth's actuality. Now that she has chosen him, he no longer really matters, since all she wants is to regard herself as starring in the movie that his appearance has enabled. As she runs into the house, leaving him amazed at her assault, there is not even a reaction shot of him, because his feelings, in this woman's film, are quite irrelevant.

"NO TROUBLE IN HANDLING YOU AT ALL"

The remainder of the plot is simple. They marry, then Lina gradually becomes convinced that Johnny, who, she learns after their honeymoon, is penniless, is trying to kill her to collect on her insurance. As in the novel, there are two deaths that precede the final attempt on her own life (successful in the book, imagined in the film). First, her father dies; then Johnny's best friend, Beaky Thwaite. Whereas these deaths occur at Johnny's hands in Cox's novel, in the film they function to expose the workings of that (so to speak) collective unconscious that motivates both Lina and her audience.

Before discussing the visual implications of her father's death, which significantly darkens Lina's vision, we should examine that vision in the first of its two phases, when it appears to be as happy as it will soon become intensely gloomy. This happiness, however, is tenuous, dependent on that fragile sense of dominance that she is able to sustain only as a spectator. It is this urge to dominate that we continue to discover in the very spectacle that both expresses and conceals it.

After defiantly announcing to her parents, over lunch, that she has been out with John Aysgarth, and will be going out with him again, she argues with her father about her lover's character (he has heard something unpleasant about that character, although he cannot remember

259

what it was), and then receives a telephone call from Johnny (whom we do not see), who cancels their date and then temporarily vanishes from the action. She therefore falls into deep melancholy, tries to call him, waits for a letter than never comes, even returns longingly to that secluded spot where she had fought him off. After this montage, we see her sitting, crushed and weeping, in her bedroom on the evening of the annual Hunt Ball, her gown for the occasion hanging on her wardrobe door. Her mother (Dame May Whitty) asks her why she is not dressed yet, and she replies that she is ill, whereupon her mother starts to search the room for aspirin. A servant then brings in a telegram from Johnny, which tells her that he will be coming to the ball, and will expect to see her there. We read the telegram through her eyes, see her hand thrust her glasses violently down onto it. Overjoyed, she jumps up and, as the music bursts into a glorious flourish, stands with a look of ecstasy in the middle of the room, where her mother also stands, off to the side, still looking for pills. [fig. 11]

Now we see her at the ball, searching the crowd with anxious eyes— an image that, like her present situation, connotes her hopeful expectancy, her dependence on the whims of her beloved, attitudes that imply the sort of maidenly modesty that befits, and is celebrated by, her chosen genre; and yet virtually every frame in this conventional depiction of passivity betrays the iron will that has determined it. A balding young man in hunting pinks, and considerably shorter than Johnny, approaches her wide-eyed and asks petulantly, "What about our dance?" Momentarily distracted, she recalls her promise: "Oh, yes," she laughs with gentle condescension. "Poor Reggie!" Just then we see her father, Gen. McLaidlaw, and another older man, both wearing outfits identical to Reggie's, standing in the doorway. They exchange comments on Lina's unusually fine appearance, and then a butler in evening dress comes over to tell Lina's father that "a Mr. Aysgarth" has arrived, claiming to belong to Gen. McLaidlaw's party.

Her father grumbles in astonishment. Hitchcock then cuts, with the usual abruptness, to Aysgarth, who is also wearing evening dress, and striding masterfully toward the ballroom door. Smiling, he presents himself to Gen. McLaidlaw, who disavows any knowledge of having invited him. "Oh, how awkward," Aysgarth replies. "I thought you had. Otherwise I should never have come all the way from London." The general starts, harrumphs, then mutters, "Why—I don't know what to say!" "Well, you'd better say something," Aysgarth answers, motioning toward the butler standing behind him, "or you'll embarrass this poor man to death!" At this delicate moment, Lina sees him, and flies over to him, leaving the downcast Reggie by himself; and then, as she stands before Aysgarth, several other women—just as on the morning of the hunt—rush up to him with bright flirtatious greetings. Stepping through the knot of his admirers, he takes Lina's hand.

Although he evinces here the same resourcefulness and daring with which he had defeated the conductor, he does so now in Lina's context, and so those disruptive qualities serve to flatter rather than discomfit her. His clothes, first of all, identify him with the butler (as does his mock-sympathetic reference to "*this* poor man"), suggesting his servile position in her fantasy, a servility to her alone: the men are bested by his good looks and his charm, the women quite bowled over. And yet it is not Aysgarth himself who derives the benefit of these conquests, but Lina, for whose sake he has achieved them. The women are without identities, mere faceless adulators who comprise a yearning horde against which Lina's easy victory seems all the more vivid. Their function, in other words, is entirely pictorial, offsetting her resplendent happiness with their collective deprivation: as they mob Aysgarth, they form an adoring circle that actually appears to include a pair of painted figures, two delighted young ladies shown running forward in a large old portrait hanging on the wall at Aysgarth's back [fig. 12]. And, like the defeat of all those females, so does the males' defeat redound to Lina's greater glory, but in a way that is psychologically more telling. In her patronizing laughter at "poor Reggie," Lina demonstrates the managerial adeptness of the child psychologist, as she will later do with Beaky and with Johnny himself. ("Johnny! I'm just beginning to understand you! You're a *baby*!") However, it is not just her peculiar strategy in dealing with all men that is exemplified by her patronizing Reggie-as-opposed-to-Aysgarth, but in rejecting Reggie with such ease she also betrays her deep and complicated hatred of one man in particular—the man who represents herself-as-spectator, he who stares distrustfully at Aysgarth just as she had stared back on the train, and who now seems to resent the interloper as much as Reggie does: her father, another short, balding figure in hunting pinks.

As Aysgarth takes her hand, a waltz begins to play as if on cue, and they, as if on cue, start waltzing. After a few turns, they steal from the house and out to his car. He takes them for a drive, and soon asks her if she has "ever been kissed in a car before." "Don't joke with me, Johnny," she replies, demurely laughing. "I'm no good at joking. I don't know how to flirt!" He insists that he is serious, and they kiss. Thus, again, elements of the opening scene recur, but now in the context of *her* story, and therefore without their prior menace. Whereas she had feared his sexual attentions on the train ("Was that your leg?"), in this vehicle his attentions please her, and she gladly yields to them. (In the film's final scene, as Aysgarth drives her, at high speed, back toward her mother's house, she sits in terror, expecting him to murder her at any moment, a situation that represents the further, and uncanny, repetition of this earlier drive.) And her amused and affectionate plea that he not "joke with" her recalls her earlier retreat from his subversive (and inclusive) comic energy (a revulsion that she had made explicit in their conversation at the cliffside: "Frankly, I don't understand men like you. You always give me the feeling that you're laughing at me.")

Despite her vigilant efforts to suppress his comic influence within the closed and somber province of her genre, her narcissism, which is the very cause of her attempt to keep that province thus sealed off, itself becomes a comic spectacle, but only once we cease to see her through her eyes. Such a moment occurs when Lina strikes her theatrical pose of jubilance upon reading Johnny's telegram, although her mother too stands in the frame, on a prosaic errand. And such inadvertent comedy becomes even more apparent in this scene, when, after they have kissed, and Johnny has alluded wryly to the many other women he has known, Hitchcock cuts from the romantic two-shot to a full close-up of her alone, as she says tenderly, looking off into space, as if addressing her own image, "I hope I'm not saying the wrong thing, but—I love you!" Johnny then admits uneasily that he too is "falling in love," as they drive on, and she effuses about how she "had pictured it all rather conventionally," as if *this* moment—including that effusion— is not itself pictorial and conventional, but unexpected, uncontrolled: an implication that is immediately contradicted by their more than fortuitous arrival at her own estate: "We're coming to my house! Would you like to come in for a drink?"

At first he refuses, as if afraid he might be getting in too deep, but then he inexplicably changes his mind and stops the car; and as they climb out and approach the house, she looks up at him with wondering uncertainty, as if experiencing the delicious helplessness of one swept off her feet by an impetuous wooer. Again, however, her apparent passivity is contradicted by the visual event that seems to celebrate it. First her butler lets them in, his clothes also identical to Johnny's, a similarity that reemphasizes her unmistakable authority. They then retire to the sitting room, where she mixes the drinks with an efficiency so marked that Johnny marvels at it. "I think it's because," she answers, "for the first time in my life, I know what I want." He sits looking up at her as she stands before him, sitting now as her appreciative audience; and then he pulls her into his embrace, and they kiss, the intimacy shot in a slow, semicircular dolly from her right side to her left, accompanied by the lyrical phrase of a single violin. The shot's movement, like the music, is hypnotically romantic; and yet the moment's tone is at odds with the images themselves, which persist in demonstrating her clear dominance. The shot begins with her visibly predominating over him, and ends by showing her in exactly the same powerful position: "Are you courting me?" she asks, looking down into his eyes. "I'm afraid I am," he answers, somewhat ambiguously. "This is a wonderful moment," she breathes, leaning her head against his so that she lovingly upstages him [fig. 13], completely covering his face with her own as she continues to exult in her containment of the scene: "Here we are in my home. The house that I was born in! Alone and together. In my favorite room," and so on.

Thus their courtship proceeds, her seriousness itself becoming comic, her presumption of passivity betrayed by the very images with which she seeks to manifest it. Moreover, components of the opening scene continue to recur, cleansed utterly of their original offensiveness now that she imagines herself as firmly in control of their new context. Indeed, it is precisely such ameliorative recurrence that the first scene itself exemplified, as Lina regressed from her fear of the actual man into her love of his photograph; and so, throughout the first half of the film, does she continue to be inordinately pleased by the mere sight of documents that she assumes to contradict or annihilate whatever real disquiet, or disquieting reality, preceded them.

The first of such reversals seems entirely understandable, as she becomes, at the sight of Johnny's telegram, as euphoric as his absence had made her miserable. A bit later, just home from their expensive honeymoon, after voicing her delight at their expensive new house, Lina is horrified to learn that Johnny has no money. As they discuss his finding a job (a possibility to which he responds with aristocratic incredulity), Lina receives a telephone call from her parents, who welcome the couple home and announce the impending arrival of a wedding present (which turns out to consist of two monstrous antique chairs, a gift that moves Lina deeply and disappoints Johnny intensely). Prompted by his wife, Johnny gets on to thank his father-in-law, whom he tells he has just been offered a job by his cousin, Capt. Melbeck. He hangs up, and Lina asks him if that bit of news was not "a fib." "Was it?" he answers with a grin, and shows her Melbeck's letter, which we read through her eyes. With a look of weary fondness, she asks him why he failed to mention that letter in the first place. "Because, dear, I never dreamed I'd be using it," he answers, with a wry glance at her parents' gift. "Any more than I ever dreamed we'd be receiving these two beautiful chairs."

Evidently, she does not pursue the question of his peculiar reticence, but lets the sight of Melbeck's letter solace her. Such acquiescence may seem a little strange, but it is far less strange than her next self-reversal at the sight of a document. Just after Johnny's closing reference to the chairs, a scene begins with Lina's coming home in riding clothes (a detail that suggests her confidence that she is clearly in the saddle, especially now that her skittish Johnny is an honest working man). In the front room she finds Johnny's old school friend, Beaky Thwaite (played, with his usual addlebrained geniality, by Nigel Bruce, another figure from *Rebecca*). While chatting with him, Lina notices that both those chairs are missing. Beaky laughingly assures her that Johnny must have sold them to pay his racing debts. Despite her mounting anger at this charge, Beaky insists, not only that Johnny surely sold the chairs, but that, once confronted, he'll "invent the most howling lie you ever heard!" Just then Johnny returns home, and, in response to Beaky's giggling question about the chairs' whereabouts, stands histrionically opposite his wife and friend as they sit beside each other, watching him, and spins an elaborate tale about "an American," an associate of Melbeck's, who had dropped in at the Aysgarths' house, and who had offered him two hundred pounds for the two antiques, an offer which, he claims, was irresistible.

Although Beaky is unconvinced, Lina believes the story, and even scolds her husband's friend for his distrustfulness. Soon afterwards, however, while shopping in the village, she sees both chairs on display in an antique dealer's window. Deeply pained, she comes home and finds Beaky out on the verandah. As she apologizes for having chastised him, Johnny interrupts them, crowing with excitement and hefting a tall stack of gifts for everyone—a walking stick for Beaky, jewels and hats for Lina, even something for Ethel, the Aysgarths' maid. Lina impatiently asks him what has happened, and he tells them exuberantly that he has won a fortune at the races, having bet two hundred pounds on the winner, "a ten-to-one shot!"—and he then cheerfully admits to having sold the chairs in town to raise the betting money.

As on the train, so now again he has taken something from her, and thereby reassumed his early mastery of her spectacle; and so, as on the train, after he took her postage stamp, here again she sits, tight-lipped, hunched and glowering, helplessly confronting him with her resentment [fig. 14]. And this reexchange of roles is confirmed further by the way in which Johnny and Beaky now treat her, trying to tease her out of her bad mood by making funny faces at her, chucking her under the chin, and otherwise behaving like two heavy-handed child psychologists facing a particularly stubborn patient. Of course, they fail: Lina bursts into tears, thus repeating her prior "flight" into the very posture which she had been trying to escape, since it is her hatred of her childish helplessness that brings on this fit of childish weeping. Johnny then deftly changes his approach, and consummates the repetition of the opening scene by taking a piece of paper from his pocket and holding it before her eyes: "Look: a receipt from a certain shop for a certain pair of chairs. Paid in full and to be delivered within the hour." To the sudden sound of violins trilling her delight, Lina's tears of rage turn into tears of joy, and in an access of relief and gratitude she throws her arms around her husband's neck.

Like the telegram and Melbeck's letter, this receipt, once she has glimpsed it, causes Lina to forget the painful circumstances that produced it, and to which it testifies. All three documents, in other words, reperform the original function both of Johnny's photograph for Lina, and of the film itself for its escapist viewers. The receipt, however, induces an obliviousness far more desperate and irrational than the erasures effected by the previous documents; for this piece of paper changes nothing. It makes no difference whether Johnny sold the chairs to an importunate American or to the local antique dealer, since in either case he has liquidated objects which, for her, were charged with sentimental value. Moreover, his having bought back the chairs does not alter the facts that he first lied deliberately about their fate, and then that he used the cash to place a bet (or so she thinks), a practice which he was supposed to have forsworn in taking on a wife and job. (And, of course, he might just as easily have lost that money at the races, a blow which would have precluded this act of restitution.) These considerations, however, although they ought to matter deeply to a woman of her class and temperament, seem to matter not at all to Lina, for whom the only thing that really counts is the restoration of her spectacle. Because he clearly knows this woman better than she knows herself, Johnny also knows that he can circumvent her scruples just by putting things before her as she wants to see them; and so he puts the chairs (themselves emblematic of the viewer's posture) back where they were, first offering her, as it were, a preview of this restoration by holding the receipt before her eyes as she sits looking up at him.

IF LOOKS COULD KILL

This, however, is the last time that such a strategy will work, because the next event in Lina's life will alter drastically the character of her interpretations. This event is preceded, its psychological truth collectively anticipated, by two encounters. One day Lina meets up with Helen Newsham (the woman photographed with Johnny), who remarks cattily that, despite Johnny's apparent passion for "the simple rural life" of domesticity, he seems not to have changed completely, since she very recently saw him at "the Merchester races." The entire encounter constitutes a dreamlike reexpression of the old anxieties: Helen Newsham represents another picture come to life—a picture, like the portrait behind Johnny at the Hunt Ball, of the defeated female

265

competition, only here that static figure is again a living threat, claiming to have been, a second time, at Merchester "with Mr. John (Johnny) Aysgarth." Lina then goes to see Capt. Melbeck, who, with his stolid manner, his moustache, and his military title, recalls the figure of her father; and who reveals to Lina (who has come to ask if Johnny has been truant) that her husband was not only fired six weeks before, but fired for having embezzled two thousand pounds—the amount which Johnny claimed to have won by gambling.

She rushes home and into her bedroom, in whose opulent gloom she begins to pack a suitcase, pauses, then sits down at her dressing table— the immense conjugal bed, luminously decked in satin, filling the twilit space behind her like a catafalque—and writes a farewell note to Johnny, which we read through her eyes as she composes it. She puts the letter in an envelope, which she hastily seals and inscribes; and then she stands up, weighing the envelope pensively until, with a look of tormented resignation, she tears it into several pieces, then turns and deliberately drops them, as the camera moves in on a medium close-up of her anxious face and rigid shoulders, backed by the predominating bed. Just then we hear a door bang shut, and Johnny, dressed in black, comes into the room and stands behind her, between her and the bed, holding an identical envelope.

"Then you've heard," he says. "Yes, I've heard," she answers, still facing us. "I'm so sorry, darling," he murmurs, moving toward her. "I'm terribly sorry. This telegram just came from the doctor. It tells how it happened." Startled, she takes this second telegram, whose message— which, again, we read with her—induces a sorrow as sudden and intense as that happiness caused by the prior telegram from Johnny: "DEEPLY REGRET YOUR FATHER DIED EARLY THIS MORNING FROM HEART FAILURE."

This crucial scene ends explicitly with the presentation of the first of several inscriptions that terrify instead of gladden her; and it also reveals, implicitly, the nexus of unconscious associations that will henceforth cause her to interpret all she reads as having basically the same grim significance that she discovers here—a discovery that is itself unconscious, since this telegram suggests far more than its sad message indicates.

Her confusion of her husband's crime with her father's death implies an equation that would seem to betray her deep belief that Johnny is her father's murderer (as he is in actuality in Cox's novel); and yet the images [figs. 15–17] suggest a suspicion still more painful and complex. The moment she obliterates her farewell note to Johnny, Johnny disconcertingly appears, as if immediately summoned by her tearing up the note that would have freed her from him; and his arrival with an envelope precisely like the one she threw away—an envelope containing the announcement of her father's death—reconfirms the implication, that is, her suspicion that by so certifying her contravention of her father's wishes she has actually committed patricide: Johnny, dressed in black and bearing the telegram, materializes both as the fatal instrument of her desire, and as the messenger who brings the good/bad news that this desire has been fulfilled.

This desire itself, moreover, is also complicated by her association of his (and therefore her own) sexuality with her father's (and therefore her own) death. Johnny stands between Lina and the bed, a massive object that is both the actual scene of their conjugal and yet (as far as she is still unconsciously concerned) illicit intercourse, and the symbolic scene of the dying breath—her father's, and, as she will henceforth fear quite consciously, her own. In thus embodying the threat of a pleasurable death, of death by pleasure, Johnny continues to evince for her precisely the same frightening ambiguity which she tried (and failed) to flee back on the train, in that persistent opening scene which even here repeats itself. Here again his unexpected and intrusive entrance begins with the sound of a door banging shut, here again he says, once he has penetrated the compartment, "I'm so sorry," and here again she first tries to escape, and then embraces him, still wearing a dark woolen suit of mannish cut.

Unwittingly convinced of her guilt, she blames Johnny, the object of the tortuous desire that has incriminated her. She therefore wants to kill him for her wrongdoing, as a tyrant rids himself of the agent of his own atrocities. However, the same repressive apparatus that determines the generic context of her story also forbids her recognition of such a bloody wish within herself, the guileless heroine of that story; and so, in keeping with the dictates of both her unconscious and her genre, she projects her homicidal longing onto its potential victim, the threat of whose sexuality is now compounded by the threat of her inexplicit and increasing rage.

Now her reading can only remind her of the hostility that she imputes to him, a fundamental change that Johnny cannot notice. Just after the news of Gen. McLaidlaw's death, Johnny and Lina attend the reading of the will, which stipulates that most of the estate will go to Lina's mother, while leaving to the Aysgarths nothing more than the large, forbidding portrait of the deceased that glared down on them in the sitting room on the night of the Hunt Ball. As they drive home along a road high above the sea shore, Johnny pulls over to admire the view, and—clearly desperate to make up the money the will denied him (he is still in dangerous debt to Capt. Melbeck)—begins reckoning aloud as to the sum he would need to develop the area. Hitchcock then dissolves from the actual vista coveted by Johnny to a photograph of that same prospect on a table in the Aysgarths' house, and we see Johnny and Beaky drawing up plans to form a corporation.

Lina comes in and begins asking pointed questions about the proposed financing (which, it emerges, will depend entirely on Beaky's assets). Visibly annoyed by her intrusive questioning, and poised with pen and paper, Johnny says, with faint contempt, "Let me show you," and begins to write, clearly still assuming that, in order to palliate her, all he need ever do is flash a calming document before her eyes. She persists in the interrogation, however; and so, with an even more marked expression of contempt (which she seems not to notice), he tries the tactic a second time: "Look, darling. Let me show you how simple it is." But the gesture can no longer make the right impression, and, moments later, livid and frustrated, he rebukes her seethingly for her impertinence.

Even if he had managed to complete and show it to her, his prospectus would not have solaced her as usual, because now her reading can only threaten her. Thus, while playing Scrabble with Beaky, who, as the game proceeds, makes plans with Johnny to revisit, early the next morning, the site of their intended purchase (Johnny has decided not to go through with the development, but wants Beaky to see the land once more before agreeing not to buy it), Lina absently arranges the word "MURDER" on the Scrabble board, then immediately reads this as a revelation of what Johnny plans to do to Beaky in the morning (although it is *she* who put the loaded word together). Later, after Beaky has gone to Paris to cancel the financial arrangements, two detectives come to visit Lina, and show her a newspaper item headed "Englishman Found Dead," which we read with her, and which also appears as proof to her (and us) that Johnny is the perpetrator. And later still, Lina intercepts, first a letter written by Johnny to Capt. Melbeck ("I'm sure I can find some other way to pay you back the money I owe you"), and then some letters sent to Johnny by two of his insurance brokers, letters which, again, we read along with her and which, again, appear to demonstrate that Johnny is a murderer, or, to put it more accurately, that the reader is not murderous.

And yet the very images that seem ceaselessly to corroborate the reader's innocence turn out, once fully read, to contradict it. For instance, on the morning after Johnny has so angrily chastised Lina for her prying, she appears, unkempt and gloomy, and wielding an enormous pair of shears [fig. 18], which she uses to trim back a hedge, her emphatic strokes and absent, bitter look suggesting that, in her imagination, it is not actually the hedge which she is punishing. Just then, her husband appears towering in front of her, on our side of the hedge, his back toward the camera, so that his upright head repeats the figuration of the twigs before her [fig. 19]. Violently startled at his greeting, she immediately shifts out of her sullenness and into a devoted, pleading attitude: "Are you still angry about last night?" she asks, after Johnny has told her that he is going to dissolve the corporation. He denies being angry, and she goes on: "You've never spoken to me so sharply before, and I was afraid—" "Afraid of what?" "—I was afraid that you'd stopped loving me!" In its particular context, this expression of fretful tenderness appears as self-serving as it sounds affecting, since the visual event implies not what she says so movingly, but what she feels profoundly: that he has turned on her (in several ways), and she would like to kill him for it, or alter him.

As the death of Lina's father activates a murderousness that she and we experience as a fear of being murdered, so does the death intensify in Lina a concomitant revulsion at her own sexuality, the force that (she unconsciously assumes) put her father in his grave, and which, like her own violence, she projects onto her husband. Again, an event in Cox's novel provides the raw material for Lina's cinematic dream, for Cox's Johnny is a sexual predator, whose philandering results in (among other things) the impregnation of Lina's maid. In *Suspicion* this crime is, like Johnny's homicidal longings, wholly imagined by the heroine; and yet, unlike those longings, Johnny's seduction of or lust for Ethel is an imagined crime that Lina suspects wholly unconsciously.

Just after Johnny has consoled her by displaying the receipt for the two chairs, she walks, with Beaky and her husband, over to a table where Ethel has placed the Aysgarths' store of liquor. Her back to the camera, Lina stands, half-visible, along the frame's left border, and, intermittently wiping her eyes, unwraps one of her gifts; Beaky, partly obscured by Lina's figure, stands adjacent to her at the table, pouring drinks; and Johnny stands opposite the table from her, next to Ethel, maid and master in full frontal view. As Ethel starts to retire with her emptied tray, Johnny stops her and opens yet another gift-box for her, taking from it a large mink stole which he wraps around her shoulders, as, moved and flustered, she protests, in her thick Cockney accent, that the gift is much too fine for someone like her: "What will my young man say?" she cries, beaming. As she starts to hurry off, Johnny tells her not to forget the box, and she pivots, takes up the box in both arms, turns to leave again, but then Johnny reminds her, "Don't forget my hat!"—and, after Ethel turns around again, Johnny rests his hat across the top of the open box in Ethel's arms [fig. 20], whereupon Ethel finally rushes from the frame, Johnny sharing a smile with his two equals, and with us (Lina faces and beholds the scene as our stand-in), over Ethel's abashment.

The scene's apparent innocence is reinforced by Lina's half-attentive spectatorship: as she watches Ethel's cute discomfiture, alternately looking at her own gift and dabbing at her eyes, her reaction to the maid's situation seems entirely one of benign amusement. Her marked placement as a viewer-within-the-frame, however, alerts us to the ever-present possibility that what she watches tells us at least as much about herself as it reveals about the spectacle, which is itself more suggestive than she notices, since it implies that Johnny could or would or did seduce her maid. As Ethel darts helplessly back and forth at Johnny's benevolent command, she appears to be his creature: because of him, "she doesn't know whether she's coming or going." The specifically sexual nature of his power, moreover, is implied by his laying his hat across her open box, a dream-symbolic gesture telling us that Lina thinks her husband has abused his upper-class prerogative, or rediscovered it.[8]

Of course, the objective situation is one in which such a trespass would not be extraordinary, as Ethel herself suggests in implying that her "young man" will become both envious and jealous when he hears about the gift. It is not, however, any actual seduction that matters here, so much as Lina's fear of such an action; nor is it simple jealousy that motivates this fear, but Lina's apprehensions that *she* will be seduced and belittled by her husband, since Ethel passes through this woman's film, not as an autonomous entity, but only as Lina's double. In this scene, Lina, much moved, opens up a gift just as, before her, Ethel, also much moved, opens up another; and when, several scenes earlier, Lina first encounters Ethel in the foyer of the Aysgarths' new home, they face off in identical positions as Johnny introduces them [fig. 21], Lina's black fur hat mirrored by the maid's starched white cap (and, when they first meet, Lina wears a large mink stole exactly like the one that Johnny later gives to Ethel).

It is therefore, once again, her fear that she will lose control of her spectacle that underlies Lina's suspicion of a crime; and, again, her father's death intensifies her suspicions of philandery just as it activates her fear of murder. Late in the film, Lina stands looking out her bedroom window early in the morning, as Johnny lies, still sleeping, in their bed. (She awaits the mail, so that she might inspect the letters from the insurance brokers.) Ethel brings the mail in to Lina, and then, on her way out, pauses by the bed as Johnny wakes up. This time excluded from the frame, Lina watches another "innocent" exchange between maid and master: "Hello!" he calls to Ethel groggily. "You here again?" "Yes, sir," she answers brightly. "I've brought the morning tea and the post." Although, in an ordinary context, this moment might not seem suspicious, here Johnny's faintly surprised, and rather surprising question—"You here *again*?"—suggests that she had briefly shared that bed with him the night before, then got up to continue serving her employer ("I've brought the morning tea and the post"); a suggestion indirectly reinforced by the otherwise unaccountable presence, on a white chair between maid and master as they speak, of that same large, dark hat, which comprises an intriguing visual link between the two [fig. 22].

Such fears as these reflect directly on Lina's sense of guilt over her father's death. In a later scene, she receives two visitors: "Mr. Hotson and Mr. Benson," a stereotypic pair of rural detectives, replete with trenchcoats and distrustful stares, who have come both to tell and interrogate Lina about Beaky's death. The older of the two hands Lina a newspaper, which she takes over to a chair across the room, putting on her glasses as she sits down to read the item headed "Englishman Found Dead." She finishes, looks up and slowly removes her glasses; and although she is clearly persuaded by the circumstantial evidence that Beaky has died at Johnny's hands, the images betray her deeper, older fear. As she prepares to read the item, Lina is posed beside the portrait of Gen. McLaidlaw, in front of which a bowl of flowers sits like a funereal tribute to her father [fig. 23], who is the crucial "Englishman found dead" at this moment, and, in her eyes, the "real" victim of Johnny's criminal desires.

The detectives question her insinuatingly (now that she has again lost control of the spectacle, it is she who is the object of the cool gazes of her own suspicious doubles), then leave. She approaches her father's portrait, and, with a mad intensity, addresses it: "He didn't go to Paris! He *didn't go to Paris*, I tell you!" What she thinks she means, of course, is "Johnny didn't murder Beaky!" (Her husband was supposed to have gone with Beaky only as far as London.) But the significance of her remark has been complicated by a previous association. Just before the arrival of the detectives, we watched a scene (Beaky's last) in which the men agreed to have an evening out in London, whereupon Johnny would stay there, looking for a job, while Beaky would move on to Paris. The scene ended on a comic note, as Beaky told a story about "a very curious incident" that befell him while "walking down the Champs-Elysées": "I met the most charming girl! Well, I took her out and gave her a spot of dinner. And it wasn't till much later—" But then Johnny warningly cleared his throat and Beaky broke off—"Put my foot in it again, have I?"—then wandered from the room as the other two suppressed their knowing laughter.

"He *didn't go to Paris*, I tell you!" Beaky's story of his encounter

with the prostitute, although seemingly played for laughs, has actually
deepened this strange moment by introducing into it the traditional
English notion of Paris as a place of rampant sexuality—a notion that
therefore charges Lina's desperate utterance with numerous entangled
implications. "He didn't go to Paris!" means, "He isn't down there
whoring!"—which means, "He isn't sexually insatiable!"—which
means, "He hasn't seduced me!"—which means, "He didn't murder
you!"—which means, "*I didn't murder you!*"

Although Lina's guilty terror of her father's gaze can surely be explained exclusively in orthodox Freudian terms, such analysis, however apt and interesting, must remain too narrow, since, in implicitly
bolstering the presumed mental health of the reader who engages in it,
this kind of analysis would actually deny the similarity between that
reader/viewer and the heroine he scrutinizes, whereas this similarity is
crucial, illuminating even Lina's feelings toward her father. For Gen.
McLaidlaw represents that aspect of Lina's spectatorship which Lina
keeps attempting endlessly, *through* her spectatorship, to annihilate.
Even as she tries at once to enter into and control the spectacle, there
also must remain within herself the disapproving onlooker, that timor-
ous and judging viewer whose conscious principles must be forever violated fictively by the agents in the spectacle, or else that spectacle
yields none of its peculiar pleasure. Gen. McLaidlaw represents her
own impulse to sit and judge (as well as ours), and continues to exert
the pull of this impulse even after he has vanished from the visual
event: he sends her those two heavy chairs, as if to let her know that he
expects both her and Johnny to do nothing more than sit and watch
throughout their lives in order to atone for their elopement; and he
leaves them nothing other than that daunting portrait of himself-as-
viewer, in which he is shown sitting, staring, dressed imposingly in his
full uniform with all its medals—that grim likeness whose baleful eyes
surveyed the lovers even as they dared, or tried, or seemed, to love
each other actively. "The 'old maid' is a respectable institution," she
had heard him say, and so discovered, if unconsciously, that he hoped
she would remain as she (and we) appeared when we first saw her: as a
sedentary fantasist.

Her rebellion against such an influence is therefore understandable;
but her method of rebellion merely proves that she is herself what she
rebels against, since she attempts to lead a daring life as if simultaneously sitting back and watching it—a daring life precisely like a life seen
in a movie, and therefore one that appears to deny the very posture
demanded by her watching it. Thus her rebellion must become as suicidal as it is impossible, a tendency that she acts out in moving toward
the violent death she keeps fearing. And her effort is doomed in still

another way. Once she attempts to live without her father's repressive gaze, both by disobeying him and taking off her spinster's uniform and glasses, she ends up the helpless victim of that gaze, and also victimizes us, a helplessness foreshadowed by the opening scene in that first-class compartment, out of which, as we have seen, she never really flees or leads us.

In his quasi-military cap and uniform, with his hooded eyes and graying cavalry moustache, the conductor, whom she simultaneously laughs at and resembles, prefigures Gen. McLaidlaw as depicted and bequeathed her [fig. 24]. Like her father, the conductor takes over her suspicion for her, frees her to enjoy what she would otherwise herself suspect. Despite his comic coldness, as long as the conductor stands stodgily between the heroine and her future husband, it is still possible for us to read with some slight enabling objectivity. Those two close-ups of the railway tickets, although apparently unnecessary, therefore serve a contrastive function, presenting the only documents we read with any accuracy, that is, the only documents we read independently of her contaminating gaze. One is a first-class, the other a third-class ticket, their unambiguous (even if trivial) significations ratified by the conductor, and by the institution that retains him. Once he storms out, however, outfaced by Johnny acting on her and our behalf, there is never another image so simply legible, since she who has willed the annihilation of that official face does not proceed to live unhindered by such an influence, but merely replaces it, ends up repeating it, with her own deluded, delusory gaze.

For it is not only all those documents that Lina continually induces us to misinterpret, but Johnny himself, whose neutral image she ceaselessly distorts with her own fear and hatred. After the moment of her father's death, Hitchcock repeatedly inserts close-ups of Johnny's perfectly impassive face, close-ups in which Johnny speaks with perfect tonelessness; and yet those close-ups, despite their individual neutrality, seem menacing to us, appear to verify Lina's (and our) worst suspicions, only because they are framed by shots of Lina's own fearful and (therefore) revealing gaze—a gaze whose revelations we cannot perceive if we look only with it, never into it.*

And, as we must misjudge the film's apparent villain in failing to appreciate the influence of Lina's gaze, so might such an underestimation of the heroine's sway induce us to misjudge the film itself, that is, to

---

*Only once—at a dinner party just before the film's conclusion—does Johnny wear an inarguably sinister expression, in a shot from Lina's point of view.

share in the critical consensus[9] that *Suspicion* is one of Hitchcock's lesser films, ruined by its hasty, unconvincing ending.

The ending is, indeed, a disappointment. On the morning after Johnny has (she thinks) tried to poison her, Lina finally resolves to leave him, and so Johnny drives her (at his own bitter insistence) toward her mother's house, speeding along that same road high above the ocean. The faster he drives, the more frightened she becomes; and then, as he rounds a sharp curve, her door flies open, and through her eyes we see him, wild-eyed and gigantic, reach down as if to shove her from the car. Hysterical, she pushes back at him, her cries finally culminating in one long scream, as, taking her point of view for the last time, we see the clouds and branches overhead vertiginously spin. Then the car stops, Lina runs out, Johnny follows.

Thus far, the action is, in its peculiar mood and multiple suggestiveness, continuous with all that has preceded it. Now her old desire to be, old fears of being kissed/killed in a car, of being raped at/thrown off the edge of a scenic precipice, appear to be orgasmically fulfilled in one last paranoid outburst, which, of course, we share with her. From this point on, however, the action is forced and unsuggestive, as if, in bolting from Johnny's car, the actors have also jumped out of Hitchcock's film and into an inferior production. In a scene that is clumsily shot and edited as well as crudely written, the actors mug and babble heatedly in an effort to make credible the moment that supposedly makes sense of everything: Johnny was going to kill *himself*, it turns out, and in a numbing series of fast-paced "explanations" the two of them collaborate in exonerating not only him, but—implicitly—Lina, whose unconscious agency now becomes irrelevant in the general accounting. As the strings vibrate, Lina repents for being inconsiderate ("I was only thinking of myself, not what you were going through!"), her narcissism reduced to simple selfishness; and so the two drive back home, to (as she puts it) "see it all through together," i.e., to deal with Johnny's debts.

This ending was only one of several that were shot, and many that were written. In a hurry to prepare the film for a summer premiere, Hitchcock quickly worked out and shot this ending after another version—in which Lina has an assignation with another man, then kills herself—was hooted down by a preview audience.[10] While Hitchcock's unwonted haste will explain the ending's general shoddiness, however, the scene's fundamental weakness is not technical but dramatic: Hitchcock simply was unable to devise a strong conclusion, and so even with a looser schedule, and therefore more attention to technique, he still could not have redeemed this ending, whose weakness was determined, not by temporal pressures or the requirements of the studio, but by the very quality that makes *Suspicion* great and challenging— its reflective subjectivity. By locating *Suspicion* within its heroine's mind, Hitchcock had written himself into a corner. He was unable to end the film convincingly because any such conclusion, answering every question and dispatching all unfinished business, demands a sudden pulling-back into the light of day, a reversion that, after our immersion in Lina's dark and too-familiar consciousness, must leave us blinking. The film's weak ending, then, is actually a necessary index of the film's extraordinary strength; a mere index that we risk confusing with the text itself, if we read as Lina reads, and ignore her authorship.

ADVERSARY CINEMA

Thus *Suspicion,* while seeming to gratify the commonplace desire for a romantic thriller, simultaneously urges us to take a closer look, and thereby to become self-conscious viewers, aware that the commercial spectacle can entertain us only by entrapping us. Like all of Hitchcock's most successful films, therefore, *Suspicion* invites us to penetrate its surface, to cease watching as escapists and attempt an unflinching (and still generally unheard-of) critical spectatorship, one that might enable us to grasp, not just the exquisite strategies of the film itself, but the less exhilarating, more efficacious strategies of spectacles far more suasive than *Suspicion* seems even to its most credulous viewers. That is, *Suspicion* asks us to become aware of the manipulations made routine by the very industry that produced it, manipulations that depend on our ignoring, not only the suasive devices of "the culture industry," but our own desires, which keep that industry alive, even now, long after *Suspicion* has been both celebrated and belittled as that quaint thing, "a great old movie." In enjoining us to notice and resist the narcotic quality of most commercial spectacle, *Suspicion* even asks us to perceive and understand its own belittlement, which is itself another stupefying consequence of credulous spectatorship, now that "the movies" have been supplanted in their suasive enterprise by the subtler, more pervasive images of advertising and TV.

Of course, there is nothing new about this general indictment of so-called "mass culture," which has been the object of much hostile intellectual scrutiny for several decades. Although not new even in 1941, however, the indictment as implicit in *Suspicion* deserves careful study by all current students of "the culture industry" in both its past and present forms, because these students must now attempt to reconceive American film history, whose greatest figures were themselves, in many cases, no less troubled by the suasiveness of cinema, or by the possible stupefaction of American viewers, than those who expressed

275

their fears explicitly in print. Ambivalent about their skill, and learned in the various devices of manipulation, such Hollywood filmmakers were not mere instruments of an oppressive industry, but its complicit critics, at once forced to satisfy the half-engineered desires of the viewing public, and yet also eager to attempt exposing or criticizing the very process whereby those same desires were managed. Thus any comprehensive understanding of that process must combine the reading of, say, Gramsci, Goldmann, Horkheimer, and Adorno with the equally close reading of Fritz Lang, Josef von Sternberg, and Alfred Hitchcock, among others, all of whom attempted variously (and so far without success) to induce the viewer to break out of his long simian trance, and discern his human face.

NOTES

▪▪▪▪▪▪▪▪▪▪▪▪▪▪▪▪▪▪▪▪▪▪▪▪▪▪▪▪▪▪▪▪▪▪▪▪

1. For a general discussion of the woman's film, see Molly Haskell, *From Reverence to Rape: The Treatment of Women in the Movies* (Harmondsworth, Middlesex: Penguin Books, 1974), pp. 153-88.

2. "The scenario" of *Suspicion,* writes Joan Fontaine, "was one that Cary felt would give him a serious acting role—unlike the comedies that he'd been making, such as *The Awful Truth* and *Bringing Up Baby.*" See *No Bed of Roses: An Autobiography* (New York: William Morrow, 1978), p. 133.

3. Other of Hitchcock's central characters, equally convinced of their own thoroughgoing innocence, are also revealingly introduced as readers on a train: Pamela when she first appears in *The Thirty-Nine Steps* (1935), Guy Haines at the beginning of *Strangers on a Train* (1951).

4. For a detailed expression of Selznick's strong feelings on the importance of remaining faithful to du Maurier's novel, see his caustic memo to Hitchcock in *Memo from: David O. Selznick,* ed. Rudy Behlmer (New York: Avon Books, 1972), pp. 306-12.

It is relevant to note that, with his production of *Rebecca,* Selznick intended to appeal to the same escapist frame of mind in which (he inferred) so many women had enjoyed the novel. Much to Selznick's horror, Hitchcock evidently hoped to make a film that would frustrate, or subvert, that frame of mind. Selznick's memo reveals how well the producer understood, and how highly he valued, precisely the sort of spectatorship that Hitchcock questions in and through *Suspicion,* which might therefore be regarded as an ex post facto reply to Selznick's charges as well as a revision of Selznick's film. This passage of the memo is especially germane to our discussion of *Suspicion* as it reflects the viewer's empathic paralysis:

> As for Manderley, every little thing that the girl does in the book, her reactions of running away from the guests, and the tiny things that indicate her nervousness and her self-consciousness and her gaucherie are all so brilliant in the book that every woman who has read it has adored the girl and has understood her psychology, has cringed with embarrassment for her, yet has understood exactly what was going through her mind. We [i.e., you, in your recent draft of the script] have removed all the subtleties and substituted big broad strokes which in outline form betray just how ordinary the plot is and just how bad a picture it would make without the little feminine things which are so recognizable and which make every woman say, "I know just how she feels . . . I know just what she's going through . . ." etc. (pp. 309-10)

5. Francis Iles, *Before the Fact* (London: Gollancz, 1932).

6. "Well, I'm not too pleased with the way *Suspicion* ends. I had something else in mind. The scene I wanted, but it was never shot, was for Cary Grant to bring her a glass of milk that's been poisoned and Joan Fontaine has just finished a letter to her mother: 'Dear Mother, I'm desperately in love with him, but I don't want to live because he's a killer. Though I'd rather die, I think society should be protected from him.' Then, Cary Grant comes in with the fatal glass and she says, 'Will you mail this letter to Mother for me, dear?' She drinks the milk and dies. Fade out and fade in on one short shot: Cary Grant, whistling cheerfully, walks over to the mailbox and pops the letter in" (François Truffaut, *Hitchcock* [New York: Simon & Schuster, 1967], p. 102).

Although it is likely that Hitchcock never really gave this crude "trick ending" any serious consideration, there may well have been, in Hitchcock's mind, some connection between such an ending and Aysgarth's flippant parting shot at the conductor: "Write to your mother!"

7. Quoted in John Russell Taylor, *Hitch: The Life and Times of Alfred Hitchcock* (New York: Pantheon Books, 1978), p. 176.

8. For the phallic significance of the hat as a dream-symbol, see Sigmund Freud, *The Interpretation of Dreams* (New York: Avon Books, 1965), pp. 391, 395-97.

9. See, for example, Leslie Halliwell, *Halliwell's Film Guide* (London: Granada Publishing Ltd., 1979), p. 890.

10. For an account of Hitchcock's problems with the ending, and with other aspects of the production, see Donald Spoto, *The Dark Side of Genius: The Life of Alfred Hitchcock* (Boston: Little, Brown, 1983), pp. 245-46.

Fig. 1

Fig. 2

Fig. 3

Fig. 4

Fig. 5

Fig. 6

Fig. 7

Fig. 8

Fig. 9

Fig. 10

Fig. 11

Fig. 12

Fig. 13

Fig. 14

Fig. 15

Fig. 16

Fig. 17

Fig. 18

Fig. 19

Fig. 20

Fig. 21

Fig. 22

Fig. 23

Fig. 24

Overviews

....

The Robot in the Western Mind

*Submission is not always overt. One of its most popular
forms is to change as the conqueror appears on the horizon,
so that by the time he arrives you are so like him that you
may hope to get by.*

—Raymond Williams, 1969

1. TOOLS AND MONSTERS

"Robots made to look like human beings were soon forgotten with the
war of 1939," write Alfred Chapuis and Edmond Droz at the conclusion
of their *Automata* (1958). "Today the robot is essentially an *automatic
machine*." Yes and no. As far as the corporate sector is concerned, this
statement is accurate: GE, Westinghouse, Toyota, Chrysler, Western
Electric, Texas Instruments, IBM, and others have begun using
thousands of "steel-collar workers" that don't goof off, get sick, or "look
like human beings." What this amounts to, according to a recent *Time*
cover story, "is nothing less than a robot revolution." These punctual
machines, "considerably more versatile than their simple-minded predecessors of just two years ago," claims another story in *Business Week*,
"could displace 65% to 75% or more of today's factory work force."

On the other hand, robots that resemble men are still more famous
than their working-class relations. For most people, the word "robot"
refers, not to gadgets that weld or sort, but to machines that look like
human beings. Centuries before Karel Čapek's play *R.U.R.* (1920) gave
them their name (from the Czech *robota*, for "*corvée*," the term of labor a serf owes his master), these creatures exerted an intense fascination, haunting the myths of antiquity and the Middle Ages: Daedalus
built statues that could move; Hephaistos, the *Iliad* tells us, was attended by two golden automata "in appearance like living young women";
Albertus Magnus had a robot servant which Thomas Aquinas piously
wrecked. This fascination has never disappeared, and even took on a
new cultural significance after the release of *Star Wars* (1977), which
seemed to inspire a pervasive cult of robotism. Indeed, as humanoid
robots began to appear in films, TV shows, ads, and gift books, their
gestures mimicked by disco dancers and New Wave musicians, it
seemed that American culture too was going through "nothing less than
a robot revolution."

BOXED IN

■ ■ ■ ■ ■ ■

There must be some connections, however oblique or deep-seated, between the renewed popularity of humanoid robots and the rise of their industrial counterparts. However, recent writings on the subject tend to belittle the significance of imaginary robots, suggesting that, as we enter this new Industrial Revolution, we have to put away such childish things. *Time*'s story, for instance, includes a short and derisive history of humanoid robots, under the title "Demons and Monsters," and in *The Robot Book* (1978) Robert Malone refers to legendary robots as "mere containers for old-fashioned thinking," which is the same message that appears in several other recent books.

That message may seem disinterested, like any other reasonable argument against the superstitious past. In fact, such dismissals serve a gross economic purpose. Seeming merely to laugh away yet another ancient prejudice, they actually promote a sort of technocratic boosterism, implying that *real* robots are good for you and me, since they are nothing like the golem or HAL or Frankenstein's monster, fantastic creatures with no factual basis. According to this subtle propaganda, the fear of robots is a mere vestige of that great Fear of the Unknown that kept our prehistoric ancestors grunting in terror and living without television. It is a simplistic notion. The fear of robots is no crude superstition, but a psychological response with a complex history. Moreover, the humanoid robots of film and literature bear much subtle relevance to the real robots that are now building cars, refrigerators, aircraft, and more robots.

Of course, the two types of robots tend to inspire very different kinds of feelings. The industrial robot is without charisma. It warms the corporate heart for purely utilitarian reasons: "improved productivity, faultless performance, and lower labor costs," as *Business Week* puts it. Among adults, the humanoid robot inspires, in general, either horror or amusement. In *Human Robots in Myth and Science* (1966) John Cohen writes that "we laugh when a true robot behaves like a man, and the closer the resemblance the more comical we find the situation." On the other hand, Jasia Reichardt, in *Robots: Fact, Fiction and Prediction* (1978), describes some experiments which suggest that the opposite is true: the closer the resemblance, the eerier do the robot's motions seem, particularly when the robot's status is unclear. "When an artificial arm of the most complex type . . . suddenly stops functioning," for instance, "this creates a feeling of unease in those who witness it."

These observations are in fact complementary: the fear and the laughter are expressions of the same surprise. Whether we applaud the precocious chatter of the ventriloquist's dummy or recoil from the

286

golem's lumbering advance, we are responding to the same bizarre transgression. In either case, an object breaks out of immobility and apes us with a startling insolence. Whether this event is comic or horrific depends on the limits of the object's strength. When the mimicking thing is undersized and clearly dependent, its performance meant to please, we laugh at its presumptuous weakness, and the more presumptuous, "the more comical we find the situation": the sarcastic dummy, the passionate marionette, *Star War*'s C-3PO fussing at his masters. Such comedy, however, borders on the dreadful. Once the creature ceases to be dependent, its cleverness "creates a feeling of unease in those who witness it"; the phrase "clever mechanism" no longer refers to the inventor's talents, but to the thing itself, with its unnatural abilities and its will to power. Thus the ventriloquist's dummy turns monstrous once it appears to take command, as in so many films and television shows; and the full-sized, autonomous robot, approaching humanity as if on equal terms, is never funny, because it seems intent on taking over absolutely, irreversibly.

The robot would "take over" not like a mere human conqueror, making threats and giving orders, but like a vampire, incorporating all our qualities into itself. Our strengths and energies drain into it, leaving us weak; it grows as we shrivel. Rather than some arbitrary prejudice, the fear of robots is an apprehension of gradual displacement. It arose along with the Industrial Revolution, perhaps as a psychic reaction to that overwhelming event, with all its philosophical and sociopolitical effects.

Although it was not widely manifest until the early nineteenth century, the fear of displacement was convolved with a much older kind of uneasiness: that the author of artificial life trespasses, like Prometheus and Faust, on divine prerogative. In *R.U.R.*, old Rossum the scientist "wanted to become a sort of scientific substitute for God," and so found out the secrets of creating robots. Rossum's antecedent is Mary Shelley's Frankenstein, who, in preparing to construct his early android, "disturbed, with profane fingers, the tremendous secrets of the human frame." When the scientist commits this sin, his robots often punish him with insurrection: "Like negroes, these powers own man sullenly; mindful of their higher masters; while serving, plot revenges." Thus Melville describes the robots' just rebelliousness in the epigraph to "The Bell-Tower" (1855), in which a massive automaton finally kills its proud inventor, Bannadonna, with a mighty hammer blow. Bannadonna tries "to rival [nature], outstrip her, and rule her," and his illicit creature pays him back for the blasphemy.

This situation has become formulaic. Although the overreaching scientist is still a commonplace in dystopian science fiction, the robot is now less compelling as a scourge of God than as a monster working on its own obscure behalf. It still seems a dangerous slave, but its tactics have become more sophisticated: it triumphs, not by outright mutiny, but through perfect service. Attended in every way by competent gadgets, man will lose his defining ruggedness and dwindle into "an affectionate machine-tickling aphid." Thus the anti-technologist in Samuel Butler's *Erewhon* (1872) uses those images of radical displacement that recur in so many influential works: H.G. Wells's *The War of the Worlds* (1896), whose Martian invaders huddle like gigantic slugs in the cabins of their "walking engine[s] of glittering metal"; E. M. Forster's "The Machine Stops" (1909), whose heroine, inhabiting a comfortable subterranean cell, is "a swaddled lump of flesh. . . . with a face as white as fungus"; Stanley Kubrick's *2001: A Space Odyssey* (1968), in which two vacuous astronauts are bested by a computer that is more "human" than they are.

Thus the fear of robots suggests the master's distrust of his capable slaves. Because the robot seems to get stronger and smarter as we decline, moreover, this fear also recalls the parent's terror or resentment of his growing child. "The dread of our actual children," writes Simon O. Lesser, in an essay on our feelings about robots, "arises basically from the fact that our early authority over them stems in part from our superior strength and from the realization that we wane as they wax in strength." This may further explain the peculiar horror that pervades those stories of power-hungry dummies and dolls, puppets that want to pull their owners' strings. Like children, these little things start out as our creatures, then suddenly appear as rivals.

In his essay on the uncanny, Freud suggests that the fear of robots might be based on the expectation of yet another startling reversal. "The 'uncanny' is that class of the terrifying which leads back to something long known to us, once very familiar." Once we repress some comforting childhood fantasy, its seeming recurrence is a dreadful thing. "The impression made by wax-work figures, artificial dolls and automatons," for example, may be the chilling repetition of an earlier, happier experience: "We remember that in their early games children do not distinguish at all sharply between living and lifeless objects, and that they are especially fond of treating their dolls like people." The child regards this "living doll" as his protective double; "and when this stage has been left behind the double takes on a different aspect. From having been an assurance of immortality, he becomes the ghastly harbinger of death."

Each of the robot's possible prototypes—the slave, the demanding child, the returning double—evinces the implacable resentment that we project onto the dead, who, we believe, "are discontented and full of envy for those they have left behind," writes Elias Canetti. "They try to take revenge on [the living] . . . simply because they themselves are no longer alive."

The robot seems an active mimic of mortality. Its humanoid motions look like cruel parody, as if an athlete were mocking a cripple: its physique is incorruptible, yet it walks like a corpse shocked back to life. And as it totters forward, stiff-necked, on rigid limbs, it wears a look of fixed surprise, which has a doubly uncanny effect: it recalls that expression of terminal bewilderment that often freezes the features of those who die suddenly; and it reflects our own cold horror at its unnatural approach, and—by extension—at approaching death. Our dread of the robot is a foreboding of our own annihilation, the end of that long, slow process of displacement.

THIS EXPECTATION OF DISPLACEMENT IS SO FAMILIAR THAT it comes as a surprise to find that its origin is fairly recent. "The fact of any human being doing anything in association with those lifeless figures which counterfeit the appearance and movements of humanity," admits a character in E.T.A. Hoffman's "Automata," "has always, to me, something fearful, unnatural, I may say terrible, about it." Such a response must have seemed quite modern when Hoffman's story was published in 1815, for throughout the previous century, humanoid automata (known as *androides*) seem to have inspired admiration rather than dread, at least among their educated viewers.

"What finesse in all this detail! What delicacy in all the parts of this mechanism!" Thus Diderot, in the *Encyclopédie* (1751), praises the mechanical flutist built by Jacques de Vaucanson, the most famous of automatists. Vaucanson had first displayed his flutist in 1738, and soon produced two other robots, a "man" that played a tabor and a shepherd's pipe, and a celebrated duck that had all of Paris quacking. The flutist, Condorcet writes in his eulogy of Vaucanson (1782), soon attracted "the curiosity of a world more eager for novelty than sensitive to great talents, inspiring either enthusiasm or disdain," until "the Academy of Science was ordered to examine the automaton," and found that Vaucanson had imitated Nature "with an exactness and perfection which those men most accustomed to the prodigies of art had not imagined possible." It was for these qualities of "exactness and perfection" that worldly viewers also praised the robots built by Vaucanson's successors: the brothers Pierre and Henri-Louis Jaquet-Droz, who exhibited a scribe, a draughtsman, and a harpsichordist; and the Maillardet family, who built three similar figures, as well as a magician that could write out answers to a few philosophical questions: "What is the most noble reward of knowledge?" "To enlighten ignorance."

289

If such machines provoked any displeasure, it was contempt rather than fear, since the *androides* seemed, to some, mere complicated trifles. In *The Rambler* (83), Dr. Johnson answered this dismissal, arguing that "the movements which put into action machines of no use but to raise the wonder of ignorance, may be employed to drain fens, or manufacture metals, or assist the architect, or preserve the sailor."

Throughout the eighteenth century, the automaton's similarity to its knowing observers was unfrightening, and probably reassuring. Before technology had cast its gigantic shadow over Western life, the automaton appeared, not as an invader from the world of machines, but as the exquisite fulfillment of Mechanism. Its popularity was coterminous with the influence of Descartes and Newton, and embodied the promise of that influence. Just as man was, in Descartes's phrase, "a machine made by the hand of God," so was the automaton an exact and wondrous creature; and that deity was so competent an engineer that he could even supervise the workings of the universe, another complex artifact in need, suggested Newton, of occasional adjustment. Playing its graceful melodies in the galleries of Paris and London, the *androides* presented men with a comforting reflection of themselves: triumphs of precise design, attuned to an efficient cosmos, all kept in order by the great Clockmaker.

Even as an atheistic doctrine, Mechanism could be a source of comfort. Whereas Descartes had called only the human body a machine, excepting mind and soul from mechanism, La Mettrie went all the way in his *L'Homme machine* (1748), calling man "a collection of springs which wind each other up," independent of God. This atheism was only nominal, however; La Mettrie, like Holbach and Voltaire, and like many deist and Christian philosophers of that era, often admired the created order with a religious fervor. They were able to preserve a fundamental optimism, Bertrand Bronson points out, through "the elevation of Nature as a surrogate for a present, immanent Deity." According to this pre-Romantic vision, man was not to be cherished for his warmth or for his flaws (as "humanity" is often sentimentally extolled today), but for his status as the most impressive of machines. Nature, writes La Mettrie, "creates millions of men, with a facility and pleasure more intense than the effort of a watchmaker in making the most complicated watch."

Whether known as "God" or "Nature," that busy Engineer was a mere metaphysical projection of the same rational power that was now wholly rearranging Western life. However crudely formulated by La Mettrie, *l'homme machine* was, Foucault points out, an ideal common to the new intellectual disciplines, which posited "Man" as an entity completely knowable, and therefore perfectly docile—a "subject" seen

eventually displace all clerks, typists, postal workers, telephone operators, stockbrokers, travel agents, and many teachers; the recording and film processing industries may disappear entirely. Although the champions of automation often promise that the machines will create as many jobs as they destroy, Osborne points out that this is false. The machines will need only a relative handful of technicians, or else automation would not pay.

And the machine "unkings" us in a less obvious way. Contrary to McLuhan's hopeful formulation, the advanced media have not extended our faculties, but have tended to deplete them. Assisted by the calculator, our students forget how to add and subtract; the telephone diminishes our fluency by letting us neglect the practice of writing; television blinds us to any visual event that takes longer than an instant to comprehend, and keeps us sitting down, staying home. The continuing expansion of technology depends on our reciprocal exhaustion, as corporate engineers keep searching for more ways to computerize our functions. "The second industrial revolution, now in its infancy," boasts a spokesman for the National Science Foundation, "involves the transfer of intelligence from man to machine."

Meanwhile, we expect technology to rectify this situation. Sickened by industrial pollution, we look to be healed by more machines; machines can now reproduce, in any home, the sights and sounds of landscapes which other machines have long since blighted; adventurous types, their energies made superfluous by automation and TV, can now arm-wrestle with a robot, or try to ride a bucking robot-"horse," and so on. The apologists for robots claim that the new machines can liberate the worker from tedium and danger, but this assurance raises more questions than it answers. Why should the job be done at all? To build how many extra thousands of which superfluous machines? And once that worker is "liberated," what challenging job awaits him? Or will he have more "free time" to spend playing video games? In fact, technology appears to help us out of the very destruction which it relentlessly causes, and on which its further expansion now depends.

As this process reaches ruinous perfection, the fear of robots undergoes an interesting change. Instead of simply epitomizing the evils of technology, the imaginary robot now comforts its desperate audience with a fantasy of manageability: C-3PO and R2-D2, the cute little "droids" of the *Star Wars* cycle, have replaced the fearsome robots of the past in the popular imagination. This does not mean that Americans have abandoned their anxiety in favor of "mature acceptance." On the contrary: the persistence of this anxiety is precisely what underlies the appeal of these robots, which is based on the subtle denial that we have anything to fear from our machines.

We don't depend on our technology, *Star Wars* implies, so much as our technology depends on us. As our heroes roam through outer space, the little robots tag along like comical pets, loyal but cowardly, in need of repairs and reassurance. In fact, their masters could not do without them, but we overlook this fact because the robots display signs of powerlessness. They are small, more like extravagant toys than our sinister doubles, and therefore cannot threaten us with rivalry.

While the little robots would assuage our fears of modern technology, Darth Vader makes those fears seem justified. He is not a humanoid robot, but a robotic human being, and therefore a compelling symbol of man half-crippled by the mechanisms that are supposed to strengthen him. In his jackboots, black cloak, and gleaming *Wehrmacht* helmet, he seems a terrific tyrant, and yet his dominance is tempered by servility: he bullies his victims, but grovels before his emperor, and fears "the Force" which he has betrayed. This ambiguity (which has made Darth Vader a sort of cult hero among the devotees of S & M) arises from his overwhelming gadgetry. Encased in hardware, he seems invincible; and yet that fortress is also his burden. The dark silver "breath screen" that hides his face is both a warrior's visor and a penitent's mask, as if this colossus feels ashamed of the perishable thing inside the armor: at one point in *The Empire Strikes Back*, as we see him putting on his head-piece, we glimpse the hidden scalp—shriveled and discolored, like a rotting apricot. This titan is half-dead in his accoutrements. The very props of his transcendence only call attention to his frailty; he never appears without that sound of labored breath, as in a diving bell or iron lung.

These figments are worth taking seriously, as the objects of a mass response which the proponents of expansion would deny. Although we are told that imaginary robots have nothing to do with those instruments now at work on the assembly lines, the two are profoundly related: the humanoid robot appeals to the fears aroused by technology at large, and by the remote powers in charge of that technology. Those who champion the use of robots tend to answer this uneasiness with a lot of upbeat, progressive rhetoric: "Now that we are no longer afraid of what the machine will do to us," gushes the author of *The Robot Book*, "we are freer to choose what we want the machine to do for us." This is the opposite of the truth. In fact, we are still helpless "to choose what we want the machine to do for us," and therefore we are still afraid. This fear is so reasonable, moreover, that we ought to examine the motives of those who dismiss it, and ask what sort of world they have in mind. A world of busy, empty factories and busy, crowded shopping malls? We should think about that possibility, and do so with the courage of our instincts. The fear of robots has always been an aid to

296

self-preservation; and so it will continue, as long as life is harmed no less than bettered by machines.

2. TURNED ON, TUNED UP, BURNED OUT

Apparently human, inherently machine, the robot is profoundly ambiguous. This ambiguity once underlay the robot's sinister image. As a tool that walks like a man, it appears to be the perfect slave: strong and clean, unable to loaf or talk back, it promises to liberate mankind from life's dull and dirty jobs. All of this makes the robot too good to be true, however; so capable a slave might just as easily become the master. This was the premise of Čapek's *R.U.R.* and of countless lesser works that also seem, today, archaic. The fear was that robots would either revolt outright, or pamper us all into tubby passivity.

Such fear depends upon our seeing the robot as an alien thing, coming out of nowhere to conquer or displace. But if we can somehow see ourselves as robotic, the robot ceases to frighten. We join its ranks, and await the calm beyond all passion and decision. When the world appears to us as a corporate, computerized machine, "human nature" will inhabit it most happily if it too can seem mechanical, or cybernetic. The cult of the robot expresses a celebration of powerlessness, a willingness to be led; and it is precisely those gestures which seem most "liberated" that serve this attitude most effectively.

But there is another dimension to the robot's ambiguity: the robot is a weakling that struts like a god. It is ostensibly a superman, unimpaired by old age, poor muscle tone, or dandruff. And it seems no less morally strong than physically perfect: "No evil passions, no jealousy, no avarice, no impure desires will disturb the serene might of those glorious creatures," wrote Samuel Butler in 1863, satirizing the machines of the future: "Sin, shame, and sorrow will have no place among them."

Incapable of fondness or regret, unburdened by relatives, gleaming all over, the robot appears as a model of striking independence—and yet, in fact, is utterly dependent. It must be taken care of lest it rust, burn out, run down. The Tin Woodman needs Dorothy to oil him, R2-D2 needs Luke Skywalker to overhaul him, the mighty golem needs the rabbi's spell. That masterful stride and calm of mind are illusory, the result of patient human ministration.

"Robotism" refers to desires or behavior inspired by this paradox of dependent independence. It is a subtle form of self-oppression, often flourishing where the best impulses of the 1960s have been perverted: at the disco, at lectures on "human potential," among the diehards of the "sexual revolution."

In the early 1970s, young blacks invented "robot dancing," the rhythmic mimicry of automatism: couples, wide-eyed and expressionless, appeared to glide across the floor, moving with angular precision, freezing into immobility like robots suddenly switched off, then gliding on. This splendid choreography contained a submerged message of protest. Like those English "punks" festooned with chains and pins, these dancers seemed to taunt their viewers with displays of mechanized subservience.

While the punk movement was too bitter to get far in this country, its faint vestiges continue to exploit a satiric robotism. The members of the rock group Devo, wearing industrial jumpsuits and goggles, jerk and twitch robotically onstage as they play their anthems of "de-evolution." (Similarly, "nuke suits" have become a campus fashion.) Robot dancing, on the other hand, found its way to fame, and so lost its dissident flavor. A black dance group called the Lockers worked the style into a slick routine; the white mimes Shields and Yarnell worked a robotic sitcom parody into their short-lived television series, whereupon the even whiter Donny and Marie Osmond did exactly the same thing. The style has become a common feature of the disco.

The disco is the temple of robotism in the 1970s. Its central fantasy is at once nostalgic and robotic, evoking old memories of Hollywood, Broadway, prewar night life. In settings of electric deco, couples dance with quick precision, smart in dress and step. The spectacle calls up romantic images later made familiar by television: a stage glittering with stars moving in perfect synchronization, Fred Astaire and Ginger Rogers wooing one another in midair, Valentino, dressed to kill in *Blood and Sand*, bearing down on Nita Naldi.

And yet all this dated romance is now mechanized and canned. The disco is an utterly synthetic entertainment; its music is bright, relentless, unmelodic, as hypnotic as the rhythms of the factory assembly line. It is the musical equivalent of the robot's uninflected speech, and its infectious precision demands a like precision in the dancers. Nothing could resemble less the hairy flailing of the hippies in the open air, to the impassioned strains of rock and roll.

Disco dancers are less concerned with passion than with a lustrous conformity; they want not so much to be like movie stars as to be like filmed images themselves, mere glamorous projections in a technological display. The disco is a place of spectacle, itself a spectacle, hermetic, automatic, inexhaustible; and its dancers, the elements of this spectacle, aspire to the same robotic state. "I couldn't get enough,/So I had to self-destruct," shout the Trammps in "Disco Inferno," using the metaphors of mechanism which have replaced, in disco lyrics, the conventional protests of love.

This is the disco as most people know it, from *Saturday Night Fever* and its glossy spinoffs: a wild party that stays orderly, release without abandon. In many discos, of course, the festivities are not so tidy. But even in the dampest of such places, the humping and sweating are contained, a part of the floor show, as it were. The dancers palpitate, the disco mediates: keeping the orgy within its dazzling confines, pulling all movement into line with its beat, breaking, with the strobe light, the fluidity of human motion into the rhythmic spasms of the automaton.

The disco ideal is a paradox of narcissism and surrender. Everybody is a star at the disco, posing in his own spotlight, catching his reflection everywhere; but this "stardom" is only an illusion, expensively maintained by an electrician and a disk jockey, under whose watchful eyes the dancing hundreds keep the disco busy. Thus the disco encourages an illusory uniqueness much like the dependent independence of the robot, which also owes its charisma to technicians.

Robotism now has a profitable analogue in the so-called "human potential movement" and in various cults: Americans yearn for steely independence won safely under the auspices of some protective force. Those who rush to be denounced by est instructors, manhandled by Rolfers, dunked by rebirthers, or beamed upon by Moonies are eager to attain the purity and contingent strength of the machine. Self-knowledge is a snap when somebody else will work it out for you, just as the robot's effectiveness depends entirely on the skills of its repairman: "It is through my experience [of Werner Erhard] that I have most completely come to know myself," says John Denver of his guide and fellow millionaire. The many psychic self-help manuals exploit the same contradiction: In order to learn how to pull your own strings, you'd better let us pull them for you.

Not too surprisingly, *Star Wars* has been incorporated into this new dogma, most notably as part of Actualizations Inc., an est spinoff that relies heavily on the oft-repeated *Star Wars* valediction, "May the force be with you." "The force" in *Star Wars* is a vague cosmic excuse for anything the good guys try to do. More specifically, "the force" is merely the robotic paradox of dependent independence raised to the level of mysticism: according to the old sage Obi-wan Kenobi, "the force" is "an aura that at once controls and obeys."

One can discover the dubious autonomy of "the force" only by ceasing to be effortful: "You must try to divorce your actions from conscious control," counsels Kenobi, teaching Luke Skywalker how to fence: "You must let your mind drift, drift; only then can you use the force." This resembles the wisdom of Zen, but also recalls est and other such doctrines in its exhortation to clear the circuits between robot and master. The self is conceived as something whose programming has

299

been haphazard and therefore wrong, whose "realization" depends on total erasure followed by more careful "input" from a commanding source.

It would be a mistake to note this self-image only in the followers of men like Charles Dederich and Jim Jones. Advertisers represent the self as robotic, an entity awaiting definition solely through the use of some transforming product. These messages further endorse robotism by representing the body as a disgusting mass of leaks and stenches. Before discovering "the Crest" or "the Secret," one goes through life in foul disrepair, like a car trailing exhaust. Once reprogrammed, one is not only odor-free and well-adjusted, but redefined as a living endorsement, like Suzy Chapstick, the Oil of Olay Woman, or the "Mouth-Whack Machine" that chomps on Tic-Tacs.

More than ever before, advertisements lure us to dependence with images of independence meant to confront us as reflections. The smoker, tanned and muscular (whether male or female), gazes into our eyes with solemn self-assurance, over a command ("Come to Where the Flavor Is") or a terse avowal that sounds like a command ("I Like the Box"). The image of the couple sharing a suggestive smoke has given way to a narcissistic icon. The jogger, in his solitary exertions,* is used to provide the same appeal in many ads. And even in commercials whose pitch is less austere, the sunny recreation proffered has a robotic character, as (for instance) teenagers in roller skates and radio headphones zip in and out of traffic, granted mobility and isolation by the hippest kind of technology.

Ads reflect as well as dictate—reflect, in part, what they themselves disperse. The same mythology used to sell Lavoris or Dentyne imbues the assumptions of real people, particularly where sex is concerned. Since the "sexual revolution" of the 1960s, we have come to assume that physical incapacity is unnatural. We no longer believe that sex involves an essential expenditure. "This is the monstrosity in love, lady," Troilus tells his Cressida with quaint regret, "that the will is infinite, and the execution confined, that the desire is boundless and the act a slave to limit." This melancholy notion would today be noted down as symptomatic of "sexual dysfunction."

"Sin, shame, and sorrow" have been similarly proscribed. *Clarissa*

---

* Jogging is conceived, by its most fervent practitioners, as a robotic pursuit of renewal with its own version of "the force." In *The Complete Book of Running*, a specialist says of the jogger: "That he is not made for the workaday world, that his essential nature and the law of his being are different from ordinary and usual is difficult for everyone, including the jogger, to understand. But once it is understood, the runner can surrender to this self, this law."

and *The Scarlet Letter* are now about as timely as medieval allegory, inasmuch as sexual guilt seems a grotesque anachronism. Sexual melancholy is also out of date, foreign to the person in touch with his/her feelings: after coitus, all creatures should be jolly. Such resilience is made possible by a bowdlerized conception of sexuality, a pastime supposedly as antiseptic as push-ups, and just as solitary: the sexual act is now idealized as a coming together without union, a mutual revving of engines. This consent without surrender is merely the robotic paradox in its erotic manifestation: You are a sexual champion if you "function" or "perform" with such strength and independence that you might as well not have a partner. And so the implicit hero of current sexual propaganda is the robot, the "sex machine" of disco lyrics, tireless, uncomplaining, odor-free and always turned on. Thus the peculiar sexlessness of the 1970s' robotic sex symbols: Arnold Schwarzenegger, bronzed and contoured like an antique car, Dolly Parton of the parodic breasts, and Farrah Fawcett, aglow with the cool sheen of aluminum.

The old prudishness and the new openness betray the same squeamishness. Basically conventional in its denial of the body, current sexual propaganda is proof of the cliché that death is "the new obscenity." As the robot cannot surrender erotically, cannot "die" in the Elizabethan sense, so it cannot really cease to be. In applauding the robot's sexual durability, however, we have not transcended the association of sexuality with death but have only repressed it. And what we repress, we find horrible.

The horror films of the past exploited an ambivalence toward the sexual act; the monster was itself an erotic menace. Dracula's nightly forays were much like Casanova's, the werewolf howled and slavered shamelessly, and Frankenstein's creature was a sort of diamond in the rough, raising hell all over town but briefly tamed by little girls. Even the mummy, all wrapped up with no place to go, had one thing on his mind once he broke free.

The 1970s' horror films present robotized monsters in whom the sexual appetite has been replaced by bloodlust. They terrify not by threatening violation or seduction but by answering the sexual thought with capital punishment. In *Halloween* (1978), the huge murderer, in blank mask and industrial jumpsuit, his movements mechanical, stalks nubile teenaged girls, but only (it seems) to kill them for their promiscuity. (Similarly, in *Alien*, the robot's assault on the heroine is a bizarre parody of sexual molestation.) In films like *Carrie* (1976), *The Fury* (1978), and *The Exorcist* (1973), among others, pretty girls of robotic prowess (telekinetic or demonic) shatter by remote control the men who approach them; and these women respond not only with violence,

301

but with rich displays of those unmentionable juices whose concealment is a veritable industry. Wreaking telekinetic vengeance on the
"fast" kids of her high school class, Carrie stands drenched in pig's
blood (a prank devised to mock her ignorance of menstruation), and
the heroine of *The Exorcist* bleeds and oozes colorfully while savaging
(without moving a muscle) her would-be saviors.

These women are "sex machines" in a rebellious mood. Their unexpected strength recalls the dummy's unexpected mutiny; it suggests
Farrah, the perfect household robot, appalling her fans with evidence of
ovulation, illness, rage or any other symptoms of humanity. Both Farrah's appeal and Carrie's notoriety betray a widespread hatred of the
body, for which the fantasy of robotism offers dubious solace.

But if the clanking robot with its glassy eyes is a paradigm of indifference, how can this culture be called "robotic" when it is so fervently
sentimental? "Caring" and "sharing" have become ubiquitous adjec-
tives of praise, as emotionalism becomes at once a fashion and a thriving business: *Feelings* is the title of both a best-selling self-help manual
and a hit single. Every sitcom now has its obligatory Moment of
Choked-Up Affection, and in commercials for big softhearted corporations like McDonald's and AT&T, people can barely get near one another without crying.

It is too self-conscious to be ingenuous: this obsession with feeling
betrays nothing more than a panicked inability to feel. It is merely another robotic phenomenon, all these people screaming "If I only had a
heart!" The jargon of the new sentimentalists is curiously revealing. To
say that someone is "in touch with his feelings" is only to point out the
distance between that person and his emotions: we "keep in touch"
with people who are far away, and we usually do so by telephone. (In-
terestingly, "Reach out and touch someone!" is the phone company's
latest motto.) Thus the precious "feelings" take up separate residence,
as if awaiting divorce.

Other colloquialisms express robotic assumptions, presenting the
self as most acute when in good working order, while weakness or confusion are described in terms that suggest faulty wiring. The tired, the
sick, the dead are "wasted" or "burned out," epithets that once referred
to the casualties of drug abuse, but now used in general parlance to
connote all kinds of decrepitude. And the person who can "function" is
a "together" person, with his "head on straight."

What these expressions fail to say is even more telling than their
figurative reverberations. To liken oneself to a whole or broken mechanism is to renounce, however subtly, the desire for autonomy. If your
head happens to be on crooked, maybe God or one of His various self-
appointed repairmen will make a house call. Robotism is helplessness

made attractive. The robotic paradox of dependent independence is another version of Susan Sontag's formula for fascism, "egomania and servitude."

The robot was a fearful thing because of its perfect looks, its relentless efficiency, its empty eyes suggesting death. It is now an exemplary thing for the same reasons. If we could only become like it, we too might exist forever, given periodic tuneups by some great technician. And who will reap the benefit of this new longing? Carl Sagan, writing in praise of menial robots, muses with unwitting relevance: "For the development of domestic and civic robots to be a general social good, the effective re-employment of those displaced by robots must, of course, be arranged; but over a human generation that should not be too difficult—particularly if enlightened educational reforms are initiated." Those passive constructions are intriguing: *who* will "arrange" and "initiate"? Will it be someone well-meaning, like the Wizard of Oz, sweetly dithering at the controls? Or will it be someone more like Dr. Strangelove? If all we want is to have things run smoothly, ourselves among them, it really makes no difference.

Afterword

■ ■

SINCE THE LATE SEVENTIES, THERE HAVE, OF course, been several superficial changes in the cultural landscape: disco is no more, *Carrie* and *The Exorcist* now seem as insignificant as the snows of yesteryear, the ads for Winston are no longer confrontational, robot-dancing has long since disappeared into break-dancing, and so on. Such changes, however, make no difference to the essay's original argument: I read those momentary fads and images merely as the symptoms of a much deeper reaction—one that continues to express itself, albeit through new ephemera.

It is such an emphasis on the abiding and underlying situation—on the anxiety, so to speak, and not on the fantasy or nightmare—that distinguishes true culture criticism from mere "trend-spotting." The worlds of marketing and journalism rely on, and continuously generate, the latter kind of pseudoanalysis, which is at once a parody of culture criticism, and its antithesis. The adfolk, pollsters, "futurists" and other pundits sell snap diagnoses of "the consumer" to the corporations, whose managers then (presumably) know which commodities to market next and how to misrepresent them. And these diagnoses are often themselves commodified for the TV-viewer and newspaper-scanner, as "think pieces" or "special segments" that supposedly "explain the facts." While there are journalists who do an excellent job on such assignments, for the most part these pieces are (necessarily, given the deadlines and ideological constraints) not only unilluminating, but dubious—based on evidence too slight, and insufficiently thought through: "Self-Denial Fades as Americans Return to the Sweet Life," runs a headline in the Living Section of the *New York Times*, 11 March 1987. "A Sense of Limits Grips Consumers," runs a headline in the Business section of the *New York Times*, 15 March 1987.

The conditions for what I called "robotism" are still very much in place, and their effects have, indeed, only intensified since the late Seventies. For one thing, developments throughout the Eighties have vindicated Adam Osborne's grim prediction of increasing unemployment as a consequence—the intended consequence—of management's "retooling." There have been the massive layoffs at General Motors,

AT&T, and other companies—and, of course, few new jobs were created by the technology that helped cause that unemployment. In February 1986, a study by the Congressional Office of Technology Assessment
reported that, of 11.5 million workers unemployed because of shut-
downs and relocations from 1979 to 1984, only 60% found new jobs
during those years; and of those who did find other work, 45% took cuts
in pay.

Since 1981, moreover, entire professions—other than those whose
disappearance Osborne foresaw—have begun to go the way of weaving,
cobbling, typesetting. "Modern machines can effectively duplicate
string sections, drummers and even horn sections," reported the *New
York Times* in March 1987, "so with the exception of concerts, the jobs
available to live musicians are growing fewer by the day" (a crisis that
relates to the increasing thinness of recorded music: see above, p. 181).
And those who ask questions for a living have also begun to feel the
competition from microelectronics: "Computer interviewing," reported the *Wall Street Journal* in October 1986, "is being used by market
researchers to assess product demand, by personnel officers to screen
job applicants and by at least one pollster working on a political
campaign."

Thus the old fear of robots, ridiculed by the enlightened as a mere
reflex of ignorance, still turns out to have been a most reasonable
unease; and the culture of TV has continued to address that unease,
seeking to allay it with robot-imagoes ever more bizarre. In the late
Eighties, for instance, there emerged a new cult of the mannequin,
which was now explicitly proffered as the consumer's double—or rather, as the double of the consumer-merged-with-the-commodity: "The
mannequin must represent the soul of the person and of the clothing.
The customer has to identify with the mannequin." Thus spake, in
1986, the "vice president of visual merchandising" for Bergdorf Goodman. And in 1987, the Units chain advertised itself by hiring female
mimes to wear its clothes and stand outside its stores, swiveling slow
and wide-eyed, like automata—a sight that would once have been appropriate in a horror movie, but that now strikes certain marketers as
somehow inviting (and perhaps it is).

There were so many horror movies released in the Eighties that a full
consideration of all their robotic elements would require a separate essay. Here I will mention only two.

Aliens (1986) played on that same loathing of female sexuality
which had earlier pervaded *The Exorcist* and the horror tales of Brian
De Palma—although the later film, unlike its predecessors, was actually touted for its "feminism." Whereas the earlier films merely play on
the manifest "evil" of Woman as a frightful, sticky mess (a device that

pops up also in the infamous *Fatal Attraction*), *Aliens* divides the female in two: there is Ripley, the tough-guy heroine, played cool and capable by the deep-voiced, strong-jawed Sigourney Weaver, and then there is her nemesis, the repulsive Mama Alien, all screams and tentacles and dripping maw (so to speak), discharging endless smaller monsters from a prolific womb. The two wage a very long custody battle over a little girl who, understandably, prefers the "father." In this fight, the Alien uses her various lethal nodes, while Ripley uses her brains and futuristic blaster, at one point yelling "Bitch!", like any manly wife-beater. Finally, Ripley manages to snuff the Alien only by turning herself hyper-masculine/robotic: she encases herself in a mammoth robot-exoskeleton, which—powerful and dry—allows her to crush the shrieking mother-figure as if it were a giant, juicy bug.

RoboCop (1987) invokes the horror of robotism only to deny it in the end. A gruesome dystopian satire, the film presents the plight of Murphy (Peter Weller), a Detroit policeman who, having been shot to pieces by a grotesque gang of hoodlums, dies and is recycled, by a giant corporation, into an invincible cyborg supercop. Murphy redivivus is intended as a prototype, because the corporation, or certain evil types within it, want to market more such robocops to city governments trying to stem the rising tide of crime.

The film is almost powerful in its depiction of the hapless Murphy, who, with his vast robotic body and bewildered human face, appears—like Darth Vader—as a striking metaphor for man "half-dead in his accoutrements." However, *Robocop* actually ends up exploiting the appeal of robotism. Despite the film's many light satiric jabs at corporate America, its real target is not that homogenizing force, but the film's own caricatures of heterogeneity: the few bad apples in the corporation (a ruthless young Jewish type and a vaguely homosexual martinet), and the multicolored gang of hoodlums (a black, a punk, a Vietnamese, etc., all led by a seeming ex-radical who wears wire-rims and calls policemen "pigs"). Simplified beyond all human difference, Murphy is strong and pure enough both to take his revenge and vindicate the corporate vision, which he does by wasting the motley group of heavies. Finally, he is a good servant to the very corporation that has mechanized him, and ends by trading a friendly grin with the honest patriarch who sits as Chairman of the Board.■

Big Brother Is You, Watching

· ·

The only comprehension left to thought is horror at the incomprehensible. Just as the reflective onlooker, meeting the laughing placard of a toothpaste beauty, discerns in her flashlight grin the grimace of torture, so from every joke, even from every pictorial representation, he is assailed by the death sentence on the subject, which is implicit in the universal triumph of subjective reason.
—T.W. Adorno, *Minima Moralia*

IN HIS COMMENCEMENT ADDRESS TO THE CLASS OF 1984 at Texas A&M University, Vice President George Bush, making a familiar point, invoked George Orwell's *Nineteen Eighty-Four.* Mr. Bush spoke of the novel as a prophecy that will not come true as long as America and her allies "stand together, firm and strong, in defense of our freedom." As he and/or his speechwriter(s) would have it, the novel is simply an attack on Soviet domination: "Big Brother may be all-powerful in Havana, but the United States will not stand idly by while Big Brother tries to extend his power and influence over our freedom-loving neighbors in Central America."[1]

This bellicose interpretation of *Nineteen Eighty-Four* is nearly as old as the novel itself. When it first appeared, some American rightists hailed *Nineteen Eighty-Four* as a vivid anticommunist manifesto—a misreading that Orwell himself publicly repudiated. But even if Orwell had not thus tried to defend his text against its seizure by the right, he had already protested any such warlike appropriation, since *Nineteen Eighty-Four* is itself a satire of the same cold-war mentality that seeks to use it as a weapon. Vowing to oppose "Big Brother" by keeping the U.S. permanently mobilized, Vice President Bush spoke exactly like the fictitious managers of Big Brother's own regime, who also strive to keep their system "firm and strong" against the current enemy. Nor is the similarity merely general, but extends down to the vice president's striking misuse of specific terms. His proclamation that the governments of, say, El Salvador, Chile, Honduras, and Guatemala are "freedom-loving" recalls the perverse official language of Oceania, where the

"Ministry of Peace" makes war, the "Ministry of Love" takes care of torture, and so on.

However, Orwell's novel does not simply expose the blindness of its own anticommunist boosters, but illuminates the whole system that threatens to eternalize such blind aggressiveness, which comes automatically from both the "left" and "right," or East and West. *Nineteen Eighty-Four* describes a triune world of endless opposition and no difference: Oceania, allied with Eastasia or Eurasia, keeps itself "firm and strong" against Eurasia or Eastasia, which, allied with Oceania, does exactly the same thing. And, as the megastates within the text are made identical by their very opposition, so do the megastates outside the text resemble one another through the very belligerence that keeps them separated. This has been demonstrated, absurdly and yet fittingly, by the official function of *Nineteen Eighty-Four* itself in both the U.S. and the U.S.S.R., each power using it against the other. Just as, according to George Bush, Big Brother is "all-powerful in Havana," so, according to a major Soviet political journal, *Nineteen Eighty-Four* indicts not the Soviet system but "bourgeois society, bourgeois civilization, bourgeois democracy—in which, as [Orwell] feared, the poisonous roots of antihumanism, all-devouring militarism, and oppression have today thrust up truly monstrous shoots."[2] In the U.S., there is "complete uniformity of view on all subjects," and "a continuous frenzy of hatred for foreign enemies and internal traitors"—horrors represented and perpetuated by the very writing that thus decries them.*

Thus Orwell's text, which captures the static agony of a world at once divided and unvaried, has been used to intensify the very face-off that it so memorably conveys. Perhaps this is inevitable. The enormous system that *Nineteen Eighty-Four* satirizes is surely too compelling to permit its managers to read with the care and detachment that might allow self-criticism. However, it is not only our vice president who has recently betrayed an inability to read *Nineteen Eighty-Four.* Throughout 1984, the novel has been at once celebrated and neglected in America, its significance for our society entirely denied in most of the TV newscasts, corporate advertisements, magazine articles, and other statements concocted especially for this Orwell memorial year. According to this barrage, *Nineteen Eighty-Four* is not satiric, not even literary, but an attempt at straightforward prophecy, like the works of Nostradamus, and therefore meant to be measured literally against the

---

*Furthermore, the novel was unavailable in Soviet bookstores—a ban that was lifted only in 1988.

present. Because the present is obviously much preferable to the novel's world, *Nineteen Eighty-Four* has been used, predictably, as the basis for hearty affirmations of the status quo.

And those, of course, who have the most invested in the status quo have also been the novel's readiest detractors. Certain corporate "advertorials," for instance, placed in many magazines and newspapers, have anxiously refused the possibility that *Nineteen Eighty-Four* might somehow pertain to here and now. "The year is here at last, one is tempted to say," begins one ad for Mobil, "so let's get on with it and let the novel rest." "Whatever merits *Nineteen Eighty-Four* has as literature," claims an ad for United Technologies, "the book has failed as prophecy." Although there is no doubt what Orwell would have thought of these mammoth corporations if he had lived to appreciate their achievements, these ads disingenuously insist that *Nineteen Eighty-Four* is only "about the dangers of big, intrusive government," "government against people." And yet, as if to protest an indictment, both ads attempt to vindicate these corporations' products—and, therefore, their existence—by extolling the liberating effects of advanced technology: "Orwell was wrong about technology. Technology has not enslaved us. It has freed us." Because of the pervasiveness and accessibility of computers, each of us is freer than ever before: "Because the chip increases our choices, it ensures individuality."

But the refusal to admit that *Nineteen Eighty-Four* might in any way pertain to our own lives reflects and bolsters an ideology that extends well beyond the confines of big business. Arthur Schlesinger, Jr., writing in the *New York Times Book Review* (25 September 1983), reacted with a telling shrillness to the suggestion that Orwell's satire might illuminate its present readers' world. "Such arguments are shallow, if not frivolous," opined the historian, who went on thus to proscribe any such interpretation: "This is what '1984' is about—not some sort of continuous, incremental evolution from what we have today, but a shattering discontinuity, a qualitative transformation, an ultimate change of phase." In an effort to bolster this remarkable assertion, Schlesinger sought next to demonstrate that totalitarianism cannot succeed, a failure that presumably invalidates the novel as anything other than a chilling fantasy. Whereas the Oceanic system seems to prevail absolutely and for good, real human beings are too wayward to permit any such political finality: "There have been countless martyrs to the unconquerable faith in life, like Winston Smith himself. Today many, like Andrei Sakharov, intrepidly affirm this faith against cruel masters."

The judgment promoted by Vice President Bush and his Soviet counterparts, by Professor Schlesinger and the Mobil Corporation, depends not just on a refusal to read Orwell's satire carefully, but on the complementary refusal, or disinclination, to read the world with equal care. That satire and this world cannot possibly be severed from each other as Schlesinger insists they must be, for no expression can wholly transcend the moment that produced it, nor can contiguous moments be neatly disjoined: Orwell's history is in his novel, and that history connects with ours.

And what are the real points of convergence between *Nineteen Eighty-Four* and 1984? Those who have labored to deny the novel's importance may have helped us toward an answer. Despite their differences in emphasis, the liberal historian and the massive business enterprises share the assumption that Orwell's vision has been superannuated by the recent efforts of enlightened minds: "Thanks to the electronic microchip and the technology that brought it into being," exults the ad for United Technologies, "1984 has not become *1984*." The ad for Mobil alludes worshipfully to "the strides society has made since Orwell's day in electronics, communication, and computerization." Professor Schlesinger invokes the ideal of Enlightenment somewhat differently. His reference to Andrei Sakharov, affirming the Russian's faith in life against cruel masters, is a depiction that suggests the heroic conceptions of Voltaire and Jefferson.

And yet it is precisely the ideal of Enlightenment that is the implicit object of Orwell's painful satire. As we shall see, *Nineteen Eighty-Four* actually illuminates the assumptions of those who have tried to dismiss it—the same assumptions, paradoxically, that must also motivate any effort to correct those dismissive readings. Because *Nineteen Eighty-Four* is not a bald prophecy—not just a simple "warning," but a subtle and demanding work of art that tells us truths about modern politics—we must read it closely, both as a literary text and as an oblique reflection on our own world. In my attempt at such a reading, I will first analyze Orwell's novel as a critique of Enlightenment (after some discussion of that inescapable impulse), and then move on to a discussion of Enlightenment as it is manifest today, for us, in the forms of advertising and TV.

THE OPENING SENTENCE OF *NINETEEN EIGHTY-FOUR* RE-calls some of the oldest of English poetical traditions, but only to imply that they mean nothing in the novel's world: "It was a bright cold day in April, and the clocks were striking thirteen." With its two trimeter clauses and marked caesura, the sentence initially suggests the opening couplet of a folk ballad; but then this familiar rhythmic evocation is abruptly canceled out. The line's quasi-nostalgic appeal is undercut, first of all, by the futuristic revelation that Oceanic clocks strike more than twelve. And the effect of this surprising news is reinforced by the ending's metrical dislocation, as that spondee "thirteen" falls jarringly in place of the expected monosyllable. Moreover, as with the sentence's balladic rhythm, so with its peculiar "April" day, another reference that at first seems half-familiar, then wholly alien. Despite its vaguely comforting reverberations, this "April" day does not exemplify that balmy, revivifying April sung by the English poets since Chaucer, but is strangely "bright" and "cold," suggesting that, within the world we are about to enter, such antique associations have been eliminated.

The sentence seems at first to beckon us back home, but ends by leaving us bewildered, as on a sunny morning when you think you are awake until you sense that you are dreaming it. And yet the dreamlike eeriness of this new world is merely the final consequence of the most clear-sighted practicality. In the world liberated by the Inner Party, all vestiges of literary culture—both popular and learned—have long since been discarded as fantastic nonsense. Those obsolete texts by Chaucer, Shakepeare, Eliot, and others, with their impressionistic references to "April," have now been modernized for good, made equally accessible and clear in Newspeak versions; and the rustic traditons that once sustained the ballad have also been wiped out, even from among the unenlightened proles. Moreover, in its drive to junk all preexistent myth, the Party has excised not only poetry, but even those arbitrary terms and structures once used to mark the passage of time. Whereas, before the Revolution, the clocks had been attuned to go from one to twelve twice every day, that purely customary sequence need not persist in the Party's readjusted world, where the military scheme of hours makes better sense. Indeed, the bright, cold afternoon that starts the novel may not, in fact, represent an unseasonable "day in April," but a day in what we still call "March" or "January," since the months need not refer any longer to the quaint divisions of the Roman calendar; nor, for that matter, does the Oceanic "1984" necessarily denote a point along our temporal continuum, which still refers to the legendary birth of a deity outmoded by the Party.

"It was a bright cold day in April, and the clocks were striking thirteen." This disorienting line of antipoetry does not just alienate us, then, but implicitly refers us to the intellectual origins of all contemporary alienation. Although in effect the sentence is surrealistic, with its sudden vision of a world that seems to have gone mad, this new world actually represents the final triumph of rationality itself, the distant source of the Oceanic madness that has so disastrously betrayed it. Thus the object of Orwell's horrific satire is not any one totalitarian regime, but a necessary modern urge that has indirectly brought about all modern tyrannies, whether of the left or right, whether centralized or pluralistic. What Orwell understood with such intolerable clarity was the appalling likelihood that the most destructive modern systems have emerged, paradoxically, out of the very impulse to transcend destruction: the impulse of Enlightenment.

Orwell had begun to intuit this paradox in the late Thirties, when he wrote the controversial second part of *The Road to Wigan Pier*; and as war broke out and then persisted, his intuition seemed to be continually reconfirmed by the massive barbarism that had somehow emerged out of civilization at its latest moment: "As I write," begins "The Lion and the Unicorn," composed in 1940, "highly civilized human beings are flying overhead, trying to kill me."[3] It was the war, a conflict at once atavistic and sophisticated, that led Orwell and certain others to contemplate the long self-contradiction of Western progress. In 1943, as Orwell was making notes toward his last novel, two other observers, although working out of intellectual traditions wholly different from Orwell's, were collaborating on a brilliant, dismal essay that illuminates precisely the same ruinous process that is the implicit subject of *Nineteen Eighty-Four*. Exiled in Los Angeles, Max Horkheimer and T.W. Adorno wrote the *Dialectic of Enlightenment* to elaborate their argument that mechanistic "Progress," as Orwell had once put it, "is just as much of a swindle as reaction."[4]

For Horkheimer and Adorno, "Enlightenment" refers not simply to the optimistic moment of the *philosophes*, but to the drive, as old as civilization, toward the rational mastery of nature; or, to put it more accurately, that drive toward mastery which is itself the source and purpose of civilization. The authors subvert complacent faith in progress by disproving the absolute distinction between primitive societies and the modern world that seems to have transcended them; for the aim of men, both then and now, has been to turn the natural world into the instrument of their own power. Just as archaic groups attempted to manage the inchoate forces of their universe through priestly ritual and human sacrifice, so too have modern men, from the time of Bacon's first intellectual prospectus, worked to make the material world both useful and predictable, through the application of technology and scientific method. What distinguishes the historical era which we call the Enlightenment, then, is not its objectifying tendency per se, but its total rationalization of that tendency, proclaimed "under the banner of radicalism."[5] Now nature will serve those who study it most coolly and relentlessly, having freed it from the obfuscations of folk wisdom, Church doctrine, and Aristotelian dogma: "The program of the Enlightenment was the disenchantment of the world; the dissolution of myths and the substitution of knowledge for fancy" (p. 3).

This program was conceived by its earliest proponents as a means of

universal renewal, "the Effecting of all Things possible," as Francis Bacon put it in *New Atlantis*. And yet the unrestrained demythifying impulse has led us not to rejuvenation, but toward apocalypse. In its
efforts to appropriate the natural world by wiping out the myths that
had made it legible, the Enlightenment began a process of erasure that
soon moved beyond the defunct beliefs of tribe and church to subvert
all metaphysical conceptions, particularly those which had justified
the process in the first place: "God" and then "Nature" went the way of
the countless spirits that had animated the global wilderness; and now
such later abstractions as "History," "Man," "the people," "social justice," etc.—also impossible to defend as strictly rational—have likewise come to seem mere sentimental fabrications. Horkheimer and
Adorno argue that "for the Enlightenment, whatever does not conform
to the rule of computation and utility is suspect. So long as it can develop undisturbed by any outward repression, there is no holding it. In the
process, it treats its own ideas of human rights exactly as it does the
older universals" (p. 6).

Enlightenment, then, is finally bent on leaving nothing extant but its
own implicit violence. As it proceeds to blast away each of its own prior
pretexts, this explosive rationality comes ever closer, not to "truth"—
which category it has long since shattered—but to the open realization
of its own coercive animus, purified of *all* delusions—including, finally,
rationality itself. Into the ideological vacuum which it has created so
efficiently there rushes its own impulse to destroy and keep destroying:
Orwell perceived the same suicidal process at work in Western
thought, and explicitly expressed this perception several years before
elaborating it in his last novel.

In a piece written for *Time and Tide* in 1940, Orwell considers that
modern moment when Christianity had finally proven indefensible. At
that moment, "it was absolutely essential that the soul should be cut
away," for religious belief had "become in essence a lie, a semi-con-
scious device for keeping the rich rich and the poor poor." The major
writers of the last two centuries, the heroic standard-bearers of Enlightenment—"Gibbon, Voltaire, Rousseau, Shelley, Byron, Dickens, Sten-
dhal, Samuel Butler, Ibsen, Zola, Flaubert, Shaw, Joyce"—proceeded
to demolish what was left of that old falsehood; but the outcome of that
just campaign seemed to be a total, irreversible injustice:

> For two hundred years we had sawed and sawed and sawed at the
> branch we were sitting on. And in the end, much more suddenly
> than anyone had foreseen, our efforts were rewarded, and down
> we came. But unfortunately there had been a little mistake. The

thing at the bottom was not a bed of roses after all. It was a cess-pool filled with barbed wire. (*CEJL*, II, 15)

Like Horkheimer and Adorno, Orwell saw the unprecedented horrors of mid-century not as the aberrant results of any single system of beliefs, but as the inevitable consequence of the dumb, persistent, onward urge that had devastated one belief after another. It was the relentless impulse of Enlightenment that had enabled the conceptions of the death camp, the atomic bomb, the machinery of total propaganda—each one a highly rational construction, devoted to a terminal irrationality. And that autonomous rationality, Orwell believed, would quickly supersede even those new myths devised to justify it in the present. Soon such notions as "the master race" and "socialism in one country" would seem as quaint as "Harry, England, and St. George," as Enlightenment approached that perfect disillusionment whereby the Inner Party keeps itself in power: "We are different," says O'Brien, "from all the oligarchies of the past in that we know what we are doing." For Orwell and his German counterparts, the expert atrocities of the late Enlightenment foretold the emergence of a world wholly dominated by the self-promoting urge to dominate, an urge whose only manifesto might be expressed in these infamous tautologies: "The object of persecution is persecution. The object of torture is torture. The object of power is power."

And yet Enlightenment is necessary. "We are wholly convinced," write Horkheimer and Adorno, "that social freedom is inseparable from enlightened thought" (p. xiii)—a conviction to which Orwell, too, always held firmly. Neither he nor the two Germans ever crudely called for the repeal of the Enlightenment; for if progress "is as much of a swindle as reaction," the reflexive movement backward can only end up in that same abyss toward which the automatic movement forward always speeds. Rather, these critical advocates of Enlightenment recognized that progressive thought, while indispensable, at the same time "contains the seed of the reversal universally apparent today"; and so it was the two Germans' project to salvage the best original intentions of Enlightenment, by encouraging "reflection on [its] recidivist element": "The point is . . . that Enlightenment *must consider itself*, if men are not to be wholly betrayed" (p. xv). Our responsibility now, therefore, must be to read and reread *Nineteen Eighty-Four*, not as a piece of cold-war propaganda, but as a work that might enlighten us as to the fatal consequences of Enlightenment, including the current glare of publicity that has all but blacked out the text itself.

"IT WAS A BRIGHT COLD DAY IN APRIL, AND THE CLOCKS were striking thirteen." Having thus adroitly engineered its total

316

severance from the past, the Party represents the demythifying mechanism of Enlightenment at its most successful; but such success amounts to failure, since the Party's efforts to annihilate the past have only re-imposed it. The Party's system, founded upon the total extirpation of cruel nature, has itself reverted to cruel nature. Life in the state of Oceania is nasty, brutish, and short, a furtive passage through an urban sprawl that is as primitive and dangerous as any jungle: London swarms with "gorilla-faced guards" and "small, beetle-like" men, and even its machines suggest the wilderness which they oppose: "In the far distance a helicopter skimmed down between the roofs, hovered for an instant like a bluebottle, and darted away again with a curving flight." And, as nature has been re-created at its most inimical, so has the patriarchal God, an overseer more wrathful and alert than ever:

The little sandy-haired woman had flung herself forward over the back of the chair in front of her. With a tremulous murmur that sounded like "My Savior!" she extended her arms toward the screen. Then she buried her face in her hands. It was apparent that she was uttering a prayer.

And even the defunct conventions of poetry reemerge uncannily from the mechanism that was built to obliterate them. Although "composed without any human intervention whatever on an instrument known as a versificator," the lines sung continually by the washerwoman outside Charrington's shop repeat that strangely inexpungible allusion: "It was only an 'opeless fancy, / It passed like an Ipril dye . . . ."

Thus Enlightenment hurries forward toward the very state from which it flees, a grand pattern that recurs in small and subtle ways throughout the novel, just as it defines the general structure of the narrative itself. As Winston Smith helplessly observes, "the end was contained in the beginning." Therefore the fateful number "101" not only designates the room wherein the hero relapses forever into primal incoherence, but also symbolizes all such reversion—the terminal arrival at the point of origin. And this process is not only temporal, but spatial and psychological as well, informing every movement and every thought with an absoluteness that conveys, more poignantly than any dissertation, the full horror of whatever is "totalitarian." In Oceania there is no possible escape from Oceania, only continual rediscoveries of Oceania where one least expects it. "It was a bright cold day in April. . . ." Although this April seems at first to proffer a venerable pastoral solace, it is merely one more of the Party's inventions, a term irrelevant to that April known before the Revolution; and so this "day in

317

April" is as "bright" and "cold" as "the place where there is no darkness," another promised refuge that turns out to have been devised by
the very forces from which it seemed at first to offer sanctuary. And so
it is with "the Brotherhood," with Charrington's retreat, with "Charrington" himself.

And, as there is no refuge for the novel's hero, neither is the hero
himself a solid refuge for the novel's readers; for even Winston Smith
embodies that cruel force which he ostensibly opposes. Like the "April"
day that chills him, he represents an exception that turns out to be the
rule:

> It was a bright cold day in April, and the clocks were striking thir-
> teen. Winston Smith, his chin nuzzled into his breast in an effort
> to escape the vile wind, slipped quickly through the glass doors of
> Victory Mansions, though not quickly enough to prevent a swirl of
> gritty dust from entering along with him.

Although until his "reintegration" Winston Smith is clearly different
from the rest of Oceania, it would be a sentimental overstatement to
insist that, once the Party has hollowed him out, it has extinguished the
world's last sturdy subject. Even at first, "the last man in Europe" is
already losing his fragile selfhood, which is entirely contingent on his
furtive, doomed refusal to accept the status quo. The figure who
"slipped quickly through the glass doors of Victory Mansions" already
seems as insubstantial as a breeze; whereas, conversely, that "swirl of
gritty dust," by "entering along with him," seems to walk in on human
legs. However, this first image of the hero implies not just that he is
losing his tenuous uniqueness and coherence, but that he loses them
precisely in attempting to retain them, since it is in making "an effort to
escape the vile wind" that Winston Smith seems to turn into mere wind
himself.

Until his final degradation, Winston Smith is repeatedly undone by
this same paradox, as his very efforts to escape or to combat the Party
become themselves the proof of his inviolable membership. In starting
a diary, he deliberately commits what is probably a capital offense
against the Party; and yet the first result of this dissident gesture is an
effusion of perfect orthodoxy, enthusiastic praise for an atrocious war
film seen the night before. Similarly, after his first sexual encounter
with Julia, he realizes that the same belligerent coldness had entered
into even this forbidden pleasure, thereby undoing it: "Their embrace
had been a battle, the climax a victory. It was a blow struck against the
Party. It was a political act." And his most explicit act of defiance—his
promise to O'Brien that he will commit whatever subversive crimes

"the Brotherhood" requires of him—only demonstrates the futility of his ardent opposition, which makes him sound less like the Party's clear-sighted enemy than like one of its deluded founders: "You are prepared to give your lives?" "Yes." "You are prepared to commit murder?" "Yes." "To commit acts of sabotage which may cause the death of hundreds of innocent people?" "Yes." And so on, with the hero recalling those steeliest revolutionaries of the past, whose self-discipline prepared the way, not for some hoped-for earthly paradise, but for the enlightened Party that would vaporize them.

In opposing the Party, Winston Smith approximates it, because the Party has arisen from the same impulse that motivates his opposition: the impulse of Enlightenment. Having long since disabused itself of every metaphysical distraction, the Party not only sees all, but—more frighteningly—sees through all. What makes the Party's gaze so devastating, then, is not just its sweep, enabled by the telescreens, but its penetration. The Party sees through anyone who would see through the Party, because the Party has seen through itself already, demythifying itself—not to defeat itself, of course, but to make itself eternal. In struggling to see through the Party, therefore, Winston Smith inadequately emulates it. Each of his rebellious actions puts him in the ludicrous position of clumsily anticipating the system that he wants to terminate. Whether surreptitiously writing, defiantly rutting, or conspiring to subvert an odious regime, he merely reenacts old battles long since fought and won by the Enlightenment on its way to Ingsoc.

Nor does the Party thus superannuate only its opponents. In its relentless onward thrust, sooner or later it simultaneously bypasses and exterminates everyone above ground level, whether they hate the Party, or zealously applaud it, or vacuously go about their business: Syme is vaporized, despite his exemplary commitment to Enlightenment linguistics, because, Winston thinks, "he sees too clearly and speaks too plainly"; but then Parsons too is vaporized—for "thoughtcrime," although he seems to have no thoughts.

To describe the Party only as a force that indiscriminately kills, however, is to mistake its sway for simple tyranny, like the reign of Caligula or of Henry VIII; the Party's sway is total, at once more subtle and extensive than the rule of any mere dictator, however bloodthirsty. For it is not the Oceanic bloodshed per se that proves the Party's destructiveness, but the object of that bloodshed: the extinction of all resistant subjectivity. As Orwell put it in "Lear, Tolstoy and the Fool," it makes no difference whether one's would-be oppressors work cruelly or seductively, since in either case their intention toward the subject is to erase him in the name of their own power, to "get inside his brain and dictate his thoughts for him in the minutest particulars." In Oceania, the victim is extinguished long before his heart is stopped by force, or even if it never is, since, even while still breathing, that victim has already become a mere repetition of the state that may or may not have him shot, redundantly, one day. Thus Syme, "a tiny creature," is nothing more than the linguistic diminution that consumes him; and Parsons, wet and energetic, is only a particle of the general flood. Once vaporized, therefore, these nonentities are still no less extant than those model citizens who have survived them—Winston's wife, for instance, without "a thought in her head that was not a slogan," or the functionary whom Winston hears "quack-quack-quacking" at lunch, each official phrase "jerked out very rapidly, and, as it seemed, all in one piece, like a line of type cast solid."

If all of these blank members of the Outer Party have succumbed to the state's hollowing process, then perhaps the members of the Inner Party, the supervisors of that process, have not themselves been emptied by it: O'Brien, a representative of that invisible elite, does seem somehow to stand above the universal nullity—or so the hero thinks, yearning desperately for some communion with this ostensible exception, who "had the appearance of being a person that you could talk to, if somehow you could cheat the telescreens and get him alone." It is O'Brien's curiously aristocratic mien that excites this vague hope: his "peculiar grave courtesy," an "urbane manner" that contradicts his "prizefighter's physique." Winston Smith is heartened by O'Brien's strange detachment, his air of irony and secret knowledge, which suggests a sympathetic rebel hidden deep within the oligarch.

And yet O'Brien too is wholly a microcosm of the system that has both empowered and undone him. "So ugly yet so civilized," he embodies Oceania itself, or rather, that process of Enlightenment whereby Oceania has been forced forward to its origins. The hero has misread him absolutely. The discrepancy between O'Brien's coarse bulk and smooth deportment is not the sign of some dialectical potential, as Winston Smith had assumed, but, on the contrary, just another instance of the same final contradiction that has arrested the whole world, its managers included. O'Brien's air of ironic detachment, in which the hero had discerned a promise of transcendence, is in fact the deadliest of all the Inner Party's secret weapons. "More even than of strength, [O'Brien] gave an impression of confidence and of an understanding tinged with irony." It is through relentless irony that the Party subverts anyone who, even inwardly, tries to resist its gaze.

Long before they have seized Winston Smith, the Party leaders have already neutralized his dissidence through derisive imitation, thereby transforming his struggle into an empty joke for their own unhappy entertainment. Since O'Brien himself helped to write the book attributed to Goldstein, that "heavy black volume"—Winston's Bible—turns out to be a satire; O'Brien's first encounter with the hero, in "the long corridor at the Ministry," is an implicit parody of the hero's first encounter with Julia in the same place. And the gentle "Mr. Charrington" is also an ironic spectacle, meant to draw the hero out—not to entrap him (an unnecessary step in lawless Oceania) but to make his desire laughable. But even if the Inner Party had never bothered to set the hero up for ridicule, it would still have played him for a laugh, simply by looking on, unseen and delighted, at the torment which he thought was private.

More fundamentally than by its instruments of torture, then, the Party is made mighty by its own mimetic subtlety and keen spectatorship—the weapons of pure irony, which is necessarily the attitudinal vehicle and expression of Enlightenment. Analogous to Enlightenment and fostered by it, pure irony denudes the world of every value, devastating—just with a little smile and deft repetition—whatever person, concept, feeling, belief, or tradition it encounters, until there is nothing left but the urge to ironize. And so the ironist, at last contemptuous even of the values that had previously bolstered his contempt, is forced to continue being ironic, because that attitude is all that can distinguish him from the nullity that underlies and enables it. Such an attitude depends, however, on the persistence of objects worthy of derision, even if all such objects have already been wiped out by enlightened thought and ridicule. The ironist must therefore revive anachronistic postures, reinvent the enemies long since put to rest, or else become depleted. Thus the ironist is forced to follow the ruinous trajectory of Enlightenment, succumbing to his own process of erasure, and in that process merely reevoking the objects which he had intended to destroy.

Posing as a conspirator, O'Brien "filled the glasses and raised his own glass by the stem. 'What shall it be this time?' he said, still with the same faint suggestion of irony. 'To the confusion of the Thought Police? To the death of Big Brother? To humanity? To the future?' " Only later do we realize that these apparent exhortations are nothing more than sardonic little jokes: O'Brien is sadistically equivocating, since—as he knows already—"the death of Big Brother" is impossible, "the confusion of the Thought Police" redundant, and "humanity" an essence that he means not to vindicate but to extinguish in "the future" (which, we learn eventually, O'Brien sees as "a boot stamping on a human face—forever"). Thus the hero's cherished, vague ideals are played for laughs by the resolute O'Brien; yet for all his resoluteness, O'Brien is, without the selfhood which he mimics, nothing. Similarly, once Winston's guardian agent doffs his excellent disguise as "Mr. Charrington," he at

321

once regresses into "a member of the Thought Police": alert, hostile, and anonymous, like the Party that deploys him.

The obsessive thoroughness with which the Party re-creates what it purports to have transcended attests to a distorted longing for it. Although intended as ironic, the spectacle of Mr. Charrington and his shop is so fully and convincingly detailed, and the agent's performance so finely nuanced, that the actor and directors must unknowingly desire the past which they have parodied so expertly. And when O'Brien finally reveals his true identity (or nonidentity) to Winston Smith in the actual "place where there is no darkness," the ambiguity of his reply also suggests that his irony is itself an expression of the desire which it keeps cruelly mimicking:

> "They've got you too!" [Winston] cried.
> "They got me a long time ago," said O'Brien with a mild, almost regretful irony.

What the Party leaders laugh at in their victim is not a desire which they themselves have transcended but a desire which they themselves still feel, and which they express pervertedly through their permanent campaign against it. Even in this perversion Winston Smith resembles and anticipates them. At the beginning of the novel, we recognize the hero's longing in his posture: "Winston Smith, his chin nuzzled into his breast in an effort to escape the vile wind," is a figure trying to evade Oceania by mothering himself, trying to escape the coldness of Enlightenment by reenacting that primal situation which Enlightenment attacks and yet restores in a warped form. Although still capable of acting on this desire, however, he is (like any other proper Oceanic citizen) both unconscious of it and, while driven by it, quick to side with every other Oceanic citizen against it—an indirect self-censure which he too carries out through ironic spectatorship.

Just after he has slipped into Victory Mansions in that revealing attitude, he writes, "only imperfectly aware of what he was setting down," an orthodox denunciation of the desire which he has just expressed out on the street, and which now continues to impel his jeering at it: "April 4th, 1984. Last night to the flicks. One very good one of a ship full of refugees being bombed somewhere in the Mediterranean." Both in the midst of this spectatorship and in recounting it, Winston Smith shares with the other members of the audience a cruel, sheltered pleasure in the methodical explosion of every figure on the screen: "a great huge fat man trying to swim away with a helicopter after him," then disappearing, torn by bullets, the "audience shouting with laughter as he sank." And yet this sadistic joy in the destruction of those fictitious "refugees" is also masochistic, as the hero unwittingly reveals in describing, still with evident approval of their fate, the next few victims, whose image expresses vividly his own desire as he has just betrayed it to us: "there was a middle-aged woman might have been a jewess sitting up in the bow with a little boy about three years old in her arms. little boy screaming with fright and hiding his head between her breasts as if he was trying to burrow right into her. . . ."

When, at the end, Winston Smith is rapt for good in credulous spectatorship, he is himself just like those refugees, a visible example of floundering and defeated opposition, shunned by all and waiting to be shot. The Inner Party is surely gratified by this atrocious spectacle—we can imagine them sitting and jeering his submersion into Oceanic non-consciousness, just like that earlier "audience shouting with laughter as he sank." But there is no ultimate distinction between such viewers and the disintegration that amuses them. In cheering the destruction of their own prototype, they cheer their own destruction. And so, in the end, all collapses into hateful liquid. Weeping "gin-soaked tears," his memory ebbing, the ex-hero is an old joke in the eyes of those who have been drenched along with him. He clings to the image of Big Brother's nonexistent face, as Enlightenment fulfills itself, and humanity breaks down into a flood as vast and absolute as the flood in which all life originated.

AS WE LEAVE THE WORLD OF ORWELL'S NOVEL DISSOLVING into its own flux, we must turn back to our more tangible society, wherein the novel now receives so much perfunctory attention, and ask how Orwell's vision reflects on American life today. Orwell was, of course, not thinking of this moment in America when he conceived and wrote his novel, nor would it make sense to demonstrate a crude equation of America with Oceania. Rather than simply itemize the world of *Nineteen Eighty-Four* into those details that have "come true" and those that haven't, we must discover within this satire of Enlightenment its oblique reflections on our own enlightened culture, whose continuities with Orwell's time and place demand our critical consideration. We can best begin this project of discovery by analyzing one explicit similarity between the novel's world and ours: in Oceania, as in America, the telescreens are always on, and everyone is always watching them.

The Oceanic telescreens are not actually televisual. Writing in the late Forties, Orwell could not come to know TV's peculiar quality; he conceived the telescreen, understandably, as a simple combination of radio and cinema.[6] Its sounds and images therefore suggest these parent media, which, beginning at mid-century, turned out to be alike

323

in their capacity to drum up violent feeling. The telescreens' voices are abrasive and hysterical, like the mob whose regulated violence they catalyze; and the telescreens' images are also explicitly suasive, arousing primitive reactions, paradoxically, through sophisticated cinematic techniques. Ingenious tricks of Eisensteinian montage enable the telescreens to inspire extreme reactions, whether foaming hatred of this year's foe or cringing reverence for Big Brother (reactions that are fundamentally the same).

Television, on the other hand, inspires no such wildness, but is as cool and dry as the Oceanic telescreens are hot and bothered. Its flat, neutralizing vision automatically strains out those ineffable qualities wherein we recognize each other's power; nor can it, like film, reinvest its figures with such density, but must reduce all of its objects to the same mundane level. In order to overcome the muting effect of TV's essential grayness, the managers of all televisual spectacle try automatically to intensify each broadcast moment through the few sensational techniques available: extreme close-ups, marvelously heightened colors, dizzying graphics, high-pitched voices trilling choral harmonies, insistent bursts of domesticated rock and roll, and the incessant, meaningless montage that includes all things, events, and persons. And yet these compensations for the medium's basic coolness merely reinforce its distancing effect. Repeatedly subjected to TV's small jolts, we become incapable of outright shock or intense arousal, lapsing into a constant, dull anxiety wherein we can hardly sense the difference between a famine and a case of body odor. The televisual montage bolsters our inability to differentiate, its spectacle of endless metamorphosis merely making all images seem as insignificant as any single image seen for hours.

Because of these formal properties, TV is casually inimical to all charisma and therefore seems an inappropriate device for any program like the Inner Party's. Televised, the "enormous face" of Big Brother would immediately lose its aura of "mysterious calm," and so those omnipresent features would appear about as menacing as Michael Jackson's. On TV, furthermore, the maniacal intensities of actual Party members would also lose their sinister allure—not by being canceled out but by coming off as overheated, alien, and silly. At those moments when his face takes on a "mad gleam of enthusiasm," even O'Brien would seem to have been bypassed, and therefore exterminated, by TV.

Thus TV would seem to be an essentially iconoclastic medium; and yet it is this inherent subversiveness toward any visible authority that has enabled TV to establish its own total rule—for it is *all* individuality that TV annihilates, either by not conveying it or by making it look ludicrous. Today's TV's would therefore have suited the Party's ultimate objective perfectly. As TV would neutralize Big Brother's face and O'Brien's transports, so would it undercut the earnest idealism of Winston Smith, dismissing his indignant arguments about "the spirit of Man" by concentrating coolly on his "jailbird's face," just as O'Brien does. With its clinical or inquisitorial vision, TV appears to penetrate all masks, to expose all alibis, thereby seeming to turn the whole world into a comic spectacle of unsuccessful lying, pompous posturing, and neurotic defensiveness—behaviors that appear to be seen through the moment they are represented. It is from this apparent penetration that TV's documentary programs derive the ostensible incisiveness that makes them so engrossing: "Sixty Minutes," "The People's Court," "Real People," and so on. And it is the need to withstand TV's derisive penetration that has dictated the peculiar self-protective mien of all seasoned televisual performers, whether they play love scenes, read the news, or seem to run the country. The muted affability and thoroughgoing smoothness that make these entertainers seem acceptable on TV also serve as a defense against its searching eye; yet by thus attempting to avoid subversion, these figures—finally interchangeable as well as evanescent—merely subvert themselves, giving up that individuality which TV would otherwise discredit.

Within the borders of its spectacle, TV continues automatically that process of Enlightenment which the Party hastens consciously—the erasure of all lingering subjectivity. Whereas the Oceanic telescreens are the mere means used by the ironists in power, our telescreens are themselves ironic, and therefore make those powerful ironists unnecessary. For it is not only *on* TV that TV thus proceeds to cancel selves; it also wields its nullifying influence out in the wide world of its impressionable viewers. Television's formal erasure of distinctness complements—or perhaps has actually fostered—a derisive personal style that inhibits all personality, a knowingness that now pervades all TV genres and the culture which those genres have homogenized. The corrosive irony emanating from the Oceanic elite has been universalized by television, whose characters—both real and fictional—relentlessly inflict it on each other and themselves, defining a negative ideal of hip inertia which no living human being is able to approach too closely. For example, in situation comedies or "sitcoms"—TV's definitive creation—the "comedy" almost always consists of a weak, compulsive jeering that immediately wipes out any divergence from the indefinite collective standard. The characters vie at self-containment, reacting to every simulation of intensity, every bright idea, every mechanical enthusiasm with the same deflating look of jaded incredulity. In such an atmosphere, those already closest to the ground run the least risk of being felled by the general ridicule, and so those characters most adept at enforcing the proper emptiness are also the puniest and most passive: blasé menials, blasé wives and girlfriends, and—expecially—blasé children, who, like Parsons' daughter, prove their own orthodoxy by subverting their subverted parents.[7]

Nearly all of TV's characters—on sitcoms and in "dramas," on talk shows and children's programs—participate in this reflexive sneering, and such contemptuous passivity reflects directly on the viewer who watches it with precisely the same attitude. TV seems to flatter the inert skepticism of its own audience, assuring them that they can do no better than to stay right where they are, rolling their eyes in feeble disbelief. And yet such apparent flattery of our viewpoint is in fact a recurrent warning not to rise above this slack, derisive gaping. At first, it seems that it is only those eccentric others whom TV belittles. Each time some deadpan tot on a sitcom responds to his frantic mom with a disgusted sigh, or whenever the polished anchorman punctuates his footage of "extremists" with a look that speaks his well-groomed disapproval, or each time Johnny Carson comments on some "unusual" behavior with a wry sidelong glance into our living rooms, we are being flattered with a gesture of inclusion, the wink that tells us, *"We* are in the know." And yet we are the ones belittled by each subtle televisual gaze, which offers not a welcome but an ultimatum—that we had better see the joke or else turn into it.

If we see the joke, however, we are nothing, like those Oceanic viewers "shouting with laughter" at the sight of their own devastation. All televisual smirking is based on, and reinforces, the assumption that we who smirk together are enlightened past the point of nullity, having evolved far beyond whatever datedness we might be jeering, whether the fanatic's ardor, the prude's inhibitions, the hick's unfashionable pants, or the snob's obsession with prestige. Thus TV's relentless comedy at first seems utterly progressive, if largely idiotic, since its butts are always the most reactionary of its characters—militarists, bigots, sexists, martinets. However, it is not to champion our freedom that TV makes fun of these ostensible oppressors. On the contrary: through its derision, TV promotes only *itself,* disvaluing not Injustice or Intolerance but the impulse to resist TV.

Despite the butt's broad illiberality, what makes him appear ridiculous in TV's eyes is not his antidemocratic bias but his vestigial individuality, his persistence as a self sturdy and autonomous enough to sense that there is something missing from the televisual world, and to hunger for it, although ostracized for this desire by the sarcastic mob that watches and surrounds him. Like Winston Smith, the butt yearns for and exemplifies the past that brought about the present, and which the present now discredits through obsessive mockery. Whether arrogantly giving orders, compulsively tidying up, or longing for the good old days when men were men, the butt reenacts the type of personality—marked by rigidity and self-denial—that at first facilitated the extension of high capitalism but that soon threatened to impede its further growth. And it is just such endless growth that is the real point and object of TV's comedy, which puts down those hard selves in order to exalt the nothingness that laughs at them. Whereas the butt, enabled by his discrete selfhood, pursues desires that TV cannot gratify, we are induced, by the sight of his continual humiliation, to become as porous, cool, and acquiescent as he is solid, tense, and dissident, so that we might want nothing other than what TV sells us. This is what it means to see the joke. The viewer's enlightened laughter at those uptight others is finally the expression of his own Oceanic dissolution, as, within his distracted consciousness, there reverberates TV's sole imperative, which once obeyed makes the self seem a mere comical encumbrance—the imperative of total consumption.

Guided by its images even while he thinks that he sees through them, the TV-viewer learns only to consume. That inert, ironic watchfulness which TV reinforces in its audience is itself conducive to consumption. As we watch, struggling inwardly to avoid resembling anyone who might stand out as pre- or non- or antitelevisual, we are already trying to live up, or down, to the same standard of acceptability that TV's ads and shows define collectively: the standard that requires the desperate use of all those goods and services that TV proffers, including breath mints, mouthwash, dandruff shampoos, hair conditioners, blow-dryers, hair removers, eye drops, deodorant soaps and sticks and sprays, hair dyes, skin creams, lip balms, diet colas, diet plans, local frozen dinners, bathroom bowl cleaners, floor wax, car wax, furniture polish, fabric softeners, room deodorizers, and more, and more. Out of this flood of commodities, it is promised, we will each arise as sleek, quick, compact, and efficient as a brand-new Toyota; and in our effort at such self-renewal, moreover, we are enjoined not just to sweeten every orifice and burnish every surface, but to evacuate our psyches. While selling its explicit products, TV also advertises incidentally an ideal of emotional self-management, which dictates that we purge ourselves of all "bad feelings" through continual confession and by affecting the same stilted geniality evinced by most of TV's characters (the butts excluded). The unconscious must never be allowed to interfere with productivity, and so the viewer is warned repeatedly to atone for his every psychic eruption, like Parsons after his arrest for talking treason in his sleep: " 'Thoughtcrime is a dreadful thing, old man,' he said sententiously. 'It's insidious. . . . There I was, working away, trying to do my bit—never knew I had any bad stuff in my mind at all.' "

Thus, even as its programs push the jargon of "honesty" and "tolerance," forever counseling you to "be yourself," TV shames you ruthlessly for every symptom of residual mortality, urging you to turn yourself into a standard object wholly inoffensive, useful, and adulterated, a product of and for all other products. However, this transformation is impossible. There is no such purity available to human beings, whose bodies will sweat and whose instincts will rage—however expertly we work to shut them off. Even Winston Smith, as broken as he is at the conclusion, is still impelled by his desires, which the Party could not extinguish after all, since it depends on their distorted energy. For all its chilling finality, in other words, the novel's closing sentence is merely another of the Party's lies. What O'Brien cannot achieve through torture, we cannot attain through our campaigns of self-maintenance—no matter how many miles we jog, or how devotedly, if skeptically, we watch TV.

Like the Party, whose unstated rules no person can follow rigidly enough, TV demands that its extruded viewers struggle to embody an ideal too cool and imprecise for human emulation. And like Winston Smith, we are the victims of Enlightenment in its late phase, although it is the logic of consumption, not the deliberate machinations of some cabal, that has impoverished our world in the name of its enrichment. As the creatures of this logic, we have become our own overseers. While Winston Smith is forced to watch himself in literal self-defense, trying to keep his individuality a hard-won secret, we have been forced to watch ourselves lest we develop selves too hard and secretive for the open market. In America, there is no need for an objective apparatus of surveillance (which is not to say that none exists), because, guided by TV, we watch ourselves as if already televised, checking ourselves both inwardly and outwardly for any sign of untidiness or gloom, moment by moment as guarded and self-conscious as Winston Smith under the scrutiny of the Thought Police: "The smallest thing could give you away. A nervous tic, an unconscious look of anxiety, a habit of muttering to yourself—anything that carried with it the suggestion of abnormality, of having something to hide." Although this description refers to the objective peril of life in Oceania, it also captures the anxiety of life under the scrunity of television. Of course, all televisual performers must abide by this same grim advice or end up canceled; but TV's nervous viewers also feel themselves thus watched, fearing the same absolute exclusion if they should ever show some sign of resisting the tremendous pressure.[8]

Television further intensifies our apprehension that we are being

watched by continually assuring us that it already understands our in-
nermost fears, our private problems, and that it even knows enough
about our most intimate moments to reproduce them for us. The joy of
birth is brought to us by Citicorp, the tender concern of one friend for
another is presented by AT&T, the pleasures of the hearth are depicted
for us by McDonald's. And on any talk show or newscast, there might
suddenly appear the competent psychologist, who will deftly translate
any widespread discontent into his own antiseptic terms, thereby representing it as something well-known to him, and therefore harmless.
As we watch TV, we come to imagine what Winston Smith eventually
discovers: "There was no physical act, no word spoken aloud, that they
had not noticed, no train of thought that they had not been able to
infer."

Television is not the cause of our habitual self-scrutiny, however,
but has only set the standard for it, a relationship with a complicated
history. It is through our efforts to maintain ourselves as the objects of
our anxious self-spectatorship that we consummate the process of
American Enlightenment, whose project throughout this century has
been the complete and permanent reduction of our populace into the
collective instrument of absolute production. This project has arisen
not through corporate conspiracy but as the logical fulfillment, openly
and even optimistically pursued, of the imperative of unlimited economic growth. Thus compelled, the enlightened captains of production
have employed the principles, and often the exponents, of modern social science, in order to create a perfect work force whose members,
whether laboring on products or consuming them, would function inexhaustibly and on command, like well-tuned robots.

As the material for this ideal, Americans have been closely watched
for decades: in the factory, then in the office, by efficiency experts and
industrial psychologists; in the supermarkets, then throughout the
shopping malls, by motivational researchers no less cunningly than by
the store detectives; in the schools, and then at home, and then in bed,
by an immense, diverse, yet ultimately unified bureaucracy of social
workers, education specialists, and "mental health professionals" of every kind. The psychic and social mutations necessarily induced by this
multiform intrusion have accomplished what its first engineers had
hoped for, but in a form, and at a cost, which they could never have
foreseen: Americans—restless, disconnected, and insatiable—are
mere consumers, having by now internalized the diffuse apparatus of
surveillance built all around them, while still depending heavily on its
external forms—TV, psychologistic "counseling," "self-help" manuals,
the "human potential" regimens, and other self-perpetuating therapies
administered to keep us on the job.

And so the project of industrial Enlightenment has only forced us back toward the same helpless natural state that Enlightenment had once meant to abolish. Both in America and in Oceania, the telescreens infantilize their captive audience. In *Nineteen Eighty-Four* and in 1984, the world has been made too bright and cold by the same system that forever promises the protective warmth of mother love, leaving each viewer yearning to have his growing needs fulfilled by the very force that aggravates them. So it is, first of all, with Orwell's famished hero. The figure who had slipped quickly into Victory Mansions, "his chin nuzzled into his breast," had tried unknowingly to transcend the Oceanic violence by mothering himself, but then ends up so broken by that violence that he adopts its symbol as his mother: "O cruel, needless misunderstanding!" he exults inwardly before the image of Big Brother's face. "O stubborn, self-willed exile from the loving breast!" And, as it is with Winston Smith in his perverted ardor, so it is with every vaguely hungry TV viewer, who longs to be included by the medium that has excuded everyone, and who expects its products to fulfill him in a way that they have made impossible.

What is most disconcerting, then, about the ending of *Nineteen Eighty-Four* is not that Winston Smith has now been made entirely unlike us. In too many ways, the ex-hero of this brilliant, dismal book anticipates those TV viewers who are incapable of reading it: "In these days he could never fix his mind on any one subject for more than a few moments at a time." At this moment, Winston Smith is, for the first time in his life, not under surveillance. The motto, "Big Brother Is Watching You," is now untrue as a threat, as it has always been untrue as an assurance. And the reason why he is no longer watched is that the Oceanic gaze need no longer see through Winston Smith, because he is no longer "Winston Smith," but "a swirl of gritty dust," as primitive and transparent as the Party.

As this Smith slumps in the empty Chestnut Tree, credulously gaping, his ruined mind expertly jolted by the telescreen's managers, he signifies the terminal fulfillment of O'Brien's master plan, which expresses the intentions not only of Orwell's fictitious Party, but of the corporate entity that, through TV, contains our consciousness today: "We shall squeeze you empty, and then we shall fill you with ourselves."[9] The Party has now done for Winston Smith what all our advertisers want to do for us, and with our general approval—answer all material needs, in exchange for the self that might try to gratify them independently, and that might have other, subtler needs as well. As a consumer, in other words, Orwell's ex-hero really has it made. "There was no need to give orders" to the waiters in the Chestnut Tree. "They knew his habits." Furthermore, he "always had plenty of money nowadays." In short, the Party has paid him for his erasure with the assurance, "We do it *all* for you." And so this grotesque before-and-after narrative ends satirically as all ads end in earnest, with the object's blithe endorsement of the very product that has helped to keep him miserable: "But it was all right, everything was all right, the struggle was finished. He had won the victory over himself. He loved Big Brother."

It is a horrifying moment; but if we do no more than wince and then forget about it, we ignore our own involvement in the horror and thus complacently betray the hope that once inspired this vision. Surely Orwell would have us face the facts. Like Winston Smith, and like O'Brien and the others, we have been estranged from our desire by Enlightenment, which finally reduces all of its proponents to the blind spectators of their own annihilation. Unlike that Oceanic audience, however, the TV viewer does not gaze up at the screen with angry scorn or piety, but—perfectly enlightened—looks down on its images with a nervous sneer which cannot threaten them and which only keeps the viewer himself from standing up. As you watch, there is no Big Brother out there watching you—not because there isn't a Big Brother, but because Big Brother is you, watching.

NOTES

■ ■

1. "Bush Says U.S. Can Avert '1984' if Allies Are Firm," *New York Times,* 7 May 1984, B8.

2. "Soviet Says Orwell's Vision Is Alive in the U.S.," *New York Times*, 8 Jan. 1984, p. 8.

3. George Orwell, "The Lion and the Unicorn: Socialism and the English Genius," in *The Collected Essays, Journalism and Letters of George Orwell*, ed. Sonia Orwell and Ian Angus, 4 vols. (New York: Harcourt, Brace and World, 1968), II, 56. (This collection will hereafter be cited as *CEJL*.)

4. "The Rediscovery of Europe," *CEJL*, II, 205. Orwell makes this point in the course of comparing the optimistic works of the Edwardian writers with the darker mood of their postwar successors. The entire passage will reproduce the specific context of the observation: "Compare almost any of H. G. Wells's Utopia books, for instance, *A Modern Utopia,* or *The Dream,* or *Men Like Gods*, with Aldous Huxley's *Brave New World*. Again it's rather the same contrast, the contrast between the overconfident and the deflated, between the man who believes innocently in Progress and the man who happens to have been born later and has therefore lived to see that Progress, as it was conceived in the early days of the aeroplane, is just as much of a swindle as reaction."

5. Max Horkheimer and T. W. Adorno, *Dialectic of Enlightenment*, tran. John Cumming (New York: Continuum, 1982), p. 92. Subsequent references will be noted parenthetically within the text.

6. Horkheimer and Adorno also assumed that television would be such an amalgam, although their remarks on the emergent medium's potential suasiveness have proven more accurate than Orwell's conception, since they expected the televisual hegemony to arise out of the medium's tendency toward total homogenization, and not out of that inflammatory capacity envisioned in *Nineteen Eighty-Four*. See the *Dialectic of Enlightenment*, p. 124. For a celebratory discussion of the same televisual tendency uneasily foretold by Horkheimer and Adorno, see Marshall McLuhan's remarks on TV and synesthesia in *Understanding Media* (New York: New American Library, 1964), pp. 274-75.

7. The absolute interchangeability forever represented on, and valorized by, TV is not, of course, only a formal illusion, but also an expression of the triumph of exchange value, which is at once the ultimate reason for TV's hectic display of goods, and a major ideological message arising out of that display. Within the televisual atmosphere, determined, as it is, by the equalizing power of money, a blasé manner is downright obligatory. "The blasé person," Simmel writes, "has completely lost the feeling of value differences. He experiences all things as

being of an equally dull and grey hue, as not worth getting excited about, particularly where the will is concerned. . . . Whoever has become possessed by the fact that the same amount of money can procure all the possibilities that life has to offer must also become blasé" (*The Philosophy of Money,* trans. Tom Bottomore and David Frisby [Boston: Routledge and Kegan Paul, 1978], p. 256). Although Simmel refers here to the jaded rich of his own era, his full analysis of the blasé attitude (pp. 256-57) also applies to TV's creatures—that is, viewers and characters alike—whose jadedness is not so much an expression of material satiation as it is a response to the flood of mere *images* of "all the possibilities that life has to offer."

8. "Cameras and recording machines not only transcribe experience but alter its quality, giving to much of modern life the character of an enormous echo chamber, a hall of mirrors. Life presents itself as a succession of images or electronic signals, of impressions recorded and reproduced by means of photography, motion pictures, television, and sophisticated recording devices. Modern life is so thoroughly mediated by electronic images that we cannot help responding to others as if their actions—and our own—were being recorded and simultaneously transmitted to an unseen audience or stored up for close scrutiny at some later time." Christopher Lasch, *The Culture of Narcissism* (New York: Norton, 1978), p. 47.

9. Although Horkheimer and Adorno, both in the *Dialectic of Enlightenment* and (separately) elsewhere, draw comparisons between totalitarian domination and the implicit coerciveness of advertising, Orwell tended, in his journalistic writings, to regard advertising not as comparable to totalitarianism but as the excrescence of a different, much preferable system. He often condemned advertising for its corruptiveness rather than for its animus against the subject. For instance, he deplored its incitements to snobbery (*CEJL,* 3:183-84, 194) and condemned its emphasis on trivialities in the midst of war (2:343-45 et passim).

However, such moralistic complaints do not express Orwell's deepest reservations about advertising, whose most pernicious effect, he argued, was its "indirect censorship over news" (2:68). He regarded advertising as the force that ensured the total fatuity of what we now call "the media," that invisible yet inescapable environment which imperceptibly blunts and diminishes every mind within it: "Between the wars England tolerated newspapers, films and radio programmes of unheard-of silliness, and these produced further stupefaction in the public, blinding their eyes to vitally important problems. This silliness of the English press is partly artificial, since it arises from the fact that newspapers live off advertisements for consumption goods" (3:35).

Although such "stupefaction" results from universal trivialization rather than from terror, it evidenced, for Orwell, the drastic reduction of the subject. "This silliness of the English press" has its clear Oceanic equivalent in the calculated inanities devised by the Ministry of Truth, whose job it is to keep the proles as dim and vacant as Winston Smith ends up, even if the proles are reduced by films, novels, and newspapers, not through torture. There is, then, a distant relationship between advertising and the moronized masses in *Nineteen Eighty-Four,* despite the fact that the Party has long since smashed the apparatus of consumerism. And there is further evidence for this relationship in Orwell's earlier novel *Keep the Aspidistra Flying* (1936), which contains this very telling description of the ideological atmosphere inside an advertising agency:

> The interesting thing about the New Albion was that it was so completely modern in spirit. There was hardly a soul in the firm who was not perfectly well aware that publicity—advertising—is the dirtiest ramp that capitalism has yet produced. In the red lead firm [where the hero had worked previously] there had still lingered certain notions of commercial honour and usefulness. But such things would have been laughed at in the New Albion. Most of the employees were the hard-boiled, Americanised, go-getting type—the type to whom nothing in the world is sacred, except money. They had their cynical code worked out. The public are swine; advertising is the rattling of a stick inside a swill-bucket. And yet beneath their cynicism there was the final naïveté, the blind worship of the money-god. (London: Seeker and Warburg, 1954, pp. 65–66)

Having blown apart the myth of "commercial honor and usefulness," the devotees of advertising, "completely modern in spirit," are now entrapped by "the final naïveté," serving wholeheartedly the very mechanism which they see through. Thus the enlightened employees of the New Albion are the prototypes of the doublethinking members of the Inner Party.

INDEX

■ ■